Teaching Us

The Class of 1960 at Moses Brown School

VOLUME I

In Class

Clifford W. Brown, Jr.

*With Much Help from Members of the Class and Many Others
in the Moses Brown School Family*

Teaching Us: The Class of 1960 at Moses Brown School: Volume I, In Class
Copyright © 2023 Clifford W. Brown, Jr.

Produced and printed by Stillwater River Publications. All rights reserved. Written and produced in the United States of America. This book may not be reproduced or sold in any form without the expressed, written permission of the author and publisher.

Visit our website at www.StillwaterPress.com for more information.

First Stillwater River Publications Edition.

ISBN: 978-1-960505-15-6

Library of Congress Control Number: 2023913378

1 2 3 4 5 6 7 8 9 10
Written by Clifford W. Brown, Jr.
Images provided by Moses Brown School.
Cover & interior book design by Matthew St. Jean.
Thank you to Amy Barrett and Marilyn Brownell for advice on cover design.
Edited by Ann Davis and Clifford W. Brown, Jr.

Published by Stillwater River Publications, West Warwick, RI, USA.

  Names: Brown, Clifford W. (Clifford Waters), 1942- author.
  Title: Teaching us : the Class of 1960 at Moses Brown School. Volume I, In class / Clifford W. Brown, Jr.
  Other titles: Class of 1960 at Moses Brown School. Volume 1, In class | In class
  Description: First Stillwater River Publications edition. | West Warwick, RI, USA : Stillwater River Publications, [2023] | Includes bibliographical references and index.
  Identifiers: ISBN: 978-1-960505-15-6 | LCCN: 2023913378
  Subjects: LCSH: Moses Brown School. Class of 1960--History. | Preparatory schools--Rhode Island-- Providence--History. | Quakers--Education--Rhode Island--Providence. | Moses Brown School--Curricula. | Moses Brown School--Administration.
  Classification: LCC: LD7501.P9 B76 2023 | DDC: 373.7452--dc23

The views and opinions expressed in this book are solely those of the author and do not necessarily reflect the views and opinions of the publisher nor those of Moses Brown School.

In honor and in memory of the extraordinary teaching and coaching staff of Moses Brown School during the 1950s.

Table of Contents

Preface and Acknowledgments — vii
Introduction — xix

Part I: The Lower School
I. The Lower School and its Leadership — 1
II. Early Years: K through Second Primary (1947-1950) — 11
III. Third Primary: The Third Grade (1950-1951) — 17
IV. First Intermediate: The Fourth Grade (1951-1952) — 47
V. Second Intermediate: The Fifth Grade (1952-1953) — 69
VI. Third Intermediate: The Sixth Grade (1953-1954) — 93
VII. Summers (1953-1955) — 119
VIII. Fourth Intermediate: The Seventh Grade (1954-1955) — 131
IX. The Lower School in Retrospect — 157

Part II: The Upper School
X. First Form (1955-56) — 169
XI. Second Form (1956-57) — 215
XII. Third Form (1957-58) — 241
XIII. Fourth Form (1958-59) — 299
XIV. Interludes (1956-60) — 329
XV. Fifth Form (1959-60) — 341
XVI. The Upper School Classroom Experience — 379

Appendices
Appendix I. The Upper School Setting — 391
Appendix II. The Class of 1960 — 395
Index — 398

Preface and Acknowledgments

This is an unusual undertaking. It is an account of Moses Brown School during the 1950s—a thin slice of its more than two hundred-year history in Providence—written from the vantage point, not of the School itself, but of its students. There are many types of school and college histories. They include: 1) traditional institutional accounts that chronologize important milestones, such as changes to the physical plant, arrivals and departures of faculty and administrators, memorable ceremonial events, curricular development, fundraising achievements, and outstanding sporting exploits; 2) non-systematic anecdotal compilations of school life, usually recounted by faculty and alumni/ae; 3) personal memoirs of important institutional figures; and, 4) the rarer "encyclopedia" of an institution, topically arranged with many brief articles about a wide range of people, events, curricula, organizations, buildings, traditions, artifacts, alumni achievements, and so forth. Each of these different accounts makes a valuable contribution to understanding the history of an institution and its mission. Moses Brown School, a Quaker school owned by the New England Yearly Meeting of Friends, is fortunate to have excellent examples of the first three types.[1]

This current work attempts to set forth something a bit different. Its aim is to present a *comprehensive* and *systematic* account of a school's activities

---

[1] Rayner W. Kelsey's magisterial *Centennial History of Moses Brown School* 1819-1919; William Paxton's *Moses Brown School: A History of the Third Half-Century* (Providence, 1974); Frank Fuller's *Shadows of the Elms* (Providence, 1983), a marvelous collection of alumni anecdotes; and L. Ralston Thomas's *Recollections* (Providence, 1994), transcribed by Fuller and Brown.

from the viewpoint of its *students,* principally the students in a single class—the Class of 1960. It presents the educational experiences, very broadly defined, that Class members underwent during a decade or more of their time there. This is a student story, told from a student viewpoint as our student perspectives evolved while we grew. It explores the topic of just what it meant to be a student in the 1950s, and just how we received an education at an excellent private school: what was taught, what was learned, and how was it learned, both in the classroom and outside of it. Moreover, even though the classroom experiences recounted here were foundationally important, a major theme of this saga is that much student learning took place after class in extracurricular activities and in sports competition. Treating student experiences in class, then after class, and then in contest on the playing field as integrated parts of a larger educational experience is yet another approach adopted here that may be somewhat different from approaches used in other accounts of primary and secondary education which focus only on one or two of these features.

Such a study is important for several other reasons. First, the decade of the 1950s was itself a significant moment in American history. Domestically, by most conventional economic standards, it was one of the most prosperous decades in the twentieth century, although that prosperity did not extend in equal measure to many American minority groups. With both the Depression and World War II surmounted, it was an era of much productive activity, growth, and widespread optimism about the future. Throughout most of the decade (with one brief interruption near its end), much of American industry operated at full capacity, although in Rhode Island itself many old industrial firms began to falter and close, directly affecting many students at Moses Brown.[2] Nationally, this was the heyday of the industrial labor union (both honest and corrupt) and a time of rapid growth in middle class incomes. Home ownership and automobile ownership expanded at exponential rates—as did ownership of American-made television sets. It was also a time when single-earner households were the norm. Although we members of the Class of 1960 were of the war baby generation, we were soon followed by the famous baby boom generation, and both groups experienced these portentous trends during their formative years.

---

2 Nicholson File, the American Screw Company, the Wanskuck Company, the Atlantic Mills (in Olneyville), ALCO, the Lonsdale Mills, BB&R Knight, and the Lorraine Mills are a few examples.

Lest we forget, Jim Crow was still prevalent (especially in the South), African Americans could not vote in many states, and large percentages of schools were segregated. Still, the 1950s saw the beginning of school integration, led by the courts and affirmed by the executive branch at Little Rock. The Civil Rights Movement was beginning, as was the drive for enhanced roles for women in the economy and the professions—although the pace of these last developments really took off during the 1960s.

The decade of the 1950s was indeed a time of recurring international tensions and the Bomb, but with the end of the Korean War, it became largely a peaceful era, accompanied by bipartisan foreign policy in Washington. Despite occasional political scandals, there was a high level of trust in American political institutions—which had successfully brought us through depression and war. President Truman, although his policies and comments were often controversial, was a personally honest and patriotic straight-shooting public servant whose highly commendable transparency left little doubt in anyone's mind as to where he stood. And when President Eisenhower assumed office in 1953, he quickly ended the Korean War, slowly maneuvered Joe McCarthy into oblivion, and convincingly ushered in an era generally characterized by growth and calm reassurance. Historians' assessments of both presidents have risen with time, and most people today would also concur that when Americans went to the polls in the 1950s to elect a president, the choice between Eisenhower and Stevenson was a choice between two highly competent and honorable men, either of whom would have been a source of national pride when in office.

The 1950s era was a time of many discoveries and scientific developments, from the H-bomb, the ICBM, and the artificial satellite, to the transistor, fiber optics, DNA, and the Salk polio vaccine. Concurrently, the decade saw many lifestyle changes, including the arrival of touch tone phones, long distance direct dialing, and the rise of television network news to dominance, as evening newspapers withered and died. It saw Hollywood's response to TV with Cinerama, 3-D movies, and drive-in theaters. It was a time of steady suburbanization (even in Rhode Island). Air conditioning was spreading, but still largely confined to public and commercial buildings (there was none yet at Moses Brown). Transportation evolved dramatically, as President Eisenhower's interstate highway system was built and jet aircraft replaced trains and ocean liners as the principal means of public long-distance travel. On a smaller scale, automatic transmissions arrived in force during our time at Moses Brown, although most of us took the driving test for our first license in a car with a standard transmission (and often with a pair of tail fins). This was the world in which we children (and later we adolescents) grew up, encouraged by our parents and our mentors at Moses Brown to observe the unfolding regional and national pageant with increasingly informed attention—as the years passed.

Second, the 1950s was an important time in the history of primary and secondary education. Although we did not know it at the time, we were standing at the end of a long era of pre-electronic instruction. There were no hand calculators, personal computers, internet sites, cell phones, iPhones or other means of rapid information access. Instant communication from nearly anywhere to nearly everywhere was unheard of. There were no transatlantic television cables—when Queen Elizabeth was crowned in 1952, American audiences had to wait a day for the film to be processed and flown across the ocean before they could witness the event. Television made its way into homes, but not yet extensively into classrooms. The slide rule and the log table dominated serious calculations in class; the pen and the typewriter dominated composition. Information came from dictionaries and other books of reference, not from screens—there was neither Google nor Wikipedia, nor the internet itself. Word processing was unheard of. Cameras still used film, and the photographs in textbooks and other class materials were largely black and white. Mimeographs, hectographs, and other stencil-based copiers were in frequent use, but direct copying of documents was not widely available in this pre-xerox era where copies were referred to as "photostats." Personal instruction and the printed word dominated the classroom.

Third, this is an account of an era when most New England preparatory schools, including Moses Brown, were single-sex—a circumstance soon to change. Moses Brown had been coed before 1926, and was to be so again starting in the 1970s, but during our time there it was single-sex, with coeducational events (such as dances and plays) strictly monitored and chaperoned. This account, therefore, gives a glimpse into the practices of an historically significant educational culture that has largely disappeared.

Fourth, and very important, this is a description of education at a Quaker school. Although the School's owner, the New England Yearly Meeting of

Friends, true to the Quaker tradition, exercised only gentle control over the School, nevertheless, there was definitely a Quaker influence that could be felt at important times throughout the experience. Several faculty were Friends, there were Friends among the student body, there were recurrent Quaker visitors who spoke on a variety of topics, and there were many School traditions grounded in Quaker antecedents. Quaker values were certainly influential in quietly shaping the educational experience.

Fifth, it is important to examine secondary education in the 1950s because that decade stood on the brink of seismic sociological and attitudinal changes that greatly affected campuses, including Moses Brown, in the years immediately following: challenges to (and redefinitions of) authority, breakdowns in status and other forms of differentiation and discrimination, changes in dress codes and in the manner of address, and, not least, the sexual revolution with the arrival of the Pill. Many century-long traditions were about to be swept away or drastically reshaped. From the standpoint of the student, what did the world of education look like before the deluge? Some answers may be surprising.

Finally, I hope this work, by showing in great detail what a liberal arts curriculum was at the primary and especially secondary levels in a quality educational institution at that time, will provide a benchmark for future scholars to evaluate how it has changed over time: what was considered important for students to know then, compared to what is considered important for students to know now or, eventually, in the future.

This is a project that has evolved. With the 50th Reunion of Moses Brown's Class of 1960 then approaching, I began to write an account of my days at Moses Brown School in the hopes that they would trigger other memories in my classmates so that a comprehensive set of recollections of the School during the 1950s could be produced. By that time, I had in my possession a set of eight lengthy tapes on which I had recorded recollections of Moses Brown. These had been recorded (while driving back and forth to Washington, DC), at the suggestion of Mr. Frank Fuller, School Historian, in the early 1980s. Expeditions to the attic and cellar at my home in Providence produced sets of School yearbooks, newspapers, and official bulletins, together with a large number of textbooks from both Lower and Upper School. Also found were many of my own School papers and artifacts. In addition, there were many communications from the School to my parents (including tuition bills), dutifully preserved.

When Doc [King] Odell, longtime School Historian, heard about this project, he offered to lend me a full set of *Delphians, Quakers,* and *Moses Brown Bulletins* from our era to supplement my own holdings. They are much thumbed. Doc's support for this project has been extensive and very valuable. Several lengthy taping sessions with him have provided much important information and insight. In addition, I have drawn heavily on the archive of *Providence Journal* microfilms at the Providence Public Library, especially for sports accounts. Mr. William Paxton's 1974 sesquicentennial account, *Moses Brown School: A History of the Third Half-Century 1919-1969*; Mr. Fuller's 1983 collection of alumni anecdotes, entitled *Shadows of the Elms*; and Mr. L. Ralston Thomas's 1994 *Recollections*, edited by Mr. Fuller and me, have also proved valuable resources—as did Kelsey's 1919 centennial history.

When we celebrated the 50th reunion itself in May 2010, the organizers, under the leadership of Tammy Worthington-Witczak, kindly set aside a couple of hours for a roundtable at which my classmates reminisced about our experiences. More than a dozen attended the session. This proved very valuable in terms of providing material, especially about faculty whose classes I had never taken, and about life "on corridor," which I had never experienced. These recollections were augmented by in-person or telephone interviews (in some cases several interviews) with faculty and coaches from the era: Doc Odell, Jerry Zeoli, Fred Pratt, and John Jeffers. I also had the pleasure of interviewing Mrs. Barrett, Mrs. Marcello (parents of classmates), and Mrs. Theodore Whitford, the centenarian widow of the late Ted Whitford, one of our Upper School instructors (to whom we dedicated our yearbook). Mrs. Pratt participated in the interview of Mr. Pratt and made many insightful observations and suggestions. Both Pratts read early drafts of the manuscript and made many helpful comments. I also wish to thank Karin Morse from the Moses Brown Alumni Office, and School Historian, for her support, her detailed comments on the manuscript, and her help in identifying Moses Brown alumni who graduated before our Upper School era. In this same connection, I also want to thank Molly Garrison and Emalyn Gordon of Lincoln School who helped identify the class affiliation of Lincoln alumnae. In addition, I wish

Preface and Acknowledgments   *xiii*

to acknowledge the help of School Archivist Anne Krive for her help in locating photographs for use in these volumes. I also wish to thank Head of School Matt Glendinning for his recognition of this project, and Interim Head of School Ron Dalgliesh, for his support and encouragement.

In addition, I interviewed and received much valuable feedback from many classmates. Vin Marcello, our Class President, who has been an enthusiastic supporter of this project from its inception, has been especially helpful in arranging meetings and interviews (including several with Coach Zeoli), in reading text, and recalling many episodes in the classroom, in student government, and on the playing field. I am also indebted to him for arranging an interview with Nancy Golden about the Proscenium Club. His support and encouragement have been very important contributions to making this project work, and the result would have been much diminished without his help.

Bill Barrett has also shared many anecdotes and has read and commented on vast portions of text. His memories of events and personalities are extraordinary. He has also shared written recollections of several sports in which he participated, and on which I draw on in Volume III. His help, commentaries, and support have been invaluable. He is also largely responsible for the annotated list of classmates that appears in Appendix II of this volume. Jack Nixon, another enthusiastic supporter of this project, read the entire text twice, made many helpful suggestions, and contributed important and insightful anecdotes, especially about Mr. Whitford and Mr. Jeffers. His interest is greatly appreciated. Dave London provided many recollections of faculty, of the tennis team, and more generally about the School and our classmates. He also carefully reviewed much text and made numerous helpful suggestions. I'm also especially indebted to Bill Brehm for his many recollections of Mr. Howe, Mechanical Drawing, and track meets, and for proofreading a great deal of this text—and to Pete Parker for his detailed memories about the swimming program. Mark Saklad shared valuable memories of managing track, the Science Club and its rocket launchings, as well as of the Camera Club and the *Mosaic*. Fred Schwartz commented extensively, humorously, and helpfully on the manuscript and shared some of his own recollections in writing. Dave Chaffee took the time to provide valuable information about the Broadcast Club. Barry Fain and Bill Carney met with me to tape many important recollections, and Barry met me again for a lengthy follow-up interview. Barry also has made valuable suggestions about the manuscript and how to bring it to fruition. Bill Criss, Bruce Perry, Jan Moyer, and Bruce Henkle, participating in a conference call, shared their experiences on the gridiron and on corridor. In addition, Bruce Henkle spent serious time on the telephone being interviewed about baseball. Al Holoff contributed many recollections about his Moses Brown experiences, and especially about his strategies on the tennis court. He also read portions of the manuscript and made numerous useful suggestions. Hernan Franco, who participated in the 2010 roundtable, provided me with a copy of Ed Corris's detailed write-up about the 1960 softball team, on which I have drawn heavily, and with which I have taken some liberties. In addition, I was very happy to interview Ed himself. Al Crandon also shared with me some excellent recollections about Mr. Cole. In addition, I had valuable telephone interviews with the late Bob Marshall, the late Roy Maletz, the late Bill Criss, and with Dan DeVlieg, Jim Rigney, Herb Sawyer, Ralph DiLibero, Steve Estee, Dick Crawford, Jan Moyer, Dick Buckley, and Jeff Forman. Recollections by Bill Goddard, Tom Clark, and Harrison Huntoon were also helpful in recounting Lower School experiences. I was also very fortunate to be able to visit with Nick Littlefield several times before his passing and receive focused and insightful comments on the Moses Brown Lower School during the 1950s.

In addition, I have had several interviews by phone or in person with alumni from other classes in our era: the late Bob Smith ('58), who recalled his time as editor of the *Quaker* and who reminisced about sports and faculty; the late Russ Carpenter ('59), who took considerable time reading drafts of portions of the manuscript and sharing his memories about faculty members. Tom Godfray ('59), Mike Knowles ('59), and Ted Armstrong ('61), all shared memories with me, especially about baseball, track, and hockey. Drew Kemalian ('59), Steve Thornton ('58), and Vic Field ('59) all spent serious time either on the telephone or in person discussing football, baseball, and basketball. Walter Ensign ('61) gave me a very detailed description of the Camera Club's activities and how he and Mark Saklad took photographs for our publications. He also helped review the text describing these events.

For the chapter on the Proscenium Club, I also wish to acknowledge the assistance of Will Mackenzie ('56), Nick Clapp ('53), Nancy Hayes Golden

(L '61), John Manera ('61), Paula Roll (L'70), Janet Chase Jones (L'60), Nancy Rapelye Godfray (L'60), Bill Applegate, Bonnie Riker Mutter, Cait Calvo, Preston and Lois Atwood, and other members of Players for their recollections of plays and directors from the 1950s era.

Thanks also go to my colleague George Gmelch at Union for many helpful suggestions, to Ken Aslakson and Andy Morris for their encouragement, to the staff of the Schaffer Library at Union College where I work, including Bruce Connolly, David Gerhan, and Mary Eiffe. Thanks also go to other colleagues in the Political Science Department at the college who have been supportively bemused by this enterprise. Thanks go as well to Jonathan Knight for sage advice and editorial suggestions, to Laura McGill, and Rhonda Becker for her work on the manuscript.

I wish also to acknowledge the very helpful assistance of Steven and Dawn Porter of Stillwater River Publications, of Ann Davis who served as an excellent copyeditor, and of Kates Mertes, who indexed this trilogy.

Many thanks also to my wife, Marilyn Brownell, for her encouragement, help, and patience, and for reading and commenting on large parts of the manuscript.

I wrote much of this account in the New England literalist style—with lots of basic description of physical surroundings and lots of cataloguing of mundane events. This method was adopted, in part, because hard descriptive evidence just might be of use to future historians at Moses Brown School and elsewhere for reasons we today cannot predict. It might be regarded as an extensive integrated transcription of many oral histories, supplemented by documentary evidence. My apologies in this regard to many current and to most future readers. For similar reasons, I have said a lot about curriculum, extracurricular activities, and sports because people in the future might wish to have a factual basis for drawing their own conclusions about the nature of an excellent liberal arts education during America's Golden 1950s.

Since much of the material in this account is based on my personal recollections, the result (of necessity) is often autobiographical for extended passages. For this I offer apologies both to classmates and to other readers who may find it more than a trifle self-centered, and its perspectives thereby narrowed. As to the factual accuracy of the narrative, please remember that my tapes were made twenty to thirty years after the events described, and my current recollections are sixty to seventy years after those events. Many of these memories, however, are quite vivid, and I have tried to indicate where there is doubt as to their validity. When memories, later on, have been put to the test by hard evidence, the record has been excellent, but not perfect. I have consulted whatever archival evidence I could find to supplement and validate recollections.

This will not read like a dime novel. Most readers—and especially those not acquainted with the times and the people described—may find many passages quite boring. Its length reminds me of a comment made to my father by Doc (then Mr.) Odell in 1956. He was referring to an interminable outline of the geographic and historical features of the United States which I had produced as part of a project in his geography class: "Clifford, in his ponderous way, has produced a lengthy tome...."

The three-volume tome that follows is divided into several parts. Volume One, "In Class," has two parts. The first part discusses the Lower School, especially from the Third Grade through the Seventh. The second part discusses the Upper School, largely in terms of its academics. Volume Two, "After Class," is divided into four parts covering Upper School social and "political" activity, intellectual and avocational clubs, public performance activities, and publications. Volume Three, "In Contest," is devoted primarily to Upper School varsity sports, and is basically divided into three parts, one for each season, followed by a final brief coda that recalls the Spring Term of our senior year.

I went to Moses Brown in the late winter of 1950 and graduated in the spring of 1960. Moses Brown at the time had many highly motivated and experienced teachers and coaches in both Lower School and Upper School who knew us, as Fred Schwartz observed, better than we knew ourselves. I comment at some length on many of them. Most were hired by Mr. Thomas before the Second World War. By this time they had reached the peak of their careers. Therefore, we were very fortunate to have the benefit, year after year, of a large number of extremely gifted people who were highly dedicated to the School, to its traditions, and to its students. They were not there on their way to another job, even though the resources of the School were inadequate to pay them remotely what they deserved. For most of them, this was their whole life and they were giving to the School—and to us—everything they had. In their honor, the Class of 1960 has established a "Master Teacher Development Fund" to encourage quality teaching at the School—and also to honor them. Members of the Class of 1960 contributing to this project wish to dedicate this current treatise to their memory.

Clifford W. Brown, Jr. '60.
180 Brown St., Providence, RI
January 2023

PHOTO CREDITS: *The photographs in this and subsequent volumes come largely from Moses Brown publications:* Moses Brown Bulletins, Moses Brown Catalogues, Mosaics, Delphians, Quakers, *and books by Paxton, Fuller, and Thomas. These are supplemented by photos lent by Vin Marcello, Barry Fain, and others. Mark Saklad was the principal photographer for many* Quakers *and the 1959 and 1960* Mosaics, *and many of the photographs in these volumes were taken by him. Also used are photographs, never published, from* Mosaic *files, most of which were taken by Mark. Also used are photos taken by Walter Ensign for these same publications. I have also used photos from the Moses Brown School photograph collection. Marilyn Brownell took the photograph of the Friends' Meeting House in Volume II. Many thanks to the School for permission to use these photographs.*

Introduction

My Brief Journey to Moses Brown

We are, most of us, born into a family, but soon begin the slow journey of emerging from it to face the world beyond. School is very much part of that process where our points of reference expand from parents, siblings, cousins, and other relatives to teachers, classmates, and strangers, some of whom eventually become as familiar to us as many in our family circle. When those of us in my generation were very young, this may have been even more the case than it is today. The family and our surroundings at home were at the center of everything. There was no television, nor any other form of animated *visual* stimulus to bring the outside world into our homes. There were movies, of course, and children occasionally might be taken to view an appropriate one, but for the most part movies were where parents went when the babysitter came. If a family was fortunate enough to have home movies, these were usually family-centered, and viewing them was a special occasion.

Of course, there was radio, and it was at its zenith in the 1940s. I personally remember it well, but not with affection. Some programs were indeed funny (although I was too young to get the joke most of the time), but many were scary or at least disturbing. I can remember the weird organ music that accompanied the *Romance of Helen Trent* that an elderly nearby neighbor was fond of listening to. I can remember a program where someone with a cane noisily fell down stairs with sequenced sound effects, and was pronounced dead after she landed at the bottom with much clatter and commotion. Scary stuff. The news broadcasts were arresting—not so much for their contents (most of which I did not understand), but for their style of presentation. I remember Walter Winchell, who delivered the news in apocalyptic tones, with each item punctuated by high-pitched beeps. To be sure, the folks, especially my father, listened to the Red Sox on weekends, but at an early age I was not yet into baseball and found the broadcasts unintelligible, although I did witness the delight on his part when Ted Williams hit a home run and his consternation when Joe DiMaggio (as opposed to Dom DiMaggio) did the same. Radio in the car was a bit more fun. We frequently visited grandparents who lived about two hours away, and it was often turned on during these trips, which were typically on weekends or in the evening. The programs were largely comedies—such as Jack Benny or *Our Miss Brooks*, or *Amos and Andy*, and even if I didn't get the joke, I knew it was supposed to be fun and was a form of "make believe." Radio, although a recurrent presence in my life, was therefore always something a bit unnatural, a bit unreal. Its arresting features kept it somehow from intruding into the structure of the family environment: actual reality consisted of home surroundings (including toys), daily routines, family, close neighbors, and occasional visitors whom I would encounter only when parents were present. I expect that this was the same for those who became my Moses Brown classmates. When one looks at the essays of the youngest students printed in the *Delphian* (the School's literary magazine), family and family experiences seem to be the central topics.

My parents and I lived in Methuen, a suburb of Lawrence, Massachusetts, until I was nearly seven; my father's job was to manage the Arlington Mills, a large textile complex. As a late-coming only child, I received a lot of attention, and was taught the alphabet and how to spell simple words at an early age. I was read to every night before bedtime, and I was also taught at an early age how to read on my own by Aunt Amey (Steere), my mother's sister, who lived with us from time to time. The folks also taught me numbers and simple arithmetic.

I remember my Methuen home surroundings very well (the house is still standing).[3] It was a two-story dwelling with a big yard in back. The house itself was not very large, but was cozy and felt secure. In the earliest of years

---

3   The address was 527 Prospect Street—an address I was asked to memorize at an early age in case I got lost. I was instructed that if the latter occurred, I was to find a policeman or postman, identify myself, and tell him my address.

I slept in a crib in my parents' bedroom near a window that looked out over a field across the street (now developed). When I was about three or four, I was given my own room, and this was very special. I had my own bed, dresser, and playthings, which included teddy bears, toy sheep, and other toys, from which I soon graduated to building blocks, little pale-red bricks, wooden toy trains, log cabin logs, tinker toys, and eventually an erector set (with which my father and Uncle George (Steere) spent as much time as I did). I also remember playing with scotch tape and cardboard shirt-boxes, with which I built ships large enough to play in on the living room floor. Noticing this, our next door neighbor gave me a heavy and very functional scotch tape dispenser for a birthday present. I also remember using crayons and colored pencils at different times to draw cars and ships.

In summers, I played outside on the lawn and in the garden. Somewhere along the way, I was given an old rusted-metal secondhand tricycle which I loved to pedal up and down the sidewalk and into the large driveway. In winter I had a sled which I used to slide down the hill from a neighbor's yard into our yard, and later used (under supervision) to slide down the lightly trafficked street a block behind our house. Parents, grandparents, aunts and uncles, some of whom lived with us from time to time, were all very supportive and fun to be around. For the last few years we lived in Methuen, the folks rented cottages at Hampton Beach, New Hampshire, and later at Biddeford Pool, Maine, where we spent a lot of time during the summer. I loved the beach, with its infinite opportunities to run from the water flowing in from the waves, search for shells, build sandcastles, and mark out spaces and territories for games. The beach experiences continued after we moved to Providence. I remember those times in Methuen as exciting, safely adventuresome, and always enjoyable—with very few worries and not many mini-crises to deal with, other than sicknesses, which were recurrent (and addressed by having my tonsils removed during that time).[4] I expect that

---

[4] Before I had this operation, at about the age of five, my parents explained to me what was being done and why, no doubt to lower the level of my angst. They also told me how the anesthesia (ether, in those days) would be administered. When the time came and I was on the table, the anesthesiologist started to use a new procedure, different from the one my parents were familiar with and had explained to me. I proceeded to tell him that he wasn't doing it correctly, and explained to him how it should be done. He took my professional criticism good-naturedly, but did insist on using his own method, which was putting a mask over my face attached to a rubber sac, (which he called a balloon) and which he had me blow up, thus inhaling the ether. His was one of the most immediate and effective means of silencing my criticisms that I have ever encountered.

many of my classmates enjoyed similar experiences at their Rhode Island homes and summer dwellings.

My earliest school experience was at a school in Lawrence called "The Garden of Children"—the English translation of "Kindergarten," probably renamed such because of the Second World War. It was run by a Mrs. Cole. I think I attended for only one year (1948-49). I was constantly sick that year, with measles, severe colds, and the like, and spent only short spells at school between illnesses.[5]

We were probably taught basic skills at Mrs. Cole's school, but I have absolutely no recollection of in-class experiences. Basically, all I remember from this first cut at school are the class outings and picnics to which we were carted in an old "beach wagon" with a wooden body, singing songs like "Row, Row, Row, your Boat," "Three Blind Mice," "Pick Up Sticks… Give the Dog a Bone" as we drove to our destinations—which included outings at Canobie Lake in nearby New Hampshire, a resort with carousels, intriguing curved mirrors, and the like.

In the fall of 1949, my father took a new job in Providence as "Agent" (general manager) of the Wanskuck Company, a textile firm owned by the Metcalf family. While the folks hunted several months for a new house in Providence, we lived at my grandparents' farm in Chepachet, Rhode Island, and I attended public school in neighboring Mapleville, where my mother's younger sister, my aunt Louise (Van Bever), became my teacher. She taught First through Third Grades in a single classroom, with each grade seated at desks in different sections of the room. There must have been about thirty students, altogether. She gave reading assignments or written work to two grades to do on their own, while she gave instruction to the other grade, rotating the process, and constantly keeping an eye on everyone. She assigned me to the Third Grade, which meant that I never experienced Second Grade. Being in a room with three grades was a bit distracting, as it was hard not to listen to what my aunt was saying to the other classes—so my in-class assignments were often neglected, for which I would be duly reprimanded. We did not buy our own books, but used the public school hand-me-downs for texts (often marked up by the

---

5   My parents wanted me to go to public school, but much to their disgust, the one-room public grammar school near where we lived in Methuen had just been closed.

My Brief Journey to Moses Brown *xxiii*

previous user), with only the workbooks being new. Nevertheless, we were introduced to the basics (reading, spelling, penmanship, and arithmetic), and had visiting art and music teachers[6] whose occasional presence lent some variety to the experience. There were no organized sports for our age group, but we had ample recess time to play tag and other games in the fall and hurl snowballs in the winter. All this was very new, and living at the farm during these months was also an exciting and different experience.

In February, 1950, the folks bought a home in Providence near Moses Brown (perhaps *because* it was near) and we moved in sometime during March. My father, who had attended Boston Latin School and enjoyed his experiences there, was a strong believer in the public schools, and my parents considered sending me to Henry Barnard, which was then presided over by the legendary Miss Thorpe. I am not sure why they decided otherwise (I was not consulted), but they settled on Moses Brown.

I remember my first experience there, when I was taken in to be screened for admission in the middle of a school year. I recall sitting in the Bird Room, fascinated by its display of a large variety of stuffed birds (some of which looked a bit ragged) while my parents went in to see Headmaster L. Ralston Thomas, to whom I was probably introduced at the time, although I do not remember this being done. I was then taken over to the Lower School building to meet Mr. J. Drisko Allen, Head of the Lower School, whom I do remember from that day. He greeted me warmly, asked a few questions, and then led me upstairs to a little room above his office, where he introduced me to Mrs. Frances Bachman, whom I later had as a teacher. She gave me some tests. I did some reading, and I remember being asked if I could do complex additions—involving multi-digit numbers of different lengths. Although I had never seen any before, I replied that I could do them, and proceeded to add the sums. A few, at least, must have been right, because I was admitted.

Moses Brown was a very different experience from Mapleville. I started out with Harriet Wilson in the spring of 1950 (with the Class of 1959), and was promoted to the Fourth Grade, taught by Miriam Pixley in the

---

6   I do not recall the name of the art teacher. She taught us how to make Christmas decorations (among other projects) with Santa faces and colorful paper chains. The music teacher was a Mr. Berry who brought a violin with him and played it for us while we sang to its tunes.

fall. This put me at least a year ahead of my age group. I attended Fourth Grade for a few weeks, still at the age of seven, and then, at the suggestion of my parents and Mr. Allen, reverted to the Third Grade, thus joining the Class of 1960—back to Miss Wilson again. Everyone tried to emphasize that this was to be my choice, not theirs (I remember Mr. Allen speaking at length to this effect) but I'm sure that the decision had already been made. It was probably the correct one. My new class (in terms of the students) seemed a lot more welcoming. I stayed with Miss Wilson for the rest of that school year, and then went through a full set of normal promotions until graduation from Upper School in 1960.[7] Thus began a decade of memorable experiences at Moses Brown School, both in the classroom and outside of it.

---

7   My tuition in 1950-51 was $425.00 plus a small "blanket fee" and a modest stipend for books. By the time we had reached the Fifth Form in Upper School, the tuition was $875 plus a $40 blanket fee and book costs.

PART I

The Lower School

I

The Lower School and its Leadership

Moses Brown School, originally Friends' Boarding School, was founded in Portsmouth, Rhode Island, in 1784. It closed after a few years. In 1819 it reopened in Providence. Middle House, still its central space today, was built at that time. Until the twentieth century, the School was primarily a boarding school for Quaker children, but in the first decade of that century a "country day school" component was added to the boarding department and the School began to admit students of all faiths, with instruction from Kindergarten through the Twelfth Grade. As a Quaker school, it originally educated both girls and boys, but in the 1920s, the New England Yearly Meeting of Friends acquired Lincoln School. Moses Brown then became an all-boys school, with Lincoln its all-girls counterpart. This arrangement lasted until the 1970s, when Moses Brown became coed once again. Both Moses Brown and Lincoln are still Quaker schools owned by the New England Yearly Meeting.

The School's very appropriate name was given to it in the early twentieth century. Moses Brown himself was a Quaker farmer, merchant, businessman, and civic activist who was instrumental in bringing Friends Boarding School to Providence and financially supporting it during the early years. His son, Obadiah Brown, left the School a large legacy. Moses came from the same family for which Brown University was named. Among his many accomplishments was the financing of Samuel Slater's Pawtucket cotton mill—which introduced the factory system to the United States and

Mr. Thomas with the Lower School faculty and staff, 1950. Front row, left to right: Miss M.P. Pixley, Miss E.E. Chappell, Mr. J.D. Allen, Mr. L.R. Thomas, Miss O.M. Woodbury, Miss E. Eastman. Second row: Mme. D. Warge, Mrs. F.M. Bachman, Mrs. E.L. Jeffers, Mrs. P. Schatz, Mrs. L.W. Moore, Miss H.M. Wilson. Back row: Miss C. Sanders, Mrs. L.C. Childs, Mrs. F.S. Cullen, Mr. G.R. Fish, Mrs. B. O'Donnell, Miss L.E. Muscente, Mrs. D.L. Robison.

The Lower School and its Leadership

launched the American industrial revolution. A devout Friend, he became a strong abolitionist.

In the 1950s, the Moses Brown Lower School consisted of Kindergarten (called "Pre-Primary") plus seven grades divided into three "Primary" and four "Intermediate" levels. Upper School consisted of five Forms (Eighth Grade through Twelfth). At that time there was no Middle School corresponding to Junior High in the public schools.[8] There were some differences between the Primary level and the Intermediate level experiences in Lower School (for example, the Intermediates had no organized naps at lunchtime, their curricula were a bit more structured, and their sports were more organized), but despite such differences there did not seem to be more than minor distinctions between the two levels—at least to us students. The jump from Lower School to Upper School was far greater than the jump from Primary to Intermediate within the Lower School.

Mr. Allen. The Lower School itself was reasonably separate from the Upper School. It had its own faculty (only a couple of teachers taught in both), its own dedicated locations, its own special events (including exhibitions and the Christmas Pageant), its own staff, and its own administrative head. During our entire time at Moses Brown, the latter was Mr. J. Drisko Allen (whose friends called him Dick). A graduate of Colby College, with graduate work at Harvard and Wisconsin, he had been hired as a teacher in 1929 and had become head of the Lower School in 1941.[9] He had numerous responsibilities, and was ultimately in charge of most Lower School affairs, including curriculum, record keeping, admissions, sports, special events, and discipline. He led and he coordinated.

Mr. Allen was well-qualified for the job, a person who could interact effectively with children, hold the hands of parents, maintain the respect of the teaching staff, and presumably move paperwork with smooth efficiency. Our student encounters with him were fairly frequent. He recurrently showed movies to the Lower School in Alumni Hall and presided at most of its ceremonies or

---

8   The Middle School, consisting of the Seventh and Eighth Grades, was created in the fall of 1958 while we were in Upper School.

9   Paxton, *Moses Brown School: A History of the Third Half-Century* (1974), pp. 30, 54.

events. During recess in springtime he used a fungo bat to hit pop flies ("fungoes") for Lower School students to catch, rewarding each successful grab with a penny. He came to our classrooms to explain things and make consequential announcements. I can remember him lecturing us on how important it was for us to wear rubbers on our shoes when it rained. Apparently the word had gotten around that it was a "sissy" thing to do, and Mr. Allen arrived in the classroom one day to dispel that myth. He explained that it was an ADULT thing to do (he never called adults "grown-ups"), that it protected the shoes, and that he himself never failed to wear his own rubbers.

He was a very calm and controlled person. He never raised his voice, but always conveyed a strong sense of authority as he talked to us in moderate, measured, and well-enunciated speech. He wasted no words. His sentences were pronouncements—stated in well-chosen and purposeful terms. They were, however, never fiats. When he announced a policy or rendered a decision he always gave a reason for it. His explanations, carefully presented, implied that he had thought the issue through (and had probably spoken in similar terms before). To us children, these explications always seemed dispositive, and combined with the firm modulations in his voice, they created a very strong impression of unassailable authority which neither rank nor emphasis by themselves would have created. In addition, Mr. Allen's explanations were often given in language that conveyed the impression that he was upholding a universal principle, or following a long-standing custom that was above challenge or reproach. His assured tone conveyed the certainty that this was just the way things were done—although he would never employ those terms explicitly. He spoke clearly and factually, and was precise in stating exactly what he wanted and why. For young children, his approach was powerfully persuasive. When he spoke, we listened. As we got older, his style seemed a bit condescending and aimed at kids a bit younger than us, but we were so used to him and his mannerisms by then, that we didn't resent it. And, from habit, we never thought of challenging him.

Mr. Allen was always polite, but he could firmly convey displeasure. On one occasion I remember he caught several of us during recess playing unsupervised on stone steps at the rear of the Upper School gymnasium, which we were not supposed to do. He firmly ordered us off the steps, explained in even tones that playing on stone steps could be dangerous, that this area was therefore off-limits to us, and that we had been told this.

The Lower School and its Leadership

J. Drisko Allen

Then, with determined strides, he herded us back to our sixth-grade classroom where we were condemned to spend the rest of the week with our heads down on our desks during recess.

He did listen—or at least gave the appearance of it. When we were in the Seventh Grade, our tennis instructor was criticized by some parents for his coaching practices. Word got around. I remember Bob Saywell, a fellow seventh grader, and I went to Mr. Allen's office and defended the coach, arguing that he was doing an excellent job. Mr. Allen began by listening, then explained to us in general terms the nature of the complaints, and asked us to respond to them, which we did. He thanked us for taking the initiative, listened to our expostulations, treated our views with respect, and was in no way either patronizing or dismissive. As I recall, the coach was not fired.

Mr. Allen was the ultimate authority with respect to discipline. Most teachers were expected to handle their own disciplinary issues with students, but if someone was truly a problem—or an offense was sufficiently great—the punishment was to be sent to Mr. Allen's office. This was a portentous sentence, and very seldom invoked. I somehow avoided it and can't give a firsthand account of what the experience entailed, but I do remember that few, if any, ever described what happened. Their silence added to the apprehension. Since Mr. Allen was a fair, sober, firm, and calm individual with no trace of vindictiveness (and a person who, no doubt, went by the book), I can't imagine he imposed anything disproportionate on the offender. He may, however, have contacted parents, and that would have had its own results. As the ultimate punishment, a trip to his office was emphatically to be avoided.

Bill Goddard, a half century after the fact, did tell me about being sent to Mr. Allen's office. His offense was not personal. As Bill recalled, we had been asked to bring some toys to school and he had brought a modern toy soldier, duly equipped with a modern toy rifle. Moses Brown, however, was a Quaker school, and toy rifles, especially military ones, were not welcome. Probably not sure how to handle this herself, the teacher sent Bill to Mr. Allen. As Bill recalled the encounter, Mr. Allen confiscated his rifle, explained exactly why he was doing so, and sent him back to the classroom.[10]

Mr. Allen's attire and mannerisms matched his proper style of address. He always wore a suit and tie, and sported well-polished shoes. Frequently, he wore an unwrinkled London Fog raincoat. Although he removed his jacket when hitting pop flies at recess, he did not remove his tie, and his well-pressed white shirt, which he never seemed to soil, was a distinguishing characteristic on these occasions. Unlike Mr. Thomas and several Upper School faculty members, he seldom wore a three-piece suit, but in all other accoutrements he was fully presentable, and to have encountered him on campus outside of his normal attire would have seemed shocking. Off campus was a bit different: it was his custom to relent slightly and remove his tie when leading a dozen or so seventh graders on summer bicycle tours from Providence to Montreal and back, but his white shirt and collar were as pristine as always throughout the trip. The one occasion when Mr. Allen did create sartorial shock was at a square dance which took place in our Sixth Grade year: he appeared in immaculate blue jeans, a striking red shirt, and red bandanna. Jaws dropped. However, it seemed that he fully understood that he was making a statement (as it would be put today), and he appeared to enjoy himself immensely. Though proper, Mr. Allen was not stiff. Though formal, he always seemed quietly confident—and comfortable both with us and with himself. We therefore respected him, but did not fear him. He did have a sense of humor, and he smiled upon occasion, but he was never effusive. To us, he was our mentor, not our pal.

---

10 Conversation over dinner, December 2016.

The physical surroundings. The Lower School classrooms over which Mr. Allen had administrative responsibilities were located in two places. Pre-Primary and Grades One through Four were located in the Lower School building itself, which had been built off the southwest corner of the main building, and was connected to that building on the second floor with an archway through which ran a hallway with a classroom to its west (shared with the Upper School). This is now called the Seth K. Gifford Building, named for the Headmaster who was instrumental in starting the country day school at Moses Brown. The building was given its present name and rededicated to Dr. Gifford's memory in a ceremony held in 1960 directly after our Commencement, with his daughter, Margaret Gifford Sisson, in attendance.

The Lower School building was a well-built edifice with fine oak or chestnut woodwork—I remember the heavy balustrades and the solid upright posts on the stairwells which were handy for swinging around the corners. Also, the large exterior walls were thick, and there existed fairly wide surfaces in front of each window which were often filled with decorative plants or botany experiments. The windows themselves were wide and tall, and all classrooms in the Lower School building had windows on the south side of the building, and hence on sunny days they were filled with light throughout all seasons. The building is still used for classrooms and offices today.[11]

---

11 On each floor there were three rooms leading off a corridor (lined with lockers), which ran east/west on the north side of the building, accessed on the second floor by two stairwells at its ends. The whole building was entered by a single doorway under the archway (and by the corridor across the arch mentioned above).

The Pre-Primary, which Miss Otla Woodbury taught, was located on the first floor of this building on the southwest corner, far to the right as you entered the building through the main door under the arch. The First Grade, taught by Miss Eleanor Eastman, was on the second floor, also on the southwest corner, right above the Pre-Primary room. The Second Grade, taught by Mrs. Dorothy Robison, was on the second floor in the middle of the south side. The Third and Fourth Grades, as described in more detail below, were in the southeast corner on the first and second floors, respectively.

Mr. Allen's office was on the first floor, next to the staircase immediately to the left upon entering the building. There was a small room above his office on the second floor that was used for special purposes, such as for the nurse when she visited, or for special testing. The bathrooms were on the north wall, on both floors, as I recall. The basement was a storage area for sports equipment, and was accessed by stairs from within and by a door accessible at ground-level from the outside near the southwest corner of the building. It had a large room lined with lockers where, according to Bill Barrett, sports (e.g. dodgeball) took place on rainy days.

Grades Five through Seven were located in the building attached to the east side of Middle House (a location now named for the late Headmaster David Burnham). This area today is no longer used for classes. Older than the Lower School building, it, too, had thick walls and wide windowsills. Beneath this classroom area were the kitchen and storage rooms; above were two floors of dormitory rooms.[12] As a child, one felt very secure in these solid structures.

The classes were small—about fifteen to twenty students. We sat at separate desks, not fixed to the floor, but mounted on boards which could slide, so that the desks could be moved and rearranged. The desks had tops on them, and all the papers, books, mimeographed reading materials, pens, pencils, erasers, etc. were stored in them. The hinged top of the desk sloped up and away from you; the front side of the desk (next to where you sat) sloped inward, down and away from you, so that the bottom of the desk was smaller than the top.

Under the cover of each desk, along the front, there was a trough for the pens and pencils. Fountain pens were introduced to us in the Third Grade. My Lower School classmate Bill Barrett recalled that before then the class had used only pencils. However, even in the Third Grade we were not yet fully trusted with ink-filled pens, and they were stored on the teacher's desk. Bill assumes that this security measure had resulted from prior catastrophes and shenanigans caused when eight-year-olds were introduced to pen and ink. I can visualize those pens now, standing upright in round holes punched through the top cover of a box.

By the time we got to the Fourth Grade, we were trusted to keep our pens in the desk. These were ink fountain pens. Ballpoint pens were still in an early stage and were not very reliable. I remember learning how to fill the

---

12 As one left Middle House, the first room on the south wall was where the Fifth Grade was located, the second room was where the Seventh Grade met, and the third (and last room on the south wall) was not a homeroom, but was used primarily by the Sixth Grade for its social sciences classes. The Sixth Grade homeroom was on the north wall of this building in the east corner. Thus the Fifth and Seventh Grade classrooms, with southern exposures, were sunny and bright. The Sixth Grade, with most of its windows facing north, was not as bright, although there were two windows on the east wall which let in the morning sun. Thus the Lower School classrooms were located so that seven out of the eight (including Pre-Primary) had bright southern exposures. This was probably by design.

fountain pens by sticking them into the ink and squeezing the ink sac which was surrounded by a thin flexible metal piece shaped like a very long "U." This was attached to the cylinder of the pen at only one end. When you pressed on the metal piece, it bent inward against the rubber ink sac. That expelled the air (often creating minute bubbles in the ink bottle); when you released it, the ink was drawn into the sac. Many ink bottles had a small pouch-like reservoir near the top on one side. We would tip a securely closed bottle to fill the reservoir, then remove the cap and inset the point of the pen into the reservoir to fill it. A Kleenex was needed to wipe the surplus ink off the action end of the pen.

For several grades we were not allowed to keep ink in the desk, but had to fill our pens at the teacher's desk. It was a rite of passage (in the Sixth Grade, I believe) when we were finally permitted to have our own ink bottle. Many desks had inkwell holes on the top right corner, but these were never used for their original intended purpose.

The desks were arranged in rectangular ranks and files, and the seating was alphabetical. In the Third Grade our names were called out with some frequency so that we soon learned those of our classmates in predictable sequence. The rooms had very high ceilings, appearing all the more so because of our small stature. Lamps, as I recall, were suspended from the ceiling in each classroom.

The blackboards were, indeed, black. As our desks were arranged, the blackboards were in the front of the classroom in all but the Fifth Grade (where there was a fireplace in front); in several classrooms there were blackboards on more than one wall. Each classroom in the Lower School building had a round clock attached high up on the wall. There was a central system, and every minute the hand would click back slightly and then a second or so later click forward to the next minute. If you were bored with class proceedings, you could look up at the clock and watch for the click. I cannot recall if there was a buzz or bell or other alarm system in the Lower School associated with these clocks that would proclaim the hour or the end of a class period. I believe that each teacher simply monitored the time. There was such a bell system in the Upper School. In both cases, classes were temporally well-structured.

Throughout the Lower School, the floors were covered with a false covering made to look like floorboards. It was probably some special form of linoleum, which warped and buckled in the winter, and which always squeaked noisily as you walked over it. This was true for all rooms in the Lower School building (as well as for those Lower School classrooms located to the east of Middle House), and for most of the Upper School classrooms as well. I also remember the steam radiators and connecting pipes, which in the winter time banged and clanged as the steam came up or went down, thereby expanding or contracting the pipes. These noises from the floors and from the heating system became so familiar that one could find them reassuring—and on a cold winter day with snow swirling around the buildings, the rooms had a warm and secure ambience to them. In fact, the whole setting was reassuring. Our homerooms were a kind of predictable "safe space." Having our own desks, books, lockers, and other items that we used every day could be comforting. It was not quite the same as having our own rooms at home (with our own toys and furnishings), but the arrangements did provide the rudiments of a sense of possession and ownership. Moreover, our routines were fairly predictable, and we soon got used to our classmates, whose desks were almost always located in the same place and whose names were almost always called in the same order. There were many opportunities to experience the excitements of innovation and developmental change, and that was what we were there for, but living in a stable and reassuring physical environment made our new experiences less threatening and therefore potentially more welcome and exciting.

II

Early Years: K through Second Primary (1947-1950)

———

I have no personal recollections to contribute regarding Pre-Primary through Second Primary since I did not attend during those years. The Pre-Primary teacher was Miss Woodbury, whose first name, we later learned, was "Otla."[13] She was a graduate of Wheelock College, with graduate work at Columbia. Bill Barrett, writing in our 1960 yearbook, comments on her smile, the sandbox over which she presided, and the swings we used (and she monitored) in Pre-Primary. I do remember Miss Woodbury herself from casual encounters during Lower School years. She was always very quiet, friendly, and encouraging in conversation. She obviously liked people, and especially us boys. She had a nurturing quality that went well with her generally positive outlook. She obviously took a great interest in us. In later years, she retired to Beverly, Massachusetts, where Tommy Clark from the Class of 1960 was the political editor of the town newspaper, the *Beverly Times*. When interviewed during her retirement, she commented that she enjoyed reading a publication every day edited, in part, by one of her "boys."

In the *Mosaic*, our yearbook, there is a photograph of the Class of 1960 taken in the Pre-Primary classroom in which several of my future classmates are

---

13 The Pre-Primary classroom was located in the southwest corner of the Lower School building on the main floor.

12 Early Years: K through Second Primary (1947-1950)

The Class of 1960 in the Pre-Primary

Early Years: K through Second Primary (1947-1950)

Eleanor Eastman

clearly identifiable.[14] Vin Marcello is playing in the sandbox (along with someone I do not recognize) under the watchful eyes of a teacher who must have been Miss Woodbury's assistant. Billy Goddard is seated on a '40s truck (which is too small for him); two class members are seated on a toy locomotive. Mark Saklad and Bill Fischer are standing at a table engaged in a joint project which is just out of view. Nick Littlefield is seated at a table with Miss Woodbury and two other boys who are intently working on separate projects. Steven Spear (whom we lost touch with) and a companion are on the floor separately building edifices with building blocks. Someone is using a toy hammer on a piece of wood held in place by a vise. Almost everyone is intently engaged in focused and purposeful activity: building, moving, altering, improving. Everyone is serious. It is a remarkable picture of fifteen five-year-olds who are concentrating on the enterprises at hand. The picture is in some way very symbolic and prescient, for if these pages chronicle anything, it is sustained, intense, and usually focused activity, undiminished throughout the decade.

In the First Grade, Miss Eleanor Eastman and a Miss Murray, according to Bill's narrative, taught simple addition and subtraction to the class,

---

14   1960 *Mosaic*, p. 20.

Otla W. Woodbury

while "Dick, Jane, Father, Mother, Spot, and Puff brightened our outlook on the English language."[15] The 1958 *Mosaic* account mentions first-grade number cards (probably flash cards of the held-up variety), which I seem to remember being used for arithmetic instruction in the Third Grade as well.[16] Miss Eastman was always very friendly. I remember seeing her off and on throughout my decade at the School, and even though she never had me in class, she knew who I was and always said, "Hello." She was a very calm person who moved with assurance, but also slowly and with deliberation. She was soft-spoken and quite correct. She was not in any way cold, but her speech was precise and her words carefully chosen. She was more like a grandparent than a parent. She had a nice smile, and I suspect that her classes were enjoyable, yet ordered. She was a graduate of Wheelock College. In the First Grade Miss Louise Muscente taught penmanship and art.

By the Second Grade, we were wearing coats and ties (often of the clip-on variety). Mrs. Dorothy Robison was the homeroom teacher. I can remember her relatively well, again from a distance. As I recall, she had red hair,

---

15   1960 *Mosaic*, p. 21.
16   1958 *Mosaic*, p. 35.

Early Years: K through Second Primary (1947-1950)   15

or was possibly a strawberry blonde. Mrs. Robison seemed to be a matter-of-fact and down-to-business-like person, intelligent, organized, and with a take-charge attitude. Some parents did not care for her, but none, I remember, challenged her competence. It was this year that "Mrs. Bachman played 'stepping stones' with us to teach arithmetic. Many were the boys who fell into the pond because eight and three made twelve."[17] No doubt there was more reading at an advanced Dick-and-Jane level. The Second Grade was the first of several years in which we had French lessons from Madame Emma Ducimetiere Warge. The 1958 *Mosaic* shows a joint art project with that class making a large mural. We might also have made one in our Second Grade year. According to Bill's account, this was the year that the yo-yo "was sweeping the country" and that Vin Marcello, one of two classmates who experienced all thirteen years of Moses Brown, won our yo-yo contest.[18] He also recalled that the class was given a tour of a dairy farm in Lincoln, "where we were treated to ice cream cones and Mark Saklad broke his arm."[19] Mark became the other thirteen-year veteran. Thus the early years.

---

17 1960 *Mosaic*, p. 21.

18 Vincent Marcello, who joined our Class in Pre-Primary, as noted, served as our Class President from the Second through Fifth Forms in the Upper School. He graduated from Tufts University and earned an MBA from Columbia Business School, working for a prominent Wall Street investment firm while at Columbia. Eventually he found his way into investment real estate with a diversified Rhode Island real estate firm. Observing that Newport, RI, was at the beginning stages of a real estate resurgence, he started his own firm there in the 1970s, with an emphasis on investments. This firm, which he ran for many decades, grew to become a prominent leader in property management, brokerage, appraisals, condo conversions, and syndications. Through its wholly owned real estate school, the firm grew to have more than 50 full- and part-time associates, and was sold to a national real estate franchise in 2011. Even in retirement, Vin is still active in Newport real estate. Like so many of our classmates, he is a devoted golfer.

19 1960 *Mosaic*, p. 21. Mark Saklad, one of two classmates who attended Moses Brown from Pre-Primary through the Fifth Form, went from Moses Brown to Beloit College and thence to MIT, where he became a highly trained engineer, and thus launched a very successful career in the high-tech culture of Massachusetts's famous Route 128—the Silicon Valley of the northeast.

III

Third Primary: The Third Grade
(1950-1951)

The Third Grade was memorable, and especially for me because it was my introduction to Moses Brown. Our homeroom, as noted, was on the first floor in the southeast corner of the Lower School building.[20] Adjacent to the classroom, and separated from it by sliding doors, was a room that featured a fireplace and a piano. It was vacant much of the time, but was used as extra space, mostly for the Third Grade. I can remember reading classes and music classes in this room. It was there that we changed clothes for sports and were adorned with red bows for the Christmas Pageant. We also used it for exhibits, pet shows, and puppeteering.

The school year always began on a Wednesday in mid-September,[21] and every year we were dismissed at noon on this day. Starting with half a day and half a week provided a good transition from summer vacation. Every morning during the school year, Lower School classes would open with The Lord's Prayer, a moment of silence, the Pledge of Allegiance, and the singing of "America (My Country 'Tis of Thee)"—all four verses,

---

20 The class faced north most of the time, although I seem to recall that occasionally the desks were rearranged to different configurations, including one experiment in which we faced each other across a central space. Miss Wilson's desk was in the southeast corner of the room, behind us (when we faced north), with the blackboard in front of us, a vantage point from which she could monitor our doings.

21 Except in the Sixth Grade (Third Intermediate) when a polio epidemic led to a postponed opening.

which we soon memorized. Lower School classes began at 8:45 a.m. and went to noon. In the Primaries, classes resumed at 2:00 p.m. and ended at 3:00 p.m. Sports went until 4:00 p.m. In the Intermediate Grades, afternoon classes began at 1:10 p.m. and went to 3:00 p.m., with sports going to 4:30 p.m., fall and spring, and to 4:00 p.m. in winter. There was one recess break during the morning, and there was a midmorning snack break at which we had milk (or chocolate milk) at our desks, accompanied by cookies, often Oreos, as I recall. The only other break was caused by an occasional fire drill, during which we would promptly march out of the building in an orderly fashion—and from which we would slowly return in a disorderly fashion.

Some of us went home for lunch. Most stayed at School. The dining area was located under the Upper School classrooms between the study hall and Middle House. This was a low-ceilinged room with many tables and posts. Since I was one of those who almost always went home for lunch, I had few adventures in the dining room, but I do remember the tasty mashed potatoes.

In the Primary Grades, there was a supervised nap during the second half of the two-hour break for those who stayed at School. Bill Barrett recalled that the nap room was on the third or fourth floor above the Seventh Grade classroom, and was reached by a circuitous route through the dining room and basement. He remembered going there sometimes, even after returning from lunch. Students lay down on cots or in rows on blankets on the floor. Few actually napped. Sometimes the teacher would read a story. After about an hour they returned to the classroom.

I managed to avoid naps totally. Even when my folks were away, I always went home in the Third Grade since someone was always there to prepare lunch. Because it did not take two hours to eat, and since naps were for sissies, those of us who did go home would return to School and have time on our hands. Nicky Littlefield, Tommy Clark, Bill Barrett, and Bill Fischer all went home because they lived nearby, and when we got back we would go into Miss Woodbury's room and make creative use of the blackboards, which were on the east wall. Underneath the blackboards were boxes or footlockers on which we would stand to reach the blackboards. Her own class left at noon, and the space was uncontested. We played tic-tac-toe,

Harriet M. Wilson

drew pictures of boats, made triangles and squares, or just made a mess of the board. This could not have been unsupervised, but I do not remember Miss Woodbury interfering with any of our efforts. When 2:00 p.m. arrived, we returned to the tender care of Miss Wilson.

One cannot begin to discuss Third Grade instruction without a description of Harriet Wilson herself—the "Redoubtable Miss Wilson," as my father called her. She was a fairly heavyset drillmaster who proceeded with the strong assertiveness of a woman from a near-southern culture who, with that background, probably had to elbow her way around to become recognized as a professional. She was more than a bit controversial among parents, although many approved of her methods.[22]

In later years I enjoyed meeting her again and engaging her in conversation. Standing with a Manhattan in her hand, she could be downright convivial while discussing her ancestor Sam Houston,[23] or telling anecdotes about her farm in Delaware. My mother got along with her very well—I think they took art classes together. But from the standpoint of a seven-year-old, she really did inspire a level of apprehension, if not hostility, and

---

22 A Moses Brown Alumnus described for me his parents' criticisms of Miss Wilson.
23 Pronounced "House-ton" as she frequently reminded us.

I did not enjoy being under her tutelage. Not that she ever laid a hand on anybody—or remotely threatened to—but her presence and manner were intimidating. As Mrs. Marcello, Vin's mother, observed fifty years later, "She was TOUGH!"[24] Moreover, she could be a bit arbitrary at times, and I could never feel fully secure in terms of what was expected of me with respect to effort and conduct. Looking back, she marked the end of my fully idyllic childhood—she forced me to take the first steps in a long journey towards maturity. In this regard, she was very good for me, no doubt, in the tradition of a bad-tasting medicine, but at the time I was not happy with the flavor. Many classmates shared this perspective.

Miss Wilson was a strict disciplinarian. She raised her voice on frequent occasions and bellowed out orders and criticisms. She was willing to single out any miscreant and make an example of him in front of the class.[25] She certainly commanded attention, and this was reinforced by her prowess with the baseball bat—not in the classroom, I might add, but on the playing field—where she could belt a home run beyond an outfielder's head. This capability, much more than her vocalizations, earned our respect. She really was intrinsically a nice person, and you had a different perspective on her when you had grown to be six inches taller than she was, but to the uninitiated third grader, she was truly formidable, towering above us like a wave about to crash. And since I repeated the Third Grade, I had a year and a third of her—more than anyone else at Moses Brown in my time as far as I know.

On one occasion I fought back. We had a periodical called *My Weekly Reader* in which there were occasional quizzes on which you could give your opinion of all and sundry. These included questions about your teacher. One was "What do you wish most about your teacher?" I responded that I wished she would not holler as much as she did. I think Miss Wilson actually got a big kick out of this, but on the next occasion when we transgressed, she looked at me, perhaps humorously, and asked, "Now do you see why I have to shout as much?" But I had scored a point, and it felt good.

---

24 Interview with Mrs. Marcello, 2014.
25 The experience was certainly a great contrast to that of the class in which my aunt was a teacher; although also a strict disciplinarian, she seldom raised her voice.

Frances M. Bachman

The stormy relationship with the thundering Miss Wilson was interrupted and counterbalanced by a much calmer relationship with her assistant, Mrs. Frances Bachman (who, incidentally, was responsible for bringing her nephew Jan Moyer to Moses Brown to become our Fifth-Form classmate in Upper School).[26] Mrs. Bachman, who graduated from Cumberland Valley State Normal School in Shippensburg, Pennsylvania, was an even-tempered and mature person. She was a very nice lady, cheerful and even friendly at times, but also strict, though not severe. She never raised her voice. She proceeded to business calmly and professionally without any fanfare. She kept order and tolerated no nonsense, but order was achieved without pyrotechnics. Mrs. Bachman never attained the "character" quality of Miss Wilson, but was in many ways a more effective teacher. She certainly gave us a lot of personalized attention. When she taught, Miss Wilson would leave the room, and the atmospheric change was quite noticeable

---

26 Jan Moyer joined our Class in the Fifth Form. He graduated from Brown (where he was elected to its Athletic Hall of Fame) and went to Kansas, where he worked for Continental Grain, a large national commodities corporation. After becoming acquainted with the commodities trade, he then joined and became a top executive at Farmarco, a large cooperative that traded in grain and grain futures. He then moved to Garvey Grain, another large commodities corporation, where he rose to become president, retiring from that position to play golf and enjoy life. From a telephone interview with Jan, May 9, 2020.

(and welcome). Although Mrs. Bachman always provided a refreshing interlude, as an assistant teacher she seemed to stand in the shadow of her formidable colleague. It was, after all, Miss Wilson's classroom—she was the homeroom teacher; she commanded the desk. Mrs. Bachman later was to succeed Miss Pixley as the homeroom teacher for the Fourth Grade.

Another counterbalance to the terror from Miss Wilson came from my classmates. Although there was no opportunity to socialize during class, there were opportunities during recess, at lunchtime, and after school, and I soon developed very friendly relationships with many of my fellow pupils. Whereas I had had rocky relationships with kids in the Class of 1959 when I was a member of it, the kids in the Class of 1960 welcomed me warmly. The contrast was striking, and the friendly associations I developed served as a social counterbalance to the diffidence I felt in dealing with our redoubtable senior teacher.

Many classmates were day students, some from the East Side of Providence, with most of the rest commuting from the suburbs. There were only a few boarders. Bill Barrett, Nick Littlefield, and later Tommy Clark, were close neighbors of ours—we all lived less than a couple of blocks from School. The East Side of Providence at the time was a fairly safe area, and even at an early age we were permitted to walk to School or over to a neighbor's house unaccompanied. The only caution was in crossing the street, and we all had received careful instruction from our parents on how to look both ways and proceed carefully. We were newcomers to the neighborhood, and soon after we moved in, several classmates dropped by to visit. I suspect that their parents had told them that this was the polite thing to do. I remember Tommy Clark inviting me to go down to nearby Thayer Street where he took me into a novelty store (probably the Merry-Go-Round) which sold toy automobiles. I had been given a little cash and he encouraged me to purchase one, which I did. Nick Littlefield, who lived just around the corner, came by frequently and we played with my toy Lionel train up in the attic (Nick also had a Lionel). Fairly early on, several classmates from the East Side began to collect stamps, and we spent much time trading them. I can remember being invited down to the Barretts', who lived around another corner. Here for the first time I encountered comic books (which were not encouraged in my household).[27] I can remember visiting the Goddards' a few blocks away to play Clue.[28] Although these relationships matured over the whole Lower School experience, they began in the Third Grade.

Math. Miss Wilson's specialty was math, and for us it consisted of addition, subtraction, simple multiplication, and simple division.[29] We were taught how to "carry" numbers in adding, and how to "borrow" them in subtracting. The former was easy for us—you made a small notation at the top of the adjacent column to the left and added it in when you did that column. The "borrowings" were more difficult for me, since (half the time) you had to cross out an existing number and write the next lower digit above it or under it. These procedures were taught as rules, and the logic behind them was never explained. This was simply how it was done—and we did it repeatedly until we memorized the routine.

---

27 Bill Barrett joined our Class in the Second Grade. He remained at Moses Brown all the way through the Fifth Form, winning the prestigious Headmaster's Cup at graduation. He went to Harvard, where he lettered in cross country. Erich Segal, his section man in an introductory humanities course and fellow distance-running aficionado later wrote the script for *Love Story* at the same time that he was writing a letter of recommendation to law school for Bill, and Bill has always suspected that Segal may have used his name as the inspiration for the name of the leading character, Oliver Barrett, while the model for the main character himself may have been Harvard All-American hockey star Joe Cavanaugh (who lived in the house where Segal was a tutor). Cavanaugh was from Cranston, RI, which may have been the reason that Segal portrayed the other leading character, Jennifer Cavalieri (note the identity of initials), as coming from Cranston in the movie. After college, Bill was on active duty in the Navy for six years (serving both at sea and ashore in Vietnam and Japan, eventually retiring as a reservist in the grade of Captain). He later graduated from Harvard Law School and practiced corporation law in both New York and Boston for many years. Since his Moses Brown days he has loved hiking and mountain climbing. He now lives in New Hampshire, where he volunteers extensively for the Appalachian Mountain Club as a trail adopter.

28 Bill Goddard joined the Class in Pre-Primary. He left Moses Brown for St. George's School in Middletown, RI, after the Seventh Grade. Following a stint at Yale, he joined the Army and saw action in Vietnam. Upon return, he became a venture capitalist, successfully following a centuries-long tradition in his very old Rhode Island family. Fifty South Main Street, the building that has headquartered his family business for well over two centuries, is one of the finest examples of authentic Federal architecture in America.

29 Not double-digit multiplication or "long division," both of which we learned in the Fourth Grade.

We also learned and recited the multiplication table solidly through ten by ten, and later through twelve by twelve. The elevens were easy.[30] A lot of this was familiar territory for me, having learned it at home (where my parents made games out of mathematical exercises) or in Mapleville. Miss Wilson used an exercise book (I remember the blue cover). It had time limits for the exercises that we were supposed to do in class or at home. She also used a book called *Learning to Compute*—which we encountered again in Fifth Grade and once more in Upper School. It was a difficult book, used sparingly in the Third Grade.

It was a world of repetition. The purpose, I assume, was to use repetition to build memory so that "hand" computations became easy to perform. There are scores of two-digit combinations for simple addition, subtraction, multiplication, and division, and we had to learn them all. Learning these combinations was not a chore for me at this time, since I already knew many of them, but I found the endless exercises in addition and subtraction to be very dull, with nothing at all enjoyable about them. Even less enjoyable was doing them under time constraint. The subtractions, though not always simple, seemed less prone to careless mistakes, and we were taught at an early age how to check the subtractions by adding the remainder to the subtrahend to get the minuend—impressive terms we were made familiar with around this time. There was, however, no easy way to check the accuracy of additions, other than by doing them twice and getting the same result (for long columns, we were told to check the totals by adding the numbers from top to bottom if initially we had added them from bottom to top). The additions were also more difficult because of the many individual items to be added, sometimes with differing numbers of digits. I was given some help on these exercises at home—I was encouraged to stick to them until done, and they might be carefully checked after the computations were completed. The whole practice of homework was a new experience to me, having had none before (in the Third Grade we did reading and writing assignments at home as well).

---

30   We were told that we did not need to learn the "eleven" multiplication table—just repeat the digit by which you were multiplying eleven. I think we were taught the "twelves" through 12x12 = 144. Somewhere along the way we were taught that when you multiplied 11 by a two-digit number, in which the digits summed to less than ten, you just added the two digits together and put the result in between them. Thus 11x12=132.

Homework and in-class exercises were corrected by Miss Wilson and returned to us with a numerical grade. "Corrected" is the right word here—mistakes were indeed corrected on the paper (usually in red pencil). This must have taken a lot of time on her part. Somewhere along the way (I'm not sure it was as early as the Third Grade) we were told occasionally to "exchange papers." The correct answers were then read out, and we graded each other's exams.

Often Miss Wilson would hand out her own worksheets which she mimeographed with an interminable number of computational exercises. I remember finding a mistake in one of them—where we were asked to subtract a larger number from a smaller number, and since we had not been introduced to the concept of negative numbers, this was clearly an error. I remember showing this to someone at home, and was duly instructed that I should indicate that a mistake had been made—and I was very pleased to have scored another point against Miss Wilson. Mistakes like this, however, rarely interrupted our routines and the math exercises were tedious and boring. Still, by the time we graduated from the Third Grade, we knew our number tables thoroughly and had mastered the computation skills expected of us.

Language skills (reading, composition, spelling, etc.), which later were called "English," were taught by both Miss Wilson and Mrs. Bachman. Reading and spelling were Mrs. Bachman's specialties. I remember looking forward to reading much more than to math. We sat in a large circle in the adjacent room and read. We used a book, *Streets and Roads*, somewhat of the Dick-and-Jane variety, although more advanced. Thumbing through it today, I remember most of the stories and I have recollections of enjoying them at the time. Even the illustrations look familiar. The book had a series of stories based on city living and country living, with children of our age being the central focus of each story. In addition, and reflecting the fact that we were still not far from the Teddy-bear era, there were tales featuring talking animals of the Peter Rabbit variety. There were also "fairy tales" in the Grimm tradition. Some stories were therefore "factual," while others were "make-believe." Almost all ended with smiling people and happy outcomes—and almost all had a "moral" to the story, such as the importance of honesty and the virtues of forming friendships and treating strangers decently. There was a similar book, *Finding New Neighbors*, which we used as well. Occasionally we would write simple stories ourselves, inspired by our reading experiences.

It Is my recollection that during the Third Grade, perhaps in the spring, we also had tracked reading—which meant that we would read with others at our own level. During my second year in the Third Grade (probably in the spring), I remember reading with the Fifth Grade—walking over to Miss Elsie Chappell's classroom every day for reading class. The texts were much more difficult than those in the Third Grade, the vocabulary was much advanced, and I remember being pushed very hard.

We were also encouraged to read outside of the classroom. I remember reading from the Landmark series, then a set of ten books, starting with Christopher Columbus, and including Jamestown, the *Mayflower*, the writing of the Constitution, and other, more recent events. In the Third Grade these were challenges, noticeably written in a style different from that of the books containing children's stories. They seemed more advanced and adult. We had to read several, and had to do book reports on them. In later years, more were published, and I remember reading them through the Fifth Grade. A somewhat more focused book that we read was entitled *They Made America Great*, a series of biographies aimed at a young audience, describing the childhood of the subjects as well as their adult contributions. It started with Columbus and went through FDR. It was intended to be an introduction to American history, and it covered many bases. The traditional heroes—Washington, Franklin, Adams, Jefferson, Jackson, Lincoln, Lee (not Grant), Theodore Roosevelt, Wilson—were given prominent treatment. FDR was lauded for his resilience in fighting polio, but his presidential accomplishments were listed very briefly in a couple of noncommittal sentences—he was still a very controversial figure in the 1950s. The book also included women's biographies (Betsy Ross, Dolly Madison, Elizabeth Zane, Clara Barton, Louisa May Alcott, Jane Addams); explorers and frontier men and women (Daniel Boone, Lewis and Clark, Buffalo Bill Cody, Narcissa and Marcus Whitman); inventors, scientists, and doctors (Eli Whitney, Alexander Graham Bell, the Wright Brothers, Henry Ford, George Washington Carver—the book's only African American—and William Gorgas); and social leaders, such as labor leader Samuel Gompers. I found this book to contain very interesting and inspiring reading. Thus, with both this book and the Landmark series, reading was used to teach history as well. We also had a book on American history *per se*, especially colonial history, but my recollection is that we did not spend much time with it.

I believe that we had a Book Fair in the Third Grade (where books for sale were displayed in Alumni Hall). These were held in the fall, with Christmas shopping in mind. I remember my mother buying me a child's book about Philadelphia called *The Cradle of Liberty*, probably at the Book Fair; my father commented at the time that this was unfair to Boston, which should have received equal billing! By the Sixth and Seventh Grades, my mother was in charge of the Book Fair, and it took on special meaning for me at that time.

Under Miss Wilson's direction, we also read a few poems. Each of us was asked to memorize one and recite it in class. My assignment was "October's Bright Blue Weather" by Helen Hunt Jackson, which I remember practicing with a parental audience. We also read a newspaper in the Third Grade called *My Weekly Reader*, as noted. I can remember seriously wondering if this title referred to its frequency or its quality, not yet being on top of the spelling distinction between the two homonyms. It had a feature story on its front page, a couple of editorial columns, a section on current events (aimed at our age group), and exercises on the back to test our vocabulary and reading comprehension. The stories were often about exotic places, interesting vocations, treasure hunts, new inventions (like skiplanes), festivals, animals, ship launchings, or patriotic celebrations. There were cartoons, a humor section, riddles, and some games. Often there would be lists of questions that we were asked to answer about ourselves or about the School.

We were expected to write papers in the Third Grade. Most were written as homework. They were typically about a page in length—but since our handwriting was quite large, a page did not contain many sentences. One important type of assignment was to write book reports which, generally speaking, were nothing more than brief attempts to summarize what the book was about. We were also asked to write brief papers on family adventures and other experiences we had undergone, including the inevitable

"What I Did Last Summer" at the opening of School. We were also asked to write about "My Favorite [whatever]." One essay I wrote was entitled, "The Bird." It went as follows: "Once upon a time there was a bird named Seedy. She was happy except for one thing. That was, she liked seeds but in winter time there were no seeds. She didn't like suet or sunflowers." A drawing of a bird sitting on a branch with leaves and seeds was cut out and taped to the top of the essay. I believe Miss Wilson was in charge of grading and "correcting" these.

About this same time I was inspired to start a newspaper at home. I think this was the result of being given a very primitive printing machine with rubber type that could be placed on a roll to produce copies about four inches in length. It may also have been the result of wanting to imitate adult behavior to feel more "grown up"—and to get recurrent praise or recognition. Every day for a while, I produced a publication entitled "Home News," in which I recounted the doings of the day. I was not very adept at setting type and operating the machine, so I soon abandoned it for a typewriter and carbon paper—which presented their own challenges when mistakes were made. Coverage included who overslept, what was served at meals, visitors, the occasional disaster (such as when someone who was interrupted while draining the washing machine forgot to close the spigot and flooded the floor), day trips, and other family events. I was encouraged to pursue this enterprise by my parents, each of whom dutifully bought the tabloid (for a penny a copy or five cents a week). I had three other subscribers: Aunt Amey, Grandpa Johnson, and Aunty Wallace. I think the folks felt it helped with writing at School. The following sample shows our level of third-grade spelling proficiency, and also confirms that New England accents ("Plumma") are acquired early in life:

January 15, 1951

HOME NEWS
Weather: WET!

This morning Igot up at 8:00.A.A.
Mamma stayed in bed until I went
to school. (and daddy went to work)
I came home For lunch, in a cab,
with mamma. I ate dinner (Mamma

Third Primary: The Third Grade (1950-1951)

> and daddy , Grandpa And Uncle Ben)
> were there of course. The Plumma
> came while we were eating dinner.
> Daddy went and saw him about some-
> thing. I went out to meat him.
> I hurryed off to school soon after
> that. Then daddy went back and
> finished his dinner.
>
> Editor: Clifford W. Brown Jr.

How long this publication remained in circulation, I do not recall—but it was still being published in May of that same year. I suspect that it folded temporarily at the onset of summer vacation after a run of five months. It resumed publication later and I have found an edition from the fifth grade.

Mrs. Bachman was in charge of spelling. I don't remember how it was taught, but I assume that phonics played a role. I do remember that we had spelling tests. On one occasion, I remember being afraid that I could not spell the word "beautiful," so I took the eraser of my pencil and spelled it out on the desk top in advance of the test. This stratagem did not go unnoticed, and I was caught red-handed during the exam looking at the desk top on which the word was spelled. Miss Bachman called me to account for this and I was told in no uncertain terms never to attempt to cheat again.

We had a few spelling bees. I do remember one in the Third Grade against a girls school—probably Lincoln or Wheeler. Bill Fischer and I were the last ones standing on our side. He was asked to spell the contraction "they're." He spelled it "the're," and was disqualified. On his way to sit down, he whispered to me the correct spelling containing the "y." The girl opposite then got it wrong, and the opportunity for success returned to me. But I was very stubborn about this—it just made no sense to put a "y" into it—so in utter folly, I repeated the wrong spelling that Bill had given, much to his chagrin, and I was sent to my seat. The remaining girl opposite then spelled it correctly, and Lincoln (or whatever school it was) won the spelling bee. These bees were sponsored by Webster's Dictionary, and there was a little gold medal for a prize. I certainly never won any prize in spelling.

Penmanship and Art. Language skills, of course, were underwritten by penmanship—a skill taught by Miss Muscente, who also taught art. A graduate of the Rhode Island School of Design, she was a striking young blonde, whose assets could be appreciated even by a third grader. She somehow seemed a bit out of place among the stolid instructresses at our Quaker school. She came in once or twice a week to teach penmanship and she used the blackboard to illustrate how to form letters. In doing so, her arms moved in graceful motions. She was an excellent calligrapher who made writing look very easy, even if it wasn't easy for some of us. There were little cards above the blackboards with cursive letters on them—capital and lowercase for each letter in the alphabet (perhaps the Palmer Method)—and they were the models we were asked to imitate. Attempting to mimic the style, we dutifully tried to copy each on paper (which we would line out in advance with our rulers). I was always bad at penmanship—and still am. I guess we were supposed to develop some free-flowing style so things would proceed comfortably, instinctively, and naturally. But instead, I remember laboring intensely over each letter and its formation, in effect almost cartooning it—and the result was (and is) terrible. Again, repetition was the method of instruction, and we spent considerable time trying to produce letters of acceptable quality. We would hand in our efforts, they would be corrected to conform to the models in front of us, and then we were told to try again. Although my teachers and some of my classmates were able to replicate the model letters beautifully, I had a great deal of difficulty in doing so. Things improved a bit with practice and as I grew older, but the end product was never elegant.

Miss Muscente also taught us art. I think we did this weekly in Miss Wilson's classroom, and not at the Studio.[31] Among other things, we did crayon drawings of trees and clouds, inevitably putting the sun in a blue sky. One of our Third Grade art projects was to take a bottle, cover it with papier-mâché, and then paint a design on it. My mother gave me a chutney bottle with an unusual shape to take to School (as something a bit novel), and I proceeded to make a mess of it. Eventually the papier-mâché (made from newspaper and paste) covered a fair amount of the bottle's surface space, but the paint job was quite random and, in connection with the papier-mâché, strikingly ugly. In fact, the whole decorated bottle turned

---

31 Its official name was the Studio of the Three Oaks, although no one ever seemed to call it that—just the Studio.

Third Primary: The Third Grade (1950-1951)

The Studio

out to be one of the ugliest art objects I have ever seen—an aesthetic judgment that I was able to make even in those days.

I gave it as a Christmas present to Aunty Wallace, an elderly lady who had been a neighbor of ours in Massachusetts and who now lived with us in Providence, but she immediately refused to have it in her room. Nobody else wanted it either. It therefore stood for years on the floor in a corner of one of our attic rooms until someone had the good taste to store something in front of it. Safely out of sight, it managed to survive, and today it remains a monument to the New England tradition that you should never throw anything away that might, someday, be remotely useful, although in this case it has had no conceivable use for more than a half century.

We also did some potato prints in the Third Grade—carving a pattern on the flat surface of a potato that had been sliced in half, and then covering it with paint and using it to replicate the pattern many times on a paper or cardboard surface. We were not all that dexterous, and so we proceeded slowly and deliberately to carve the patterns, hoping to mimic the example shown to us.[32] Somehow there was always a disconnect between what we were trying to do and what we actually could do, and that was both a bit frustrating and a bit puzzling. I also seem to remember finger painting in the Third Grade, but that memory is dim, and perhaps wrong.

Just before Valentine's Day (for several years) we made cards with lace and red construction paper to give to our parents, and with just red construction paper to give to our classmates. One year we all had photos taken at School, and these were pasted into the Valentine's cards. I therefore received a card from Nicky Littlefield with his picture in it asking me to be his Valentine. He probably received a similar card from me.

Music. Mrs. Louise (Winsor) Moore, from Greenville, taught us music in the Third Grade.[33] She was a nice person (and a distant relative) with a businesslike approach to her task. She herded us into the room adjacent to the Third Grade classroom and kept us busy, with no time available for nonsense. This recurrent break from ordinary classroom routines was refreshing. There was a piano in the northeast corner of the room tucked up against the wall. Although my memory is a bit vague on this point, I recall that we stood in line and sang songs as she played the piano. I do not remember if the singing was from memory or if we had a songbook. Selections included "My Country 'Tis of Thee" and "America the Beautiful." There were probably children's songs that I do not remember. No doubt we practiced in preparation for the Christmas Pageant and for Commencement exercises.

What I do remember quite well about this class was Mrs. Moore's attempt to form us into a rhythm band. We were given tambourines and drums that we were supposed to rattle or whack at the appropriate tempo. To structure that tempo, she put a large diagram on the board featuring half notes, quarter notes, eighth notes, and whatever else there may have been,[34] with stops and pauses, and everything else—all of which was completely mysterious to

---

32 The potato prints might have been in the Fourth Grade, but the chutney bottle was definitely in the Third.
33 She had received her musical training at Yale's Norfolk Music School.
34 The notes were not formed with a circle at their bottom, but with a "V" at their bottom. Each had the requisite number of crossbars at the top to indicate the length of the note.

Third Primary: The Third Grade (1950-1951)   33

me at the time. The result was visually intriguing, almost like Chinese calligraphy, but I never really understood what was going on, except that we made a lot of noise banging on our tambourines and drums. Without my being able to read the calligraphy, and without my really knowing what this was all about, my best clue for success was to imitate what everyone else was doing—which meant I was never quite up to beat. We did not perform in a concert. Whether this was because we were all so bad, or whether a concert had never been contemplated in the first place, I do not know.

Science instruction was cursory in this pre-Sputnik time. We did have a little science book, *The Wonder World of Science*, but we did not use it often. All I can recall is learning from that book that if you put a round goldfish bowl near the window, the sun's rays can be concentrated into a point and a fire may start. I think the book also mentioned dinosaurs. I can remember several experiments where we followed frogs' eggs hatching into tadpoles. I also remember seeds being planted between two plates of glass so we could watch them sprout and form roots. We ourselves were encouraged to plant seeds. I remember doing this in a yellow bowl and bringing it to School with a maple sprout to show that I had done it. One useful "scientific" thing we were taught was how many days there were in each month (a traditional poem was employed for this purpose: "Thirty Days hath September ..."), and the reason for leap years.

Shop. We had "Shop" (Manual Training) with Mr. Leo Cole, a graduate of the Massachusetts School of Art. This was over in the basement of the Studio which was filled with exciting woodworking equipment, most of which we were forbidden to use due to safety concerns. We entered this room from a side door on the south side of the building, reached by a few steps down from the outside, with a few more inside to bring us down to floor level. On the left, at the bottom of the steps, was an enclosed area walled-off by a metal and glass partition with a door immediately to your left as you entered the basement. This was the mechanical drawing room, filled with high sloping desks and blueprints on the inner walls (which we could only see when the door was open, since we were not tall enough to

Leo H. Cole

look over the metal part of the interior wall). Bill Barrett recalled that on the south wall to the right of the outside door as one entered the room there were two soapstone sinks. Bill was on partial scholarship (due to four siblings at Moses Brown and Lincoln and low earnings for pediatricians at the time) and thus was expected to perform a small task during each year. One year it was to clean paintbrushes in these sinks on Saturday mornings; another year it was to put out the Lower School swings each morning.

The shop area contained many work benches, cut and bruised from years of sawing, hammering, and the like. Students had carved their initials or names on them, and in places had sawed notches into the sides. Some were speckled with old paint. There was a vise on each bench. There was also a shallow depression on the bench, probably designed to hold nails and tools so they would not fall to the floor. I also remember metal pieces shaped like three-dimensional "T"s with rectangular tops and cylindrical bottoms that fitted into round holes, permitting the entire piece to rotate. These served as adjustable braces against which you could place a piece of wood to steady it. In the Third Grade we were barely tall enough to see the surface of these benches. Believe it or not, fifty years later (2010) some of these old tables were still there in the shop, probably the last remaining pedagogical artifacts still in use from our time.

Third Primary: The Third Grade (1950-1951)

To the right of the entrance door near the corner of the room was a lathe. To the left over in back was the memorably ancient band saw with two large drive wheels. We were not permitted to use either machine ourselves in the Lower School, but were instructed how to use each with care in Upper School.

I can remember that our Third Grade project for the fall was to saw out a breadboard made in the shape of a pig. The pattern was penciled for us on inch-thick boards. We clamped them into vises mounted at about eye level on our tables and proceeded to saw away with a hand jigsaw. Progress for me was slow—about an inch of sawing for each class, which would be about an inch per week. I was able to do the belly area between the legs, and some of the front leg and chest up towards the throat, but by the end of the term, I had failed to saw more than a quarter of the pig. Others fared better, but I was not alone in failing to finish. Much to my astonishment, Mr. Cole completed the project, and even drilled a hole at the rear creating the illusion of a curlicue tail, so that we could proudly take them home and make Christmas presents of them. It was actually a very good breadboard, and is still fully in service.

At some point during the breadboard process Tommy Clark was walking down Thayer Street, and saw Mr. Cole. "Hi! Cole-ee!" he said with enthusiasm. This was not deemed to be proper decorum for a Moses Brown student, and we were told by Miss Wilson in no uncertain terms that none of us was to do anything like this ever again![35]

Class projects and events. In the Third Grade, we had a series of class projects. Each year the Lower School had a fair (or exhibition), which was held in Alumni Hall during the spring. In 1950, when I first arrived in the Third Grade, the theme was transportation, and we made a large model of Union Station in Providence. The class took a trip down to see the station, but I was ill and did not go. My father, however, took me down later and

---

35 Tom Clark joined our Class in the early years of Lower School. He left Moses Brown after the Second Form and graduated from Belmont Hill. He later served in Vietnam and returned to work at the *Beverly Times* on Massachusetts's North Shore as Political Editor. He then worked for the *Salem Evening News*, covering political and legal stories for twenty years. He later worked in the mortgage departments of two Beverly banks.

Third Primary: The Third Grade (1950-1951)

1951 Safety Exhibit (L–R) Bill Goddard(?), Hank Levaur, Tommy Clark, and Maurice Chen, all from the Class of 1960.

Third Primary: The Third Grade (1950-1951)

gave me a tour. It was very busy, with many train arrivals, bustling waiting rooms, and a well-patronized restaurant. In 1950, the old shed out over the tracks was still there, but was taken down shortly thereafter.

We used matchboxes to build this model. As I recall, it was very well done. John Richardson ("59) worked hard on it, and it was auctioned off after the exhibit was over (I don't remember how). Someone took it home for use with his model trains.

In the spring of 1951, when I was in the Third Grade for the second time, the theme was safety. Bill Barrett recalled the Providence Fire Marshal coming and lecturing us on this topic. Again, we were asked to create an exhibit. I recall we third graders took a large cardboard box and created a cutaway model of a house (like a dollhouse) with rooms upstairs and downstairs (and a staircase). In this "house" we placed a large number of safety violations, such as little roller skates on the stairs, people smoking in bed, and other things like that. It was convincingly done. Miniature furniture was placed in the rooms. It was decorated with maroon wallpaper with gold dingbats on it. Viewers were asked to list how many violations they could find. We used it later for a marionette show. Nicky Littlefield and Tommy Clark, as I recall, brought the marionettes, and we used the "safety house" as a kind of theater for them.

Miss Wilson also sponsored a pet show. I can remember we were importuned to come with our pets. I brought a bowl of goldfish; someone else brought a black cocker spaniel. Bill Goddard, I think, brought a snake. Miss Wilson herself brought a former classmate of ours, Bill Batchelder, who had left the School earlier that year.[36] We were happy to renew acquaintances. We also had a hobby show, and I can remember bringing in plastic cereal box figures, together with some cardboard buildings that I made for the event.

We went on class trips. One was to the Roger Williams Park Museum where we were especially interested in the exhibit on the Narragansett Indians. In addition, we went to the Science Fair at Hope High School.

---

36 Bill Batchelder returned briefly to Moses Brown later in the Lower School and then went to St. George's where he became a football star and competed against us in Upper School. After that, we lost touch with him.

38 Third Primary: The Third Grade (1950-1951)

The 1954 Christmas Pageant, with the Class of 1960 in the center rows. Bill Fischer, rear right, is the reader of the Christmas Story.

Third Primary: The Third Grade (1950-1951)   39

Miss Wilson also made note in class of the fall election. I was interested in elections by the Third Grade. I had already become aware of them in 1948—before we lived in Providence. I remember being put to bed that year and being told by my very Republican parents that the wrong person (President Truman) was ahead and probably winning. I also remember a neighbor of ours taking me with her to the polling place when she voted that year. In 1950, two years later, Miss Wilson explained to us that there was an election in Rhode Island for governor and for the United States Senate. In the latter case, Senator John O. Pastore was being challenged by Republican Austin T. Levy. I can remember vaguely that Miss Wilson asked our preference in that election, and the class was predominantly Republican. My folks had worked for Mr. Levy many years before in Harrisville, knew him personally, and supported him. The Rhode Island voters, however, recorded a strong victory for Senator Pastore.

Another "event" in the Third Grade was Maurice Chen's getting the chicken pox. We were all quarantined for a day or two, but no one else got it, as I recall.

The Christmas Pageant. A major annual event was the Christmas Pageant, which was staged a week or two before Christmas in Alumni Hall. The entire Lower School from the Second Grade up took part in this.[37] The Second and Third Grades constituted the Junior Chorus; the four Intermediate classes constituted the Senior Chorus. I can remember participating in these events every year through the Seventh Grade.

The hall was very tastefully decorated for the season with wreaths and other greens. The windows, at least in the front section of the hall, were covered with transparent colored paper to make them resemble stained glass windows. A few students (with questionable voices) were selected to act out the nativity story. One seventh grader was selected to be the narrator, and he read the Christmas story from the *King James Bible*, a special

---

37   The 1958 and 1960 *Mosaics* erroneously state that the Third Grade was the first year in which Lower School boys took part in the Christmas Pageant. The programs list Second Grade participation.

honor that fell to Billy Fischer in our Seventh Grade year.[38] During some years, there may have been a student soloist.

We wore dark blue suits and large heavily starched white collars with a significant red bow attached to the front of the collar. The hall would be full of parents and other visitors. We marched over from the Lower School building and then down the center aisle of Alumni Hall, where we took our respective places, class by class, in the front of the auditorium facing the audience. Preliminary carols were sung, and then the narrator would begin to read the Christmas story. As the events unfolded in scripture, they were accentuated by more carols and illustrated by the actors, who would march down the center aisle in full costume and up onto the stage: the Holy Family, the Shepherds, and eventually the three Wise Men, processioning at times to "March of the Kings," and at other times to "We Three Kings of Orient Are." The program, which varied from year to year, would mix familiar Christmas carols (like "O Come, All Ye Faithful," "Silent Night," and "Joy to the World") with less familiar tunes. The Pageant typically featured carols and traditional songs from "many countries," including Germany, Scotland, France, Italy, Austria, and England. All were beautiful; some were much less familiar than others.[39] The production was well-staged and well-directed by Mrs. Thomas, the Headmaster's wife, who would play the electric organ throughout the event.

One year, about the Fifth Grade, the Pageant took place in a huge thunderstorm, unusual for the season. This led to a family episode. Grandpa

---

38   Bill Fischer joined our Class in Pre-Primary. He was one of our top students and left Moses Brown after the Second Form to enter Exeter Academy. I believe that he went to Yale and then followed in his father's footsteps to become a very successful physician, practicing in Connecticut.

39   The 1951 program included *"Puer Nobis Nascitur,"* "Lo how a Rose E'er Blooming," *"Cantique de Noel,"* "No Room in the Inn," "Mid Ox and Ass," and "Shepherds! Shake Off Your Drowsy Sleep"; as well as the more familiar, "Away in a Manger," "The First Noel," "Angels We Have Heard on High," "What Child Is This," "Bring a Torch Jeannette Isabella," and "Joseph Dearest,"; in addition to the very familiar "Silent Night" and *"Adeste Fideles."*

The 1954 program included: "No Room at the Inn" (German); "A Child is Born" (Old Scotch Air); "Children All Rejoice and Sing" (German – 14th Century); "As Out in the Fields" (Traditional Austrian Carol); "When Christ the Lord was Born" (Italian); "Cradle Song" (British Museum Mss. – 15th Century)"—as well as the more familiar "Jesu, Joy of Man's Desiring," "Once in Royal David's City," "Away in a Manger," "Bring a Torch Jeannette Isabella," and the "Coventry Carol."

Johnson, my father's stepfather, and Aunty Wallace were in the back seat of the car. Both were in their eighties at the time, and Grandpa was not a fan of Aunty Wallace, who was an idiosyncratic character and the source of many family crises. My father drove up the circle in front of Alumni Hall and stopped in the pouring rain as close as he could to the door. Aunty Wallace got out and decided to make a run for it, so she hurled her umbrella back into the car, hitting Grandpa on the shin.

Grandpa was a retired English sea captain (and chief engineer), with a vocabulary to match, and he exploded with "Damned Awkward B-----," aimed at Aunty Wallace, and which at least a few passersby heard as they hastened in the rain towards Alumni Hall in their quest for the spirit of the season. I was not informed as to the precise linguistic details of the episode for several years, but the story was too good to be forgotten by the family. Thus, the Christmas Pageant.

Grandpa Johnson was memorable. He was a naval architect and a retired vice president of the Sinclair Oil Company, responsible for designing and building their tankers.[40] When I was in Third Grade, some of the upperclassmen used to pester several of us as we walked down the long concrete path to the Hope Street entrance, this despite the presence, and occasional efforts, of Phil Coutanche, the School policeman, who was stationed there to help with street crossings. I remember being knocked down by David Palmer ('59) in a fight. So Grandpa undertook escort duty. Standing at six foot two, with his very aggressive Edwardian beard groomed to a point, Grandpa was not to be trifled with. He was a tough old Briton, an admirer of Churchill, and one look at a picture of him in his prime will show you why Hitler lost the Second World War. As he marched down the street (Grandpa never walked, he always marched), he gave the impression of a majestic, yet formidable, British battleship under full steam heading

---

[40] In later years I came to the conclusion that he had also worked with British Intelligence during the Second World War. His office was in Rockefeller Center, and I cannot imagine that William Stephenson, head of British Intelligence in America, and whose office was also in Rockefeller Center, did not know this former British subject who was about as pro-Churchill and anti-Hitler as one could get. He went to England frequently during the war (traveling on tankers). I remember him once telling me that he had been asked to memorize a long list of numbers and repeat them to someone down in Texas.

*Phil Coutanche
School Policeman*

for Jutland. Waiting for me at the Hope Street Gate, he used to regale Phil from his repertoire of jokes and sea stories. They hit it off famously and often, when Grandpa was away on one of his trips to England, Phil would ask about him and say how much he missed their talks and Grandpa's stories.

I can remember to this day being instructed by Grandpa at a very early age on how to use what he called a "Murphy stick"—a cane with a leaded top. This was probably in connection with my having been involved with the fight at the Hope Street Gate. "Now, chum," he would say—he always called me "chum"—"if you are carrying this stick and someone attacks you, don't try to hit him over the head; when you raise it up to strike, he will be at you with a knife. Instead, come up swiftly under his jaw with the head of the cane—then, while he is spitting his teeth out, you will have enough time to whack him on the coconut." This advice was accompanied by a demonstration. There usually was a twinkle in his eye, but he was not someone to cross.

Third Primary: The Third Grade (1950-1951)   43

Grandpa did, however, have a marvelous sense of humor, and was one of those rare individuals who could tell an off-color story in any company without giving offense. He used to march around the house, singing little sea chanteys from his very large repertoire, and I can remember secretly memorizing several of them. One day at Sunday school we were asked if we knew any poems. Up went my hand, and I repeated one of Grandpa's chanteys. I still remember it, and it was actually not all that bad (and certainly not bad at all by today's standards), but it was bad enough for eyebrows to be raised at our Baptist Sunday school, and inquiries were made of my parents from the church as to where I had learned such a song. My father actually got a big kick out of the episode, but it was quietly suggested to me that in the future I be somewhat more selective in my choice of poems to recite in Sunday school.

Father and Son Day was another major annual event. This took place on a Friday in the spring. It consisted of sporting events, a lunch, and exhibits. Fathers were invited to School for the day, and each boy was to be accompanied by his father. If his father could not attend, then he was assigned a surrogate father. My father made a special point of attending every year, even though it was a work day for him, and one year he served as a surrogate for Bruce Pansey ('59).

There were athletic events in the morning. In the very low grades, through the Third Grade, I think, there was a potato race. Four or five potatoes were placed at even intervals in a row on lines perpendicular to the starting line if it may be called that. There was a box at the starting line with a small shovel placed next to it. The contestants stood at the starting line, one to a box. When the signal was given, they picked up the shovel, ran out, scooped up a potato in their row, carried it back, and dropped it into the box, potato by potato. The winner was the first to gather all the potatoes, return to the starting line, and place the shovel down next to the box. Another event, Bill Barrett recalled, involved rolling a giant inflated ball (probably six feet in diameter) around a course.

Yet another event was the ball toss. This involved a board containing three holes with netting behind each, forming pockets. It was set slanting at an angle (with the top further away than the bottom). The contestant stood behind a line at a specified distance. The object was to toss a ball (a softball, as I recall) into any of the pockets, which were of different sizes and scored variously for difficulty. Everyone was tossing overhand, but I tossed underhand, and won second prize in the Third Grade—I still have the red ribbon—which was certainly the high point of my athletic achievements in ten years at Moses Brown.

There were many traditional track events for the upper grades during the morning. Everyone participated in these, whether or not they were going out for sports. I remember my father for several years provided Mr. Allen with yarn from the mill to be used at the finish line. After lunch there was varsity track and varsity baseball to watch.

The luncheon itself was excellent, featuring sandwiches and a memorable chicken soup—my father and I agreed that it was the best we had ever eaten. Year after year this was served piping hot from huge coffee urns with large spigots that you turned, just as you would for serving coffee. It was made right there at the School. One of the cooks had a special recipe of which he or she, no doubt, was justly proud. I wish that this recipe had been preserved, or if it has, that it might be used again at an event to which I was invited. It seldom rained on Father and Son Day in my years and the luncheon was almost always served outside. It was often held in the "grove" adjacent to Lloyd Avenue.

There were exhibits on display that could be visited throughout the day. Some were housed in the Lower School Gymnasium. I remember one year there was a mounted cat skeleton, whose original owner, we were told by Mr. Cole, had been euthanized "humanely." There were also exhibits of student work in each classroom—usually in notebook form placed on our desks. In the Third Grade we had a request to bring pictures of our fathers when they were our age. My mother dug out such a picture and I brought it in. Others did the same, and these surprised the fathers when they entered Miss Wilson's classroom.

I remember that on one Father and Son Day afternoon there was a presentation by a professional wrestler (might he have been an alum?) who described all the tricks of his trade. Many of us were shocked to learn

Third Primary: The Third Grade (1950-1951)   45

that the outcomes of the matches were predetermined. My father found it very amusing. There was a varsity baseball game to end the day, weather permitting. My father was a big Red Sox fan and greatly enjoyed any well-played baseball. We usually watched the whole event, win or lose. I remember on one occasion when I was in the early years of Upper School my cousin Bradley Steere, ('57) from Chepachet, played on the varsity team and was in a Father and Son Day baseball game. His father, Phillips, was there for the game, and we sat with him in the stands. Brad made a spectacular catch—center field, as I recall. My father turned to Phillips and said, "Phiddy (that was his nickname), let's stand and give a good hand for Chepachet!!" And they did.

Parties. There were numerous parties during Lower School years, especially birthday parties. I can remember going to a birthday party at Bruce Pansey's house in Third Grade, and one at Tommy Clark's over on George Street. There were also parties at Nick Littlefield's, Barry Fain's, Bill Fischer's, Jack Nixon's, John Dieroff's,[41] and Vinny Marcello's. These were imaginatively decorated events (with lots of crepe paper) that invariably featured special hats, horns, whistles, and a curled-up device (called a tickler?) shaped like a fiddlehead that unfolded dramatically when you blew into a mouthpiece attached to it. There were often games at these parties, occasionally hide and seek, and on more than one occasion we played "pin the tail on the donkey." Always there was a birthday cake, punch, ice cream, and often "favors" on the table that would make a loud noise when a protruding string was pulled.

I remember Mark Saklad in the Third Grade had a birthday party right in the classroom. Mrs. Saklad brought over a cake, candles, ice cream, napkins, hats, and "all the fixings" for us. We may have had others in class later, but this one I remember especially well. My folks had several birthday parties for me at our house. I remember a Fourth Grade party and a Sixth Grade party. We invited the whole Class, and I think almost

---

41 John Dieroff, who was in our Class for several years in Lower School, joining us in the Fifth Grade, as I recall, left us at the end of First Form in the Upper School, and we lost touch with him. He was the grandson of our next-door neighbor, and I knew him in that context, although he lived at a distance and we did not have a lot of contact outside of school.

everybody came. Both were held in the basement, with my mother cooking dinner for the entire Class and its teachers.

A memorable birthday event was at George Kilton's—possibly in a higher grade. The Class arrived in several cars at the same time. George had fashioned a large pile of snowballs in advance, and was ready for us. When we alighted, he started throwing them at us in rapid succession. He was, however, outnumbered, and we soon responded more than in kind.[42] Mrs. Kilton was not amused by the melee, and George received a stern reprimand.

---

42 George left Moses Brown in the Fourth Form, and I lost touch with him. He did return for a reunion, and I learned that he had become an executive at Connecticut Light and Power Company, a large utility centered in Hartford.

IV

First Intermediate: The Fourth Grade (1951-1952)

The Fourth Grade classroom, as noted, was located on the second floor right above the Third Grade in the southeast corner of the building.[43] Our principal teachers were Miss Marion Pixley and Miss Patricia Jensen. Miss Pixley was in charge of math and English and was the homeroom teacher. She was a very warm and positive person, but seemed to have relatively low expectations. She was fun, she liked me, and she was much more friendly than Miss Wilson (and I truly enjoyed the change), but she did not have the strong personality that we encountered in almost all of the other Lower School teachers. She was solid, but not inspiring in terms of how she developed our classroom activities. She was getting on in years, and this may be the explanation. She retired after teaching one more year.

Miss Jensen was in charge of social studies which consisted of both history and geography. She also taught spelling, as I recall, and on occasion, she helped Miss Pixley with reading instruction. She was young, competent, responsive, and quite energetic. She was always very interesting (and especially so when she got a severe case of poison ivy),[44] but at times she seemed a bit high-strung and insecure. This may have been her first year at Moses

---

43 The class faced west, with the blackboard in front of us on the west wall. I believe that there was a blackboard on the north wall as well. Miss Pixley's desk was near the north wall of the classroom on our right.

44 1960 *Mosaic*, p. 21.

Brown. A year later in the Fifth Grade she seemed much more sure of herself and in control of things.

Miss Pixley was not a disciplinarian. She was soft-spoken and never raised her voice. Miss Jensen, on the other hand, was a bit short-tempered at times, and could really crack the whip. Her favorite form of punishment was to ask us to write a hundred times "I will never speak out of turn in class again" (or whatever it was we did that we were not supposed to), and she would sit there and count them. Sometimes we did this at the board; more often we wrote it out on paper. Perhaps this exercise also served to improve our penmanship. I remember this practice more as a penalty for the entire class than as a punishment directed at an individual student. Some may have been singled out, but mostly the whole class would stay in at recess or after school and do its penance. On one such occasion, when it was pouring rain outside and we were kept late, Miss Pixley said to me as I was finally leaving, "Nature is weeping for us." The Fourth Grade was tough for me in many respects. For example, I had teeth to be adjusted, and spent a lot of time wearing braces, with many visits to an orthodontist in the old Union Trust building downtown.

Math. Throughout the school year, Miss Pixley posted two signs above the front blackboard—one read "Tolerance" and the other, "Cooperation."[45] It was beneath these noble sentiments that we learned "long multiplication" and then "long division." We had been exposed to simple multiplication from the time we learned our "times tables," and to simple division in the Third Grade. Now we were exposed to multiplication with multi-digit multipliers and multiplicands and to division with multiple-digit divisors and dividends. The multiplication process involved both multiplication itself and addition; long division was even more involved—employing estimation, multiplication, subtraction (and even addition as part of the multiplication process). These were lengthy and tedious procedures, easily prone to mistakes. To learn the processes, we were given seemingly endless sets of exercises which we were asked to plow through. Oh, for the hand calculator to have been invented!

---

45 Bill Barrett's recollection.

First Intermediate: The Fourth Grade (1951-1952)   49

No doubt all these repetitions were necessary, and no doubt we all learned to multiply and divide as a result of them, but nobody could say that it was a pleasant experience, even with the little song that Miss Pixley taught us to help with the division. Bill Barrett recalled that its opening lines went as follows: "When into long division you've started, When into long division you go, When into long division you've started, Divide by the first number in the row" (or at least something like that).

Instruction was straightforward. Miss Pixley described and illustrated the process to be followed on the blackboard, using several examples. For both multiplication and division it was a strict rule-based process—a procedure to be memorized and then followed as a matter of routine.[46] The reasoning behind the procedure was not mentioned—just the procedure itself. After the process had been explained, we then went up to the board and tried it ourselves, either in cohorts or as a whole class. Our efforts were watched and evaluated while in process. If we were not proceeding properly, there was prompt criticism and assistance in doing it right. Repetition was the key—we did exercise after exercise at the board and also on paper at our desks. For exams, the computations were written on the board; we copied them onto a paper, and did our best to figure out the proper results. There were also generous amounts of homework, again with exercises.

At one point, to make things a bit more interesting, my father asked me to multiply 12,345,679 by 9. This was simple multiplication, and I quickly proceeded to do the calculation. Not far into the process, I began to realize that something interesting was going on, and when the process was over,

---

46   In multiplication: 1) you placed the two numbers to be multiplied under each other with their right-hand digits lined up, and the smaller number underneath; 2) you placed a line below them; 3) starting with the right lower digit, you multiplied the top number by it, placing the result under the line with its right-hand digit under the right-hand digits of the two numbers being multiplied; 4) you then took the second number from the right above the line and did the same, placing the result one digit over, with the right-hand digit of the result under the number you were multiplying by; 5) you repeated the process until all bottom numbers had multiplied the top number; 6) you then added the set of results under the line to get the overall result; 7) if the result involved more than three digits, you used commas to set the numbers off in groups of three. Since the process of multiplying involved superscripts, you might end up with lots of them over the top number (unless you erased them as you went along), adding to the messiness or confusion of the process. Lots of tasks! Plenty of opportunities for error! I will spare the reader the exact long division process, but it was complex. Estimation involved trial and error; with practice, however, you began to get better with estimation.

Marion P. Pixley

the result, amazingly, was 111,111,111. He then asked me to multiply the same number by 18. This was long multiplication, and a bit harder, but the result was 222,222,222. When 12,345,679 was multiplied by 27, the result was 333,333,333, etc., up to 999,999,999, using multiples of 9 as multipliers. Upon discovering the results, I was anxious to rush off to School and share these computations with my classmates.

I believe that in the Fourth Grade we also began to solve "problems" as they were called. Later on such problems were subject to solution with algebra, but in the Fourth Grade there was no use of symbolic manipulation for this purpose. They were simple thought problems—if you had so many pecks of this and so many quarts of that, how many bushel baskets could be filled, etc. There were quite a few of these simple exercises that year. By the end of the term, we had mastered our multiplication and division techniques sufficiently that wrong answers had become the result of carelessness, rather than ignorance of method.

Language, Reading, and Spelling. I have very little recollection at all of what we did in "Language." We had a text, *Developing your Language*,[47]

---

[47] McKee, Paul, and McCowen, Annie, Boston: Houghton Mifflin, 1951.

First Intermediate: The Fourth Grade (1951-1952)   51

which had exercises in pronunciation, usage, basic storytelling, and report writing. We did write short stories. The *Delphian* of that year contained a short story by Nick Littlefield entitled, "Mr. Red Box," about a fire alarm box (in the town of Barton in the state of Klickatat) that was very lonely and neglected until a fire occurred in the vicinity—at which time he became a local hero, and much appreciated. We also had two short poems in the *Delphian* about Halloween, one by Nick and one by me. They both seem to rhyme well and make their descriptive points![48] We also wrote brief histories of Christmas.

I was still reading Landmark books at home and reporting on them. I assume many classmates were doing the same. There may have been other books as well. I have found my brief reports on several of them: Dorothy Canfield Fisher's *Our Independence and the Constitution*, Quentin Reynold's *The Wright Brothers*, and May McNeer's *The California Gold Rush*. The focus of these reports was on describing the part of the book that we liked the most. With respect to in-class reading itself, again we were tracked at different levels. I can recall most of that year reading in the little arch room over the walkway, often with Miss Jensen as the reading teacher. We still used the *Weekly Reader*.[49] I don't recall what else we read, but we were tested in reading class on vocabulary and on reading comprehension.

Miss Pixley was much taken at the time with a book called *Dorna*, from which she read to us every afternoon. As I recall, it was a kind of gothic romance about the Berkshires—to which Miss Pixley had a connection. I think her family came from there. There is today a "Pixley Hill Road" leading off of Route 41, south of West Stockbridge, and this may well have been named after her kin. *Dorna* seemed to be a story without end. I forget the plot entirely. I do remember that there were skunks and other animals in it (and they were of some interest), but to me the people were boring, the story pointless, and the time wasted—although it did divert attention away from other class routines.

Miss Jensen taught spelling. By now, we were expected to spell all the days of the week and all the months, including the difficult "February" (which, we were instructed, was not to be pronounced "Febuary," the way

---
48   *Delphian*, Vol. L, No. 1, Christmas 1951, p. 25.
49   At this level of development, it had dropped the "My" from its title.

everyone seemed to). About this time we also had to learn how to spell all of the then forty-eight states (yes, there is that additional unpronounced "c" in the middle of Connecticut), and the principal American cities. Spelling Mississippi and Cincinnati out loud was always fun—there was a marvelous (and similar) cadence to each. Schenectady was also on the list—I still have to pause when spelling this, even though it is now part of my New York address.

In the Fourth Grade, we began to learn spelling rules. One was as follows: when you add "ing" to a word, keep a "y" at the end but drop an "e" (e.g. hurrying, coming). We were taught that a "q" was always followed by a "u." We were instructed in the "ain" rule for words like mountain, captain, villain, fountain, etc. We were also drilled in contractions. Looking today at the list of words in our spelling tests, I would conclude that the words we spelled were principally words we encountered in our reading. Most had no more than two syllables—with the exception of words in lists of familiar things (banana) or words we used in class (e.g., arithmetic, multiplying, valentine, sincerely).

Miss Jensen also had us play a game in which we made words from the letters in a longer word. For example, from "everything," you could get eve, thin, ivy, there, tin, rye, give, and many more. I think there was a prize for the one who brought in the longest list. Strictly speaking, it was not an anagram, because we did not have to use all the letters—and in one exercise, we could use letters more than once. I remember this as homework, with my folks sitting around the table and reeling off all manner of variations of words from the basic letters in the initial word. I suspect that other parents were equally involved. They probably were not supposed to help on this, but mine had a lot of fun doing so. To me, this type of exercise was an enjoyable puzzle.

Penmanship. I do not remember who taught penmanship in the Fourth Grade, but my papers show that we spent serious time on it. We practiced both lowercase and uppercase letters and we learned to print. Occasionally we wrote paragraphs for penmanship. Again, the method was endless repetition. In some cases there were rows of slanted lines, in other cases there were repeated letters—forty or fifty at a time. Lines of short words like noon and moon gave us practice in combining letters. The capitals of "Q," "X," and "Z" were quite fancy, and more fun to make. Those I was fairly good at. I was impatient with a lot of this, however, and I think that when I was interested in *what* I was writing, I forgot about *how* I was writing. The endlessly repeated letters in penmanship were of a higher quality than those in the paragraphs I wrote for penmanship itself—and much better than the letters in papers I wrote for other subjects. Still, it was important to learn cursive—and still is if someone wants to be able to read letters and documents from the past.

History. Miss Jensen (in later years, she became Mrs. Williams, and then reverted to Miss Jensen again) also taught geography and ancient history. In the Lower School, we alternated, year by year, between American history and ancient/medieval history. Hence American was in the Third, Fifth, and Seventh Grades, and ancient/medieval was in the Fourth and Sixth. European history came in the Upper School, although we had some with Mrs. Bluhm in the Sixth Grade, and some English history with Mrs. Monahon in the Seventh.

Our Fourth-Grade history text had a maroon cover that I always remembered.[50] The stories started with Egypt and the Fertile Crescent, and thence to Greece and Rome, the Middle Ages, and the Era of Exploration. Miss Jensen was very interested in Egypt, and we spent a lot of time on it, learning about the Nile, the pharaohs, and the pyramids. I wrote a page-long paper on the importance of the Nile River to Egyptian civilization, citing water, nutrients, and transportation. She read to us in class from a novel about ancient Egypt that she had recently read herself. It was entitled *The Egyptian*. From this, we learned a lot about the culture and the economy. I also remember her reading to us a graphic passage describing how corpses were mummified, including (to us) a shockingly memorable rendition of how the brains were removed from the skull through the nose. We spent a lot of time talking about Egypt. I think that we even went down to the Rhode Island School of Design Museum to see the Egyptian collection.

---

50 Cordier, R.W., and Robert, E.B., *History for the Beginner*, New York: Rand McNally, 1948.

After Egypt, we passed on to Greece and Rome, and then to the Middle Ages. Greece was presented as a civilization that loved "beauty and learning," and we learned about how Athenian boys were taught in school. We were also introduced to Athenian democracy and the Olympics. The section on Rome emphasized the Roman army and Roman engineering—including the Forum, highways, and aqueducts. In the section on the Middle Ages, we learned a lot about chivalry, with its squires and knights.

I was inspired by this instruction and decided to write a novel under the title "I Dub Thee Knight," derived from the caption of an illustration in the book. This was to be a major project. I had some vague idea of the plotline, and began writing forthwith. I got about a page written, and suddenly decided that writing a novel was a lot more difficult than I had bargained for. Imagination and capacity for accomplishment were two different things. The project got stalled with a juvenile form of writer's block, and I never made it to page two. Nicky Littlefield used to chide me about this from time to time, asking how my novel was coming along. The project was quietly abandoned.

Geography. In geography, we had a text dealing with the world outside of the United States.[51] It was organized like a trip for us to take. Early on we visited Latin America and learned all about the Amazon. In fact, we spent a lot of time at Belem at the mouth of the Amazon. We then went to Central Africa and up to Egypt, thence to Greece and thence to Western Europe. Somehow we also journeyed to the Far East as well.

We were held responsible for the reading, some of which we did in class, and some of which we did as homework. There were also discussions in class by Miss Jensen. I don't remember that we took notes in any formal way, as we did in later years with more formal classroom presentations or lectures. Largely we were expected to remember what was said and what we read in the book. I don't have strong memories about this, which may itself be significant. I do know that we were introduced to latitude and longitude and compass points, and we were taught a few geographic terms, like isthmus, peninsula, delta, and gulf.

---

51 McConnell, Wallace R., *Geography around the World*, New York: Rand McNally, 1948 edition.

First Intermediate: The Fourth Grade (1951-1952)   55

In this class we had a project on Brazil, which we worked on every Friday. This consisted of two major parts: one was to copy down an outline of Brazil's geographic, civil, and economic features; the other, to make a series of maps. With respect to the outline, this was written by Miss Jensen on the board, and we copied it down onto three-holed ruled paper. It consisted of geographic features, such as the longest rivers and highest mountains; political features, such as its population and its major cities; and economic features, which listed the major products of the country. I think there was also a section on Brazil's history, listing by date some of its most important events.

This outline had to be letter-perfect, written legibly, with everything spelled properly, and all the appropriate indentations made under the right lines. If we made an error (and it seemed that we always did), we had to go back and do it again. I can remember recopying some pages several times. We learned a little from this exercise in a vague way, but it was not very instructive, because all we were doing was copying the material down off the board. The accuracy of style and presentation was as important as the content. Although we presumably learned something from copying this all down a dozen times (fewer times if we made fewer mistakes), and although we presumably learned a lot of facts about Brazil, it is not a set of recollections that persists.

The other part of the project was making maps. First, we made a physical map of Brazil—actually, we did one of South America as a whole. This was done in different colors, from red in the mountains down to green in the lower areas—which were extensive in Brazil, what with the Amazon Valley. We also drew the continent's major rivers. Again, we worked until we got it right. This was not coloring in contour lines, but, in effect, copying a physical map using our own shapes and colors—it was not an exercise in coloring (like those in earlier years), but in copying off another map. When the coloring was done, we then labeled the rivers and mountain chains.

Second, we made a political map, again of the entire continent. This was an exercise in getting the right countries and the right cities in the right places, spelling them correctly, and not blotting the ink while doing so. We traced the maps from an outline in the back of a workbook, and having traced them, we proceeded to fill them in. Third, we made a commodities map. I can remember putting little symbols in for coffee, rubber, oil, tin, and things like these all over the place. We were taught that symbols were "things that stand for real things." Again, this map was for all of South America. I don't remember where we got the information to make this—presumably from another map or from the book. Of the three, the physical map was the toughest to do, in the absence of pre-drawn contour lines.

We took the outline and the maps and bound them up in a booklet with a card-stock cover, using pins in three punched holes. On the cover we put a cutout map of Brazil, as I remember. I assume this volume was placed on display for Father and Son Day or its equivalent.

French. Madame Warge taught French, and she taught it to us throughout most of the Lower School experience. She must have been in her seventies or eighties at the time. She was a delightful person, a real character who endearingly referred to us as "her little bumblebees," although most of us did not like that appellation. She wore a fascinating little black hat with a feather stuck in it, which she removed upon entering the classroom. I think it was held in place by a hat pin. She was quite short—taller than we were when we first knew her, but shorter when she last taught us. She was with us off and on during the years from the Second Grade through the Seventh Grade (I don't recall that we had French in the Sixth Grade). Near the end, there were some questions as to whether she would be well enough to teach, and by the Seventh Grade there were a few disciplinary problems,[52] so that Mr. Sprague would sometimes remain in the classroom while she was teaching, but all came off well.

After attending the Universite de Lyon, Madame Warge had come to Moses Brown from France in 1917,[53] and lived on Congdon Street with Monsieur Warge, her husband, whose first name I have forgotten. Now

---

52 During a telephone interview with an alumnus from earlier times, he recalled that his Seventh Grade class had teased Mme. Warge when she described and spoke about Alsace and Lorraine. The class repeated back to her, "Al's Ass and Lorraine." She would correct the pronunciation, but students would still insist on calling it "Al's Ass." He assumes that she didn't understand the significance of this pronunciation.
53 Paxton, p. 11.

and then I would encounter her on my way home, walking up Barnes Street. On one of these occasions she told me a story about her first experience with poison ivy. She had just arrived in Rhode Island from France, and it was a beautiful day, so she went for a long walk and she spotted a wall with this lovely ivy growing all over it. It was hot, and she had walked quite a distance, so she lay down on it to take a rest. Lying there with her head propped up on one elbow and casually gazing into the field beyond, she even chewed a bit of it before resuming her journey. Well, it nearly killed her. She broke out all over. It was on her legs, arms, and face, and in her mouth—everywhere. She took several weeks to recover. From that point on, she said, "I was much more careful about trying new things in America."

On another such occasion, I remember her being apologetic for something that had just occurred in French politics at the time—she did not defend it, but she said to me, "You must sometimes excuse what the people do. They have been through so much. When the Germans were in Paris, one day all the people in the neighborhood were told to put their silver out on the sidewalk to be taken. Next week, it would be their paintings, and then they would come for the good furniture, or the jewelry. In poorer neighborhoods, it would be tools or other belongings. If you didn't satisfy the Germans, they would ransack the house. Sometimes they would take off the people themselves and they might not return. They suffered so much."

Madame Warge talked very rapidly and her whole teaching style was highly animated. Her hands and arms were constantly in motion. If we made a mistake or mispronounced a word she would stamp her foot for emphasis as she corrected us. *Plus Vite, Plus Vite, Plus Vite*—Hurry, Hurry, Hurry— was one of her favorite expressions. Her basic method of teaching was to have us memorize words, sentences, and poems by repeating them out loud. Often we sang them. We did copy each down from the blackboard, but only once. Repetition in French was oral, not written. This practice may have been mnemonic, but it also may have been to teach us proper Parisian accents. As I recall, she was very fussy about our enunciation. We learned simple greetings, such as *Bonjour, Mademoiselle,* [or *Madame, Monsieur], comment allez-vous?* Over the years, we learned simple words, such as parts of the body: *le nez, la bouche, la tête*. We learned simple French table words like *bonbon, fruits, pain, beurre, serviette,* etc. She taught us the

Mr. Cate congratulates Madame Warge, teacher of Lower School French

French for familiar household animals. She also taught us a child's prayer, *"Bonne Nuit, Bonne Nuit,"* by Victor Hugo, and later the Lord's Prayer, both of which we memorized and repeated frequently in class. She gave us a little poem highlighting all the days of the week, and we also learned the months. She taught us the hundred numbers from *un* to *cent*, and these we repeated out loud in deciles or in full sequence many times. We memorized and sang *"Frere Jacques."* As I recall, someone, adopting her style, started to sing *"Alouette, Gentille Alouette,"* but this did not meet with her approval. In later years we learned and sang *"La Marseillaise."* In the Seventh Grade, she gave us a geography lesson on Paris and a description in French of the American flag.

To help us with our words, she also played a game, popular with us, called "hangman." I suspect it was from a long-standing tradition in the European classroom. It was a guessing game, and as we correctly guessed the various words she was asking of us, she filled in the various pieces of the man on the gibbet (or maybe it was the reverse of this—if we failed to get the word properly she would add to the drawing). I can remember how it looked: she started with a primitive gallows made of a vertical line with a horizontal line to the left at its top supported by a diagonal brace. She

First Intermediate: The Fourth Grade (1951-1952)

would then draw in parts of the body, adding in sequence a head or leg or arm or nose or hat or pipe until it was complete—it actually looked more like a snowman than a corpse. I don't know what the symbolism was, but I suspect that this was a very old European teaching technique.

Her teaching methods were greatly at variance with today's language techniques. It was far from total immersion. The class met only once a week or maybe once every two weeks. I don't recall any homework, exams, or grades in Lower School French. There was therefore nothing demanding. It was merely an introduction and appreciation of the language. Still, Madame Warge was a very alive presence in the classroom; she provided welcome variety to the day's schedule, we looked forward to her visits, and most of us worked faithfully with her in class to master our songs and recitations.

Memorably, every year Madame Warge prepared by hand a Christmas card and envelope for us to color, inscribe a greeting, and address to our parents. It was always the same, with a Christmas tree on the front (which we would shade in green with pencil strokes carefully diverging from a central line), a colored candle on each branch at its side, "Noël! Noël!" printed beneath it, and a gold star at its top. Inside, Mme. Warge lined the card faintly so we could write a Christmas greeting with some semblance of proper decorum:

> Joyeux Noël!
> Bonne Année!
> Ecole de Moses Brown
> Clifford W. Brown, Jr.
> Le 25 Décembre 1950.

The paper stock was very fine, and when the tree and candles were finished and the message written according to her very precise instructions, the result was actually quite elegant. She herself addressed, stamped, and mailed these to our parents.

If there was a life lesson she wished to leave with us, it was the importance of manners. She talked frequently about this: "Manners! Manners! Manners! Always be polite—even to those you do not like." If she said this once, she said it dozens of times. To us it meant that if you wanted to be considered an adult, you had to be polite.

Mme. Warge passed away in May of 1956, while we were in the Upper School, and I remember Mr. Whitford, the principal Upper School French teacher, on the verge of tears when he delivered his moving eulogy to her one morning in Chapel. Bill Barrett recalled that several of us were chosen to attend her funeral at the Chapel in Swan Point Cemetery. He recalled that for some it was their first funeral, and it proved to be a troubling experience.

Science. The science instruction in the Fourth Grade was marginal. I don't even remember whether it was Miss Pixley or Miss Jensen who did it. I think it was the latter, but I cannot say for sure. The book was in the same series as the one in the Third Grade. It was a question of reading it from time to time. Looking back at it from today, I think we just got through the first two sections: plants and animals of the present, and those of the past. I do remember studying about beavers and ant colonies—and about trilobites and dinosaurs. We were told what an amphibian was. We were read a story in class about tar pits and how animals became trapped there and were fossilized. We were also taught about sedimentary rocks.

We did not, however, get to the sections in the book on electricity, light, and the solar system. This was still pre-Sputnik, and science was an afterthought. It is possible that we were obliged to cover animals because animals were the subject of the annual exposition in Alumni Hall that year. Perhaps the priorities were correct in terms of getting our multiplication and division skills developed, our reading and writing skills practiced and improved, and our awareness of other cultures launched or extended, but certainly more might have been done with science, even in conjunction with math or reading.

Music. Music in the Fourth Grade was under the direction of Mr. William Pickett, who had been trained at the New England Conservatory, and who had been organist and choirmaster at the Mathewson Street Methodist Church in downtown Providence for four years before coming to Moses

First Intermediate: The Fourth Grade (1951-1952)   61

Brown. He was a youngish guy. He seemed to be an English native, perhaps South African, and he spoke in an accent. He was at Moses Brown only this year. As best as I can remember, all we did was sing songs. He was a good pianist. He would sit down and bang out the pieces on the piano with great gusto, and we proceeded to sing them. I don't recall that we had music in front of us. He would sing out the lines as he played, and we would repeat them until we had the whole song down pat. One song I recall him teaching us was "We Are Marching to Pretoria," which we sung with enthusiasm, even though we did not know at the time where Pretoria was or why someone would want to march there. Looking back, this song must have originated in the Boer War. We sang several songs of that variety, lively and rhythmed. I think we had our class in Alumni Hall, since I recall him seated at a grand, not upright, piano. We ourselves did nothing instrumental. Perhaps Mrs. Moore had thrown up her hands the previous year at our instrumental potential, and the powers that be had decided to take another approach.

I remember Mr. Pickett got sick on one occasion, and we had a contest in class to see who could make the best get-well card for him. I remember Bruce Pansy and I worked together on one of these—which had a fairly decent looking piano on it and an encouraging message on the inside. I'm sure all of these were signed, and the whole set was sent to him.

Art and Shop. In the Fourth Grade, Miss Muscente was succeeded by Miss Emily Swide as our art teacher. Up until then, we had done our artwork in our homeroom classrooms. From now on, we went over to the Studio. Art was taught on the upper level; shop, as noted, was taught in the basement. You entered the upper level by a door on the southwest corner of the building. Just inside, there was a bust of Sophia Pitman, who had taught art there for many years.[54] The upper level of the Studio building, where art was taught, consisted of a single large room with big northern-light windows. As I recall, it was a "cathedral ceiling" with exposed beams and lighting fixtures (suspended from the ceiling) that, I suspect, had originally been designed for gas. The whole place at that time was

---

54 I think there was also a bust of Lucretia Mott in the Studio as well, although she was subsequently moved to Alumni Hall.

cluttered with art objects and works in progress. There were Bunsen burners, tools, and art materials all over the place. Wooden desks were located throughout; these were scratched and scarred from much use, and spotted randomly with different flecks of paint. Musty charcoal sketches graced the walls.

The Studio always seemed a bit dark to me, and In some ways mysterious with all the clutter and confusion. In front, on the east wall for many years, there was a large, well-executed, attention-grabbing mural of College Hill in colonial times that had been painted by a student—with the First Baptist Church and the Market Building prominent. Aside from that, and despite the north windows, the whole room always seemed very dingy with its dark brown and dark gray motif. Although I came to have a very high regard for Miss Swide in the Fifth Grade, there is not much I can remember about art in the Fourth, other than the clay animals we made for the annual exhibition that year.

Mr. Cole continued to teach us shop. Again, I was slow to get the hang of it, but over the whole Lower School experience I actually made a lot of things in shop class. I cannot remember what was made when, but I can remember making the following: a board with sandpaper on it for striking matches—for anyone who still used non-safety matches at that time; a seed box—for holding seed, I guess; simple matching bookends made from two small boards nailed together at right angles; a pipe stand that held several pipes (my father smoked a pipe); a three-shelf corner knickknack holder (this was actually useful—and is still in use); a mailbox (with which I instituted a mail delivery system at home—drop a letter into the box, and I would walk to the corner and post it); a parallelogram-shaped hollowed-out pen or pencil holder; a useful book rack that sat on top of a table and held a dozen or so medium-sized books; a Christmas present consisting of a painted green board rimmed by indentations made with a round file, with a reproduction of a famous Middle Ages Madonna pasted on it (Aunty Wallace, who received this as a Christmas present, promptly announced that she considered it to be suspiciously Catholic—to which my annoyed mother made an appropriate response and added that, anyway, it was "art" and it shouldn't bother her); and a birdhouse (which remained unoccupied outdoors at the farm in Chepachet for many years). All of these were made with simple tools—hand jigsaws, files, and hammers. I don't think we ever used screws and screwdrivers in Lower School. In the case of the pencil holder, we used a simple gouge. We used no power tools in the Lower School. Most completed projects were stained and then lacquered.

To a fourth grader, the benches still seemed very high, but they diminished in height as the years progressed. Instruction was basically in how to make the specific piece we were working on, and not more generally in how to do carpentry. The design was given to us and we would follow it. By the Sixth and Seventh Grades, there was more choice and we could, with supervision, do a bit of designing ourselves. In the early grades we all worked on the same project, even to the point where there was an attempt to have everyone in the class work simultaneously on the same part of that project. Making these artifacts took serious time, and we had shop only an hour a week, as I recall, so we did not do a lot of them in a given year. Mr. Cole was always friendly and helpful. He had a good sense of humor, and a lot of toleration for our shortcomings. It was always an enjoyable experience to which we looked forward each week.

The Exposition. I remember there was an exposition (or fair) in the Fourth Grade similar to the transportation and safety fairs in the Third Grade. This time it was about animals: "The Animal Kingdom on Parade," a conventionally descriptive title, selected as the result of a contest in which everyone in the Lower School was asked to participate. The runner up was "Animals, Animals, Animals, WOW!"—a title which Mr. Allen mentioned with amusing approval, but which apparently lacked the decorum which the occasion demanded.

I remember we made clay animals for this. I forget what we actually did with them. They may have been put into a forest that we made, or some such setting. I can remember attempting to make a deer out of red-brown modeling clay, although the final product looked more like a sawhorse. I got the legs onto it, but the head and projected antlers never quite materialized—or just fell off. I also remember Billy Goddard making a deer—and he did an excellent job. His deer retained its head and antlers, and actually resembled the intended ungulate.

I also recall making a snake, perhaps inspired by a Brazilian python. It was not, however, very scary. It looked more like the burner on an electric stove or a coil of garden hose, but I do remember it was a lot easier to make than the deer: you rolled out a long round piece of clay, about halfway in size between spaghetti and macaroni, and then curled it up, leaving a projecting piece in the center for a tail and a somewhat higher projecting piece on the outside for the head—which in my model resembled a nail's head a lot more closely than a snake's head. Clay modeling was frustrating. You knew what you were trying to create. You knew what it was supposed to look like. But what you could do with your hands would never produce the intended result—at least not at the level of imitation you could envision. It was all like that novel I started to write—imagination was way beyond capacity.

These clay animals were displayed in the Animal Fair over in Alumni Hall. I don't remember a lot about the fair itself. Many of our other projects may have been put on display at the same time. I don't remember what else we did, although I have found a couple of short stories about animals I wrote at this time—one about how a little peccary was caught by a jaguar (the story ends with the peccary squealing—I suspect I couldn't bring myself to polish him off definitively). The other had a happier ending, with a mother antelope outwitting and killing a coyote who was trying to eat her children.

Activities. In the Fourth Grade we all became participants in a School-organized Junior Audubon Club. I believe that Miss Elizabeth Weeks, Mr. Thomas's very efficient executive secretary, had something to do with this, or at least sponsored it. She had been a longtime observer of birds, a member herself of a Junior Audubon Society in grade school and of a bird walk society at Vassar. As a recognized amateur ornithologist, she was very active in the Rhode Island Audubon Society and a participant in its bird census activities.[55] She was also a prominent member of the Narragansett Chapter of the Appalachian Mountain Club.

What on earth did our Fourth Grade Audubon Society do? I can remember the mechanics, but not the substance. We had officers and meetings,

---

55 *Providence Evening Bulletin,* January 10, 1951.

secretary's reports, and all of that, but, for the life of me, I can't remember anything we did that involved birds. I guess people reported on them. We never went out on bird expeditions or anything like that. Maybe we drew pictures of birds or had someone read to us about birds, or whatever. Our yearbook reports that the Club sponsored an art exhibit during the Fourth Grade. No doubt it was impressive, but I have no recollection of it. I do remember that we had dues, but what they were used for I do not recall—maybe they were turned over to the Rhode Island Audubon Society. I believe we did not have class officers in the Fourth and Fifth Grades, as we did in the Sixth and Seventh Grades. Instead, students were simply elected to Audubon Club posts.

Another activity was contributing to the Red Feather campaign, the forerunner of the United Fund, which was, in turn, the forerunner of the United Way. Mounted up in front of the classroom was an outline picture of a large feather with horizontal percentage lines across. As we brought our money to School, the feather outline was shaded in with red coloring from the bottom up, the way fundraising thermometers are filled in today. As a reward for our contributions, we got a red feather to wear in our lapels. In later years, as the Feather gave way to the Fund, we received little metal pieces shaped like uneven dumbbells with one end circle printed for display, and the other end circle, much smaller, punched through the center to create a semi-sharp point. These we would bend over and affix to our lapels.

About this time—I think it was in the Fourth Grade—we were taken to a hockey game over at the old Rhode Island Auditorium on North Main Street, colloquially referred to as the "Arena." I don't know if this was a Class project or just an event sponsored by a bunch of parents. I'm not sure who was playing, but I think it was Harvard-Brown. I do remember sitting there, enjoying the action, and sipping a Dixie cup filled with Coca Cola. Later on, in the Seventh Grade, we went as a Class to the Auditorium to see the Celtics play. Bob Cousey was the star at that time, and, as I recall, someone arranged for us to meet him afterwards to sign autographs. This was Mr. Sprague's project. He was a huge basketball fan, and Bill Barrett remembered him and Vinny Buonanno egging each other on about basketball.[56] As Bill Barrett recalled, the Celtics in those days played three

---

56   Vin Buonanno left the Class of 1960 for the Class of 1961 soon after we entered Upper School.

or four home games a year in Providence—occasions that Mr. Sprague eagerly anticipated. The Arena was primarily a hockey venue, not often used for basketball. The Celtics' parquet floor was therefore brought from Boston and set up, without insulation, directly on the ice. At the game we attended in the Seventh Grade, the air in the Auditorium was especially humid, and moisture condensed on the cold hardwood floor, causing it to become very slippery. Several players took some spectacular falls, causing the game to be played with much more caution than normal. Even though attempts were made to mop the floor dry with every stoppage of play, they did not appreciably improve the playing conditions. Soon after this, the Celtics ceased playing in Providence.

On one of these two Class visits to the Arena, my father stood outside waiting to pick me up and had a long chat with Mr. Marcello, who was waiting for Vinny. Afterwards he told me how much he had enjoyed the conversation they had, although he provided me with no details. Apparently the two of them had hit it off very well. Vinny's father died not too long after that, and my father at that time spoke once again of the time they had met and talked outside of the Auditorium.

Collecting baseball cards was all the rage at this time, and everyone in class, it seems, was involved in buying and trading them. I was less involved than most, but I do remember having some and trading duplicates for others. Since we frequently went to Chepachet to visit my grandparents, I was importuned by my classmates to search for baseball cards at drugstores out in Greenville (or Chepachet) because they might have different players from the ones sold in the city.

We also collected postage stamps and traded them. Many parents encouraged this because they thought that the hobby contributed to an understanding of geography, which I guess it did. There was a neighborhood stamp shop named Zeke's, located on Thayer Street, and later on East Avenue near the Providence-Pawtucket line. Our parents bought envelopes full of used stamps there and we would sort them and paste them in an album by means of small wax-paper-like stickers. Classmates and I traded them, and for a year or two at this age we were heavily engaged in that enterprise.

First Intermediate: The Fourth Grade (1951-1952)   67

One summer my mother took the Class, or a group from the Class, out to the family farm in Chepachet for a picnic and a swim. I remember Tommy Clark cut his foot in the course of things and we took him up to see Dr. Potter (Chepachet's old country doctor) for some iodine (ouch!) and a bandage. He did not enjoy the injury, but he did get quite a kick out of meeting Dr. Potter in his old dispensary.

Nick Littlefield, Tommy Clark, Bill Barrett, Bill Fischer, Chad Gifford (who joined us in the Fifth Grade), Harrison Huntoon, and I all went home for lunch. Several of us walked in a group, going down the long concrete "West Walk" that led from the Lower School building to the Hope Street gate. At times we raced down this path (which is still in existence). Sometimes we asked Phil, the School policeman, who stood at the gate, to time us as we raced down the sidewalk; he would take out his watch, signal us to start, and announce our time upon our arrival at Hope Street. As we grew, we learned to ride bicycles, and this skill came in handy for those who lived at a distance. Chad pedaled a dozen blocks or more down Brown Street and across the Brown campus to Charles Field Street with a green book bag over his shoulder. Bill Barrett remembered Bill Fischer running over to Olney Street and spending about three minutes at home eating lunch, then immediately returning to School—for a very long recess. Most of this group was in the same Cub Scout Den together and later in the same Boy Scout Pack. I can also remember tricking and treating with them, accompanied by parents, and coming back to our house afterwards where we created a commodities market on the living room floor and traded our loot.

With respect to the Cub Scouts themselves, we met monthly at various different houses where the "Den Mothers" were. I think we met at the Clarks', the Barretts', the Giffords', and at the Littlefields'. I don't remember a lot of what we did, but it was some form of instruction, often given in the form of a game or contest. I do recall visiting the various homes. On one occasion—at the Giffords'—we were asked to take a pencil and draw a pig, blindfolded. The idea was to do an outline drawing. The breadboard training was a useful resource here, but if we were asked to draw an outline, how could we ensure that the pencil would eventually end up completing the loop, so to speak, where it began? I remember attempting this by holding a finger of my left hand on the paper while I drew the outline with the pencil in my right hand. I started with the stationary finger on the paper and ended with it. The procedure somehow worked, and I was duly commended by Mrs. Gifford for the attempt. It was certainly a much more successful endeavor than my earlier efforts to pin tails on birthday party donkeys.[57] Bill Barrett recalled that on days when we had Cub Scout meetings, we were permitted to wear our uniforms to School. We would also wear them there once a year during Scout Week, even if there was no meeting that day. This group, largely from the East Side of Providence, was fairly cohesive. Later, when we became Boy Scouts, we went to meetings at Central Congregational Church.

A major event for me In April of 1952 was a trip to Cuba, Panama, and Colombia on a banana boat. My parents had to get special permission for me to miss a few days of school. We took the train to New York and sailed from there. It was a great adventure for a nine-year-old. I remember the Morro Castle and the Maine monument in Havana, the locks on the Panama Canal, the Hotel Panama in Panama City, and banana plantations in Columbia. Sailing on the *Veragua* itself was adventuresome. When we returned, I was asked by Miss Pixley to give a full report to the class. We had brought back many souvenirs and pamphlets, so I could show as well as tell. The class seemed interested, and there were many questions. To them, it was probably a welcome diversion from long division.

---

57 Mr. Gifford, Chad's father, was a banker, starting at the Phoenix Bank in Providence which merged with the Rhode Island Hospital Trust Company. Mr. Gifford rose to become president and CEO of that bank, and was the moving force behind the construction of its main office building in downtown Providence, which is now a prominent feature of that city's skyline. Chad followed in his father's footsteps. He went to work for the First National Bank of Boston (which later became Bank of Boston), and rose to become its president. When Bank of Boston merged with Fleet, he became president of the latter, and when Fleet, in turn, merged with Bank of America, Chad became president—thus attaining the top position at one of America's largest banking corporations.

V

Second Intermediate: The Fifth Grade (1952-1953)

The Fifth, Sixth, and Seventh Grade classrooms, as noted, were located on the main floor of the building attached to Middle House on the east. This whole area in our time was accessed by students through a single door on the north side of the building that led to short halls; first, to locker areas and bathrooms, and then to the classrooms beyond in three directions. Although there was a door providing access, we never went through Middle House to get to our classrooms. The Second Intermediate (Fifth Grade) was taught by Miss Chappell and Miss Jensen. It met in the room directly adjacent to Middle House, with windows opening south out onto the traffic circle.[58]

Elsie Chappell was a remarkable person. She came from Carthage, Indiana, a small town east of Indianapolis. A graduate of Earlham College in Richmond, Indiana, with further studies at Columbia, she had been at Moses Brown since 1921, and we were her last class before retirement. She was a strong character, very much of the old school, but still at the top of

---

58 The class faced west. There was a fireplace in front, and to its right there was a door opening directly into Mr. Thomas's office. I remember once he appeared silently through this door while Miss Jensen was teaching a class, but that was the only time I ever saw this door opened. There were three other doors in this room. Miss Chappell's desk was in the rear of the room between the door and the outside wall. The blackboards were on the north wall and on the east wall in back of us.

Elsie E. Chappell

her game, and extremely helpful to me personally in terms of my development because it was in her classroom that I began to acquire a sense of independent self-confidence. She paid me a lot of personalized attention, and it is my recollection that she did so to others as well. Both the 1958 and 1960 *Mosaics* commented that she "made men out of us," reflecting higher levels of expectation in the maturity department. In a very real sense her classes were the beginning of my mature Moses Brown education. She was among the best teachers in the Lower School.

Miss Chappell was a very strong presence in the classroom, constantly expressing her views on things. She was not above singling people out, either for praise or criticism. This would probably violate modern methods, but it kept our attention. She was a strict disciplinarian—she took nonsense from nobody—but unlike Miss Wilson she never raised her voice.

Miss Chappell did not like excuses or "alibis" as she called them. I remember once being late to class. It was winter, my father had volunteered to drive me to school, and his car had become stuck coming out of the driveway—the city snowplow had piled up a heap at the entrance, he had tried to drive over it, and the car had become hung up with its rear tires off the ground. By the time he got things sorted out, we were late. Miss Chappell asked me quite pointedly in front of the class—did I have an alibi? Since alibis were clearly such bad things, I did not want to admit to having had one, even though I had a perfectly good excuse for being tardy. So I denied having an alibi, thinking to myself that I would never want to be caught with one. I forget what the penalty was for lateness, but no doubt there was one—probably staying in during recess. I don't think Miss Chappell ever sent someone to Mr. Allen—she never needed to.

As far as instruction was concerned, her fields were math and language. She also taught reading, but I was reading at a higher level (with Miss Stapleton), having had Miss Chappell when I was in the Third Grade, as noted earlier.

Math. Miss Chappell in the fall gave us a serious review of long multiplication and long division, which she thought we needed. *Learning to Compute* again appeared, and was used this time much more systematically. She then proceeded to teach us fractions and decimals. We learned how to use a fraction to express the result of a long division computation—instead of just leaving a "remainder." We learned how to add and subtract fractions, finding and using "common denominators." I don't think we learned about multiplying fractions until the Sixth Grade. Fractions were fussy and difficult, but the thought of moving to the more advanced topic of "decimals" seemed frightening. The very word was scary to me. People used the word "fraction" in ordinary conversation—but who ever used the word "decimal"? I remember my father reassuring me in this regard by telling me that decimals were actually easier than fractions: all you had to do was know where to put the decimal point, and the rules for doing so were always quite simple. At first, I didn't believe him, but he was right—decimals were a blast. In fact, they seemed like a little game that was fun to play. After decimals, we learned percentages. I can remember my father telling me that the word meant "per 100" or "by 100." Ten percent was ten over 100 or one tenth. Decimals, of course, made percentages easy.

Miss Chappell also gave us math *problems* in a serious way. Looking back on Lower School math, we did a lot of computations and we gradually began to solve more and more problems throughout—but I really never connected the two until late in the game. Had someone early on told us that the reason we did all the computing was to be able to solve problems—and that solving problems would be useful in the adult world—we would have seen the point of all our repetitious labor with computation. As far as I recall, nobody ever did, or if they did, I missed the point. I think teachers assumed we knew this all along (as they did), but in my case I did the computations because I was told to (or it was expected of me), not because I would eventually find it useful.

We studied measures (such as pecks and bushels and how to add them), conversions of Fahrenheit to Centigrade, dollars and cents and how to add them (decimals to the rescue!),[59] pounds and ounces (and how to add them)—not easy—and converting things from one measure to another. Importantly, we were introduced to calculating simple square measure—by multiplying the sides of a rectangle—and I believe we were shown how to compute the circumference and the area of a circle using pi. I was always well-disposed to pi because I have always been well-disposed to pies (which, being circular, somehow seemed related).

The problems we had were simple, like "how many apples can you buy for 35 cents if apples sell for five cents per dozen," but they did take some thinking to figure out, and this was more interesting than simply doing the rote mathematical computations we had had in the past. Instead of just being given exercises to do, we were now selecting the numbers needed to solve the problem—and deciding ourselves which computations to make.

Miss Chappell's math instruction was along the same lines as that of Miss Pixley—"Here's how it is done." She would show us at the blackboard how to manipulate fractions and calculate, as my father explained, the much more simple results for decimals. She used the board at the side of the room, and also in back. I believe at times we went up to the board ourselves to do exercises. The math book we had was really an exercise book, so we used this for practice in class, and, of course, there was always homework.

---

59 Mercifully, we did not have to add and subtract pounds, shillings, and pence: thank you, George Washington and Alexander Hamilton!

Language, spelling, penmanship, and reading. Our language text was *Enriching Your Language*.[60] Although there were sections in it on discussion, conversation, and word usage, Miss Chappell largely ignored them and concentrated on composition. The language of our well-spoken parents had, right across the class, been the model for all of us, and I recall none of us having problems with respect to word choice, diction, grammar, or good usage. Good language was spoken at home. We imitated it. Had one or two of us had some problems with usage, immersion in the class itself would have corrected this fairly quickly. Needless to say, our vocabularies needed development, but by now simple grammar was second nature. Few, if any, used double negatives or "I is…" or "ain't."

Miss Chappell therefore focused on composition and the mechanics of written language. We wrote a lot, principally stories and book reviews. Many topics were anecdotal, describing experiences and family activities. The *Delphian* for Spring, 1953, contains a short piece by Bill Fischer entitled, "The Funniest Thing that Happened to Me," about a trip to Litchfield, Connecticut, that he took with his folks to visit his grandparents—while at the same time, his grandparents were taking a trip to Providence to visit the Fischers, each hoping to surprise the other. Kent Painter from our Class also had a piece in the same *Delphian*—about rowing a boat in a pond, slipping in his seat, losing the oars, and finally getting them back again.[61] Some of these stories were written in class, others at home.

Again, we had book reports, and we had a reasonable number of them. Even though we were reading in another class, we were expected to read books for Miss Chappell and write reports on them. The Landmark series had expanded, and I remember reading many of the new ones in the Fifth Grade—those that come to mind include *The Pirate Laffite and the Battle of New Orleans, The Monitor and the Merrimack*, and *The First Transcontinental Railroad*—all of which I enjoyed.

I do recall we had a "Tree Essay" for several years in the Lower School. It may have started as early as the Third Grade. We were asked to write an essay about one species of native tree. I remember doing the white oak in the Fifth Grade—describing it and then discussing its uses in the New

---

60   McKee. Paul, and McCowen, Boston: Houghton Mifflin, 1951.
61   *Delphian*, Vol. LI, No. 4, Commencement, 1953, p. 177.

England building and maritime industries. In the Sixth Grade, I chose the Red Maple. There were several recommended books we could read to learn about native trees, and there was an annual prize for these essays in each Class—in memory of Obadiah Brown.

To improve our composition style, we were introduced to coherent paragraph design: begin each one with a topic sentence—and make sure all sentences support that topic. We were even given examples of paragraphs that contained nonrelevant sentences, we were asked to cross those out as a test. Miss Chappell emphasized writing mechanics a lot. She taught us how to write a letter properly: how to punctuate a greeting (personal letter, a comma after the greeting; business letter, a colon), how to close (personal letter, close with "Sincerely," or "Sincerely yours,"; business letter, close with "Very truly yours,"), and so forth. We were taught how to address an envelope (either with the lines straight above each other or on a diagonal).

We also learned about how and when to use quotation marks, the difference between common nouns and proper nouns (the latter were always to be capitalized), and which words to capitalize in essay and book titles. We were told that when we wrote essays we should underline the titles of books and put quotation marks around the titles of stories. We were discouraged from using contractions in essays—unless they were used in dialogue—but were instructed in how contractions were properly formed. In this connection, we were shown, more generally, how to use apostrophes and how to punctuate, indent, and paragraph dialogue. All this was taught to us in the context of "This is how grown-ups write," and we certainly wanted to be more grown up.

In the Fifth Grade we memorized the School song: "Where the walls so tall and stately of our Alma Mater rise ...." We also had to memorize the School Psalm (the 121st): "I shall lift up mine eyes unto the hills from whence cometh my help..." In addition, we memorized several verses of the Quaker poet John Greenleaf Whittier's hymn, "Dear Lord and Father of Mankind, forgive our feverish ways...." (modern versions say "foolish ways"). Bill Barrett recalled that we also memorized several stanzas from "The Eternal Goodness," another Whittier hymn that contains the lines, "I know not what the future hath of marvel or surprise..." All these were sung or recited at the Lower School Commencement exercises every

Second Intermediate: The Fifth Grade (1952-1953)   75

year—from this time forward, and throughout the Upper School, we could now add our voices to Moses Brown ceremonial singing.

Miss Chappell also taught spelling, a subject that I was not very good at. Somewhere along the way, perhaps at this time, Aunt Amey tutored me in spelling. She herself taught spelling, working with dyslexic and linguistically challenged students at St. George's School in Middletown, and she gave me many spelling rules to help overcome my own (relatively mild) dyslexia: "i" before "e" except after "c" or sounded as "a" [long "a"], as in "neighbor" or "weigh." In this context, we were also instructed to "seize the protein-fed heifer before she breaks the weir." It was also in the Fifth Grade that we were expected firmly to have sorted out some common spelling and usage confusions: to, too, and two; there, their, and they're; and four, fourteen, and forty. Miss Chappell also introduced us to the difference between affect and effect, but that didn't sink in fully with me until later on. She also taught us how to spell the stylistic schools to which Miss Swide introduced us in the Fifth Grade, including such challenges as "impressionistic."

I remember the dictionary we had in the Fifth Grade, although I don't recall its name. We kept it in our desk. It was a student dictionary—I believe we had the same dictionary throughout the whole Lower School. We were taught how to look up words in it to check their spellings.[62] It was fairly primitive. I can remember Miss Chappell using words too advanced for it. One of these was "sward," as in green sward, which was in the Moses Brown Alma Mater. I remember we looked it up in our dictionary and it was not there. I wondered if she had made a mistake—after all, the word was not in the dictionary. She explained that this was an abridged dictionary—and what that meant. After looking it up at home in *Webster's*, I finally had to concede, with some reluctance, that "sward" was a word, and not just an oddity found in the School song.

We continued to have penmanship and reading. In Miss Stapleton's reading class we read adventure stories, including Richard Connell's "The

---

62 By the Fifth Grade, if I didn't know how to spell a word, I was told to look it up in the dictionary. This seemed odd: if I didn't know how to spell it, how could I look it up? When I asked that question, it was deemed impertinent. Slowly I adapted to trial and error techniques, but I was never given a systematic method to use, and my haphazard efforts seemed far from satisfactory.

Most Dangerous Game" and one (whose author and title I forget) about a plantation owner in the tropics confronting an invasion of killer ants which ate his livestock and nearly ate him—until he was able to reach and open a sluice gate and flood them away.

We had exams which tested both reading comprehension and vocabulary. These exercises may have been conducted by Miss Chappell or Miss Stapleton. The following vocabulary words, drawn from several tests, show that we in the Fifth Grade were advancing into the world of adult reading and conversation: extricate, trundle bed, whit, cartouche, damask linen, epithet, sundry, martial, propitious, repudiate, stratagem, municipal, emaciated, palings, infinitesimal, predatory, undulating, vicarious, pinion.

Geography. Miss Jensen taught us social studies in the Fifth Grade. For whatever reason, she seemed to me much more engaged and enthusiastic in the Fifth Grade than in the Fourth—and much more in control of her classes. It may simply be that I was more mature by then, it may be that she had experienced another year of teaching and had improved her style, or it may be that teaching with Miss Chappell created a different atmosphere than teaching with Miss Pixley—and we were better behaved. Also, Miss Jensen may have liked the subject matter more. Whatever the reason, her classes seemed more interesting and enjoyable.

I remember our Fifth Grade American geography textbook quite well, and I have refreshed that memory.[63] It started in the Northeast with New York and New England, which were familiar. There were black and white pictures of Boston and New York City. We worked our way south and west through the rest of the country, its cities and its rural areas. As the story unfolded, we made political maps of the various regions. We put in state capitals, other major cities, rivers, and so forth. We also made national topographical, rainfall, and "natural vegetation" maps, and maps of where crops like corn, wheat, and cotton were grown. When making these maps, we used colored pencils. The textbook also had stippled maps of population density and crop production. By this time, we were expected to be able

---

63 McConnell, Wallace R., *Geography of the Americas*, New York: Rand McNally & Company, 1950.

to fill in an outline map of the country with all the state names, correctly spelled—and another outline map with major American rivers, correctly spelled.

Our text emphasized economic geography, and it went into great detail about the manufactured and agricultural products of each region. At this time American industry was principally in the Northeast and Midwest. We also learned about raw materials and the products made from them. We were introduced to hydroelectric power, blast furnaces, oil wells, pipelines, irrigation and crop rotation. We made product maps of the various regions. Eventually we covered the whole country from coast to coast. Although the text included Canada and Latin America, we did not get that far.

About this time my folks bought me a *World Book Encyclopedia*, and this came in very handy for doing homework assignments in Fifth Grade geography. Bill Barrett remembered his folks buying one about this same time—perhaps the School encouraged such purchases; perhaps they could be ordered at the Book Fair. I can remember writing brief essays on various industries based on articles from this very readable reference work. American economic geography was loosely tied to American nationalism. This period saw the apex of American manufacturing in relative terms globally. We were number one in many areas of production (steel, oil, cars, telephones, appliances, radios, televisions), and national pride was generated in our geography classes by an awareness of these statistics.

We did some "show and tell" with respect to industry. My father was in textiles, and I remember bringing in some wool and woolen yarn. A good friend of my folks, who was in the cotton business, gave me some cotton samples to bring in while we were studying the South. We also wrote papers on different cities, industries, and crops.

There was an auxiliary geography text—I think it was an auxiliary text, although it may have been a book given to me—about a family that pulled up stakes in California and then drove across the country meeting various people in many regions as they traversed the continent, until they finally arrived on the East Coast. I remember them visiting West Virginia and meeting a little girl who had two dolls: one of her father in a soiled miner's uniform and the other with him cleaned up in normal clothing. The moral of the story, I assume, was that workers with dingy jobs were to be respected, and were no different from everyone else.

We also did a project with Miss Jensen on the State of Maine. It was especially interesting to me because we had spent our summers there when I was younger, and, in fact, we were still to spend one or two more. If she had chosen Vermont or New York, the case might have been different. I was curious at the time as to why we were doing something on Maine—not that I objected—but why not Rhode Island? The simple answer may have been that she originally came from Maine,[64] had developed this project before coming to Rhode Island, and had not had time to make a parallel effort for Little Rhody.

In any event, we went into impressive detail on the Great State of Maine. We were now making physical maps of Maine instead of Latin America. We also made political and economic maps. I remember having to memorize Maine's sixteen counties. We really went into great detail. Again, the outline form was used to create material to accompany the maps—we took notes in class from her and arranged them in outline fashion on ruled paper. We copied over the rivers, the cities, and the products—textiles, lumber, paper, lobsters, sardines, and so forth.

As was the case in the Fourth Grade, we put all these into a folder (in this instance with a cutout map of the state of Maine on the cover) to be displayed on Father and Son Day or on other occasions, such as parents nights.

Looking back, Miss Jensen really should have had us study Rhode Island. Maybe there was too little space on a Rhode Island map to display its products! At that time Rhode Island actually produced things—woolen, worsted, and cotton cloth; lace; rubber products; jewelry; silverware and silver artifacts; machine tools, especially precision tools; files for wood and metal; wire for the telephone company; screws, fasteners, hand tools, and other hardware; even milk, poultry, vegetables, fish, lobsters, and quahogs.

---

64 Lewiston, Maine.

Second Intermediate: The Fifth Grade (1952-1953)   79

History. We also studied American history in the Fifth Grade.[65] In this class we started with the Age of Exploration and the Colonial Period, and we carried it right through the Revolution, the settlement of the West, and briefly, the Civil War. We did not get down to the level of the Wilmot Proviso, but we were taught about the Louisiana Purchase, the Erie Canal, and the Mexican War. The only post-Civil War material was on inventions, like the telephone, the light bulb, and mass production.

It seemed that all American history courses started with Columbus and ended with Lincoln—this until we reached Mr. Everett Raines in Upper School who managed, barely, to get into the twentieth century. Mrs. Monahon in the Seventh Grade made some forays into more modern matters, but her greatest interests were in colonial history and the pre-Civil War period. So we had good grounding in the period before the Civil War, but less grounding in the period, say, between the Civil War and the First World War.

It Is Interesting that In the Fifth Grade we were given a list of "understandings" in history. These were concepts used by historians and included continuity, interdependence, common impulses, cumulative[ness], responsibility, and the dependence of tomorrow on today. I don't remember anyone explaining what all these meant, and if they were explained, it is doubtful that any of us understood them at any level of sophistication (or really remembered them afterwards)—but someone, at any rate, was interested enough in such larger dimensions of historiography that they were motivated to share them with us.

Near the beginning of our Fifth Grade year, we copied a chronology, starting with 1488 when Bartolomeu Dias rounded Cape Hope, and ending when Washington was elected president. I think this was for reference and not for memory, but certainly we did memorize many of the people, events, and dates it contained. We were taught about the early explorers: Marco Polo, Prince Henry, Dias, da Gama, Columbus, Cabot, Balboa, Ponce de León, Cortez, Hudson, Magellan, Pizarro, de Soto, LaSalle, and Drake. We were told about Amerigo Vespucci and the origin of the name America. We were told about Mercator and his maps. I don't remember

---

65   The text was Cordier, R.W., and Robert, E.B., *History of Young America*, New York: Rand McNally, 1951.

being told about Verrazano, who is now credited with being the first European to visit New York Harbor and Narragansett Bay. We were given the dates when many American cities and colonies were founded, and who founded them. We were told about the French and Indian War, and quite a bit about the American Revolution. In my file, I find papers written about Marco Polo, the colonial economic differences between northern and southern colonies (which we also discussed in class), the Boston Tea Party, the Battle of Saratoga, and John Adams.

I can remember reading at home about the world wars—Life Magazine's *Pictorial History of World War II* was a book that fascinated me during Lower School days—but we really did not get much of that in class.

I do not recall what we did for US history projects in the Fifth Grade, if any. I just remember Miss Jensen teaching it and the textbook we used, as noted. I do remember an exchange with her about the causes of the Civil War and the motivation of "slavery" versus that of "states' rights." The standard procedure was that we would be responsible for readings in the textbook, then Miss Jensen would talk about it in class, and then we would have a test. One major task was memorizing various names, dates, and other facts, but I enjoyed that, in part because my folks found ways to make games out of history as well as out of geography.

Current events and the election of 1952. We held a mock election in the fall of 1952: Eisenhower against Stevenson. I can remember Stevenson got only one vote in the Class—Tommy Clark announced that he was voting for Stevenson. When asked why, he said that it was because everyone else was voting for Ike.[66] Eisenhower therefore carried the Class with near unanimity.

Later, in the Upper School, I remember Mrs. Paxton telling us that in 1936 her daughters were going to Lincoln School and there was a mock

---

66 In addition, his family may have had some sentiments favoring Democrats—I remember Tommy proudly telling me that Senator Theodore Francis Green, a Democrat, was the oldest man ever to sit in the Senate, adding to his record every day. I think Carl Hayden dethroned him later on, with Strom Thurmond ultimately surpassing Hayden.

Second Intermediate: The Fifth Grade (1952-1953) 81

election there pitting FDR against Alf Landon. Mrs. Paxton told me that the Class voted overwhelmingly for Landon, and one daughter came home and said, "I really feel very sorry for President Roosevelt. He's such a nice man, and it's really a shame that he is going to lose." Well, in 1936, FDR carried every state save Maine and Vermont in one of the largest landslides in US history. I guess that Lincoln students (and, no doubt, Moses Brown students) were not fully representative of the public at that time.

We had campaign buttons which we wore at School, and there seemed to be a contest to see who could amass the most buttons. Tommy, of course, had a Stevenson button. I remember my mother saying she should get a Stevenson button to go with her large collection of buttons promoting presidential losers, stretching back to Hoover in 1932 (including Landon, Willkie, and two sets for Dewey). Also, we thought it very special that Ike had nominated Nixon to be his running mate because we had Jack Nixon (no relation) in our Class.[67] I can remember we were very proud of this special circumstance that was nearly unique (Jack had an older brother Bruce Nixon at Moses Brown at that time—the only two Nixons most of us knew). Bill Barrett recalled that Jack on one occasion displayed his Nixon button upside down: "Look, Miss Chappell, you have a new student (NOXIN)."

I can also remember that in Miss Stapleton's reading class we had a periodical called *Current Events*, which was a more advanced version of the *Weekly Reader*. This explained the Electoral College and the presidential nominating conventions, and I can remember becoming very interested in both at that time. I also recall an article in this paper about a young television reporter who was just coming onto the scene and who was pioneering the technique of having an "anchor" coordinating other reporters at the convention. That article was my introduction to Walter Cronkite—before I saw him on TV.

I was allowed to stay up later than usual the night of the election. I remember my father being excited by the early results, and when the Democrats

---

67 Jack Nixon joined our Class in the Fourth Grade. After graduating from Upper School, he went to Brown and subsequently earned an MBA from the University of Rhode Island. He then enjoyed a distinguished career in banking, rising to the position of Executive Vice President at Fleet Bank in Providence. Concurrently, he spent 30 years in the US Navy (27 years in the Reserves) and retired as a Captain, serving as a commanding officer for six different commands in the Southern New England region. Like so many other members of our Class, he is a devoted golfer.

Watching Eisenhower's first inauguration
(Moses Brown's first all-school television program)

conceded New York, he was ecstatic. To him this was the turning point of the whole evening, and that proved to be the case. I was sent off to bed before the full result was in, but found out the next morning that Ike, indeed, had won.

When Eisenhower was inaugurated, a television was set up in Alumni Hall, and we all went down and watched the inauguration. His inaugural address made a point-by-point presentation of his program or priorities, maybe a dozen or so. I remember when we got back up to the classroom, Miss Chappell, in a remarkable feat of memory, reviewed those points and tried to explain to us their significance in reasonably understandable terms.

Nineteen fifty two saw the climax of the Korean War. It started while we were in the Third Grade and ended in the summer after the Fifth Grade, so all during this period we were experiencing war, but the School did not discuss it much. Perhaps it was the Quaker tradition, perhaps we were deemed too young for such discussions, but I don't remember a lot mentioned in class about Korea—although Bill Barrett did recall Miss Chappell telling us at this juncture in the Cold War solemnly and regretfully that she thought the Soviet Union would be the next great world power.

I was aware of Korea, however, from the television evening news, the newspaper, and discussions at home, although it was still to me a fairly remote episode. I especially recall the stories on television. Newscaster John Cameron Swayze reported every night on how many MIGs had been shot down and what was happening at Pork Chop Hill, Old Baldy, or other such interestingly named locations. I remember television maps of the Korean struggle—the line moving down the peninsula at the beginning, then up, and then back down to the center near the Thirty-Eighth Parallel, an oft-repeated phrase. I do remember Ike pledging to go to Korea, Stevenson saying he should go to Moscow instead, and Aunt Amey, who liked Stevenson, commenting unfavorably about Stevenson's rejoinder. I also remember the news coverage of Ike's trip to Korea after the election.

I suppose that if you wanted to trace my interest in political science and politics it went back to pre-school times when my parents taught me all forty-eight states and their capitals, and we played all sorts of geography games, but it was certainly enhanced by the social studies classes at Moses Brown as they were called.

Science. Miss Chappell did not teach us much science. In fact, as noted, we did not have much science instruction in the Lower School. But it was clear that she was interested in science. A friend of hers who taught astronomy at Smith College came to town, visited the School, and visited our classroom. We probably did have a little formal science in the Fifth Grade—I have found a science exam from this year quizzing us on the planets.

We also had a session on trees and leaves taught by Miss Jensen. It may have been in conjunction with the Tree Essay. She had a book that demonstrated systematically how to identify a tree by using such clues as the shape of its leaf, whether leaves were ribbed on the back or not, whether or not the twigs were arranged opposite each other on the stems, and so forth. She asked us to bring in some leaves to be identified. In response to that request, my folks drove me out to the farm one evening and we brought back some sassafras leaves. Miss Jensen proceeded to go through the steps and identified them correctly. Tommy Clark brought in a whole branch which he had torn off of a maple tree on his way to School! We all thought his gesture was wonderful, but the powers that be frowned a bit.

Elisabeth G. Weeks

If we didn't have a lot of instruction in science, we at least had the Junior Audubon Club—and, once more, my memories are a bit vague as to what we did. I remember class instruction being suspended on a few occasions for this purpose. I think Miss Weeks came in to talk to us. We may have had another speaker. Students also spoke about specific birds. At one meeting there was discussion about installing a bird feeder outside one of our windows—which did not happen, as I recall. I do remember being taught how to identify New England summer songbirds about this time, but I think this was done out at the farm, where live examples could be seen.

These Audubon meetings presented an opportunity for us to learn democratic procedures and how to conduct a meeting. In the Fifth Grade, Nick Littlefield was elected President; Vin Marcello, Vice President; yours truly, Secretary; Kent Painter,[68] Treasurer; and Bill Barrett, Correspond-

---

68 Kent Painter left us after the Sixth Grade. As was the case with so many other Lower School students, we lost touch with him.

Second Intermediate: The Fifth Grade (1952-1953) 85

ing Secretary. I do have my notes for the September 29 meeting (which consisted entirely of the election), and for a subsequent meeting at which substance was discussed—both sets of notes being edited by Miss Jensen. The following minutes give a flavor of our Audubon meetings:

> Nicky Littlefield opened the meeting with a ruler as we had no gavel. Just then Tommy Clark came in with the gavel. Billy Barrett, the Corresponding Secretary, read the Secretary's report. There were no errors of major importance. Under Old Business, the matter of the station was brought up. Hank Levaur[69] suggested we put a feeding station up outside the window. Miss Jensen suggested to Nick Littlefield that he ask about raising money for the bird seed. Kent Painter told an interesting story about his grandfather's bird seed. Kent said that his grandfather had a pet shop. Billy Goddard added that birds like peanut butter.
>
> Miss Jensen suggested that we end the discussion [about the feeding station] and go on to the program. Hank Levaur said that [a] bird and animal combination was a Duckbilled Platypus which we were going to study. He [later] assigned a bird to each boy and asked each one to write a short paper. During the program Nicky Littlefield went around paying no attention to the program, rapping on people's desk[s], telling them to keep quiet. At 2:55 someone made the motion that the meeting be closed. It was seconded. The President, Nicky Littlefield, then declared the meeting adjourned with the sound of the gavel.[70]

---

69 Hank was in our Class for only a brief time; we lost touch with him and do not know his career trajectory.

70 Nick Littlefield (Bancroft Littlefield, Jr.,) joined our Class in Pre-Primary. He left Moses Brown after the Second Form in the Upper School, went to Milton Academy, and then to Harvard, earning his law degree from the University of Pennsylvania. He also studied at the London School of Economics. Nick had a brief, but successful career on Broadway, and then joined the law firm of Hughes, Hubbard, and Reed in New York. After serving as an assistant US attorney in the Southern District in New York, he returned to New England and became Chief Counsel to the Massachusetts Special Anti-Corruption Commission from 1978-80. After joining the law firm of Foley Hoag and Eliot, he went to Washington to become one of Senator Ted Kennedy's chief advisors, serving as the Staff Director of the Senate Committee on Labor and Human Resources. Nick was the coauthor and principal historical source for the very important biography of Senator Kennedy entitled *Lion of the Senate*, which appeared in 2015. Nick passed away after a long illness in 2017. I was very happy to reconnect with him and his family while doing research for this Moses Brown memoir.

Art. Miss Swide, our art instructor for the second year, was a graduate of the Massachusetts College of Art, and she was a remarkable teacher. She certainly demonstrated real professional training, and for us she expanded the whole concept of art beyond simply dabbling with paint. In the Fifth Grade, she offered some special classes on Saturdays at which, for the first time, we began to paint with oils. I can remember painting a covered bridge and attempting to paint a lighthouse. Bill Goddard, I remember, did a very fine painting of a lighthouse which I could not begin to match. He had real artistic talent. We were taken to the Rhode Island Philharmonic that year for a concert—and Miss Swide thought that this would be a wonderful occasion for us to do an interpretive painting of the experience, perhaps something abstract. I'm not sure exactly what she had in mind, but she was severely disappointed in my effort, which was a poor attempt to show Beethoven sitting at his piano composing the Fifth.

I remember she took the Class, or at least part of it, to Boston, where we went to the Museum of Fine Arts and across the street to the Isabella Stewart Gardner Museum. That was a very interesting trip. At MFA, we saw Revere silver, Egyptian artifacts that brought back memories of the Fourth Grade, and portraits by Copley. At the Gardner, we saw Sargent's painting of the Spanish dancer, and visited all floors of that palazzo. It was explained to us who the painters were and to some extent the significance of their paintings. There were several carloads from School. I remember my mother drove and I think two or three other parents drove as well. The Class at the time was probably only twenty to twenty-five boys; I think most went, which would probably be four or five carloads. I believe that Miss Chappell went with us.

We began to learn a little bit about various painters and a little bit about art history. We learned such terms as "Realism," "Impressionism," "Surrealism," "Expressionism," and "Futurism." There was an art appreciation show on television that year, and we were encouraged by Miss Swide to view it. I remember talking with her about Seurat, after vewing this show (since the television program mentioned his name many times, but never showed it in print, I had mistakenly thought that his name, quite appropriately, was Sir Art; she set me straight). I think that if this kind of instruction had continued and subsequent art teachers had shown the degree of interest in teaching art appreciation that she did, it would have been a valuable experience for all of us. After Miss Swide, we continued painting and doing other interesting things, but never again at Moses Brown did we have an art appreciation course. Even though I was not good at painting, I really did enjoy Miss Swide's classes. That year for Christmas, we printed cards from linoleum blocks on which we carved a picture. Mine had a set of three trees with a star on top at the right. Miss Swide was married in June, and, regrettably, did not return to Moses Brown in the fall.

Music. In the Fifth Grade, we had Mrs. Thomas for music. I can remember Miss Chappell telling the class one morning that she had a wonderful surprise for us. And, when we were all on the edge of our chairs, so to speak, she announced that Mrs. Thomas was going to be our music instructor. Of course we were acquainted with Mrs. Thomas as the Headmaster's wife, and she had played the organ for the Christmas Pageant. But most of us knew little about her, although we had probably seen her around School walking Shawn, the Thomases' quite gentlemanly Irish red setter. We did, however, look forward to her teaching us music.

Mrs. Thomas was one of the most delightful, enthusiastic, and alive persons you could ever know. She had been an actress and had never lost her panache or her persona. In fact, she was very active in The Players (an amateur theater group) down on Benefit Street. There was never a dull moment in her classes, and everyone was so riveted by her performances and by her personality that she never had a disciplinary problem. She was always one step ahead of us all. We thoroughly enjoyed learning with her for three memorable years.

In music, we spent a great deal of time singing and memorizing songs. In the fall we prepared for the Christmas Pageant. In the spring, we prepared for Commencement. We also spent time learning how to read notes, and how to understand sharps and flats. She discussed the chromatic scale and showed us what she called the "Musical Clock or the Circle of Fifths." I have my hand-drawn version of this impressive-looking figure—and haven't the faintest idea of what it was all about.

In addition to all this instruction at School, Mrs. Thomas took us down to a concert at the Veterans Auditorium to hear a special performance by

William Turner's retirement party
(L–R) Mr. Jurnquist, Mrs. Thomas, Mr. Turner, Mrs. Turner

the Rhode Island Philharmonic, and later to the Rhode Island School of Design Auditorium to hear another concert, perhaps also by the Philharmonic. I think this was part of a statewide program for students. Beforehand, she taught us the various different orchestral instruments in their four main classes. She introduced us to five strings (including the harp), seven woodwinds, four brass, and fourteen of the many percussion instruments (including the piano). She showed us pictures of them and described in interesting ways how each was played, and how each made music. She also shared brief recordings with us to give examples of how each sounded. She then described how they were integrated and how the orchestra was built up. By the time we went to the concert, we could recognize and identify the various instruments, understand their significance, and were well-versed in how the symphonic orchestra itself was structured.

I remember Mrs. Thomas playing the piano for us, often while we attempted to sing. It was always a riveting experience. The lessons were in Alumni Hall, and the piano was over on the left of the stage (audience left). We sat in wooden chairs down front near the piano. We remembered Mr. Pickett, our music instructor the previous year in the Fourth Grade, as an excellent piano player. His style was very loud and assertive, and he beat out the tunes with speed and authority. Mrs. Thomas, however, was a musical genius, and the pianoforte—soft and loud—was transformed completely into an extension of her vivacious personality, or into the personality of someone she was imitating. For us fifth graders, she was constantly having fun with it, playing this tune, playing that tune, many of which we were familiar with, but playing them with improvisations that fascinated and entertained us. She explained the pieces, gave us some history, and often told jokes about them. Victor Borge, step aside. She was a presence, and whenever she sat down at the keyboard, we could expect to have fun because she herself was having so much fun. She played, we sang. We sang, she played. If some of us knew a tune she had not heard, we sang a few bars for her and she easily improvised, picking up the tune right away and playing it as if she had heard it many times before. We were impressed by that. If we were singing in ways that needed improvement, which was often the case, as I recall, she would stop, and in the most engaging and encouraging way lightly show us how it should be done and ask us to try again, often singing along with us to get us into the right mood and mode. The time went very fast in those music classes.

Once, around Christmas time, we were singing "Hark the Herald Angels Sing." I can remember raising my hand and telling one of Grandpa Johnson's stories. It was about Beecham Pills. As the story went, the Beecham Pill Company in England offered to buy hymn books for a parish church—and asked for absolutely nothing in return. All was fine, until Christmas—when the minister announced that the congregation would sing "Hark, the Herald Angels Sing." The song, as it was written in the hymnal, went as follows:

> Hark, the Herald Angels Sing
> Beecham's Pills are just the thing
> Peace on Earth and Mercy mild,
> Two for an adult, one for a child
> Etc.

Mrs. Thomas was delighted by the story—and was not to be outdone. She informed us all that Sir Thomas Beecham—perhaps related to the pills—was a famous conductor of the London Symphony. She told us—possibly a true story—that once he was conducting the music for an opera which was being performed by a visiting company of which he apparently had a very low opinion. During the performance, a horse lifted its tail and plopped onto the stage. Beecham stopped the orchestra, turned to the audience, and said, "Ladies and gentlemen, that horse may be lacking in manners, but, Gad, what a critic!"

Since the Thomases retired in 1955, we were the last graduating class in the Lower School to have Mrs. Thomas for music.

Movies and television. I think it was in the Fifth Grade that the Avon Theater had a Saturday morning movie series aimed roughly at our age group—and above. By and large, these were adventure films. A great number of us East Side Moses Brown kids attended. I remember *Robin Hood*, starring Errol Flynn and Basil Rathbone. I also remember *Kit Carson* and a film called *Down to the Sea in Ships*. There may have been other westerns, including one on the Oregon Trail. Bill Barrett remembered *Kidnapped*. Perhaps we also saw *Treasure Island*. I remember seeing *The Thin Man* at the Avon about that time, but this was with my parents.

We also had films shown in Alumni Hall during this period. They were documentaries, and not very memorable. Mr. Allen ran the projector. I do remember one about George Washington, probably made in the early 1930s. It showed his mission to Fort Duquesne on behalf of the State of Virginia, requesting that the French abandon that outpost. I remember it made a point that the French "were very polite, but firm." I don't remember how it treated Braddock's debacle, but Washington himself was portrayed in a very formal and stuffy way.

There were films about other American heroes, about other lands and peoples, about manufacturing processes, and other topics to supplement our geography and history courses. Bill Barrett remembered that every year Mr. Allen convened the older students from the Lower School in Alumni Hall to show a film featuring the highlights of the most recent World Series games (often a contest in those days between the Yankees and the Dodgers).

One movie featured the demise of the Hindenburg, and that footage was riveting. I remember, however, Mme. Warge afterwards being very critical of it being shown—I guess she didn't approve of disaster films. Some films turned out to be insufferably dull, but they did get us out of the classroom, and we enjoyed the change in routine.

Television, as noted, was just coming into vogue when we were in the Lower School grades, and most classmates soon had access to a set at home. The programming started late in the afternoon (earlier in the day there would either be nothing at all or a "test pattern" on the screen). There were two Boston stations (Channel 4 and Channel 7) and one Providence station (Channel 10, I think). There were baseball games (I remember the Boston Braves on television, as well as the Red Sox), and in the evenings there were the featured programs like *Milton Berle's Texaco Hour*; *Martin Kane, Private Eye*; *I Remember Mama*; *The Big Story*; *The Life of Riley*; *Henry Aldrich*; *The* [Friday night] *Gillette Cavalcade of Sports*; *The Hit Parade*, etc. I was allowed to stay up late on Friday nights only.

Every afternoon, however, before supper and the news, there were programs aimed at our age group. One was the famous *Howdy Doody* with Buffalo Bob and Clarabell the clown. Howdy himself was a marionette, who performed and interacted with Buffalo Bob in front of an admiring "Peanut Gallery" of children. Sometimes they showed silent movies of the Keystone Cops variety. Less well known, but for a slightly more mature children's audience, was *Kukla, Fran and Ollie*, which my parents urged me to watch. Kukla and Ollie were puppets, Ollie being an intelligent dragon. Fran was a live person. I somehow looked at both shows. There was also a film series, *Crusader Rabbit*, which I enjoyed a lot. There was *Flash Gordon*, which I did not. Just about everyone in the class was watching one of these programs and we used to talk about them in School. They occupied our time just after we came home from School, and before we were summoned to the supper table. We never ate in front of the TV. After supper was homework time, interrupted by frequent telephone calls to and from classmates.

VI

Third Intermediate: The Sixth Grade (1953-1954)

The Third Intermediate comes back to me in strong memory.[71] It featured a very organized curriculum, and, thinking back to the whole Lower School experience, it was my most important year. I think that Mrs. Florence Cullen, our homeroom instructor, was the best teacher I had in the Lower School, and there were many good teachers there. A graduate of East Stroudsburg Teachers College in Pennsylvania, with subsequent work at Rutgers, she was a very professional instructor, had obviously thought a lot about her teaching techniques, knew her subject matter very well, and was a calm disciplinarian. In her quiet (but firm) way she conveyed to us that we were there to learn and that the learning experience could

---

71 The Sixth Grade homeroom, as noted, was on the northeast corner of the building stretching east from Middle House. Most windows faced north towards the art studio; one faced east so you could see along the side of Alumni Hall towards the Lower School gym. It was the only Lower School classroom with no southern exposure. The class itself faced south, with the blackboard in front of us. Mrs. Cullen's desk was on the east wall to our left.

Adjacent and to the south of the Sixth Grade classroom (in front of us as we sat), was a room with metal and glass partitions separating it from the Seventh Grade classroom to its west. In this room we had Sixth-Grade Geography and History with Mrs. Bluhm. Here we faced north, and her desk was on the north wall in front of us. The blackboard was behind her. This is the same room in which I had had a reading class with Miss Stapleton. I don't remember if the room had a name.

There were locker rooms and a bathroom to the west of the Sixth Grade classroom. The lockers (and the ones over in the Lower School building) had no locks on them. Each was assigned his own locker, and we used them to store overcoats, rubbers, and boots.

Florence S. Cullen

be exciting and fun. Like Miss Wilson and Miss Chappell, Mrs. Cullen would stand for no nonsense, but unlike Miss Wilson, she seldom raised her voice, and unlike Miss Chappell, she organized classroom decorum carefully and systematically, rather than simply demanding it as occasions arose. Her expectations were very clear, and she held us to a constant set of standards. She was therefore exceedingly fair to everyone. It was through ordered, structured procedures and calmness of method that she established unquestioned command. Her subjects were English and math.

Mrs. Cullen was assisted by Mrs. Ellie Bluhm, also a superb teacher, who obviously enjoyed teaching us our geography and history lessons, and who put a lot of personal effort into both. She was cheerful, vibrant, enthusiastic, and engaging. Her friendly personality and love of subject made each class interesting and enjoyable. Geography and history can be dull, but there was never a dull moment in her class. She did not use gimmicks, but did use imagination. Overall, it was her enthusiasm and sunny personality that carried the class and made it an experience we looked forward to every day.

Eleanor K. Bluhm

Mrs. Bluhm was well trained, with an undergraduate degree from Vassar and a master's degree from the Fletcher School of Law and Diplomacy at Tufts. She had taught at the University of Chicago. Her husband taught political theory at Brown, and later at the University of Rochester. I was to meet them in later years, and in the 1980s he wrote in support of my tenure at Union College. In terms of learning, I grew more in the Sixth Grade than in any other Lower School grade with the extraordinary combination of Mrs. Cullen and Mrs. Bluhm. I believe that I was not alone in this respect. It was here that learning began to move gradually away from repetition and performing the exercises we were told to perform—to thinking a bit more on our own, making some decisions, and understanding in some cases why we were being asked to perform the required tasks.

Homework and study habits. We always had homework at Moses Brown, but much of it had been exercises in math and English. By the Sixth Grade, we were given homework in every subject. To keep the assignments straight, I carried a small notebook in my jacket side pocket, and jotted them down for the next day. Reviewing one such notebook recently, I see math assignments listed by page and number in the text, names of locations to include on a map, and spelling or vocabulary words to learn (e.g. "chaotic"). Sometimes we wrote down lessons from class. We also made note of when quizzes and exams would occur. At the beginning of the year we listed the books and pieces of equipment to buy.

By the Sixth Grade, homework took quite a lot of time during the evening hours. But inevitably, that time would be punctuated by telephone calls. Virtually no evening went by during which I was not on the telephone for at least a half hour—usually with Nick Littlefield, Bill Barrett, Tommy Clark, or Harrison Huntoon. This was the case for most of my classmates. I can also remember calls from other classmates asking for help with homework, or from someone who had forgotten an assignment, or from someone who just wanted to chat—but I don't remember a lot of social gossip in these calls. They were usually about something that had happened in School that day or was expected to take place in School tomorrow. The practice was to continue throughout the rest of the Moses Brown experience. Since call-waiting was not yet an option for telephone subscribers, I'm sure that our parents were vexed by their phones lines being tied up—and the people trying to reach them, no doubt, were even more vexed by the recurrent busy signals during much of the evening. Some parents (not mine) actually put in a second line, just for their children to use. Although inconvenient for the folks, their kids' evening telephone networking was very much part of the '50s culture and it was a relatively new way in which we expanded our social horizons beyond the family itself. We became closer friends with our interlocutors than would have been the case without the telephone, and the exercise helped expand our world beyond the family in ways that would not have been possible a generation before. In fact, we got to know our phone pals at least as well as we knew many of our close relatives in this, our life's gradual journey out from the family.

English. By the time we reached the Sixth Grade, reading had become part of "English" (spelling was still taught separately), and we still did some cursive penmanship exercises (in one of these, I tried to be smart and wrote my capitals with a backward slant, and was severely marked down for doing so). English *per se* was taught for the first time in a formal way. Before this year, we had done a lot of reading, had learned to write letters, compose brief essays, and use a dictionary. We had practiced simple usages. But in the Sixth Grade we had formal instruction in grammar, wrote more extensive essays, and embarked on a *very* ambitious program of reading. As I later learned, reading good English is an excellent way of learning to write good English. I am sure Mrs. Cullen understood that very well.

Her first love was English, and she gave us the fundamentals. She taught us the basic structure of a sentence (subject/predicate or subject/object). We learned the difference between definite and indefinite objects, and the difference between a phrase and a clause. She taught us the four types of sentences: declarative, interrogative, imperative, and exclamatory.

She then taught us the eight parts of speech, and spent quite a lot of time on them. She had us write them in a notebook, and, as I remember, there was a little poem using them to help us remember each. We reviewed proper nouns and common nouns. We memorized the complete list of pronouns, and did exercises in how to use them with precision (this, that, these, those). We learned about singular and plural verbs and their tenses. We spent serious time on exercises designed to teach us the importance of using singulars and plurals in conjunction with each other. For example, "The boys were well prepared because each brought *his* own drinking cup; everybody did *his* best to keep it full of water."

We were told the difference between the active and passive voice. We learned the several dozen prepositions[72] and what a prepositional phrase was. We were taught the difference between adjectives and adverbs, and how adverbs modified verbs, adjectives, and other adverbs (in fact, we spent a lot of time on modifiers). We were taught about comparatives and superlatives—and how both adjectives and adverbs could be used to form them.[73] We were taught to identify conjunctions. And then there were those interjections, the odd ones sitting off there somehow by themselves—many of which we were not even supposed to use in polite conversation! We also spent a fair amount of time reviewing possessives and contractions and studied anew how to place apostrophes in their proper locations, which could be tricky with plural possessives.

With these fundamentals in place, Mrs. Cullen taught us how to divide sentences into parts—not just subject and predicate, but also phrases (to be put into parentheses). As exercises, we wrote out sentences, identified the part of speech represented by each word, and divided the whole into subjects and objects. When we were on top of that, she taught us how to diagram simple sentences. We did this both on paper and up at the board. All these exercises, and especially those involving diagramming, were like solving puzzles, and they could be a lot of fun. We did not diagram infinitives, participles, and gerunds. That we did later on in the Eighth Grade. In addition to diagramming sentences, we were also taught how to outline paragraphs—and condense them.

---

72 Bill Barrett remembered that we memorized the whole set in alphabetical order (about, above, across, after, and so forth, as he can still recite), but I have suppressed that memory! However, I have recently found a test which endorses Bill's recollections. I listed 43 on this exam; since I did not get full credit, Bill's recollection that there were at least 50 is probably correct.
73 Good, better, best; well, better, best; big, bigger, biggest; soon, sooner, soonest.

Grammar served more than one function, as I recall. It did help us with proper speech and gave us the rules needed to ensure that our speech was indeed grammatical. As we internalized good usage, our own speech evolved: "It was *she*"; "What counts is *whom* you know." To some extent, I suppose, it gave us a sense of superiority over those who used improper speech. In a related vein, it also gave some structure to our thinking. Exercises in grammar were exercises in logic, paralleling those in math, and this was one reason why they could be viewed as puzzles and entertaining games. Interestingly, in a sense, they also became a source of authority for us. Grammar, in its own area, like math, was unambiguous (almost always). Rules defined what was right and what was wrong—and did so impersonally, although the teacher served as judge. As we studied both disciplines, our sense of authority began to shift away from the personal (as represented by our parents and by our teachers as persons) and towards the impersonal (as represented by the abstract rules of logic and social convention)—from the rule of "men" and "women" to the rule of law, so to speak. This process, however, was very slow, and the distinction between the teacher as a personal authority and as the articulator of abstract authority never became total at this age.

In Sixth Grade English we also wrote a reasonably large number of essays or stories (usually 200-250 words in length), and in the evaluation and correction of these essays we were given further instruction in grammar. A lot of them were experiential: "How I Irritate my Father," "The Panama Canal" (describing a trip there), "My Favorite Dinner," etc. We were also asked to write a series of autobiographical essays about pre-school and early school experiences. We wrote essays about historical figures, two of which made it into the *Delphian* (Herb Sawyer wrote a piece about an Army surgeon who pushed back the frontiers of medical knowledge, and I wrote about Henry Ford).[74]

Some writing exercises were imaginative stories: "A Christmas Scene through a Window," and "Our Vacation in 1900." One assignment was to write an essay describing (in the first person) life as an inanimate object. In response to this request, I wrote "A Table Conversation" (between a fork,

---

74 *Delphian*, Vol LIII, No. 2 [sic], Commencement 1954, pp. 74-75. Note that this issue should have been denominated Vol. LII, No. 2, but was mistakenly labeled Vol. LIII. Thus there was no Vol. LII, No. 2. The subsequent issue was designated Vol. LIV, No. 1.

Third Intermediate: The Sixth Grade (1953-1954) 99

knife, and spoon)—using and punctuating conversational direct speech. Three of these made it into the *Delphian*: 1) a tragic tale by Nick Littlefield of a tennis ball that was happily married to another tennis ball by a tennis ball minister from the same can—but unfortunately all three eventually lost their bounce and rotted away; 2) a happy tale by David Stenmark of a football that adjusted to his life of being kicked around and actually came to enjoy it;[75] and 3) an exasperating tale by Leon Najarian of a necktie whose daily adventures included being spattered with food, ducked into soup, and dipped into ice cream.[76] Other *Delphian* issues reveal that with some classes Mrs. Cullen encouraged sixth graders to write adventure stories.

Other writing exercises were book reviews, reflecting the fact that reading was very important in the Sixth Grade. Mrs. Cullen had a little file box containing cards with the names of books she deemed to be classics for our age group. We were encouraged to read a large number of these both during the year and the summer afterwards. I can remember devouring a whole series of adventure classics at this time: *Tom Sawyer*, Stevenson's *Treasure Island* and *Kidnapped*, Verne's *Around the World in Eighty Days* (before the movie was made), Defoe's *Robinson Crusoe*, Wyss's *Swiss Family Robinson*, and Villiers's *And Not to Yield*. I believe we also read Kipling's *Jungle Book* at this time. We did book reports on these, and even gave oral book reports in front of the class (I remember doing one on *Treasure Island*). Often the assignment required an answer to the question, "What part of the book did you enjoy the most?" I have found a book review of *Island of Peril*, of which I have absolutely no recollection whatsoever, although I do remember the story lines of the other books listed. Towards the end of the year, I tackled *Moby Dick*. We had a Book-of-the Month-Club edition, bound in black, and illustrated with multiple heavy-line black and white woodcut drawings by Rockwell Kent. The entire book seemed to present striking contrasts of black and white. Looking back, I assume that this was no coincidence.

---

75 David Stenmark left us after his junior year in Upper School. We have been very happy to welcome him back to many Class reunions! Working nights, Dave earned a degree in architecture from the Rhode Island School of Design while also working for the Industrial Trust Company in Providence. His job at the bank was to work on the planning, design, and upgrading of the bank's branches throughout Rhode Island, representing the bank as it dealt with the various architectural firms who worked as contractors for the bank. He continued in this position, as the bank changed its name to Fleet, and then went thought many mergers—with RI Hospital Trust, Bank of Boston, and Bank of America.

76 *Delphian*, Vol. LI, No. 1, Winter, 1954, pp. 29-30.

At the time I was unaware of the symbolism, but the arresting illustrations and the large black typeface seemed to make this a different kind of book than the ones I had previously encountered. It was all a bit scary. The book itself was also tough going, with its adult vocabulary and its story line continually interrupted by diverting episodes and descriptive material about whales and whaling. It was long. Nor did it have a happy ending. All this added to the challenge. The books I had read up to this point had either been entertaining stories or historically informative narratives with positive messages. *Moby Dick* was unsettling.

Thus we had a very strong and concentrated program of reading, all outside of the classroom, concurrent with Mrs. Cullen's philosophy that the best way to develop writing skills is through reading and internalizing examples of good writing. We probably read at least a dozen books during the school year and more in the following summer. The emphasis on reading built vocabulary. We learned new words through context, and only occasionally did we need to revert to a dictionary. However, learning words off the printed page, as opposed to learning them through conversation, could occasionally lead to mispronunciation. I can remember thinking for quite a while that "epitome" was pronounced "epi-tome," and "albeit," "all-bite," but I was eventually straightened out in these regards.

One major encouragement to reading was the annual Book Fair, in which Mrs. Cullen took a very active role. It was an important event in the calendar of the School, and I remember it well. My mother was involved during the Sixth Grade and was in charge of it during the Seventh Grade (and possibly the Eighth Grade). From that perspective, it was especially interesting to me. I remember those involved all went up to Boston to select books. I didn't go, but I heard about the trip.

The Fair lasted a few days. Books were set up and put on display in Alumni Hall. There were tables for different levels of reading in the Lower School— and then other tables for mature readers of all ages. I assume the School received a percentage on the sales. My mother made a lot of purchases, especially during the years she was in charge.

One year they also sold records, and we took our old Edison record player that played cylindrical records over to Alumni Hall. My mother located a statue of "Nipper," the "His Master's Voice" RCA dog, which she borrowed and set up next to the big horn on the record player. Another year there was a full display of nice looking internally lit globes which created quite an impression as you entered Alumni Hall. Another year, the theme was "There is no Frigate like a Book to Take Us Lands Away," and the stage was decorated to look like the deck of a ship.

I also remember that one year there were copies of the *Bible* for sale. Mr. Cole prepared a nice sign to go in front of the *Bibles* saying "Always a Best Seller." My mother told him in no uncertain terms to go back and make a new sign saying "Always *The* Best Seller." He beat a hasty retreat and soon reemerged with the new sign.

During the years my mother was in charge, everybody involved came over to our house afterwards to figure out the sales and prepare the orders and deliveries.

I don't remember if this was in conjunction with the Book Fair or not, but one year the Class put on a set of one-act plays based on scenes from famous books. I was in Dickens's *Great Expectations*. I don't remember who else played whom, but I played Pip and was bullied by the Convict. He yelled at me that if I told anyone about him, he would cut my throat. This message must have been delivered so effectively that I blocked him out of memory, and totally forgot who played him.

Spelling. We had a lot of spelling exercises and a test once or twice a week on which we were asked to spell twenty to thirty words. Often the set of words reflected a topic or a theme. They were read to us and we wrote them down. Some words were repeated in subsequent exams, sometimes more than once. By this stage, we were spelling mature words found in adult conversation and in good reading materials: catalogue, machinery, lettuce, ceiling ("i" before "e" except, as here, after "c"), companion, favorite, advise/advice, temperature (not "temprature"), luncheon, altogether (mnemonic: al-to-get-her), auger, laundry, journal, judgment (no "e" after "g"), argument (ditto—drop that "e"), patient, principle/principal (the latter was your pal), straighten, excursion, prominent, cashier, receipt (and recipe), neighbor, grammar (no "e"—and not your mother's mother), peculiar, especially, carriage, refrigerator, libraries (not "liberries"), deceive, business, chorus, hymn and rhythm (still can't always get that one right), belief, college (no "d"), scissors, agriculture, effect/affect, whether/weather, immediately, unfortunately, athletics (remember only one "e"), wreath, Democrat and Republican—*never* say "Democrat Party" (as Joe McCarthy was doing at the time)—niece, nephew, "all 'E's' in cemetery existence," etc. We also learned how to spell Czechoslovakia in geography class: you start with "Czech" (remembering the Cz); you then add "oslo" (the capital of Norway), and end with "slovakia" (which is spelled phonetically). Bill Barrett remembered frequent "intramural" spelling bees during class time. He recalled one lasting about twenty-five minutes which he won after spelling numerous words correctly. When it was over, we immediately began another one. Bill was the first to spell, and he missed the first word, "ladder," spelling it "laddar." As he now puts it, "Pride goeth before ... a fall."

Math. In Sixth-Grade Math, we started with a review of long multiplication, long division, fractions, and decimals, including percentages. This may have been diagnostic to see who knew what. We soon moved on to very complex fractions, and learned how to multiply fractions—and to convert fractions to percentages. We learned to work with percentages exceeding 100 percent. We were introduced to the concept of negative numbers, and we were taught about squares and square roots (we learned how to hand calculate the latter, a complex procedure). We reviewed how to add and subtract units of measure not based on decimals—like pints, quarts, and gallons; and quarts, pecks, and bushels.

We began to move slowly away from raw computing, with an increased emphasis on problems. We did not learn algebra to solve those problems, but we did begin to learn formulae (A[rea] = L[ength] x W[idth]). We learned how to calculate areas and perimeters, including those of rectangles, triangles, and circles. We learned about proportion.

In most of these cases, it was made clear just why the procedure was useful—to determine, for example, how many square feet there were in a rug that was sold by the square foot, or how many feet of fencing would be needed to go around the perimeter of a field whose shape and dimensions we were given, or how high a water tower was from the length of its shadow compared to the length of a shadow cast by a fence post of known height. We learned less familiar units of measure, such as rods and fathoms. We learned how to calculate volume: how many bushels of grain would fill a grain bin 8 feet long, 2 1/4 feet wide, and 4 feet high at 1 1/4 cubic feet to the bushel?

Although we had been introduced to *pi* in the Fifth Grade, we used it more extensively in the Sixth. We learned how to compute the volume of spheres and cylinders, building on the formulae to compute the areas and circumferences of circles. Thus you could figure out how many cubic inches of Coke were in a can. We also learned the Pythagorean theorem, and used it to solve problems. Many problems involved money. We calculated the cost of specified amounts of goods at so much per pound or so much per square yard. We calculated the commissions salesmen would receive for certain amounts sold. We calculated mortgage interest rates. We calculated simple interest on bank loans (and were told that if you borrowed a dollar for one year and paid your lender $1.05 at the *end* of that year, it was 5 percent real interest. Today's banks and credit unions—please take note!) We also were introduced to the concept of compound interest, and the compounded percentages by which bank accounts increased or decreased over time. We were asked to explicate why a 10 percent decrease in one's allowance followed by a 10 percent increase did not get you back to the original allowance. We were introduced to tax rates and told what a "mill" was. We calculated distance and speed: "A test pilot traveled 90 miles by flying 6 minutes at half speed and 6 minutes at full speed. Find the full speed of the plane in miles per hour."

These practical applications of math made the subject more immediate and relevant, and began to convince us of its eventual usefulness to us in our lives. Moreover these new exercises in "applied math" actually developed practical skills that better prepared us for the "real world."

In developing these skills and practices, there was in-class instruction of the "how-to" variety, plus lots of in-class exercises and tests, and lots of homework—typically three or four serious at-home computational exercises a week.[77] Occasionally we would exchange papers and correct each other's. I sat next to Chad Gifford; he corrected mine and I corrected his. Confirming this, I have found one exercise with "Corrected by Chad Gifford" written on it in his handwriting. We also began having standardized tests in the Sixth Grade, such as the Stanford Achievement Test, which were fairly math-intensive. All in all, we were now building the capability to use mathematics to meet serious daily household requirements and even simple business needs.

Geography. In Sixth Grade we had a very intensive social studies program—both geography and history—taught by Mrs. Bluhm. The subject areas of our geography class were principally Europe and Asia; the subject areas of our history class were principally the ancient and medieval worlds.

I found Sixth Grade geography fascinating. We had a text called, *Our Earth and Man*,[78] dated 1951, which I have always remembered very clearly, and which I have just reviewed for writing this piece. This was the first textbook that I remember having glossy colored illustrations (along with some black-and-white pictures). It had colored physical/political maps, beautifully executed, showing mountains, plains, and the major cities. There were also economic maps showing things like population density and crop production. There was something about the format, maps, and illustrations that I found very attractive.

Early on, we revisited longitude and latitude and were asked in a homework assignment to estimate the coordinates of cities and other specific geographic features like the Suez Canal. As I recall, we also did a review of the equator, the Arctic and Antarctic Circles, the Tropics of Cancer and Capricorn, and how each was defined. We were reintroduced to the world's major rivers and the seas or oceans into which they flowed.

During the Sixth Grade, the Cold War was at its peak, and our textbook began in earnest with the geography of the Soviet Union. It went into real

---

77 Mrs. Cullen had a formatting style for these assignments. We were supposed to do each on a plain paper we ruled horizontally between each computation, with vertical margin lines on each side. The answers for the questions were copied into the right-hand margin.
78 Whipple, G., and James, P., New York: Macmillan, 1951.

detail, first about Soviet Europe, and then about Soviet Asia in separate sections. We learned the country's physical features, its rivers, and its cities. We also learned about its principal products and its manufacturing centers. The book described the Trans-Siberian Railway. It also mentioned in several places the important role Russia had played in the Second World War. Although there were references to state farms and collectivization, there was really not a lot about its planned economy and its politics (although both were mentioned briefly). There was only a hint or two about its being a repressive or aggressive state—the latter primarily in the chapter on Eastern Europe.[79] We knew it was not friendly, and we knew what the Iron Curtain represented, but the Soviet Union was never portrayed in class as an outright enemy—and we were not taught to fear it. We made a series of maps of the Soviet Union, and it was a tough country to map.

We then studied Western Europe, and this was the part of the course that I enjoyed the most. Perhaps it was the easiest external region to which an American sixth grader could relate. We studied Scandinavia, France, the Low Countries, Germany, Switzerland, and Austria. We learned about fjords, polders, and buffer states; about the historic lakes and rivers of the continent (and into which bodies of water the rivers flowed); we learned the principal European mountain ranges, and about Matterhorn, Mt. Blanc, and Mt. Erebus. We learned about the major products of each country, and where in each country they were made or grown. We learned all the Western European capitals and other major cities. The text was upbeat, with an emphasis on Europe's recovery from World War II. Somewhere along the way we were asked to color in an outline map of the European countries, labeling each, and identifying the major rivers. Africa, regrettably, was mentioned in the text only briefly as a colonial appendage to Western Europe.

We then did a section on "Central Europe," where we were introduced to Poland, Czechoslovakia, Hungary, and the countries of the Balkan Peninsula. We spent a fair amount of time on Czechoslovakia (and its three parts at that time), and on Poland. Again, we learned the principal rivers, cities, products, and lifestyles of the region, and were reminded that it was under Soviet control.

---

79 Reading it now, I find that the teacher's introduction to the book (included in our edition) is filled with a lot more Cold War rhetoric than the text itself, although there were references to it here and there throughout.

In all these cases, Mrs. Bluhm spent serious class time explaining what she thought to be the most important features of each country we studied—and quizzing us on the reading. I remember especially her descriptions of the Soviet tundra, taiga, and steppes. She also used take-home exercises that she made up herself to test us on the reading. These we filled out and handed in at the beginning of class.

Unaccountably, Britain, Ireland, Spain, Portugal, and Italy were omitted from the textbook's chapters on Western Europe, and Greece from the discussions of Central Europe. They were included in the introduction text where the countries of Eurasia were listed. Perhaps there was to be a chapter on the Mediterranean countries that never got completed—this would account for some of the omissions, but not all.

We then studied the Middle East and the importance of its oil. I remember reading about this area while at home sick. We made maps of Syria, Israel, Jordan, and Saudi Arabia. The edition of the text we used was dated 1951. Israel had been independent for only three years. Its independence was noted in the text, but the section apparently had not been completely re-written, and, under the subheading of "Israel" it discussed "Palestine" as a whole. Again, we learned the major cities, rivers, and products of the region. When we came to the section on Egypt, we were already familiar with the ancient monuments mentioned, as well as the Nile and its annual flooding, but now we were introduced to the Suez Canal and the Aswan Dam,[80] which controlled that flooding, but simultaneously eliminated a positive by-product of the old inundations: the depositing of nutrients brought down from the mountains above that fertilized the fields. Given our focus on Egypt in the Fourth Grade, and its seeming centrality to ancient history, modern Egypt seemed quite diminished in importance compared to its historic ancestor—now just one country among many.

Next we came to the countries of South Asia. We studied their physical features and were required to learn their major cities and products. We spent serious time on India and Pakistan (which then included East Pakistan, now Bangladesh), learning about their history as well as their geography. We studied in detail their crops and exports (rice, jowar, sugar cane, coconuts,

---

80   Not to be confused with the Aswan High Dam, built later.

peanuts, cotton, jute, and tea). I still have tests in which we were asked to write a paragraph about the special different features of Bombay, Madras, New Delhi, Karachi (then the capital of Pakistan), Calcutta, Darjeeling, Simla, and Lahore. We were also tested on the principal rivers of the region (Indus, Ganges, Brahmaputra), and, of course, the Himalayan Mountains.

Again, this section of the text was well-illustrated and was enjoyable reading. French Indochina was included in the region, and the text reads "They are seriously threatened by an army of communists who, supported by China, are trying to gain control of the country." That was not to be the end of that story.

We were supposed to cover Indonesia and Japan, but we ran out of time, and didn't reach them. A big omission from the discussion of Eurasia in our textbook was China, which had fallen to the Communists two years before the publication date (and five years before the class). It was mentioned briefly in a few sentences and described as a major producer of rice, a pawn of the Soviet Union, and a participant in the Korean War. A black-and-white map presented a partial view. Diplomatically, the United States did not recognize China then, and the near non-recognition of China in this geography text was parallel. Perhaps the omission of China could be excused somehow by the omission of the other important countries mentioned above. In the list of Eurasian countries in the back of the book (giving their areas, populations, major cities, etc.), Italy, Spain, Portugal, and Greece are omitted, but China, the United Kingdom, and Ireland are included—along with small places like Luxembourg and Nepal, so it's not clear what was going on here.

Although geography class involved a lot of memorization, successful internalization of factual knowledge was based far less on rote and repetition than had been the case with early math and English. Then memory was tied to sameness; now it was tied to difference and distinctiveness. In this regard, a major aid to memory was a sense of space or of place or of unique location. You would remember the place of different features on a map the same way you would remember the way different houses were placed in a distinct pattern throughout your neighborhood, or how boulders were placed differentially in a pasture, or lawn chairs in a yard, or even complex patterns on a rug. Spatial perception strongly added to repeated encounters to create familiarity. This applied not only to maps, but to the social and economic features of different countries, which seemed to meld into a matrix, with an awareness of that matrix itself adding decisively to the ability to remember. Thus success in memorization was based much more on association (how items were associated with each other or how items were associated to the matrix) than on repetition. This same phenomenon applied to history, as we built temporal matrices into which we fit new data points while we learned more and more about a time period. Thus what we remembered from earlier history courses became an armature on which to hang new facts and deeper interpretations in current courses. This same spatial and associative phenomenon also applied strongly to memorization in Upper School biology, where we were asked to memorize parts of cells and larger organisms, and then asked to memorize the functional relationships of those different pieces and parts to each other. None of this was perfectly done, and reality was less neat than this description portrays, but I think it does to some extent get at what was going on.

In Sixth Grade geography each of us had a project. We were assigned a country or set of countries. Herb Sawyer and I paired off on Austria, Switzerland, and Liechtenstein.[81] The project consisted of making maps of these countries, collecting newspaper clippings about them, and putting the collection into a file folder or scrapbook. We then put everything on display for Father and Son Day. We had to read a book about our countries. I think Herb read about Switzerland. Somehow, there was no book on Austria available in the School library (and certainly none on Liechtenstein). Someone found me a boring book about Hungarian farm life as a geographically proximate substitute, which I remember not enjoying at all. Perhaps books about Austria were scarce in 1954, the very year it emerged from Big-Power occupation. The class itself, however, was very engaging, and most students enjoyed working on their projects. It gave us an interest in Europe, and this was an important period for Europe, as it recovered from the Second World War.

I remember sitting in the Sixth Grade next to a very large map of the world just over my shoulder, which was part of a current events program. The

---

81 Mapmaking was a frequent occupation during and after school throughout much of the Moses Brown Lower School experience, a practice continuing into the Upper School. I enjoyed it greatly, and found it a useful skill when engaged in political consulting later in life.

Third Intermediate: The Sixth Grade (1953-1954)   109

British Empire and Commonwealth was splashed in red all over the world in those days—and there was a fair amount of French purple, especially in Africa. These were traditional colorings for mapmakers at that time. The map had boxes with short descriptions of important recent events throughout the world, often with arrows pointing to the location. A new map would come in every couple of weeks or so. I remember memorizing countries and capitals. It was fun to sit there and look at it if I was not doing anything better.

In the Sixth Grade we continued to read the magazine *Current Events*. Although it occasionally featured materials about domestic issues (such as whether eighteen-year-olds should be permitted to vote), it seemed to concentrate this year on international affairs, and therefore was quite relevant to Mrs. Bluhm's class. Highlighted were foreign leaders and countries. It contained interesting news items from around the world and feature stories about the United Nations, Foreign Aid and Foreign Trade, Nobel Peace Prize winners, the St. Lawrence Seaway, Russia getting the H-bomb, the India-Pakistan dispute, and (approvingly) the overthrow of Mossadegh in Iran. There were side boxes with factoids about American history. There were also lots of quizzes and puzzles—including crosswords that many of us could actually do. As I recall, from time to time we discussed a selection of these articles in Mrs. Bluhm's classes. This was really the first time that "current events" became an important systematic feature of classroom instruction.

One innovative instructional device Mrs. Bluhm used was the geography bee. We would stand up in two facing rows on opposite sides of the classroom, as in a spelling bee, and she would ask us questions, back and forth. If we answered correctly, then we remained in line; if not, we would sit down. I remember winning at least one of these—and I remember the question that secured the victory. My success was a bit unfair to my predecessor on the opposite side. The question was, "Into what body of water does the Elbe River flow?" He responded, "The Baltic Sea." This made sense to me, since the Elbe was in the middle of Germany, it flowed northward, and the Baltic lay north of Germany. It was the answer I would have given, had I been asked it first. It was, however, the wrong answer. As my opponent headed for his seat, I had a few seconds to think it over. Remembering the mistake I had made insisting on the wrong spelling of "they're" in the Third Grade, I hesitantly answered, "The North Sea" as the only other possible option, even though this seemed to make no sense to me at all. Well, that was the correct answer, and I won. Immediately after we were finished, I went to the map in my textbook and confirmed the surprising result. These bees were a lot of fun—you continually tried to answer a question in your mind before the person to whom the question had been addressed responded, and you kept a running score of how many of the questions you could answer. Mrs. Bluhm must have put a lot of effort into composing these questions—I'm sure she made them up herself.

I also remember Mrs. Bluhm doing a section on the United Nations in this class. We read a lengthy pamphlet on the UN, which discussed its various functions and agencies. This I found to be very dull. Fortunately for me, we only spent a week or so on it at the end of the year. Just as the study of geography and history in this class really inspired a lifetime (and, indeed, professional) interest in such matters, this UN book, in the opposite direction, created the impression that the UN was intrinsically dull, and somehow, even to this day, I find it such.

Ancient and Medieval History. Mrs. Bluhm also taught ancient and medieval history through the Renaissance, and did it imaginatively. The text we used, which I have reviewed briefly for this piece, was entitled, *Out of the Past*.[82] It started with "cave men" and ended with the era of New World exploration. We learned about the Java man, the Peking man, and the Piltdown man, the last of which is now known to have been a hoax—and about Neanderthals and Cro-Magnons and other stone age ancestors (some of whom we now believe may not have been ancestors). We then proceeded to the ancient civilizations of the Middle East (Babylonia, Assyria, Judea, and Persia—as well as Egypt, our old friend from the Fourth Grade).

A lot of time was spent on Greece, both its politics and its culture. We were taught about the Persian Wars and the battles of Marathon and Salamis. We learned about the *polis* and Athenian democracy, and were told that Socrates, Plato, and Aristotle were great thinkers. We also learned

---

82 Wilson, H.E., Wilson, F.H., Erb, B.P., and Clucas, E., American Book Company, 1950.

Third Intermediate: The Sixth Grade (1953-1954)   111

about the Olympic Games and some of the major Greek gods. In addition, Mrs. Bluhm taught us about the Acropolis, Greek temples, and the classic orders of columns—Doric, Ionic, and Corinthian. She gave us a homework quiz in which we were asked to have our folks drive us around Providence identifying the different orders of columns on various buildings (Moses Brown front entrance = Doric; Manning Hall at Brown = Doric; Providence Athenaeum = Doric; John Carter Brown Library = Ionic; 233 Bowen Street = Corinthian).

We also spent time on Alexander the Great and especially on the Punic Wars and Rome. I find a colored-in map of the Roman Empire at its greatest extent in my papers. In addition to studying Rome's rise to power and its military victories, we studied Roman engineering, including roads, bridges, and aqueducts.

There was a book called *A Child's History of the World*[83] that Mrs. Bluhm read to us in class. She was an excellent reader and the class enjoyed this light, perhaps irreverent, but very informative tale. Ultimately someone gave me a copy, and I read it cover to cover. It was written in a very conversational, chatty, anecdotal way, and it presented history as a sequence of stories. I enjoyed it. I believe that my classmates did also. It started with cavemen, and moved up through Greece and Alexander to Hannibal and thence to Caesar—and then down into the Middle Ages and modern Europe. I forget how far we got in class, but it kept our attention. It was filled with much more interesting detail than our textbook was—and since it presented all events and movements as narratives or stories, rather than as dry factual episodes, chronologies, or abstract historical theories, it kept our attention. The events narrated were historically accurate, and I think we learned a lot more from Mrs. Bluhm's reading of these narratives in class than from our text.

I can remember Mrs. Bluhm reading to us from this book about the battle of Zama, which took place in 202 BC, and in which Scipio Africanus defeated Hannibal in one of the decisive battles of antiquity. The book said he devised an interesting stratagem to overcome the Carthaginian forces. I raised my hand and asked what that stratagem was. The next

---

83 Hillyer, V.M., New York: Appleton Century Crofts, 1951.

day she reported on how Hannibal had used elephants to charge an opponent's line. The traditional Roman legion was deployed as a solid block of soldiers diagonally arranged, like the stars on today's American flag. At Zama, Scipio arranged them instead in vertical lines—with troops standing directly in back of each other, several men deep, and with lots of space between the lines (like the arrangement on the forty-eight-star American flag). The elephants, being intelligent beasts, and not being interested in running into spears, all headed for the spaces between the lines of soldiers, and passed through the body of troops with little damage to Scipio. After the elephants were safely in the rear, Scipio then closed his ranks, resumed his diagonal pattern, and went on to defeat Hannibal. I met Mrs. Bluhm again about twenty-five years after this and she remembered the episode. We got a good laugh out of it.

A Child's History of the World was also my introduction to modern European history. Its stories included very helpful background information that came in handy in Mr. Pratt's class five years later in Upper School. Our early history texts had emphasized what children had done in historical contexts—children in Egypt, in Greece, in Rome, and in the Middle Ages. These presentations may have been made based on the (perhaps) erroneous view that children are more interested in *children* in other cultural settings than they are interested in *adults* in those settings. Perhaps this is the case for many children, and perhaps children can relate to other children better than to adults, but from an early age, children want to be "grown-ups," want to imitate adults, and fantasize about acting in an adult world. To the extent that this is the case, they will be interested in *adult* behavior (or imagined adult behavior) in cultures being studied—and perhaps more so than in *children's* behavior. The *Child's History* was not primarily about children, instead mainly focusing on adults, but the narrative was told in anecdotal form in ways attractive to those who had learned to enjoy a good story. In this regard, Mrs. Bluhm never talked down to us, at least not in recognizable ways.

We spent a fair amount of time in class on the Middle Ages, starting with the fall of the Roman Empire and Charlemagne's attempts to restore it. We studied the social structure of the feudal system, with king/queen, nobles, clergy, serfs, and merchants—as well as squires and pages. We briefly studied the manorial system—and the guild system. We wrote papers on the process of becoming a knight. We were quizzed on chivalry, jousting, and tournaments. We learned about castle design with keeps, dungeons, and moats, and how nobles residentially graduated from castles to palaces as the centuries unfolded and conditions became safer. We were introduced to the Vikings, who disrupted the peace of the later Middle Ages—and the Hanseatic League which later helped to restore it. We were also introduced to important figures like Joan of Arc, Louis the Spider (who could ever forget someone with a sobriquet like that?), and Alfred the Great. Somewhere along the way we were taught about Magna Carta, trial by jury, and the origins of representative government in early English parliaments. Mrs. Bluhm read to us from the *Child's History* about the crusades, including, as I recall, about the infamous Fourth Crusade—the Children's Crusade. In the context of the Crusades, we were taught, approvingly, about the Arab culture of that period and its contributions to mathematics and science. We had learned a bit about the Middle Ages in Fourth Grade, but by now we were a lot more mature, and could learn in greater depth. The earlier encounters, however, gave us some background, so that when we arrived at a topic, we already knew something about it, and the new encounters were therefore less daunting.

With the Middle Ages behind us, we proceeded to the Renaissance era, with brief introductions to Chaucer, Dante, Cervantes, Petrarch, Erasmus, Shakespeare, Da Vinci, Michelangelo, Rembrandt, and even Stradivarius. We didn't read any of the authors directly, but we were told about them and what kinds of works they wrote (or, in the case of Stradivarius, what kind of violins he made)—presumably so that they would not be strangers when we met them again. Concurrently, we were taught about the rise of literature written in modern languages—and how this was an important development. Finally, the class was told about the Reformation and Counter-Reformation, with their principal figures—Luther, Calvin, Knox, and Henry the Eighth on the one side and Ignatius Loyola on the other. The text ended with the Age of Exploration, but we did not get there. Although its focus was heavily on ancient and medieval Western history, the text commendably included a selection of non-Western topics as well. There were chapters on ancient Indian, Chinese, and Pre-Columbian American societies. Although not a lot of space was devoted to many of those topics, the book did introduce us to a few non-Western cultures and their accomplishments. Generally throughout, I was more interested in the politics than the arts, and some sections of the course were more fascinating than others, but as taught by Mrs. Bluhm, it was a very enjoyable class.

Science. I have very little recollection of science instruction in the Sixth Grade. I have found a few science papers—about one per month—in which we were answering questions about fluoridation, substance abuse, medical equipment, and how animals protect their young. We also wrote an essay on dandelions and milkweed. We did have a bit of astronomy, learning about Galileo, comets, their orbits, and the Arizona Crater that was formed when a comet's orbit took it too close to earth. We were taught the principles of the six simple machines.

Around this time there were a few special programs with a science theme on prime-time television.[84] There was one, I believe, that focused on astronomy; another was on human biology, including an interesting account of blood and the human bloodstream. This was long before PBS, and these were presented as specials by one or more of the networks. The host was an actor, not a scientist, and they were for a lay audience. We were encouraged at School to watch them.

Even though science was not emphasized during this year, my folks did make a contribution of sorts to the study of astronomy. They held a birthday party for me in the basement to which the entire Class was invited. The Cullens and the Bluhms were also there. My mother set out a large buffet in front of the furnace and all helped themselves. The scientific contribution was from Dr. Charles Smiley, Professor of Astronomy at Brown, who gave an entertaining talk on astronomy, and then invited all of us down to his planetarium for a show. He was a wonderful lecturer to audiences of all ages, and I think that his presentation was quite a hit with most of my classmates.

Art, Shop, Music, and French. In art, we had Miss Virginia Holmes, who was new to us and to the School. She was a graduate of Boston

---

84 It is possible they were a few years after Sputnik, but I think they started in the pre-Sputnik period.

University, College of Arts and Letters. She had taught in the Newton, Massachusetts, public school system, then one of the best in the country. Unfortunately, I don't have a clear memory of her or what we did in studio. In shop, we continued to have Mr. Cole; in music, we continued to have Mrs. Thomas. In French, we may have had Madame Warge, but I really have no recollections of her teaching us in the Sixth Grade—it is probable that we had no French that year. She did teach us again in the Seventh.

Other School recollections. We had a square dance in Alumni Hall during the Sixth Grade called "The Hacker's Hoedown." We were given square-dancing instruction in advance, and again at the start of the proceedings. We invited dates. There were lots of chaperones. Mr. Allen, as noted, arrived in jeans and a bright red shirt—and seemed to have a wonderful time.

We had a Class newspaper in the Sixth Grade. It was ambitiously entitled *The Student Weekly News*. I have a copy of two editions; whether there were any more, I do not know. I can't remember if this was an official or unofficial publication, but I do remember that at least one edition was produced in our basement on a gel-based mat that I believe was called a hectograph. Later editions were mimeographed, perhaps at School. It sold for four cents. Nicky Littlefield was Editor-in-Chief, Jack Nixon and Chad Gifford were the Sports Editors. Harrison Huntoon was Education Editor and in one edition wrote a piece about Scandinavia. Tommy Clark was World News Editor and in that same edition, among other things, wrote about the Bricker Amendment's being "doomed" in an arresting summary of congressional activity. This proposed constitutional amendment was an attempt to limit the president's authority to reach "executive agreements" with foreign powers. I was business manager for the newspaper, wrote the first part of a mystery story, and composed a crossword puzzle with the help of my father. Billy Goddard was illustrator. I think Bill Fischer, Barry Fain, Vin Marcello, and Mark Saklad may have been involved, but they don't appear on the masthead. In one of the editions that I found there was a lot of basic information about movies and TV programs—perhaps that section may have been the responsibility of one or more of these four classmates. The publication featured jokes—perhaps cribbed from *The Reader's Digest*. High Honors recipients for the term were listed. There was also a piece in one edition about the composition and first meeting of the Lower School Student Council. It was a publication with much variety!

We had Class elections that year. I remember being promoted for Vice President. I do not remember who my campaign manager was, perhaps Chad Gifford, perhaps Tommy Clark, but he put up a large sign on the west wall of the classroom reading, "Cliff for Vice." This sentiment was subject to misinterpretation. Mrs. Cullen quickly pointed out that it did not necessarily convey the right impression, explained to us the meaning of the word "vice," with which most of us were unacquainted, and promptly removed the sign. After this episode, I think, no one was elected to "Vice" that year. Nicky Littlefield won the race for President on the fifth ballot, edging out Bill Fischer. Bill, in turn, beat Jack Nixon on the fourth ballot for Secretary. Jack then beat me on the fourth ballot for Treasurer. As to what these officers actually did, I have no recollection: I don't think we ever had another Class meeting at which the president presided or the secretary took notes; nor did we collect any money for the treasurer to handle, but at least we had officers in place had an occasion arisen calling for democratic action. The election was not a total waste. Some of these officers also became representatives to the Lower School Student Council, which met with Mr. Allen at least once. At its inaugural meeting it was decided to set up committees to study bicycle parking, to improve the lost and found system, to set up cots for the First Grade, to keep school grounds neat, to secure sports schedules, and to secure a rubber stamp reading "Student Council." Whether this ambitious agenda was ever carried out, or whether another meeting was held, I do not know.

I also remember that in the Sixth Grade, no doubt to enhance our literary skills, we began the practice of sending notes to each other in class, passing them surreptitiously from desk to desk. On occasion, we also resorted to airmail for delivery purposes by making paper gliders and winging them across the room when no one was looking. A penny in the nose gave them added accuracy. If we were caught, and this did happen, the penalty was to stay in during recess. Mrs. Cullen soon put an end to the practice, although many of us did refine the art of paper plane construction, and I think we had some contests in this regard outdoors.

I also remember that at the beginning of each recess Mrs. Cullen would ask one of us to take the day's attendance slip over to Mr. Allen's office and give it to his secretary. I often was selected to do this, and remember the routing out through the Sixth Grade locker room, through the hall into Middle House, down the stairs in Middle House to the dining room, through the dining room into the locker area beyond it, and then out the door under the arch and into the Lower School building—and then back the same route. It must have taken an eleven-year-old about three or four minutes each way, and there was not a lot of recess time afterwards, but it was a bit of an honor to be trusted with this task.

As to recess itself, we usually played soccer out in the field north of Middle House. This was the year when a group of us strayed from the assigned playing field and was caught by Mr. Allen, reprimanded in that decanal tone of his, and condemned to stay inside during recess with our heads on our desks for a whole week.

Finally, I cannot leave the Sixth Grade without mentioning the time that George Kilton grabbed Leon Najarian's earmuffs—nice fluffy ones held together with a steel band curving over his head—and deposited them in a hole in the low crotch of the tree in front of the Hawes Gymnasium, from which they proved irretrievable. I assume they remained there for sixty years until the tree was cut down to make way for the Woodman Center in 2016.[85]

---

85 Leon Najarian was a good Lower School friend. We used to play together after school. I remember visiting his house on East Avenue in Pawtucket quite a few times, and he visited ours. I believe he left us at the end of the Third Form in Upper School, and we lost touch with each other.

VII

Summers

(1953-1955)

During the five-year passage from Third Grade to Seventh Grade, we grew physically (more than doubling our height), intellectually (from scrawling simple sentences to understanding the main elements of English grammar), and emotionally (from the insecurities and hesitations of young children to the confidence of twelve-year-olds on the cusp of adolescence). To our parents, these five years probably went by swiftly, but to us they seemed more protracted, unfolding richly day by day, season by season, as new experiences were added to our collection of memories. At that age, as someone once explained to me, each year was a truly significant part of our whole remembered experience. If we were eight in the Third Grade, and if our serious recollections stretched back to the time when we were two, the Third Grade year constituted one-sixth of our recollected life—and that is quite a bit. Even at the Seventh Grade level, a year was about a tenth of our remembered experiences. School lasted a long time, year by year—and so, too, did summers.

The Lower School experience was an important part of our journey outward into the world, as we began to emerge from our families and acquire new acquaintances, experience new surroundings outside of the home, and find adventures beyond those shared with our parents, siblings, and close relatives. The process was gradual. We originally came into a world composed primarily of family members in stable home surroundings. When we went to school, our world expanded to include teachers and classmates. And from there, our world expanded, in a mediated way, to those peoples and places we studied. We then began to interact directly with people out in the "real world" around us—which in our case included girls of our age, who were missing from some families, and missing at School for all of us. This expansion was not as neat as presented here, and the stages overlapped, but there was a sense of development and growth as our families and our schooling gently pushed us into new realms of relationships and awareness.

Summer adventures added to this process. They offered other ways of experiencing new surroundings and making new acquaintances. Rhode Island is a marvelous location in which—or from which—to vacation, since even in those pre-Interstate days the whole state and most of New England was easily accessible. Thus coastline, countryside, lake, forest, and mountain range were summer options for nearly everybody at Moses Brown. Looking at the summer activities listed in the *Moses Brown Bulletin* for those years following the Fifth, Sixth, and Seventh Grades, members of the Class of 1960 were primarily engaged in recreational activities, with a few summer jobs mixed in. As we grew and moved into the Upper School, the percentage of summer jobs, not surprisingly, steadily increased.

For the three summers we spent after our Fifth through Seventh Grade years (1953, 1954, 1955), there are numerous accounts of vacation experiences from classmates in the August *Moses Brown Bulletins*.[86] There were often reports of more than one activity. Not everyone who was enrolled reported on summer experiences, but those who did recounted activities that provide good examples of how we spent our time during the summers of the last three years of Lower School.[87] The list of activities and their locations also attests to the affluence enjoyed by many of our families and their commitment to providing engaging summer opportunities to their offspring.

Interestingly, only eight summer reports during the three-year period mentioned travel outside of New England (aside from the Moses Brown bicycle trips to Canada in which Ed Corris, Mark Saklad, and David Stenmark

---
86 Passages quoted in the following paragraphs come from these *Bulletins*.
87 The earlier years had only a few reports.

participated from our Class). Frank Abella planned to go to California before returning to his home in Puerto Rico;[88] I went to Cape Breton; Bill Batchelder took in the New York City sights; Bob Dean stated that he was traveling to Fort Benning, Georgia; Hank Levaur went on a fishing trip to New Brunswick; Jeff Plante expected to go to Florida's St. Petersburg;[89] Ned Young anticipated a trip to Virginia; and Steve Koffler hoped to "tour the country."

Not surprisingly, several classmates played Little League baseball during the summer. Bill Batchelder was a catcher for the Barrington Little League team. Nicky Littlefield played on the Little League team in Princeton, Massachusetts. Jack Nixon played for the Blackstone Valley Little League. In his letter to the *Moses Brown Bulletin* written in August 1953, Jack reported that "our team is now in first place, leading by two games." He was to play with them again the following year.

One major summer destination was the New England summer camp—and summer camp was one institution that pushed us out and away from the confines of family surroundings. Most camps were in rural areas, many on lakes surrounded by woods; only a couple listed by Moses Brown students were near the seashore. Many of these camping experiences were the first occasions when members of the Class of 1960 were separated from their parents for an extended period of time. Eight classmates went to Camp Yawgoog, the Rhode Island Boy Scout Summer Camp in Hopkinton.[90] This camp taught basic survival and first aid skills, wildlife recognition, outdoor cooking and camping, and other Boy Scout achievement skills. Kent Painter had "a wonderful time" at the YMCA's Camp Westwood in Coventry. Two other summer camps were in Massachusetts: Bob Dean went to Camp Monomoy in East Brewster on Cape Cod; Steve Oster attended Camp Bauercrest in Amesbury.[91] Two more were in New Hampshire: Bill Barrett went several years to Cragged Mountain Farm in Free-

---

88 Frank Abella joined us in the Lower School and stayed with the Class about halfway through Upper School. Like Hernan Franco, he came from Puerto Rico. We lost touch with him after he left.
89 Jeff Plante, I recall, was with us for only a brief time in Lower School, leaving after the Sixth Grade.
90 Bill Barrett, Tom Clark, Ed Corris, John Dieroff, Chad Gifford, George Kilton, Nick Littlefield, and Alan Volkmar.
91 Steve Oster left Moses Brown early in Upper School.

dom; Dutch Vetterlein "played sports and games" for at least two years at Camp Tecumseh, Center Harbor, on Lake Winnipesaukee.

The other camps were in Maine. Barry Fain "learned many games and crafts" at Camp Brunonia, located in Casco; George Kilton enjoyed fishing, horseback riding, and winning medals for archery at Wavus Camps in Jefferson (which was supervised by Mr. and Mrs. Allen); Robert Saywell and Vin Marcello also went there; Mark Saklad went to Camp Wigwam in Harrison; Hank Levaur enjoyed camp life at Kennebec Junior Camp in North Belgrade. One year Harrison Huntoon went to Camp Winona in Denmark, Maine, reporting that "I am having a wonderful time. Today we had Sports Day with Camp Wyonegonic, our sister camp. The girls were here from 10:00 AM 'till 4:30. Saturday we have a dance, and in a few days I hope to be on another canoe trip. Having such a lot of fun I wish camp wouldn't end in a month."

For those who did not go to camp, many vacationed with their families at summer homes in Rhode Island near the seashore. The Batchelder family summered in Newport near the water—and near a handy golf course. Vincent Buonanno and John Dieroff summered at Bonnet Shores on Narragansett Bay. John wrote to the *Bulletin* that "I have been at my summer cottage at Bonnet Shores since the fifteenth of June. Each day I go swimming. We have a variety of activities here. Among them are bowling, fishing and many different sports. The other day my grandfather took me and my brother Jay ... fishing. Jay caught a flounder which was large enough for our dinner. Derric Chesebrough ... spent the day with us." Joey Franklin had fun "swimming, sailing, and riding his bicycle" at Bay Ridge, East Greenwich. Harrison Huntoon spent many days swimming in Little Compton: "my favorite sport is spear fishing. I was runner up in one of the golf tournaments and came in second in one of the boat races." Leon Najarian stayed with his family at Shore Acres: "I fish and go sailing with my brother on our Woodpussy, the *Tri-Lee*." Bob Saywell spent time in the fishing village of Jerusalem across the inlet from Galilee, where Kent Painter spent time in summer.[92]

Three classmates spent their summers close to each other near the water in the Wakefield and Matunik areas. The Goddards had a summer home

---

92   Robert Saywell, I believe, left us at the end of Lower School.

in Wakefield which I visited. It was a very tasteful residence with lots of windows that overlooked a salt pond. I remember Bill used the pond to sail a beautiful model boat that he had handcrafted. The Goddards were very gracious hosts, and Mrs. Goddard, an excellent cook. Bill and I spent much time playing Clue. The Chesebroughs also had their summer place in Wakefield near Matunuck where Derric "enjoyed the seashore and its activities" and sailed his boats.[93] The Marcellos also summered nearby at Potter's Pond in East Matunuck. As Vin wrote about his adventures, "One of the first things I learned to do was to jump off a twelve-foot diving board, and to improve my swimming a great deal. Derric Chesebrough, one of my neighbors, was supposed to teach me how to sail my sailboat, but his boat-launching was delayed because of the death of Captain Hanson. As I was anxious to learn, I called on Tommy Bain, another one of my friends, and asked him to teach me. After a few hours with Tommy, I think I have learned to sail quite well. I have also been doing a lot of fishing and crabbing. Here comes Derric Chesebrough across the pond—now the big race is on!"

The following year, Vin's father bought him a twelve-horsepower outboard motor. As Vin wrote about it, "With this motor and my 14-foot Amesbury boat, I have explored the small islands of Salt Pond. I have been fishing and doing a great deal of sailing, swimming, and spear fishing, and I have been diving for an aeroplane engine which crashed in Potter's Pond in the early forties while dog-fighting." Vin, still at a fairly young age, took his fourteen-footer out through the narrows at Galilee and sailed it over to Block Island, accompanied by a younger neighbor, Chris Ogden, later a biographer of Margaret Thatcher. This was adventurous—and unauthorized by his parents. The outward bound trip on the calm sea was uneventful, but during the afternoon Block Island Sound became rough, and the return trip was indeed adventuresome with a small boat, a trailing wind, and a serious swell. Vin was quite relieved to clear the Point Judith breakwater and deliver his passenger safely home.[94]

---

93 Derric [Frederic Read] Chesebrough left Moses Brown for St. George's School in Middletown, RI, after the Seventh Grade. He was a good friend, and I missed his presence in our Class. He graduated from Brown University and then served in the Army. Having been purposefully sent into a very dangerous area by a superior officer who did not like him, Derric was killed in Vietnam while serving as an artillery forward observer in the Army's 9th Division. His name appears upon the Wall in the Vietnam Memorial in Washington, and on a memorial on the Brown University campus in Providence.

94 Telephone conversation, July 2017.

Chad and John Gifford with Nantucket catch

Several classmates had summer homes on the shore in Massachusetts. Ed Corris vacationed with his family at Harwichport on Cape Cod. Tommy Clark spent his summers at Land's End in Rockport on Cape Ann, doing "all kinds of things" and taking part in all the fun. The Kofflers vacationed at Nantasket. As Steve recounted his summer adventures, "I am doing quite a bit of fishing off the State Pier. The mackerel that I caught, and mother broiled, was the best I ever tasted. I have been doing a lot of swimming and playing miniature golf, and felt quite proud when I got a score of forty-one when par was forty-six. It's an eighteen-hole golf course with lots of traps and very exciting." Chad Gifford spent summers on Nantucket, enjoying activities at the Yacht Club, while engaged in sailing, tennis, fishing, and swimming. Jack Nixon boated with his family on Buzzard's Bay.

Not everyone needed a summer home to enjoy the water. Jim Hoye stayed right in Barrington where he enjoyed both the water and the "cool breezes" that refreshed his home.[95] Similarly, Herb Sawyer enjoyed the cool bay breezes that refreshed his home in nearby Edgewood.[96] He also worked on his father's boat during the summer.

---

95 Jim was with our Class for only a year or two, leaving after Lower School; we have lost touch with him and do not know his career trajectory.

96 Herb Sawyer joined our Class in the Sixth Grade. He graduated from Mitchell Junior College in New London (where he met his wife, Judith) and later from the University of Miami. He worked a year for Fleet Bank, and then joined the advertising firm of Potter & Hazlehurst in Providence, where he remained for 30 years. The firm had many regional clients, including A. T. Cross. Herb rose to the position of full partner in the agency. After retiring from this firm, he went to work for Daly & Wolcott, a software company in Providence, from which he definitively retired in 2002. He and Judith now live in South Carolina. Telephone interview with Herb, May 10, 2020.

Summers (1953-1955)

There was a sailing club at Moses Brown during our Upper School years. The School was not as active in this regard as St. George's in Newport (where several of our Lower School classmates eventually went), but sailing was a pastime that alumni and many of our Class enjoyed—and continued to enjoy throughout much of their lives. For example, Bill Murdoch, who joined us in the Upper School, later in life operated a business selling nautical equipment and spent much time on the ocean near his Jamestown home. Halsey Herreshoff ('51), who graduated a few years before us, came from a boat-building family and was a crew member on one of the successful defenders of the America's Cup.

During many of the Lower School years my folks rented a cottage on the beach at Biddeford Pool, Maine. Some years it was for the whole summer. It was a mile-long beautiful private beach, with much open space. There were guest rooms in the cottage, and lots of relatives came up to visit, including many my own age.[97] Friends of my folks also visited frequently. Although we did not sail a lot, I expect that my other shoreline experiences were similar to those of my classmates: wading up and down the beach looking for different kinds of shells; splashing in the warm tidal pools with their rippled bottoms; learning to float on inner tubes, and then learning to swim in the waves; building forts and sandcastles; digging wells and canals; running races on the hard sand at low tide; marking out the wet sand for hopscotch and other games, many of which we invented for ourselves; watching the adults play horseshoes and badminton. And then there were the cookouts on the beach, fired with driftwood, at which hot dogs, hamburgers, steaks, or kettles of lobsters (boiled in sea water) would be prepared. On the Fourth, fireworks were legal and everybody up and down the beach seemed to set some off. By August, there were corn roasts. On rainy days, there were magazines, crayons, coloring books, and other books to read—in my case, the Dr. Doolittle series—as well as card games, checkers, Chinese checkers, solitaire, and even chess. After a rainstorm, it was fun to walk on the beach, stepping through the wet sand crust to the dry sand underneath. Rain or shine, it was always interesting to watch the ocean and its contents (birds, seals, boats). At night, we fell asleep to the sound of the surf, and in the morning woke up early to the screeching of the seagulls.

---

97   As I recall, all of my mother's six siblings visited us at various times, and many of my 16 first cousins came as well.

Some of us also went up-country. Bill Fischer spent his summers with his family at his grandparents' home in Litchfield, Connecticut. Nick Littlefield's family built a house in Princeton, Massachusetts, north of Worcester. The house was located "in the middle of a large blueberry pasture." As Nick recounted, "I have been earning spending money by picking and selling quarts of blueberries. I have also been playing a bit of tennis with three other boys who like it a lot, too." Dave Stenmark's family had a place in West Glocester, Rhode Island, where he spent summers "swimming, fishing, and boating at Bowdish Reservoir."

Skipper Mays didn't have to go up-country, he was already there. He spent his summers at home in Greene "working a little, playing a little, and generally enjoying the vacation," but also at times "farming it up—plowing, cutting hay, cutting lawns, and acting as a hired man at Holden Hollow Farm...."[98]

Some of my summers paralleled those of Skipper. When we were not at the beach, I spent lots of time on my grandfather's farm in Chepachet. It was a working dairy farm, and during Lower School days, my time was divided between play and work. By the time I was in Upper School, it was all work. There were several cousins of my age nearby, and as kids we played all sorts of games together. Tag was a favorite. We invented variations on tag—one was "Sea Lion" in which someone played that animal, while the rest of us played seals which the sea lion attempted to catch (tag). Where we got the idea for this, I do not know. We also played a lot of croquet. In the days of loose hay, we jumped off upper haymows into the mow below.

There were many other activities, recreational and instructional, that took full advantage of the farm itself. We waded in the brook, swam in the pond, and climbed the hill behind the house. At a respectful distance, we observed (and listened to) Grandpa (John) Steere operate his water-powered sawmill—and his water-powered electric dynamo, located in the gristmill, which generated the electricity for the farm. We explored the woods and swamps—and were taken on nature walks by grandparents and aunts. These no doubt paralleled the nature walks that many classmates had at camp. I remember being introduced to cowslips (which we were told

---

98 Skipper Mays, who was somehow related to Maxwell Mays, the artist, left us after Lower School, and we lost touch.

were officially called "marsh marigolds"), checkerberries, sweet fern, mayflowers (which we were told were officially called "trailing arbutus"), lady slippers, cattails, ferns, and mushrooms (which we were told not to eat). We were also shown how to distinguish poison ivy from other ivies, and poison (swamp) sumac from normal sumac. I remember we were taught how to identify trees: white, black, and red oak, maples, walnut, ash, white pine, hemlock, sassafras, ironwood, chestnut oak, and even American chestnut (saplings of which still grew on the farm). Aunt Amey was a member of the Audubon Society, and over the years she showed me how to recognize several score wild birds which lived at the farm. I imagine that a lot of my classmates learned many lessons like these at their New England summer camps.

At the farm, my cousins and I made good use of the pasture in which about fifteen cows and heifers resided during the day. They were friendly and harmless, and we were allowed into the pasture (except on those days when the cattle breeder came around with a bull). The pasture was about three or four acres in size, filled with rocks and boulders of various dimensions, together with a few trees, old chestnut telephone poles, and some clumps of thistles and bull briars. It bordered a brook, a swamp, and a pond. We turned this territory into a country: Pastureland. The cow trails became railroads that we would run up and down. Different boulders became stores, shops, museums, and stations. We had a capital with municipal buildings. To avoid cousinly rivalry, we elected the attentive family dog as president. The rest of us became cabinet members. The cows, ever present, were too large to be part of the game, but they did faithfully maintain the railroad rights-of-way, for which we were truly grateful.

We kids also began to do useful work on the farm at an early age. One skill we acquired in our preteens was to herd cows; they will usually respond predictably to a small stick if well-handled by a kid. During late summer they were "baited" (pastured) in a large unfenced field, where we would watch them, usually accompanied by an adult. At the age of eight, I was instructed on how to plow a level field with a small Ford tractor with hydraulic plows attached.[99] I learned how to drive a Model-A hay truck

---

[99] *Moses Brown Bulletin*, August, 1953: "Clifford Brown is 'having a wonderful vacation on my grandfather's farm, driving the tractor, swimming, and working in the garden. I am busy picking raspberries during the season.'"

as soon as my legs could reach the pedals—steering it around the hayfield while others loaded the hay. The reward for doing this was to ride on top of the load back to the barn. Also, during this time I was taught how to ted hay—you just drove the tractor around in an evolving pattern of elongated loops, dragging the tedder behind you while it kicked the hay up to help it dry. We were kept off side hills until we entered our teens. At some point we were old enough to drive a tractor that pulled hand-operated cultivators behind it. Here the trick was to avoid driving on the young corn and crushing it. In the fall, we were allowed to go into the silo as it was filled, and help level and stomp down the silage. In this operation, given our weight, it was more fun for us than it was useful work.

I can remember also helping out in the garden. We were shown how to plant radishes and carrots at a very early age. I remember being given a small hoe and rake to use for getting rid of weeds. It was fun to watch the vegetables grow—and to begin to harvest them in midsummer. We also were permitted to pick raspberries and blackberries—and to pick and shell peas.[100] With all the garden vegetables and fruit available, there were frequent picnics, cookouts and corn roasts throughout the summer, and a major Fourth of July clambake with lots of homemade Rhode Island quahog chowder, homemade clamcakes, steamed clams, watermelon—and relatives.

Some of the above may have been work, but it was enjoyable work. It was probably more enjoyable to me than to my cousins because I was not there 24-7. At this age, I might stay there for a few days on end, but never for more than a week without a break. Even later, during high school, when I was doing serious work at the farm, there were always breaks. I had another life in Providence, and was not under the constant pressure of daily chores. Nevertheless, the farm experience was valuable. It did teach responsibility at an early age—and made us feel important because we were contributing something useful to the family that the family appreciated. In addition, it gave us an opportunity during our preteen years to imitate adult behavior—and not just in a "make-believe" fashion.

The farm work Skipper Mays and I did may have been work—or it may have been fun—but some other classmates spent their summers, at least in

---

100 A less pleasant task in the early 1950s was to harvest Japanese beetles, using a can of kerosene.

part, earning spending money. Accounts in the *Bulletin* list some summer jobs. Ed Corris worked in a bait shop. Billy Batchelder, Billy Fischer, and Jack Nixon caddied—and Bill Batchelder ran a cola shop on weekends. Nick Littlefield, as noted, picked and sold quarts of blueberries. Joey Franklin mowed grass and sold fish. Leon Najarian did minor radio repairing and washed cars. It is highly likely that many others had summer part-time jobs and just did not report them.

The School itself was tied to the camp culture, both through occasional efforts over the years to become actively part of it,[101] and much more directly through frequent faculty participation in the culture itself. Many faculty, both Lower School and Upper School, supplemented their incomes by working at summer camps. Some of these offered remedial academic opportunities, while others offered more traditional sports and other recreational activities. In the Lower School at least five faculty members (Mr. Allen, Mr. Sprague, Miss Pixley, Miss Jensen, and Miss Moore) were camp counselors or instructors. In the Upper School, at least six faculty members with whom some of us were later to interact (Mr. Whitford, Mr. Tinker, Mrs. Full, Mr. Armstrong, Mr. Howe, and Mr. Hutton) spent summers as counselors or instructors at New England summer camps. These represented noticeable percentages of both faculties. In each case, most of these camps were in northern New England, and they included facilities both in the woods by lakes and at the shore. The nature of the programs themselves and the active participation in them by trained faculty members attest to their perceived relevance to our formal developmental and educational experiences.

---

101 The School was given property in Maine by Arthur Anderson, a friend of the Thomases, for this purpose during the 1940s. It was eventually sold. Just after we left Moses Brown, a camping facility for boarders was established at Indian Hill in Little Compton and was used for recreational activities during the school year.

VIII

Fourth Intermediate: The Seventh Grade (1954-1955)

The Fourth Intermediate (Seventh Grade) was the culminating year of Lower School. Our principal teachers were Mr. Lloyd Sprague and Mrs. Eleanore Monahon. Mr. Sprague was a young person, perhaps in his thirties, a graduate of Keene State Teacher's College in New Hampshire, with further studies at Springfield and Columbia. He was an excellent instructor, professional and interactive. There was always enthusiasm in his methods, and classes were therefore engaging. He was very much into sports. He had a good sense of humor and was a very genial person most of the time. He was friendly, relaxed, mature, and very knowledgeable. He was the first male homeroom teacher we had; indeed, aside from Mr. Cole and Mr. Pickett, all our instructors had been women. Mr. Sprague therefore became a sort of role model to us, perhaps sending a subconscious signal in the culture of the time that we were becoming more adult. He taught math and English, with math being his first love.[102]

Mrs. Monahon taught history and science. She, too, was a truly excellent teacher, and we found her equally inspiring—I loved her erudition,

---

[102] The Seventh Grade classroom, as noted, was located directly to the east of the Fifth Grade classroom. As was the case with the Fifth Grade, the class faced west. Mr. Sprague's desk was on the west wall in front of us. This was the first time that a homeroom teacher faced the class from a desk (although Mrs. Bluhm also faced us). There were blackboards on the west and north walls, and a small one between the windows on the south wall.

Eleanor B. Monahon

her enthusiasm, her knowledge of history, especially Rhode Island history, and her dry sense of humor. Most of our Lower School teachers could be viewed as fairly strict substitute parents under whose care we spent seven or eight hours each day. Not Mrs. Monahon. She was much more like an eccentric great aunt who might visit the family on occasion, an interesting person whose visits were looked forward to by a child because they were fun—in part, because they were routine-breaking and out-of-the-ordinary, and, in part, because, in subtle ways an aunt treated you differently than your parents did. Mrs. Monahon was a real character, also reminding you of someone from a Dickens novel, with her hair in a bun and her glasses hanging down from her neck on a chain most of the time—an arrangement I had not previously been familiar with. She spoke slowly, articulating every word, but you paid attention to those words because she was always saying something memorable. You looked forward to her classes every day—just as you looked forward with pleasant anticipation to those visits from the iconoclastic great aunt. Somehow you sensed that she was treating you differently than the other teachers did, and that in itself was intriguing. Thus with Mr. Sprague and Mrs. Monahon, in very different

Fourth Intermediate: The Seventh Grade (1954-1955)

Lloyd F. Sprague

ways, we slowly separated from the matriarchal tradition that had dominated our classroom experiences from the early days of the Lower School. It had served us well, but we were beginning to move on.

Math. With our background in computation, decimals, and fractions, Mr. Sprague's emphasis in Seventh Grade math was on review problems and practical applications of what we had learned previously, building on the problem-solving experiences we had acquired in the Sixth Grade. The textbook we used was *Basic Ideas of Mathematics*.[103] Its emphasis was on the practical and useful. We started off with exercises in estimation and rounding which would be of use in the world of business. We reviewed how to convert fractions to the more easily manipulated decimals. We learned how both could be used in measurements—and were introduced to the

---

103 Lankford, Francis G., and Clark, John R., published in Yonkers-on-Hudson by the World Book Company, 1953.

metric system. In fact, we spent a lot of time on measurement. We then spent serious time reviewing percentages and how to calculate interest, skills to which we had already been introduced. We reviewed how commissions were figured. Bill Barrett recalled that Mr. Sprague also explained to us the concept of insurance, including life insurance, and how to write and endorse a check (correctly spelling out the amount—and making sure with a line that no one could write something in to alter that amount).

We were taught how to add and subtract using negative numbers and were introduced to the concept of infinity—what you got when you divided by zero.

In addition, Mr. Sprague taught us basic geometric constructions with a compass and ruler—how to bisect angles, draw perpendiculars, construct squares, hexagons, and even pentagons. He showed us how to create parallel lines. All of these skills had practical applications in designing. They also could be used to make simple paper constructions, such as five-pointed stars to go on an American flag or six-pointed stars for snowflake art, or for the Israeli flag.

Mr. Sprague also gave us a little trigonometry—at least he reviewed with us how to use proportion to measure the height of a tree, building, or chimney. He also began to teach us algebra. This was in our text, but he gave us a lot of in-class instruction to accompany it. What we did was very formulaic, in that we really did not know what the purpose of it was (that would have helped). But we understood that it was important, and it certainly was a challenge. Algebra, after all, was what high school students did, and learning even the rudiments made us feel important. I can remember plenty of X's written out on the board up front and being given rules for manipulating them. We also had simple equations that we solved by adding and subtracting equal amounts from each side of the equals sign. He explained to us that if the sides were equal to begin with and you did exactly the same thing to each side of the equation, then both sides remained equal afterwards. Made sense. Interestingly, we did not return to algebra until the Second Form in Upper School.

Basically, however, the emphasis throughout the year was on problems, problem-solving, and practical applications, both in class and in the homework. Mr. Sprague was not a showman, but was still a very alive presence in class, always somehow in motion. There was an air of assurance about him that commanded respect. He answered questions clearly and crisply without hesitation. His sessions were full of instruction and demonstrations. If something was explained in the text, he still reviewed it for us in class. He used lots of examples. Nothing dragged, and the time went fast.

English. In English, the emphasis was upon reading. We also wrote lots of book reviews. I finished most of Jules Verne's works that I had not already read—*20,000 Leagues under the Sea*, *Journey to the Moon*, *Journey to the Center of the Earth*, and most memorably, *The Mysterious Island*. I found the latter fascinating, and the most enjoyable of Verne's works. I think the focus on mechanical inventiveness and individual resourcefulness resonated with my own understanding of our New England cultural inheritance. I think I also read Blackmore's *Lorna Doone* that year. I had already read Sherlock Holmes, but read it again. Somewhere along here (I think it was Seventh Grade), I read *Gone with the Wind*. The movie had been shown downtown, and the family had taken me to see it. We had a copy of the book, and I began to read it. I could not put it down. We had been assigned another book to read for class (Walter Edmond's *Drums along the Mohawk*, I think), but I ignored it and read *GWTW* cover to cover. It was interesting to see how the movie had condensed parts of the book and had omitted other parts—but my overall conclusion was that the movie had been very faithful to the text. I also read Dumas's *The Count of Monte Cristo*. This was tough going at my age, with lots of unfamiliar terms from French society and culture (what was "damask" anyway?), but I persisted and enjoyed the adventure passages and the final outcomes. I also started to read several of his six D'Artagnan romances around this time, beginning with *The Three Musketeers*, which I read during the summer after graduating from the Lower School. Again, they were a lot harder than, say, *Treasure Island*, but they were filled with action, and I enjoyed this.

We spent a lot of time in class reporting on books we had read. We also spent serious time building on the grammar we had learned in the Sixth Grade. We studied nominative and objective parts of the sentence, various

136 Fourth Intermediate: The Seventh Grade (1954-1955)

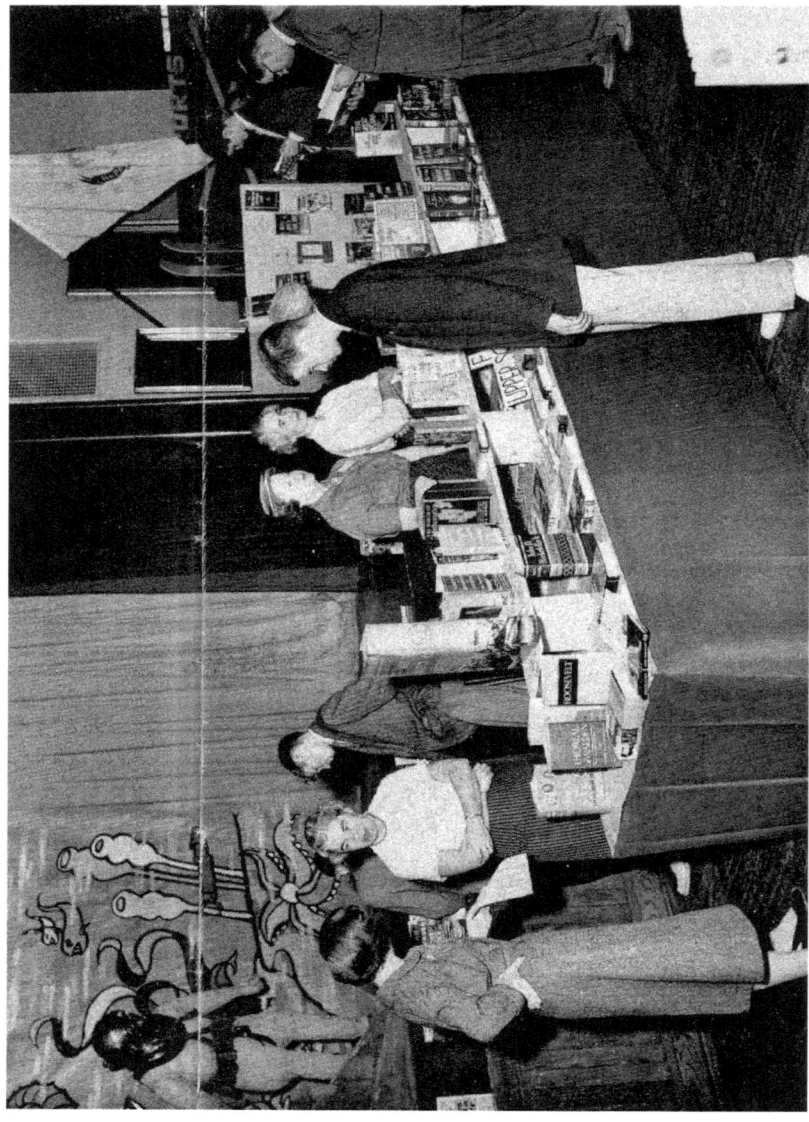

The Book Fair, 1956

Fourth Intermediate: The Seventh Grade (1954-1955)

verb forms, gender and case, and other aspects of grammar. We did more of sentence diagraming. All in all, English classes kept us almost as busy as math classes did. And we still had spelling exercises.

We continued to write essays. The *Delphian* that year contains a narrative essay by Bob Dean on the events of 1954, including the Rhode Island hurricanes, the McCarthy hearings, the Bikini H-Bomb explosion, and the Giants's four-game triumph in the World Series.[104] Bill Goddard wrote an essay on the adventures of a skunk in a henhouse, and[105] Vin Buonanno wrote a short autobiography of a postage stamp which had several adventures before fulfilling its intended ultimate destiny.[106]

Rhode Island History. Mrs. Monahon's instruction style was memorable. She chiefly taught us history. She may have taught a section of reading that year, and she also taught us some science, but her main area of personal interest was history—both Rhode Island and American. She lived at the John Brown House mansion with her husband, Clifford Monahon, who was executive director of the Rhode Island Historical Society (which she called the "Hysterical Society"). She knew the state's historians on a personal basis, as well as many other people who took an interest in Rhode Island history.

"Half Deck," her classroom, was tucked away between the first and second floors of the building (hence its name) halfway up the stairs in the northeast corner of the Alumni Hall wing near where it joined the main building. It was a very small space, and we were packed in tightly. There were windows on two sides. Sometimes in winter the snow would swirl around outside, giving a cozy atmosphere to it all.[107]

Her half-year course on Rhode Island history included political history, industrial history, and cultural history (furniture, artifacts, etc.). It was a

---

104 Bob Dean stayed with us into the Upper School. He left in the Third Form, as I recall, and we lost touch with him.
105 *Delphian*, Vol. LIV, No. 1, Winter 1955, pp. 20-21.
106 *Delphian*, Vol. LIV, No. 2, Commencement, 1955, p. 49.
107 The room no longer exists.

thorough rendition of Rhode Island through the middle of the nineteenth century. We did not make it to the twentieth century, but her discussions of Rhode Island industrial history did explain how the State had become the industrial center it still was in the early 1950s.

In this course, we used as a (sort of) text the Old Stone Bank series on Rhode Island history, of which there were three or four volumes. Each book contained separate unconnected essays about some important building or artifact, or some significant event that had occurred. Examples included the burning of the *Gaspee*, the building of the Arcade, the Dorr Rebellion, why capital punishment was outlawed in Rhode Island (an innocent man was hanged for murder), etc.

Mrs. Monahon supplemented these stories from her own vast knowledge of Rhode Island history, organizing the whole topically and chronologically. She taught history, not as events but as a sequence of stories, which at our age made it interesting. And since we were in relatively happy circumstances, the larger story clearly had a happy ending. She personalized her stories, when possible, with reference to places and people with whom we were already familiar. And she spiced the stories with anecdotes, often a bit irreverently and conspiratorially, as if she were letting us in on a secret or sharing a bit of juicy gossip with us. Continually expecting such, we paid attention.

Rhode Island had a fascinating political history for us to study. We began with Williams, Clarke, Gorton, Coddington, the Pequot War, King Philip's War, the Great Swamp Fight, Hutchinson, and the Quakers. We discussed religious liberty, separation of church and state, and the two Charters—and then moved on to Rhode Island's involvement in the colonial wars: King William's, Queen Anne's, King George's, and the French and Indian. During these, the state had sent soldiers to Crown Point and Ticonderoga in New York, and to Louisbourg in Cape Breton, and she discussed those expeditions. We then moved on to Rhode Island's role in the Revolution. She mentioned the *Gaspee*, of course, and reminded us that Rhode Island Independence Day was two months before the national one. We studied the Battle of Rhode Island, Esek Hopkins and the Colonial Navy, Rochambeau at Newport, and Stephen Olney's regiment at Yorktown. She mentioned the visits of George Washington to the state—and the lengthy constitutional ratification process that delayed the state's accession to the

Union. She also talked about Rhode Island's Oliver Hazard Perry and the Battle of Lake Erie in the War of 1812. We were taught about the Dorr Rebellion in the early 1840s, and Rhode Island's contributions to the Civil War, which included the famous General Ambrose Burnside (of sideburn fame) whose statue is in what is now Kennedy Plaza. I remember that when we got to Burnside, Derric Chesebrough appeared in class with Burnside's inkwell (which his family had inherited). Burnside was Rhode Island's most prominent general, although he was the loser at Fredericksburg.

Mrs. Monahon also went into some detail about Rhode Island commercial and industrial history. She talked about the triangular trade (molasses, rum, slaves), the China trade, and the activities of the early merchants. Rhode Island's role in the slave trade was discussed in class. I can remember her also discussing extensively the origins of the Rhode Island textile industry, with Samuel Slater being financed by Moses Brown—and the machine tool industry, started by the Wilkinsons and Jenckses, and later fully developed by Brown and Sharpe. She told us about the Blackstone Canal. She mentioned the devastation of the Great Gale of 1815—timely, because Hurricane Carol had devastated Rhode Island in 1954, during the summer just before we took this class.

As part of the course, we also did a project on contemporary Rhode Island industry. Jack Nixon and I worked together on this, writing to various companies, asking for information about their products and processes. Jack got some good responses; I was less fortunate. My father got us some materials about the textile industry. We made posters and created a very extensive notebook from this Rhode Island history course for display at the end of the year.

In this same connection, we also took a class trip by bus to Saugus, Massachusetts, to see the Saugus Iron Works, a working model of one of the original iron producing sites in the US. We were told that US Steel had put $1 million into reconstructing it. We saw it operate, with the bellows blowing a stream of air to put oxygen into the furnace. I don't remember the furnace itself actually making iron (it was just a case of the bellows operating from the waterwheel), but at least some of the mechanics were demonstrated. There was also a museum there that we visited. This was not in Rhode Island, of course, but Joseph Jenckes, who started Rhode Island's iron forging industry, was the son of the ironmaster at Saugus—so there was a Rhode Island connection.[108] This trip provided the material for the Class's Commencement program at the end of the year.

Finally, Mrs. Monahon taught us a lot about Rhode Island cultural history. For example, I remember that she took us down to the John Brown House and showed us the extraordinary Townshend desk and other pieces of furniture; she was an expert on old furniture and shared this expertise with the class. I can remember being told how to identify Duncan Fyfe and Chippendale chairs (I probably couldn't now). She took us to the Carrington House across the street from the John Brown House and showed us the Chinese art and artifacts there, bought with the profits of Carrington's shipping business, which included the China trade, and which was based on ships called "Carrington's Coffins" because many were unseaworthy. She talked about different types of pottery, such as Wedgwood and Spode. She took us on a walking tour of the Benefit Street area and described its architecture (e.g., the Sullivan Dorr mansion—Federal). It may seem strange that anyone could interest thirteen-year-old boys in Chinese pottery, but she could. In this same cultural context, I remember going on a trip to Newport with Mrs. Monahon, Mrs. Barrett, Bill—and perhaps Mrs. Sisson, Bill's grandmother, who was Mrs. Monahon's good friend and the daughter of Dr. Seth K. Gifford. This was not a School trip, just an outing, and it may have been a year or two later. Mrs. Barrett drove. I remember Mrs. Monahon taking us to the Wanton Lyman Hazard House and other Newport colonial homes and giving us well informed guided tours.

Throughout, we had tests and wrote papers—biographies of Rhode Island heroes and things of that sort (I remember writing a paper on Oliver Hazard Perry—and mounting a postage stamp commemorating him on its front). By mid-season, we knew something about many aspects of our Rhode Island heritage.

American History. Mrs. Monahon's American history course was equally absorbing. Here we had a regular text, and it was both interesting and excellent in terms of comprehensiveness (at least through the

---

108 See Beers, J.H. *Representative Men and Old Families of Rhode Island*, 1464.

Fourth Intermediate: The Seventh Grade (1954-1955) 141

mid-nineteenth century).[109] It could well have been used in an introductory high school class. Even though it carried the story to modern times, about two-thirds of its pages were devoted to the period through the Civil War, and that is about as far as we got in class. Nevertheless, Mrs. Monahon's course in US history was very strong and detailed—I remember that when we had US history again five years later in Upper School with Mr. Raines, it was more like a refresher course for the period through the Civil War than something really new. Even in college, much of US history was like a refresher course of both Monahon and Raines.

In class, Mrs. Monahon provided a strong factual basis for understanding history—the events, the dates, the wars, the battles, the treaties, the presidents, the significant issues and legislation, the national acquisition of new territory and what it cost, and also the inventions and the engineering accomplishments (e.g., the Erie Canal, the Transatlantic Cable, the Transcontinental Railroad, and the Brooklyn Bridge). Yet her instruction, as in her Rhode Island history course, was entertaining. Her quirks and many idiosyncrasies contributed to the learning process. There was never a dull moment. She used to talk about her "one acre estate in the Berkshires" (she actually owned a large property there). She filled her lectures with many lively anecdotes. I remember her referring to King James I as the "educated fool." In fact she was very big on English kings and queens, and we had to familiarize ourselves, at least, with the Tudors through the Windsors. In a national context we also revisited Queen Anne's War, King George's War, the French and Indian War, and the American Revolution, all of which we had studied earlier that year in a Rhode Island context. About this time, we memorized the American presidents and when they served (remembering the latter is not as tough as it seems—you can tie their mostly four-year terms to other important dates and events).

The course included the exploration era, colonial history and culture (including the founding stories of all thirteen colonies), the early Republic (with tariff and slavery issues), and the Civil War. The text was thorough in terms of presenting important events, major economic and social developments, and leading figures in the colonial period and afterwards

---

109 Wilder, Howard B., Ludlum, Robert P., and Brown, Harriett McCune, *This is America's Story*, Boston: Houghton Mifflin, 1954. I do not know if the Robert Ludlum was the spy novelist, but probably was not.

up through the Civil War. We were by now indeed operating at the level of the Wilmot Proviso, though not yet at that of the Peggy Eaton Affair, which we would learn about with Mr. Raines in Upper School. There was some cultural history (which tended to extol the virtues of the English colonies and their traditions over those of the French and the Spanish). I read Theodore Roosevelt's history of the War of 1812 in this class. In addition, the Westward Expansion was emphasized, as was the arrival of Jacksonian Democracy, although his treatment of the Cherokees was omitted.

The Civil War received a lot of attention, including its remote and proximate causes. I remember we discussed the events leading up to the Civil War in some detail, and that Mrs. Monahon mentioned a prominent Providence abolitionist Quaker lady (Edith Buffam Chase, as I recall) who journeyed to Harpers Ferry to see John Brown hanged. That a proper lady would take a long train ride to then western Virginia to view a hanging was rather intriguing. The slave system was described in some detail in our text, and some of its horrors enumerated, but the presentation was cautious, and at times, qualified. The text went to some length to describe the contrasting perspectives and different points of view held in the South and in the North. Slavery, however, not states' rights, was identified unequivocally as the cause of the Civil War. We also studied the war's strategies, its battles, and the many reasons for the Union's victory. We had to memorize the sequence of northern generals in the east: McClellan, Pope, McClellen again, Burnside, Hooker, Meade, and Grant. Lincoln was rightly portrayed as a great national leader.

Reconstruction was treated cautiously, although the text did mention the KKK and its violence, and conceded that in modern times many blacks were still disenfranchised.

The post-Civil War era was treated more in terms of social forces than in terms of political events. The text discussed inventions and industrial expansion, some of which we had already been taught in a Rhode Island context; the arrival of immigrants and the many contributions they made to American society; and then the American expansion into the world—first into Latin America, and then globally with the two world wars. The New Deal was treated accurately, but briefly. All American presidents were treated with respect.

Although the book did contain some negative aspects of American history, they were not given prominence. Jim Crow may have been mentioned, but it was not highlighted. Nativism and religious discrimination were largely overlooked. Scandals, such as the XYZ Affair, were relegated to early history—although Mrs. Monahon shared a few additional ones with us. Clearly the positive was accentuated.

The text presented history in an attractive manner, with maps, cartoons, action drawings, old photographs, and a very readable story line that emphasized the heroic, the successful, and the happy ending. It was Mrs. Monahon who provided the iconoclastic, the whimsical, and the skeptical interpretations. Without question, however, this class, both its instructor and its text, was a very important one for me, and gave me an excellent events-based and story-based background for future interests in American history.

Geography. We also studied geography in the Seventh Grade. Our text was *Geography of a Working World*,[110] and it focused on agricultural and industrial production. It is my recollection that we did not read this cover to cover, just sections in it, especially those dealing with agriculture and industry in the United States. The focus was on industry, and we all had projects related to this. I wrote a piece on the Bessemer steel process and undertook a major project centered on the petroleum industry, producing a booklet on it. This included sections on the geological creation of oil, how it was discovered, where it was produced, methods of drilling, what an oil well looked like, how oil was refined, and what by-products came from it. The *World Book Encyclopedia* was very useful in making this enterprise a success. Technology was portrayed in this class as a very positive and very American phenomenon. I can remember reading (in the *World Book*) the statistics which pointed to American industrial and technological dominance during this era—when, as noted, we had half the world's telephones and radios, made half its steel, produced half of its oil, produced more than half of its automobiles, built most of its generators, and led the world in industrial technology. American agriculture was not doing too

---

110 McConnell, Wallace R., and Harter, Helen, New York: Rand McNally, 1951 edition.

badly either. Some of these statistics presented a distorted view because the Europeans were recovering from the devastations of war, but to a seventh grader, they were a source of great pride. Consistent with the Quaker tradition, national achievement was tied more to measures of mass production and mass consumption than to military power and prowess.

Science. Mrs. Monahon also taught science. She was a trained biologist who had been an instructor in the Upper School. She had a terrarium, among many other things on her little cluttered desk. She taught us a bit of astronomy and geology. We learned about sedimentary, igneous, and metamorphic rocks. We were asked to bring in samples, and we brought in so many that she remarked that she was being stoned like St. Stephen. We were taken as a class down to a geology display room at Brown and shown different rock samples, including some fascinating crystals. For a text, we had a pamphlet entitled "Stories Read from the Rocks"[111] that discussed geologic formations from the ice ages, petrified forests, fossils, volcanos, crystals, and other types of rocks. We also had a little instruction in chemistry (e.g., water came from oxygen and hydrogen), but there was no experimental or lab work. Once again, science was not emphasized in the curriculum. All in all, however, our many encounters with the memorable Mrs. Monahon were marvelous learning experiences that demonstrated the many contributions that personality can give to instruction.

Art, Shop, Music, and French. Finally, we continued to have Art, Shop, Music, and French once a week. For the first of these, we had Miss Carolyn Moore, for the second, Mr. Cole, for the third, Mrs. Thomas, and for French we had Madame Warge. Miss Moore was the only one of these instructors with whom we were unfamiliar. She was a highly qualified teacher, with a master of fine arts degree from Penn. I have only the vaguest of recollections of her classes. Among other artistic efforts, I think, we did some drawing with charcoal.

---

111 Published in 1948 by Row, Peterson and Company, Evanston, Illinois.

Civil Defense. We had occasional fire drills throughout the whole Lower School years, but somewhere along the way we experienced something novel in a related category. We were required to practice measures promulgated by the Office of Civilian Defense to protect us against an atomic attack. I don't recall being asked to get down under the desk, but I do remember the entire Class being conducted down into the bowels of Middle House near the kitchen. There we did kneel down on the floor and put our hands in back of our bowing heads. I think we did this only once.

Looking back, this was a bit silly. Although the Russians had exploded a nuclear device in 1949, they had no real capacity to attack Providence in the first half of the 1950s—or, really, until they acquired missiles in 1957. Even then, they probably lacked the number of missiles to make an attack on Providence likely. Alternatively, if they had somehow found the means to drop even a Hiroshima-style bomb on downtown Providence, its one-mile radius of destruction would certainly have included Middle House, which would have provided four to five stories of beams and brick masonry under which to bury us. It would have been far better to go up to the cupola, watch the show, and depart in style.

Lower School Sports. Any memoir of the Lower School would be incomplete without an account of our organized sports activities, which took place every day after class, beginning in the early years.

The playing fields for the first four grades were located to the southwest of the Lower School building, extending south all the way to Lloyd Avenue in one direction and west more than halfway to Hope Street in the other. In the far corner of this large area was a house-lot-sized field that went down to the corner of Hope and Lloyd. This entire area sloped gently in the direction of Hope Street, so none of the playing fields was truly level. The whole expanse, probably a couple of acres in size, contained football fields, soccer fields, and baseball fields, converted from one to the other as the seasons changed. We probably shared this space with upper classes.

In the Third Grade, we changed into old clothes in the room next to our classroom. That year we played a version of touch football. Bill Barrett also remembered games of Red Rover—and the occasion when he was the only one left untagged, after which he had to run through a gauntlet of the entire Class, and to his amazement still did not get tagged! Sometimes we played soccer, and Bill recalled Derric Chesebrough as being an ace goalie. In spring, we played softball, in which I inevitably struck out. In the Third Grade we played mostly in that subsection of the field which was at the corner of Hope and Lloyd. For some reason (that I don't remember—and probably never understood) I was elected (or selected to be) captain of one of the softball teams. They were divided into the Blues and the Whites, the School colors. I was captain of the Whites. I do not recall what duties, if any, this entailed. Most of the good players were on the Blues. There was, however, one exception, and that was Vin Marcello, who was the best ball player in our Class. We were very lucky to have him on the Whites. He was an excellent hitter, and if he connected with the ball, which he did quite frequently, it would inevitably be a hit, and often a home run—sometimes over or through the fence onto Hope Street.

To combat Vin's prowess, the opposition invented what they called the "Vinny Switch," modeled, no doubt, on the "Williams switch" designed at that time to frustrate Ted Williams at Fenway. I don't remember whether Vin was a right-hander or left-hander, but the Blues moved their entire team to the opposite side. Since he was almost our only successful hitter, this cut down on our score. I do not remember if we won the final game—but we probably lost (otherwise I would remember), despite Vin's own memorable accomplishments.

I also remember a game called pushball that we played in the Third Grade. The object was for the Blues and Whites to push on opposite sides of this very large ball (it was as tall as we were) until one side succeeded in pushing it over a line—sort of like tug-of-war in reverse. I do not remember being terribly helpful in that event either. We would lean on it. Often it slid out between the two groups to the side. I suppose it kept us busy.

Our coach in the Third Grade (and maybe Fourth Grade as well) was Mr. Mustard, who lived at the foot of Barnes Street. He was one of several Brown students (hired by Mr. Allen) who supervised our Lower School sports. We were always instructed to address them as "Sir," and we referred to these coaches collectively in the third person as the "Sirs." Mr. Mustard

Fourth Intermediate: The Seventh Grade (1954-1955)

was very polite and very tolerant of our behavior. He had a whistle, which he had to use fairly frequently. Another Sir was Mr. Richard Coveney. Bill Barrett recalled that in a later year a Sir was seriously injured in one eye from a snowball hurled by Jimmy Hoye during an organized snowball fight (which would never be allowed today).

While playing sports down in that lot at the corner of Hope and Lloyd, we often wandered off and devised our own games under a big copper beech tree (which is still there in 2021). We were not supposed to do this, but the tree's fascinating root systems created many possibilities for creative use, and we could secretly bring in toys and play with them in this novel environment. We could dig, build dirt walls, run our toy cars around the roots, and let our imaginations run free—all while we were supposed to be elsewhere playing in a more organized fashion. In the Fourth Grade we began to play real football, with tackling permitted. I remember being taken downtown by my parents to be fitted for a uniform with real shoulder pads.[112] We changed into our uniforms in the basement of the Lower School building, where we had special lockers for them. We played in the field just south of the Lower School building along the woods separating it from the traffic circle. I can remember playing in the line and being tackled by David Campbell—which knocked the wind out of me.[113] I don't remember if we played another school or just did intramural football, but I think it was the latter. In the spring, we graduated from softball to baseball—I think this was phased in, because I do remember some softball played that year.

There was a Lower School gymnasium located to the east of the main building complex across a driveway, a lawn, and a paved parking area. This originally had been a barn. Mr. Thomas before our time had converted it

---

112 In the Fourth Grade, we used fields towards the Lower School building. There was a small wooded area between these fields and the traffic circle, and I can remember football being played along this wooded area with the field perpendicular to Lloyd Avenue. Also, this was used for softball, with the plate near the wooded area. In addition, I can remember Lower School softball games with home plate at the northwest corner of the field near the trees that separated it from the long concrete walk that went down to Hope Street from under the archway. Bill Barrett recalled that this large field had a single tree in the center, no doubt constraining an optimal layout of playing fields.

113 David was a classmate who was the son of the minister at Central Congregational Church. He left Moses Brown shortly thereafter, and we lost track of him.

148 Fourth Intermediate: The Seventh Grade (1954-1955)

Lower School football
Southwest of Lower School building

Fourth Intermediate: The Seventh Grade (1954-1955) 149

to a gymnasium to replace an earlier Lower School gym a bit further down the hill towards Weymouth Street. I remember it as a single-room facility with a high ceiling, wooden floors with lines on them for different activities, and basketball hoops at each end. I think it was used primarily for the Intermediate grades. I don't, however, remember playing organized sports of any kind there other than calisthenics and running. It was probably used only during bad weather. I do remember the Class being taken there on occasion and being marched around it—with groups from other classes—but I do not remember many indoor sports activities taking place there during Lower School. Indeed, I remember the facility more for its Father and Son Day exhibits than for its athletics.

In the Fifth Grade, most classmates played football and baseball, but a few of us played tennis. We used the courts in back of the barn down by Lloyd Avenue. These were not in the best of shape, but we made do. I can remember being taught the rules and how to score. I wasn't very proficient at tennis, but it didn't seem to matter, since we never had real competitions, or at least none in which I was asked to compete. I never could produce a good overhand serve. Since there were only a couple of tennis courts, and since they were for the use of the whole Lower School, we sat on the benches a lot, or went up and used the west wall of the Lower School gym to practice against.

We also created our own diversions. There were dense bushes between the tennis courts and Lloyd Avenue, with paths running through them. These we explored. There was a nearby hill sloping sharply down to a playing field at the corner of Lloyd and Weymouth. This we rolled down. I think we had more than one tennis instructor during the three years I took tennis, but I do remember Barry Blank, a very proper naval ROTC student from Brown. He was a good instructor when we paid attention, and a good tennis player. Although several of us played tennis again in the Sixth Grade, most of my classmates played football and softball. We had a good football team with an undefeated season—beating Friend's Academy 12 to 0 and 19 to 0 in two of the games. According to Chad Gifford's account in our Sixth Grade newspaper, Jack Nixon was quarterback; Chad Gifford, left halfback; Nicky Littlefield, fullback; Tom Clark, right halfback; Billy Batchelder, right end; Kent Painter, right tackle; Skip Mays, right guard; Joey Franklin, left tackle; and Billy Fischer, left end. Bill Barrett, not listed by Chad, recalled being center (like his grandfather at Brown). Although the paper does not mention Vin Marcello, I can't imagine him not being part of this team—unless he was playing then at a more advanced level. Jack Nixon scored touchdowns in both of the above-mentioned games, and seemed to have engineered the victories. The coaches were Mr. J. Parker Scott and Mr. Coveney.

On several occasions in the Sixth and Seventh Grades, the football team went off to play other schools. Parents, including mine, were asked to drive. I remember one trip to Friend's Academy—down near New Bedford—for which we have home movie footage. I think we also played Gordon, Country Day, and possibly St. Andrews. Several of us, not on the team, went and cheered. I find no records of intramural Seventh Grade games, although I am sure there were several.

At some point during the Sixth Grade, possibly for winter sports, sets of Third and Fourth Intermediate teams were merged into one league for intramural competition (perhaps for speedball), and four teams were formed: the Hawks, the Eagles, the Bulldogs, and the Scorpions. The Seventh Grade's Tom Godfray ('59) led the Hawks to first place. Nick Littlefield and Chad Gifford were the top scorers for the Eagles. In the Seventh Grade we had our own football and baseball teams (I don't remember the organized winter sports that year). Tennis was still available for those of us who did not want to participate in either of the main sports.

We also played games in a semi-organized way during recess. These included "speedball" and soccer—games you could instantly start and finish without set-up time. All you needed was the soccer ball, and no other equipment. There were two teams in the Sixth and Seventh Grades for these recess soccer games. One was called the "Union" and the other was called the "Robots." The Union was largely composed of those who had been all the way through the Lower School and the Robots were composed of the relative newcomers. I was active in the Union—the president, as I recall, despite my lack of athletic prowess. I even drew up a constitution for it.

Somewhere along the way one Union member decided to create a revolt from within, successfully sought support, and formed a third group: the

Rinky Tinks. This secession was not envisioned by the constitution. Many remained loyal to the Union, and at this point, with three teams on the playing field, the situation became increasingly confused. So the instructors moved in, reorganized the whole situation, and broke up everything. I was very much involved with this, being very active in the Union. There was even a Class meeting where our arrangements were discussed at length.

During the post-lunch recess in the Spring Term for the Sixth and Seventh Grades, Mr. Allen hit "fungos" for us to catch. This exercise was called "pennies from heaven" because you received a penny for each ball caught. In addition, those who caught a certain number received a huge free Awful-Awful frappe (or cabinet) at the Newport Creamery in Wayland Square. Later on, by the time we were in Upper School, Mr. Allen was applying the pennies directly to the thirty-six-cent price of an Awful-Awful.[114] Bill Barrett recalled that some students were very aggressive and hogged more than their share!

Mark Saklad reminded me that Mr. Sprague headed the bicycle club, an organization primarily for boys in the Seventh Grade. Mr. Allen had started the club in 1932, and had led it until shortly before our final Lower School years. Anyway, on Saturdays there were bicycle trips several miles in length starting at School and even venturing as far as East Providence. After Commencement, Mr. Sprague led a bicycle tour to Quebec. Mark remembered that the group took their three-speed bikes on a train to Montreal. Then they travelled through Trois-Riviéres to Quebec City and thence down through Quebec into New Hampshire and then back to Rhode Island. He recalled that the Quebec hills were too much for the axle in the transmission of his bike, which broke *en route*, necessitating a serious delay for repairs. He also remembered the group going into a Quebec diner where no English was spoken. Mr. Sprague, who did not speak French, was not daunted by this minor obstacle, and he somehow managed to negotiate an arrangement whereby he ended up behind the counter frying eggs on the griddle for the whole group.

---

114 *Quaker*, May 27, 1959. "Awful Big and Awful Good." If you could finish three, you received the fourth for free.

L. Ralston Thomas

Mr. Thomas. Near the end of the Seventh Grade, Mr. Thomas came to our classroom and told us about the Upper School and how different it would be (no homeroom teacher, subjects new to us, study hall, etc.), and what might be expected of us. He described the demerit system and Saturday punishments for misbehavior. Someone asked him what would happen if they could not come on Saturday to make up the demerits. He responded in his very calm, but definitive voice, "You will come."

Mr. Thomas was a quiet and soft-spoken person, but a very strong presence nevertheless. This was his last year at Moses Brown as Headmaster. From the viewpoint of the Lower School student, he spoke with enormous magisterial authority. He had gathered together and held together a very dedicated faculty, and it was clear to us that they venerated him—whenever a teacher referred to Mr. Thomas, it was always in very quiet and respectful tones. This level of respect gave him the ability to lead quietly and firmly, and to ensure that everyone on staff was performing appropriately as part of a well-coordinated team. That always seemed to be the case during the Lower School years. Neither in the classroom nor on any informal

Fourth Intermediate: The Seventh Grade (1954-1955)   153

Editha Maxham Thomas

occasion, did I ever hear anything critical from a Lower School faculty member regarding either the administration or another faculty member. Nor to the best of my knowledge did my parents. That speaks very well of Mr. Thomas's leadership skills in creating a cooperative atmosphere among his staff. He had been Headmaster since 1925, succeeding Dr. Seth K. Gifford, and he had a long record of accomplishments, including, most notably, high-quality faculty recruitment, the building and modernizing of the sports program and the science curriculum in the Upper School, and bringing the School through both depression and war when enrollments plummeted nationally and many similar schools folded.

From our standpoint, Mr. Thomas didn't have a lot to do with the Lower School on a day-to-day basis. Mr. Allen handled the administrative, the disciplinary, and often the minor ceremonial functions, and it was he who gave us instructions on the mechanics of Lower School expectations. But Mr. Thomas, although he seldom visited our classrooms, was present on major ceremonial occasions, and throughout the Lower School we never forgot that he was Headmaster. His distance added greatly to his mystique.

Mr. Thomas's office was in Middle House just to the right of the door when you came in the front entrance, and administratively he ran a tight ship. He had very few assistants. Miss Weeks was his executive secretary, assisted by Mrs. Allen (Mr. Allen's wife), Miss Margaret Littlefield, and Miss Elizabeth Rose, who served as receptionist; Mr. E. Harold Jernquist was the treasurer; Miss Nancy Keach handled the books and served as assistant treasurer, as I recall. There were also Miss Ruth Cook, the School nurse, and Mrs. Gertrude Seidel, the house manager, whose specific duties I do not remember. Miss Thelma Young ran the kitchen and dining room. Mr. Wilfred Goff presided over buildings and grounds. Mr. William Turner served as custodian and special assistant to the Thomases. He also was a remarkable pianist. In the Upper School, many of the other administrative functions were performed by faculty—Mr. Herman, for example, was Director of Testing. He and others served as coaches, and yet others served on corridor duty. This was not a large bureaucracy—but the School seemed well-run. The grounds were well-kept, and the ancient buildings were well-maintained. It presumably handled its finances in a good solid Quaker fashion. It raised money from donations, although not until the postwar years. Most importantly, the School enjoyed an excellent reputation for placing its students into the top colleges. All in all, in the Thomas years, Moses Brown was run smoothly by a very small, but efficient and highly motivated team that functioned well, was remarkably well coordinated, and strongly, but quietly, led.

Commencement. The Seventh Grade brought us to the end of the Lower School experience, and so Commencement that year marked a rite of passage. Not only were my folks there, but a cousin and several aunts and uncles also attended. I'm sure the families of my classmates were equally well represented. The Commencement exercises for the Lower School were always held in Alumni Hall. Students from the Intermediate grades marched down the aisle and sat near the front behind the Lower School faculty; parents were seated in back. Mr. Thomas presided at a Victorian-style oak lectern (on the floor, not the stage, as I recall), and Mr. Allen took part. A Class gift to the School was presented to Mr. Thomas by Class treasurer, Derric Chesebrough. Prizes were awarded. Almost always the prize was a book with a specially engraved bookplate bearing the seal

Fourth Intermediate: The Seventh Grade (1954-1955)   155

of the School and stating the name of the prize and its recipient. This was elegantly wrapped in white tissue paper and tied with a blue ribbon—probably by one of the assistants to Miss Weeks mentioned above. There were three or four speeches by the seventh graders. I do not believe that there was an address by anyone from the outside, but probably Mr. Allen and Mr. Thomas made substantive remarks. We recited the 121st Psalm and sang the Alma Mater and the other songs we had learned in the Fifth Grade and practiced subsequently, including "America the Beautiful," "My Country 'Tis of Thee," and "Dear Lord and Father of Mankind." The music was from the organ. It was a very dignified and appropriate ceremony.

When we were in the Seventh Grade, Mrs. Monahon was in charge of the Commencement Day exercises, and several of us were selected to give talks. It is my recollection that Bill Barrett was Class president that year, and hence the spokesman who led the Class portion of the program and introduced the speakers. Bill Fischer, Nick Littlefield, and I each gave a talk (in that order), so I had to sit there and sweat out the other speeches. The four of us sat in a line on the stage. I don't remember what the other topics were, but mine was a discussion of Rhode Island industry (starting at the beginning of the Industrial Revolution), its manufacturing accomplishments, and how they contributed to the growth of the economy. Although textiles were given some prominence, the speech centered more on the growth of the tool and machinery industry in Rhode Island, briefly tracing its development from the early days of John Brown's Hope Furnace through David Wilkinson's building of machinery for the Slater Mill—up through the many Rhode Island-invented improvements to textile machinery, and on to Nicholson files, Corliss steam engines, and Brown & Sharpe precision tools. The speech ended by quoting Jeremy Bentham's famous phrase, the "Greatest Good for the Greatest Number," in support of how Rhode Island inventiveness and manufacturing skills helped bring a high living standard to Americans.

We were supposed to write these speeches ourselves, but we worked on them with Mrs. Monahon, and, frankly, I think she did most of the writing. The typescript for mine runs three double-spaced pages. Spoken deliberately, the speeches must have been something like five or six minutes long. We had to memorize them, and we stood to deliver them. We were dressed up with blue coats and white duck pants—at least those of us up on the podium were. We were instructed not to stand with hands folded in front since that gave an impression of having stomach distress. I remember that in the rear of Alumni Hall there were a couple of classical busts (Homer, Demosthenes, or whomever) that used to sit on the top of the library stacks. We were told to look at them while we delivered the speech, and not make eye contact with the audience. The one exception to this rule was that we were occasionally to glance at Mrs. Monahon, who was to be seated in the audience, so that she might signal to us during the speech if we were speaking too fast, too slow, too softly, or whatever. Pursuant to this instruction, I remember looking down at Mrs. Monahon, and receiving only an encouraging smile—so I concluded that there was no need to adjust the pace or volume. Everyone (eventually) remembered his lines.[115]

Afterwards we went outside for a reception, where the sunlit grounds were at their most beautiful—with the rhododendrons in full bloom down by Lloyd Avenue, well cared for by Mr. Goff, who inherited the very successful horticultural tradition of the legendary Joe Sargent, recollections of whom were frequently shared by Lower School teachers.[116] It was a memorable rite of passage.

---

115 Bill Barrett remembered that Bill Fischer momentarily forgot his lines, recalling that he did not lose his composure, but stood in silence for a brief moment until he remembered what came next and then resumed his speech. I have totally forgotten this, but since Bill Barrett was presiding over our efforts, I will defer to his recollections!

116 Joe Sargent, originally from Cape Cod, was the quintessential New England artisan. Hired by Dr. Gifford, he was in charge of buildings and grounds at Moses Brown, including everything from running the electric plant to plowing the snow to maintaining the shrubs (his greatest love). Dr. Gifford paid him the supreme compliment when he said, "At Moses Brown, Joe Sargent could do everything but teach Greek."

IX

The Lower School in Retrospect

As I recall it, the Lower School experience was excellent preparation for the Upper School—or for any alternative to the Upper School.

The overall focus was on training in foundational skills. Math was heavily emphasized every year, and there was a clear development, starting with basic computations, then moving on to more complex computations, and finally to problem solving. These were followed by the teaching of more esoteric ancillary skills, including square roots, geometric constructions, primitive formulae, and a little algebra. Toward the end of this process, as we reached the Sixth and Seventh Grades, math became much more decidedly applied math, and we were introduced to examples of the kinds of problems we might encounter in the home and in the business world.

Looking back, there must have been a fully integrated curriculum design to cover the whole Lower School math experience—and it was an intense experience—with lots of time spent in class and lots of homework. In class, as noted, we did things not because we enjoyed them particularly, but because we were told to do them. Math wasn't put into a fun-and-games type of mode—this was before the controversial experiments with the "new math"—and for us basic computational skills were much more emphasized than the underlying logic of math. You were told what to do, not why. There was some reward for getting things right and much blame for getting them wrong. Nevertheless, most of us plugged away at them—and we did learn.

There was also a strong emphasis on reading—tracked reading. This was a basic skill that was pushed very hard. It started with children's stories, and grew in difficulty year-by-year as we matured, using mostly short stories in the middle grades, book-length adventure stories by the Sixth Grade, and real novels by the Seventh. During the last two years of Lower School we were encouraged to acquire the habit of reading extensively outside of school—and to enjoy it.

Writing was also emphasized as a skill throughout the entire experience, but in a slightly less structured way than math and reading, with individual teachers having a bit more leeway in terms of how they taught it. The emphasis, however, was still on acquiring basic skills, starting with penmanship and punctuation. These included spelling, vocabulary development, paragraph design, and especially sentence structure. We were taught useful applications (such as letter writing). We also had serious instruction in grammar—the latter providing an excellent underpinning (that many students today lack) for subsequent instruction in both English and other languages.

We did write essays on our own—the practice certainly was important, and we did more of it as time passed—but there was no attempt during these years to teach creative writing, other than on a random basis by assigning paper topics. There was much more emphasis on avoiding outright mistakes than on creativity (or even enjoyment) in writing, in contrast to the emphasis on enjoyment in reading. Perhaps the teaching of creative writing would have been developmentally too early for us, but we might have been taught in a rudimentary way how to make essays more interesting and how stories might be written reflecting the same level of enthusiasm that we experienced when we verbally shared stories with each other.

Writing (and especially creative writing) came much more into its own in the Upper School, where English, including both critical reading and creative writing, was central to the curriculum. I don't wish to be unduly negative here—Moses Brown did have a philosophy of "language" or English that apparently had been well thought through. It carried out its program effectively. There is a lot to be said for mastering the basics before proceeding to apply them, and we certainly did have a strong grasp of the basics by the time we left Lower School. Nevertheless, English, like math, was occasionally more of a task than the joy it might have been.

The social sciences were also emphasized. Instruction in them was strong and extensive. With American history in three grades and ancient and medieval history in two (followed later, incidentally, by Upper School courses in each), we did cover serious territory. It was well covered from the perspectives of the time, and the strategy of having us revisit a topic recurrently meant that our teachers were building on our previous acquaintance with the subject while adding depth to it, a layering exercise which certainly aided the learning process. The history we were taught was taught well and in remarkable depth.

Basically our Lower School trajectory of history topics started with the ancient civilizations of the Middle East, traveled to Greece and Rome, passed through the Middle Ages in Europe, and then crossed the Atlantic to North America during the "Age of Discovery," where it focused on the emerging United States, from its colonial period to the nineteenth century—all largely in isolation from other contemporaneous cultures, including the modern European civilization (from which two world wars were to emerge, greatly to affect America).

The emphasis on ancient history—the classical tradition—was probably also designed to give a cultural context to support the teaching of Latin in Upper School. Moses Brown did not require Greek in our time (although some studied it on their own in the Upper School with Mr. Cate), but Latin was still strongly recommended for college admissions in those days and all of us took at least two years of Latin. Ancient history also introduced us to the culture from which ancient historiography, philosophy, and theater emerged, and Thucydides, Plato, Aristotle, Sophocles, and Euripides, not to mention Homer, were very important parts of the college curricula for which we were being prepared. The classical emphasis was therefore probably, in a major way, college-driven.

This left a lot of gaps, of course: little Native American history (although we did get a smattering of it from Mrs. Monahon, primarily in a Rhode Island context), little serious Latin American history (on the Incas, Aztecs, or Mayas, for example, although we were briefly made aware of their existence), only a smattering of Asian history, and virtually nothing about sub-Saharan Africa except as a source of slaves and as a colonial adjunct to

Europe.[117] Most interesting in this respect was the lack of twentieth century history, American or otherwise (even though the century was half over). We were taught hardly anything about the two world wars in history class, and certainly those wars had been very important in shaping our lives, and especially the lives of our parents.

Of course, there is only so much time in a curriculum that can be spent in studying history, and subjects taught in serious depth have to be prioritized. In this context, many may argue that the most important historical episodes for a child to know (and can easily understand) are those that seemingly led directly to his own culture or subculture—his own historical, political, and cultural inheritance, so to speak (and in those days we Lower School students were not a very diverse lot). On the other hand, a good case can be made (and should be made) that exposure to the cultural and political history of people not in one's own principal line of historical causation can be a very important, relevant, interesting, useful, and broadening experience. And in addition, as we now know well, our actual American cultural inheritance has always extended far beyond the narrow line of sequence indicated above. Today the Moses Brown student body is commendably much more diverse and no doubt exposed to a much broader range of historical experience.

Geography was more world-based, with parts of Latin America, Africa, and Europe taught in the Fourth Grade, the United States in the Fifth, a lot of Eurasia in the Sixth, and economic geography (American and to some extent global) in the Seventh. Mr. Odell was to give us an intense "capstone" geography course in the Eighth, so taken as a whole, this curriculum was more comprehensive than the history curriculum, and those who went through the Eighth Grade—and most of us did—had a strong grounding in geography, especially physical, political, and economic geography.

We must not forget that this was a period of amplified patriotism in the United States—it was the height of the Cold War. In both history and

---

117 In the Upper School the only serious addition to the historical topics covered in Lower School was modern European history—there were no opportunities to study Latin American, African, Middle Eastern, or Asian history, so the above observations pertain largely to the Upper School as well.

geography courses, American achievements were certainly emphasized much more than American failures and deficiencies. History was taught as progress—with generally positive outcomes where problems were surmounted and things moved in an upward direction. Political corruption and political failure were usually taught in the context of successful reform movements that overcame them. There was indeed recognition of slavery and its burdens, as well as its economic and political importance, but it culminated in a Civil War to eliminate it. The unfinished business of that war, full equality for African Americans, was only lightly discussed—this at a time when Jim Crow produced segregated schools in the South and denied blacks the right to vote (*Brown v. the Board of Education* was handed down when we were in the Sixth Grade, and although I remember Earl Warren on the cover of *Time* magazine, I recall little being mentioned about this decision in the Lower School at that time).

I would suggest, however, that this perspective of history taught as progress and achievement fell short of triumphalism. We were not taught to boast. We said the Pledge of Allegiance every morning, but any American "nationalist" perspective was muted. Pride was instilled, but not aggressive pride. Perspectives were formed around past and present American achievements, such as winning independence and freedom, establishing rights, and economic achievements—from taming the wilderness to building the world's leading economic system. As noted, in discussing current, as well as historical, events, there was much more emphasis on America's economic and technological achievements than on her military achievements; in the latter case, those mentioned in our history classes were remote in time. As taught to us, pride in America was much more evoked by our being the freest country in the world—or by our being number one in manufacturing or commodity production (or in the number of telephones installed)—than evoked by being the country with the largest number of aircraft carriers, the fastest fighter planes, or the most nuclear weapons.

And, in this regard, also as noted, there were no triumphalist accounts of the world wars—and the Soviets were not portrayed as particularly evil or even as dangerous enemies. References in class to communism as an evil doctrine were few and far between. Of course, communism was not taught in any positive way, but I do not remember in the Lower School any lectures or presentations to augment the prevailing negative perceptions of the Soviets or of communism in general. Perhaps this was thought to be unnecessary, given the broad consensus at that time and our middle class social backgrounds. In any event, we were not taught to hate. Nor was fear instilled regarding the nuclear threats of the Atomic Age. We were not given a naive view of the world, but we were not given an alarmist one either. Although our textbooks and our instructors were largely secular, the above perspectives were certainly consistent with a Quaker outlook.

Science was not emphasized in this pre-Sputnik era, as mentioned recurrently above. This was a substantive area not extensively developed—in strong contrast to the Upper School where science under Ralston Thomas's leadership had been very much emphasized for decades. Foreign languages were also largely ignored in the Lower School. Today there is a widely acknowledged perception that early exposure to a foreign language may be the best way to develop lifelong speaking and reading skills. This may not have been fully understood at the time. Mme. Warge was a nice person, and no doubt a fine practitioner of the French language, but she did not offer us systematic or extensive instruction in French. Lower School French introduced us to some French culture and acquainted us with a few rudimentary words and phrases, but it was a thin basis for further development. French was more of a teaser, and many were not teased.

With respect to the other areas of instruction, aside from Miss Swide, there was no art appreciation, and her efforts in this direction were probably her own special contributions and not a part of a school-wide curriculum or plan. Shop encouraged the development of motor skills and possibly contributed to a sense of practical accomplishment. It was probably a holdover from the days when many students were from farms or from working families. Together with Mechanical Drawing in the Upper School, it might have been a residual curricular component from an earlier time when more attention was paid to vocational training to meet the needs of some students.

Sports were emphasized. I was not very good at them, but most others were, and this was considered an important part of our development.

Overall, there was a sustained level of intense activity. School kept you busy. There were very few courses, if any, in which you could really slack off and still do well. There was also a very strong premium on excellent academic performance. You knew that a lot was expected of you. You also got the feeling that your teachers knew what they were talking about, that they believed in their stated principles, and that they were interested in you and your accomplishments. They understood you on a personal level, and they wanted you to learn and succeed. Things were genuine; no one was trying to put something over on you—and these qualities carried over to the Upper School.

Some with contemporary perspectives would argue that the Moses Brown Lower School educational experience emphasized the acquisition of basic skills over the encouragement of creativity and self-expression, and they could make a serious argument to this effect. Math computation, reading skills, spelling, penmanship, basic English composition, and fact-laden geography and history were indeed emphasized.[118] There was a very strong sense that the way one acquired the basic skills in math and even English in the early years was through drill and repetition. The method of instruction was highly structured, and the classroom, for the most part, orderly and disciplined. Development was guided along a prescribed path, rather than rising spontaneously. On a social level, we were taught to respect our peers, and especially our superiors, at School. We did not always follow these social strictures, but they left their mark, and were reinforced by our parents, who had brought us up in the pre-Spock era.

And yet I would find it hard to argue that creativity was unduly stifled, growth constricted, or our potential seriously narrowed as a result of this approach. Curiosity was widespread among us; we were never discouraged from asking questions, nor did our questions go unanswered. Our teachers usually took pains to explain how things worked and why things occurred, and many of our texts contained attempts at such explanations. Tales of historical experiments and inventions were ever-present throughout our classes, and for the most part positively presented. We were continually encouraged to do things on our own outside of the classroom. We did not feel that our freedoms had somehow been denied us, and I think it fair to say that few, if any, felt that the School had let them down.

---

118 In this context it must be remembered that at this time there were no handheld calculators, no word processors with spell checks and grammar checks, no facility for texting, no Google, no Wikipedia, and no "Hey, Siri." Educators believed that the basic facts and skills they taught would always be useful.

What the Moses Brown Lower School experience did bring to us on a positive level in varying measure (and in addition to the skills and knowledge we acquired) were the development of task-oriented attitudes, a sense that accomplishment would be rewarded (and slacking off punished), an awareness of standards and quality, a measure of intellectual discipline, a sense of self-esteem (in most cases), a competitive spirit, and in many cases, a drive to achieve. Academic aspirations and achievements were lauded both by teachers and, importantly, by peers. Getting an "A" was as recognized as much as hitting a home run in softball. The tradition of *arête*—excellence—which the School emphasizes today, was very much present in the Moses Brown Lower School during the 1950s, but it was a standard that developed over time as we matured. In the early years, the primary distinction was between incorrect and correct, not between ordinary and excellent—although in the early years when you had lots of correct answers, the result was denominated "excellent." The standard of excellence itself emerged throughout the Lower School years as our tasks and methods became more complex and individualized, as our awareness grew, and as our values deepened.

The teachers in the Lower School indeed taught values—more by example than explicitly. Truth was in the School motto—although at this level of development, it meant telling the truth, not seeking it. Our teachers, whatever else one might say about them, were uniformly sincere. What you saw was what you got. They were frank and did not play games with us. They were also fair. Although I'm sure they had their favorites, I don't remember any serious instances of favoritism—or any instances of a teacher picking on someone or making an unfair example of him. Miss Wilson may have picked on all of us, but she was very careful to make no exceptions. Clearly there were standards—classroom rules, skills to be acquired without shortcuts, exams fairly and uniformly graded, and aspirational levels of achievement. Finally, there was just a basic atmosphere of decorous decency about the place. All this was foundational for true excellence.

I think it could be argued that had we walked out into the world after the Seventh Grade and had no more formal schooling, leaving aside questions of maturity, emotional development, and, of course, credentialing, we would have had many basic practical skills to survive (or to develop other skills needed to survive) in many real-world surroundings at that time. We had the computational ability to handle household finances—and to run many small businesses. We understood the rudiments of borrowing and lending. We had the measurement skills to handle many retail transactions from both sides of the counter. We had the communication skills to correspond with acquaintances and write to customers. We had the ability to read a newspaper, a road map, a catalogue, many an instruction manual, a driver's license written test, and a novel. We had a reasonable level of civic awareness and understood the basic requirements of citizenship. We knew a bit about the world. There were a lot of blanks to fill in, but in many cases we had the rudimentary skills to develop the ability to do so.

The commitment to ensure that the curriculum gave us these practical skills was probably deeply grounded in the traditions of nineteenth century education. It was taught by teachers, some of whom had been trained in the 1920s by teachers themselves trained in the 1800s. I believe that this practical foundation—and an emphasis on acquiring useful knowledge—was salutary. It provided a good background for our eventual entry to the adult world. It gave us motives to learn and it encouraged realism.

Still, to put this point into perspective, a Lower School education was primarily and realistically regarded as a good grounding for what was to follow. We could not have walked out of Lower School and into any serious profession, even at that time, nor would anybody have expected us to. We had no scientific skills to speak of. We still lacked the math to become engineers. Only a few of us had the rudiments of design. Our understanding of the world was more factual than interpretive. We knew no foreign languages. Our understanding of English itself lacked sophistication and nuance, even though we knew the basic dimensions of its structure. Our public speaking skills were primitive. Much remained to be learned before we could enter college, let alone enter the late twentieth century world of increasing vocational specialization. As we entered Upper School, we were now to continue our steps on the long journey leading from training to education, and in many cases to professionalism, but that journey, although it had followed a somewhat narrower path than it would follow today, had been well launched.

PART II

The Upper School

The Class of 1960, First Form

First row: Clark, Treasurer; Littlefield, Secretary; Marcello, Vice-president; Brown, President. Second row: Buonnano, Sawyer, Nixon, Dieroff, Sanderson, Ahmed, Schwartz. Third row: Ladd, Brehm, Forman, Fain, Neal, Marshall, Saklad, DiLibero. Fourth row: Darrah, Saywell, Carney, Dean, Barrett, Volkman, Abella. Fifth row: Najarian, Kindelan, Huntoon, Young, Franco, Stenmark. Sixth row: P. DeSano, Corris. (Not in picture: Fischer, Oster.)

X

First Form

(1955-56)

On September, 21, 1955, our Moses Brown experience began anew. After the opening exercises in study hall, half of us First Formers traipsed back to the rear of that room, out into the adjacent hall, and over to the Arch Room located above the archway that led to the Lower School building. The space was familiar to many of us because we had had a reading class there with Miss Jensen in the Fourth Grade. We flocked in, sat down, and began to chat excitedly, exchanging summer tales and fall expectations—full of our own importance, now that we were Upper Schoolers.

In front, at a desk on the south side of the classroom, sat Mr. King B. Odell, a large man with rounded shoulders and dark hair neatly combed across an impressive dome. His full, round face was adorned with thick-rimmed glasses through which he looked out at us intently. The whole apparition reminded one of a fairly aggressive owl. When the bell rang, he stirred and then barked, "Shut up, you babbling bunch of babies. You're now in the Upper School." And so we were.[119]

---

[119] Mr. Odell, with the exception of a four-year hiatus during which he earned his doctorate, remained on the staff of Moses Brown School for more than 65 years, teaching and coaching for a half century, and then serving as School Historian. When Matt Glendinning, Head of School, was featured in an imaginative video announcing a snow day in song (a video that went viral nationally), Doc Odell appeared near its end with an extraordinary look of incredulity on his face. Whatever might have crossed his mind on that occasion, he did not, however, utter a similar instruction to his boss.

Moses Brown's Upper School at that time consisted of five grades called Forms, with the First Form (Eighth Grade) the earliest.[120] Day students in all five forms had their desks in the same large room—study hall—and they traveled from there to their classes, which met in a dozen or so rooms, mostly nearby. There was consequently a different feel to the classroom experience than in the Lower School where we had our own room with a homeroom teacher and a regular assistant. Now we had four or five principal instructors in different rooms and a communal home base which we shared with most of the Upper School.

The Class of 1960 and its companion classes in the Upper School were larger than those in the Lower School, and they were therefore divided into two or three sections, each having its own separate schedule. Thus sets of classmates took the same courses at different times of day, sometimes with different instructors for the same course. Most of these classes were interspaced by time spent for what was called "study hall."[121] Although classrooms might be used by different instructors, some of the senior faculty (including Mr. Herman, Mr. Paxton, Mr. Raines, Mrs. Full, Mr. Cate, Mr. Fuller, Mr. Hutton, and Mr. Whitford) had rooms that were primarily their own.

The Upper School academic curriculum, with some individualized variation, basically consisted of five years of English, five of math (through pre-calculus), at least two years of Latin, three years of modern language instruction (typically French or German), a four-year science sequence (general science, biology, chemistry, and physics), and a history sequence (ancient, modern European, and American, the last having a serious civics component). The science sequence began in the Second Form and the modern language sequence in the Third Form. The science curriculum tracked with the math curriculum so that students in science courses would already have had the required background in algebra, geometry,

---

120 By the mid-1960s, Moses Brown had six forms—starting with the Seventh Grade in Middle School.

121 My basic schedule of courses in the First Form will serve as an example: Chapel; Geography with Mr. King B. Odell in the Arch Room; Study Hall; Latin with Mr. Frank Fuller in Room 1; Study Hall; Math with Mr. Howard Roberts in Room 4; Lunch break; English with Mr. William Taber in Room 2; Study Hall; Dismissal. I also had Studio with Mr. Leo Cole; Shop with Mr. F. Warren Howe; Music with Mr. William Reifsnyder; and *Bible* with both Mr. and Mrs. St. John in Alumni Hall. These last four classes met once a week during some of the time allocated to Study Hall on other days.

First Form (1955-56)

and trigonometry. These central courses were supplemented by courses in *Bible*, geography, art, shop, music, speed-reading, and Mechanical Drawing. The last, together with general science, provided some background for engineering. Occasionally students would take specialized instruction in another language (such as Spanish, Russian, or ancient Greek). Some students worked with faculty on an individual basis in music and art. Advanced placement courses began to be taught during our years at Moses Brown. This curriculum was obviously designed to prepare students primarily for a liberal arts college experience and, no doubt, reflected the requirements and expectations of the Ivies, the Little Ivies, and other good colleges. It also probably resembled closely the curricula of other New England prep schools at that time, although the larger ones would have had more language opportunities, more history courses, and a greater variety of specialty classes.

The account that follows is organized by year, not across years by subject, so that topics not taught across the full five years are described in their proper chronological sequence and appear in the same chapter with those taught to us during the same year. This arrangement also allows the narrative to integrate the classroom experience with outside school events that took place year by year, and also accentuates the growth over time of our intellectual and social skills. For the First Form, after a brief introduction to Chapel, I describe the four principal courses of geography, Latin, math, and English (which met every day); and the supplementary courses of studio, shop, music, and *Bible,* which met once a week. This was my own menu of courses that year and the menu of most other students in the Class of 1960. The eight-course load (four principal, four ancillary) shrank to six in the Second Form (five principal, one ancillary), and then to five principal and no ancillary in the Third Form—where it remained for the rest of the Upper School experience. In special cases, courses that were ancillary in the early years (music or studio art, for example) were sometimes taught as principal courses in the later years on a tutorial or mini-class basis.

Chapel. The school day opened with Chapel, which we attended every morning in the study hall throughout the entire Upper School experience. It began at 8:30 a.m. and lasted no more than fifteen minutes. The

Headmaster usually presided.[122] Day students sat at their desks. Boarders sat on benches up front to the left. The faculty and Assistant Headmaster sat on benches a bit behind the Headmaster to his left against the wall. Thus the top administrators, the full faculty, and the entire student body all met together for a few moments each day. We always opened with a hymn.[123] Mr. Frank Fuller, our Latin instructor, played the piano which was located up front on the right as we faced it. Chapel singing was not always a concerted effort. Some of us knew the hymns; others did not. Many made a serious effort to belt them out; some did not. While standing on our feet with hymn books in hand, especially if we were among the older crowd in the back of the room, we could exchange notes, gossip a bit, or make irreverent comments. These were not frequent practices, but they were recurrent.

The singing was followed by a prayer, which always included a silent component. Then came an address—a short talk on a topic of interest (not always religious, but usually with a moral lesson to it). The content of this message stemmed from whatever moved the spirit of the speaker that morning, and that could be just about anything, sacred or secular. This talk was given sometimes by the Headmaster, more often by a member of the faculty, and in our senior year, occasionally by students themselves. Doc Odell recalled that the faculty dreaded being tapped for this duty.[124]

There was great variety in the Chapel messages. Some were well thought out; some were more spontaneous. I remember that one morning Coach "Army" Armstrong (chemistry teacher, baseball coach, and Director of Athletics) forgot it was his turn to deliver the Chapel address until he had arrived at the study hall. He grabbed a *Bible*, thumbed through it quickly, and read randomly (as he admitted at the time) from the book of Proverbs. The result was not all that bad. Mr. Everett Raines (senior history teacher), always well-organized, read several times from John Graham's admonitory letters to his son Pierpont. William Taber (English instructor) on one occasion gave an interesting talk on the decline and fall of the British Empire, styling it as one of the most benign empires in world history. An ardent Quaker, he also gave a passionate message at another time in

---

122 Today, this title has been appropriately changed to the gender-neutral "Head of School."
123 We sang from *The New Hymnal for American Youth*, New York: Fleming H. Reuell Company, 1930.
124 Interview, March 22, 2012.

First Form (1955-56)

George C. St. John, Jr.

support of conscientious objectors (of which he had been one), using as his text the passage from the Sermon on the Mount that called us to turn the other cheek. Walter Jansen (English instructor and World War II veteran) promptly responded at the next Chapel session, also invoking the Sermon on the Mount, and highlighting the passage that urged people to go the second mile. As examples of those who had done so, he extolled the virtues of soldiers who, at great sacrifice, had acted heroically in battle. I think there was a second scripture-based clash between the two men along these same lines not long thereafter. Thus we heard many points of view.

On one occasion, Mr. George C. St. John, our new Headmaster that year, preached memorably from a Biblical text—the passage in Exodus describing Moses and the burning bush. He said that he had had a similar recent experience. While walking down the sidewalk towards Hope Street, he had seen smoke emerging from behind a bush. Although his initial reaction had been to wonder if this was a new Mosaic miracle, he had discovered to his horror that some seniors had chosen the wrong time and place to light up. Smoking was forbidden on School grounds. This rule had been carved in stone at the highest level, and consequences had followed. Mr. St. John concluded by telling us with emphasis to go forth and puff no more.

Incidentally, Mr. Robert N. Cunningham, who succeeded Mr. St. John as Headmaster, relaxed this rule, as I recall, and by our senior year smoking was permitted in some locations on campus.

Current events often provided material for Chapel topics. Sputnik, launched during our Third Form year, had a very big impact on the American consciousness, and numerous Chapel messages reflected this. Many speakers, citing Sputnik, discussed the need to teach more science and technology—and to improve education more broadly. I can remember Ted Burton ('58) comparing Elvis Presley's annual income to that of a scientist or an engineer, and concluding that this was an example of a warped national reward system. In this same context, speakers made comparisons between Sparta and Athens—how the Russians were Sparta and we were Athens, the first a disciplined country that paid attention to science and engineering, the second, a happy-go-lucky country devoted to frivolous activities that squandered its resources. With respect to Sputnik itself, I remember Professor Smiley taking some of us over to the Ladd Observatory to watch for it (more accurately, watch for its orbiting launch vehicle). Fred Schwartz was among us, and we did spot it.[125]

We also had outside guests who spoke at Chapel. I remember an interesting series when a minister, a rabbi, and a priest were brought in to speak during consecutive weeks. Occasionally seniors delivered Chapel talks. I

---

125 Frederic Schwartz, who joined our Class in the First Form, went to the University of Pennsylvania for several years and then transferred to the University of Rhode Island after a brief illness. He graduated from Boston University Law School where he picked up enough awards to be drafted by the newly formed federal Department of Transportation (DOT) where he had a number of bureaucratic titles; including Special Assistant to the Assistant Secretary for Environment and Urban Systems and Staff Assistant to the Secretary. He was also the legal/legislative member of the DOT team which started the federal bicycle program in the '70s. During this period he also found time successfully to sue the National Park Service when it banned kite flying in Washington. As a result, he was given the task, for several years, of helping to choose the fireworks on the National Mall. He also founded the Annual Washington Croquet Tournament. After leaving DOT he entered (and continues in) private practice where he specializes in appellate law, employment law, property law, immigration law for extraordinary and exceptional applicants, and assorted conundrums. He has been a trustee or board member of a number of cultural organizations and president of the Washington English-Speaking Union. He and his wife Jill have been married for over 30 years. I am greatly indebted to him for permitting me to occupy a room at his Watergate cooperative when I was Research Director of the John Anderson presidential campaign in 1979-80, and for many other courtesies over the decades.

suppose all this was grounded in the Quaker tradition—people could and would speak what was on their mind as, indeed, the spirit moved.

Mr. St. John had problems with discipline and on occasion this became manifest in Chapel. He was a very nice and very erudite person. He knew his subject matter, was splendidly versed in educational philosophy, and could well address curriculum issues, but he was not cut out to handle adolescent high school boys, numbers of whom tried to put things over on him. Students in Chapel services led by him could be restless and the ceremony could lack order. He was often unable to deal with this effectively. I remember that we had an epidemic of Atomic Pearls. They were little pearl-shaped balls which would explode like a firecracker when stepped on, or even when thrown vigorously against a hard surface. I'm not sure who was responsible for introducing them to the Moses Brown School environment, but they did become a presence in the study hall, and in Chapel a speaker's remarks might be punctuated by a sudden explosion. The usual M.O., according to Bill Barrett, was for an upperclassman to roll one diagonally up the aisle so it would go under a desk in hopes that a lowerclassman would unwittingly (or wittingly) step on it. This happened recurrently.

Mr. St. John was not able to handle this casting of pearls, nor was he willing to relate it to scripture. I remember Mr. Taber in a Chapel talk once asked everyone who had Atomic Pearls to put them on the floor and step on them—and let that be the end of things. This did not, however, solve the problem. In our Second-Form year, Mr. Raines was given the title of Dean and put in charge of discipline. This helped. Things calmed down further after Headmaster Robert N. Cunningham took charge. He was willing to crack the whip. Chapel-goers could get restless under Mr. Cunningham, but no student defied him openly—and the Atomic Pearls passed into history as examples of a successful disarmament effort based on the threat of massive retaliation.

Geography. Returning to the Arch Room where our Upper School narrative began: Mr. Odell was there to teach us a capstone course in geography, and he was to offer one of the most intensive and fast-moving courses

King B. Odell

that I ever took anywhere.[126] After a few sessions of shock therapy, the likes of which we had not seen since Miss Wilson, we grew quickly to admire this fascinating character who was such an intense and engaging instructor. There was a directness about him that immediately commanded both attention and respect. It quickly became clear to us that he stood for no nonsense (and was fully capable of recognizing it when he saw it), yet he also came across as a genuine person with a great sense of humor who was interested in all of us as individuals and who was there to help us learn important things. His fairly ancient white T-Bird by that time was a School legend, and that added immeasurably to his mystique among us eighth graders.

He had an interesting teaching style. There is an ancient question in pedagogy: is it the job of an instructor to teach a subject, or is it the job of an instructor to teach a student? Odell did both. He was intensely involved with the subject—he lived it, as one colleague later recalled. But he also came to know us very well as individuals, and he treated each of us as unique personalities. When you sat in his class, you always felt he was

---

126 Mr. Odell left Moses Brown at the end of the 1955-56 school year to go to graduate school at the University of Missouri on a Fulbright, and became "Doc" Odell with a PhD four years later, returning to the Moses Brown classroom in the fall of 1960.

talking to you personally, and in almost every class he called on you. Initially, we dreaded this, but as our confidence built, we came to enjoy it. He saw through us very quickly, and he was not shy in commenting about our foibles—such as my tendency to write lengthy tomes. To this very day, he retains a remarkable set of recollections about the personal characteristics of hundreds of alumni—which he draws upon at convivial roasts. Bob Smith ('58), later president of the Harvard *Crimson*, recalled him as the "best teacher I ever had—including Harvard ... with great techniques for making you remember something."[127]

There was passion in his presentations. He was heavily engaged with his subject matter, and he was willing to speak his mind on just about anything in direct and forceful ways. Moreover, you knew that what he said was what he meant. You knew where he stood. He could indeed use hyperbole for effect, and often did so, but it was identifiable as such. There was basic honesty here, and even at our age we understood and appreciated it. The intense engagement, the forcefulness, the straightforwardness—all combined to send the message that knowing world geography was important to him, and therefore should be important to us. Thus conveying a sense of importance was the link between teaching the subject and teaching the student.

But it was not all ardent intensity. There was also humor. Mr. Odell's constant mixture of serious points and humorous comments helped keep our attention—you never knew quite what was coming next. His humor lightened the intensity of the class, but it was often sardonic humor, filled with gentle ironic comments and delivered with a Cheshire-cat-like smile—a smile like the one that comes after the parakeet has disappeared, or, to mix the metaphor a bit, the one on the tiger who has just digested a sacred cow.

His humor was often directed at us. He had an uncanny knack for reading people, and he enjoyed reading each of us—you seldom could put one over on him. He always called us by our last names (even in private conversation), and he constantly put us on the spot. He joshed us. When we made mistakes, he never let us forget them, humorously reminding us of our foibles on recurrent occasions—but in such a way that we learned to enjoy

---

127 Taped interview, March 26, 2014.

laughing at ourselves. Bill Barrett recalled that Mr. Odell had a lot of fun with Bob Dean. At this time a high prelate in the Church of England had become a communist and was widely referred to in British circles as the "Red Dean." Somehow Mr. Odell managed to affix this title to Bob, much to the amusement of everyone, including Bob himself. He also had a lot of fun with another student (Ted Vetterlein?) as they discussed the details of Ecuador's guano trade. The repartee was not all one way. When we were talking about India, someone asked him if Lahore was one word or two. That was one question he dodged.

There was a bit of a drill instructor in Odell, and he did shape us up. But he always treated us fairly, and we all looked up to him and wanted to earn his respect. He was a strong authority figure—but an irreverent one—and he created quite an impression. You could grow in this class, and your growth would be recognized. I think everyone in the course not only learned a lot about geography, but also learned a lot about themselves.[128]

First-Form Geography was supposed to cover the whole world outside of the USA (even including a bit of China), but the focus was on the Western Hemisphere, Europe, and the Soviet Union, with a brief introduction to the Middle East and South Asia.[129] The class filled in many gaps left over from Lower School and also took familiar things to new levels. Mr. Odell gave us very detailed descriptions of all the continents and most of the independent countries then in existence. We reviewed latitude, longitude, great circles, and the prime meridian. We learned the significance of different kinds of map projections (Mercator, Goode, etc.). We learned about equinoxes and solstices. We learned about climate—including cyclonic storms, trade winds, horse latitudes, and doldrums. We learned about minerals and their economic significance. We learned about soils and their agricultural importance. We learned lots of mountain ranges (distinguishing, for example, between Alps, Apennines, and Dolomites). We memorized the

---

128 The Class was dismayed to hear that at the end of the year he was leaving Moses Brown. Four years later, those who had known him were overjoyed to learn that he was to return, but disappointed that we would just miss having him again. Upon return he taught French and Russian, as well as geography, and coached tennis and track. Moses Brown was lucky that he continued to serve there for more than 50 years.

129 I have many materials from this class which I have consulted in preparing this description. These include extensive country notes, exams, and homework ("Guides to Study") which were exercises we did from the (now-missing) textbook.

First Form (1955-56)

highest mountains in each continent (McKinley, Aconcagua, Elbrus, Everest, Kilimanjaro, and whatever the one was in Australia). We learned the principal rivers of the world and various other geographic features—great deserts, rain forests, central plateaus, massifs, savannahs, deltas, basins, fiords, gulfs, isthmuses, peninsulas, barrier reefs, seas (Red, Yellow, White, and Black), and even the Great Australian Bight. We reviewed memorably strange locations, such as Patagonia, the Outback, the Great Canadian Shield, the Gobi Desert, and our old friends from Mrs. Bluhm's class, the taiga and the steppes.

We also learned capitals, major cities, famous railroads (like the Trans-Siberian), and canals (like the Suez, Kiel, Panama, and Volga-Don). Not that all of this information was vital to success in life (unless you worked for a travel agency), but at times it did come in handy. I can remember learning from Mr. Odell about Comodoro Rivadavia in Argentina, and then not hearing about it again for a quarter of a century until the Falklands War broke out in 1982. I suspect that at the beginning of that war the alumni of Mr. Odell's geography class were the only Americans outside of the Foreign Service, a few tourists, and Paul Theroux, who had ever heard of Comodoro Rivadavia. As a further help in understanding Mrs. Thatcher's war, we recalled that Mr. Odell had also covered a great deal of Patagonia, had familiarized us with Tierra Del Fuego, and, indeed, had told us that the only important fact anyone needed to know about the Falkland Islands themselves was that sheep there outnumbered people at about the same ratio as cows outnumbered Yankees (at that time) in Vermont.

Mr. Odell also had us make maps which were graded with a great deal of precision—and on their neatness as well as their accuracy (the former was always a problem for me). We started with maps of Canada and North America. Then there were more detailed maps of Central America, the Caribbean, Argentina, Brazil, several countries in Europe, and the Soviet Union. We were running out of time when we reached Asia, and I recall (and can find) none from South Asia, Australia, or Africa. Different countries were colored appropriately. The maps showed political boundaries, major cities and rivers, mountain chains, bodies of water, other geographic features, and national products, both agricultural and industrial. For example, on the South American map I made there were symbols for 41 products: 6 animal, 15 mineral, and 20 vegetable.

These maps reflected an emphasis made throughout the course on the major products of each country, the reasons why those products were produced, and the resulting patterns of world trade. Included in the discussion of why countries produced what they did were such factors as natural resources, climate, geographic features, history, and culture. What made economic geography interesting was not simply the variety of products and the variations by country and region, but the ever-present explanations of why the differences existed. We were therefore not just asked to memorize lists of national products, for example, but also to understand why countries specialized in producing them.

The concept of comparative advantage itself was not mentioned in so many words, but the perspective that countries specialized in their economic activities for specific reasons—and then traded their products for other products they did not produce—was ever-present. This was especially true in the case of agriculture, where we were taught about all manner of different natural conditions, including geographic features, soil quality, and weather (especially temperature and rainfall). But the reasons for industrial specialization (or the balance between industry and agriculture) often took us into the realm of history and politics. For example:

- With respect to Britain, we learned about the industrial revolution (coal, textiles, steel), the growth of its empire, its shipping industry, its traditional role as middleman in world trade, and London's historic role in world finance.

- In the case of Brazil, we learned about its colonial experience and subsequent independence, the rubber boom, the development of the coffee trade, the Amazon economy, and the country's modern industrial efforts.

- In the case of Germany, we learned about the growth of its steel and chemical industries, with the latter's history of developing synthetics in response to commercial and military needs.

- In the case of the Soviet Union, keeping in mind that this class took place during the Cold War, the emphasis was on its agricultural and industrial capacities, and not on its military prowess. We learned about the Russian Revolution, the fall of the czar, agricultural collectivization, industrialization and the five-year plans—their successes as well as their failures. The Soviet Union was certainly presented as a dictatorship and its economic and political control over Eastern Europe was discussed in some detail, but we did not learn a lot about the Red Army or the atom bomb. This class was pre-Sputnik. We did, however, briefly discuss Stalin and his regime.

Not only were we taught about products, but also about trade and transportation. Principal exports and imports were taught for virtually every country we studied—and often in the context of their trade relations with the United States. Transportation networks (roads, railroads, rivers, canals, pipelines) were emphasized, including especially the status of a country's railroads and current efforts to expand them.

It was actually a very interesting class, and made the more so by the instructor's mastery of detail, his anecdotes, and his often humorous way of presenting the material. He took things well beyond geography itself, narrowly defined. Bill Barrett remembered being assigned to find out the process by which pencils are made and report back to the class. Mr. Odell had a lot of fun with that one.

We also discussed World Wars I and II. Mr. Odell described many of the causes and geopolitical considerations that led to the wars—as well as the aims, strategies, and conduct of the participants. We talked a bit about the Cold War, the nuclear age, and the six-year-old NATO, although these were not the focus of the course. He worked in a lot of twentieth century history and current events. We talked about the politics and political systems in many countries. We discussed democracy and totalitarian dictatorships. We learned a bit about the differences between the American and British systems of government. He did not miss the opportunity to comment humorously about the travails of the French National Assembly (and the sequence of premieres) in that Fourth Republic era—or the "riot in the Diet," which had just taken place in Tokyo, for that matter. This was really the first time in our experience that the twentieth century had been discussed in a Moses Brown class at any level of detail. This was more than "current events." It was "current events" contextualized.

Mr. Odell was a tough, no-nonsense grader. In the Lower School many of us had been used to getting lots of As, and if you got a B it was almost considered to be a source of shame.[130] He altered that complaisant expectation. I got off to a bad start by misspelling his name (O'Del) on the first homework assignment. It came back corrected. On the first quiz and on the first set of homework (his soon-to-be-notorious "Guides to Study," as he euphemistically referred to our take-home exercises) we got generous helpings of Cs, which we were not at all used to. This got our attention. We also had to be very careful with our cartographic efforts—the devil was in the details—because they, too, would be graded down severely if items were misspelled, missing, or their presentation sloppily inaccurate.

The geography textbook, which I cannot seem to locate, was the source of these "Guides," which were offered in the form of questions at the end of each chapter. They were largely subjective, and he graded them rigorously and carefully with lots of comments, explaining the deficiencies in each answer. These careful comments enabled us to improve our performance because they indicated what was expected.

The problem was that we were used to simple factual answers in our Lower School social science classes (e.g., What is the capital of Belgium?; What is the longest river in Africa?; What country is the chief exporter of attar of roses?). Now we were expected to answer more complicated questions (e.g., How does the geography of Argentina shape the nature and value of its exports?; How do the natural resources of Germany aid its industrial production?; Why did the Russians dig the Volga-Don Canal?, etc.). We had to think, sort things out, and organize our presentations—as well as memorize and present the basic facts.[131]

After getting several—to me—annoyingly unsatisfactory grades on these Guides, I decided to go on the offense. I took a whole evening (and then some), and wrote very lengthy answers to each of sixteen questions,

---

[130] For comparative purposes, I am taking some liberties here. Typically, Lower School teachers graded on a scale of E (Excellent), G (Good), F (Fair), and P (poor).

[131] The large majority of Guides that I have found cover the first half of the class—only a few near the end are country specific. Most are about cartographical, geological, meteorological, and economic topics.

First Form (1955-56)

submitting twenty pages, compared to the usual two or so.[132] I was going to show him! Mr. Odell was very amused by this. I think he liked the aggressiveness of the gesture. He commented to me later that he had left reading my answers to the end of the pile, stating that he could usually find at least something to take credit off for, but in this case he apparently did not. He gave me the coveted 100. I regarded this as the top accomplishment of the Eighth Grade. I never again got 100, but I had made my point and had learned something about answering subjective questions. My subsequent grades were generally a lot better than my previous ones.[133]

Mr. Odell's in-class exams were typically a combination of short answer identifications and paragraph-long essays. I find one exam on Latin America consisting of 100 identifications, together with several essays, including one on the agricultural and mineral products of Columbia and another on the production and shipping of bananas.

Mr. Odell also gave us other projects. We were required to compile extensive notes about each country studied. I have my set of these. Whether they were created from class notes, the textbook, or other sources (e.g. the *World Book Encyclopedia*), I do not remember, but they are comprehensive with respect to the geography and economics of the country.[134] Each was accompanied by a map we drew. I typed them on my mother's new electric typewriter. They were graded with check marks, not letter grades. We wrote most of these after Christmas, during which time we wrote far fewer Guides. Hence our principal homework during the fall was writing the Guides, and our principal homework after Christmas was compiling these notes—together with other exercises. We assembled the notes at the end of the year for exhibit.

---

132 I have found a full folder of Guides, including this one, which was dated October 26, 1955. My recollections did not exceed reality. Sixteen questions are answered, totaling twenty pages of handwriting and four pages of maps or diagrams. Mr. Odell's comments on the top were: "Far more than is required. This is excellent work, but do not overdo it."

133 This recollection was also accurate. Grades subsequent to October 26 Guides were mostly in the 80 range.

134 For example, the Canada outline is eight single-spaced typed pages; the Mexican is four. The Brazilian is five, the British is eight, and the French is five. Virtually all of Latin America and Europe are covered, as well as several countries in the Middle East and India. As to content, these outlines include very detailed lists of geographic and economic features: climate, advantageous/disadvantageous location, important historical events, agricultural products, mineral products, industrial products, trade patterns, internal transportation features, major cities, colonies (where relevant), current issues, assets, and problems.

Another special project was to make facsimiles of national flags. I think each of us did two. In my case, I did Britain and New Zealand. These were about four feet by two-and-a-half feet or so. We used a large oilcloth with a smooth surface and a textured backing. We painted on the backing, using a special paint. We drew the outlines to scale and then painted in the colors. These were for display at some event (in the fall I believe), perhaps Parents Open House, but I do not remember exactly.

A more ambitious special project was to make a large map of a given country. Of course, I chose (or was assigned) the United States (why my flags were of Britain and New Zealand and my map was of the US, I can't remember). This was also done on the back of oilcloth, but instead of paint we used India ink—in my case black for names and boundaries, colored ink to fill in the states. I remember this well. It was a really large project. The map had to be scaled and then drawn onto the oilcloth. I put a small-scale grid on a National Geographic US map and a much larger grid on the oilcloth with the same number of lines. I then drew the map by hand, using a pencil, following national and state coastlines and boundaries, proportionally reproducing the shape of the lines from within the small squares on the National Geographic map in the larger oilcloth squares. My father had taught me this technique for enlarging drawings. There was a sizeable table in the attic that I used for this purpose. That was the easy part.

When I was satisfied that the lines were where they should be and my map in this respect resembled that of the National Geographic Society, I then traced over the pencil lines with India ink. This was harrowing because the only remedy for error was some form of white-out that really did not cover India ink unobtrusively—if you covered it successfully, the white-out stood out like the proverbial sore thumb; if the white-out was appropriately subdued, it did not cover the wretched ink. So this was a slow process. The textured back of the cloth also gave me problems, since it was impossible to do fully precise lines; the pen sputtered over the warp and filling of the fabric.

When the black ink outlines were finished, then a color scheme had to be devised so that no adjacent states had the same hue.[135] Colored India ink was

---

135 Bill Barrett reminded me of the four-color conjecture—that a map of any number of areas (e.g. states) in any configuration can be colored with just four colors so that no two adjacent states are the same color (barring more than four states meeting at a point). I had not heard of it then, but have since. It has now been proved. I didn't get my color scheme just right and had to recolor a state.

First Form (1955-56)   185

then used to fill in the states. I had several bottles. It is a miracle that I did not spill at least one—there were a few near misses. You had to work from the top down to avoid blotting. This was not always easy or successful. I drew up a schedule, and colored about three states per day. When the states had been colored in, I then used the black India ink to write in the names, the capitals, and the major cities. That would have been the easy part, except for the fact that the ink tended to run, and my printing was atrocious. Finally the miserable thing was done. I think this was the occasion when I first learned to experiment with adult swear words. It was not my best production at Moses Brown, but at least the Great Lakes were at the top, and hence, on careful examination, you could distinguish it from a map of Canada.[136]

In addition to the map, we had to prepare a booklet on the same country, stating its major geographic features and giving an historical sketch. For the USA, this was a special project, taking even more time than the map, but it was much less frustrating.[137] I remember thinking that if I made a major production of the booklet it might atone for the sins of the map. And so I produced a monster. I can remember even now sitting in the den downstairs writing this thing night after night, trying to produce as many relevant pages as possible. This was the undertaking that Mr. Odell, as noted, described to my father as "a ponderous tome." Indeed.

But aside from all my concurrent (and retrospective) complaints, this was a wonderful course and one of the most memorable in those memorable years. It was nonstop intense activity from beginning to end, driven by a rigorous curriculum and energized by a riveting personality. Looking back in detail on what we did, it seems astounding that we covered as much as we covered. The exams confirm that we learned most of it—at least for the time being. Odell challenged us in ways that we had never been challenged before, and most of us, I recall, responded positively to that challenge.

On January 20 of that year, we held a First-Form Geography Banana Party.[138] My folks invited the whole Class,[139] and all the First-Form teach-

---

136 I still have this map, but time (and possibly a mouse) have degraded parts of it with a few tears and holes.
137 I cannot find this booklet.
138 *Moses Brown Bulletin*, April 1956, p. 8.
139 The boarders were given special permission to attend.

ers to come over to our house one evening near the end of the first term for what today would be called a theme party. It was probably their substitute for the traditional birthday party that had been a frequent occurrence in the Lower School. I had also just been elected Class president, and they may have been mindful of that.

We were studying Central America in geography class, and I mentioned to Mr. Odell that my folks had taken me on a trip there several years before. He asked if we had any pictures, and I replied that we did. One thing led to another, and my folks decided to have the Class over to see the pictures. United Fruit lent a film and we asked Dorothy and Hubert Latham, friends whom we had met on the voyage, to come over and show theirs as well.

My mother set up tables in the basement and arranged a nice sit-down meal for fifty-five people or so, catered by Carr's, an East Side institution located a few blocks from our house.[140] She did some cooking herself as well, and decorated the room appropriately. She also ordered an entire stem of bananas from the United Fruit (Chiquita Banana) folks (who refused to charge her anything for it). This was hung prominently in the room.

The dinner started with a coconut fruit cup appetizer—tropical fruit in a fresh coconut shell with the coconut meat still in it.[141] During the appetizer course, the boys started humorously razing Mr. Odell. They sang "Happy Birthday" to him. They chanted, "We hate geography," and echoed with "We like shop" (Mr. F. Warren Howe, the shop teacher, was there), and "We like studio" (Mr. Leo Cole, the art teacher, was there). "We like Latin" and "We hate Latin" were also yelled in Mr. Fuller's presence. "We hate compositions" brought a smile to the face of Mr. Taber. My father, in a short introductory speech of welcome quipped that if he were Mr. Odell he would give the whole class "Ds."

"We get them anyway," someone lightly shot back.

---

140 Carr catered frequently for Brown and was given an honorary citation by the college upon his retirement from the business. His building at the corner of Angell and Brown is now owned by Brown. My mother was a frequent patron of Carr's.
141 I draw here on an account of the party written by me at the time for English class.

First Form (1955-56)

Presently the noise quieted down and the main course arrived. It consisted of an excellent chicken à la king in patty shells, accompanied by appropriate vegetables. Naturally, the dessert was a banana split, after which the tables were cleared and preparations made for the movies.

My father introduced Mr. Odell who told everyone to pay attention to the films and promised that, "There will be no test on Monday."

"There will be a humdinger on Tuesday," someone piped up from the side. Mr. Odell did not demur.

Shortly thereafter the movies began, first the United Fruit documentary explaining the life cycle of the banana, followed by the Lathams' home movies taken on the trip, narrated by my father. An alcohol-free planter's punch was served during the films.

It was truly a festive occasion, with everyone helping themselves to large amounts of bananas afterwards. Some classmates, near the end of the evening, even used a few as projectiles, and a three-foot-high (quite ugly) Jamaica jar somehow became a casualty (much to my father's amusement). Things, however, did not get totally out of hand, the jar was never missed (its twin remains in the basement today), and all passed off pleasantly. Everyone gave the impression of having had a great time.

Latin. All Upper School students were required to take at least two years of Latin. It was the tradition in a preparatory school at that time. Our instruction in this seminal language was from Mr. Frank Fuller. He was a calm and careful professional, seldom ruffled, who knew his Latin thoroughly, and who taught it quietly and methodically. In some respects he reminded me of Mr. Allen, given his deliberate manner, his ability to speak in a quietly authoritative voice, and his willingness patiently to repeat things until he was satisfied that we understood them. Now that I think of it, they both were graduates of Colby College, and were no doubt brought up in the old Maine manner. Mr. Fuller also had a master's degree from the University of Michigan. His nickname among students was "Doc Fuller" during the days before Doc Odell became "Doc."

Frank E. Fuller

He was a very careful person in many respects, and meticulously honest. Consistent with the subject he taught, he led a structured life. I'm sure that his mastery of Latin, with its tenses, cases, modifiers, and the need to assemble all this with great precision, reinforced both a strong sense of order and a careful attention to detail. In classical Latin, it was either right or wrong, and although there could be marvelous variety in expression, there were very clearly recognizable limits beyond which experimentation could not go. Mr. Fuller carried this approach to language over into English. He was advisor to the *Quaker*, the School newspaper, and was a careful critic of English expression, as many a *Quaker* editor can testify. He also taught French on occasion.

In later years I worked with him on Mr. Thomas's memoirs, which involved taping, transcribing, organizing, editing, and then copy editing the text. He was right in his element here, judiciously assessing what was—and was not—appropriate for public presentation, how the material should be arranged, and how the final text should be paragraphed (and even punctuated). It was an exercise in being true to Mr. Thomas's own words, and yet presenting them in a written, not spoken, format. I did a draft; Mr. Fuller took it from there. He was a superb editor and copy editor. I believe he had help from Mrs. Cullen in this task.

Despite his calm, formal, measured, and quite low-key persona, Mr. Fuller could relax and let his sense of humor quietly surface. He was a lot more aware of the facts of life on campus than he often let on. In private, he would occasionally recount anecdotes about student and faculty foibles and misdeeds that he never would recount in more formal and public circumstances. His sense of humor was gentle, not rollicking, but his proper Maine way of telling a good story made it all the more funny. He also liked to step out of character on occasion—relaxing with a cocktail, or putting on a fancy apron and flipping hamburgers at School events. At his retirement party, Doc Odell roasted him in front of his hundred-year-old mother, and we learned that on occasion he could break a rule or two, such as when using a forbidden hot plate to make his coffee. Only once in my experience did he lose his temper. I forget the occasion or the source, but he exploded at some group infraction and slapped a table surface full force with a yardstick. His audience was so shocked that it had a big effect. There was never, in my experience, a repeat performance.

Mr. Fuller was very interested in current events and especially recent developments in literature and the arts. He was an avid reader of the *New York Times*, its cultural portions, and especially its Book Review section. He stayed on top of his own field, but also on top of developments throughout the humanities. In his quiet New England way, he passed careful judgment on the evolving intellectual and cultural trends of the day with a commendably open-minded conservatism that tried to recognize where others were coming from. His devotion to the *Times* was deep-seated. Every Sunday morning, as a matter of routine, he would walk down to Thayer Street, buy his *Times*, and read it at a local coffee shop. Doc Odell remembered that if it was sold out on Thayer Street, Mr. Fuller would drive over to a store in Taunton, Massachusetts, which he knew would still have the Sunday edition. Sometimes Doc would accompany him.[142] I remember that when a book of mine was reviewed in the Sunday Book Review section, Mr. Fuller spotted it and called my father that same Sunday morning.

---

142 Interview, March 22, 2012.

In his class, we were taught what I assume was a standard first-year Latin curriculum.[143] Mr. Fuller followed the text closely. It began with very simple sentences, most of which used cognates. Nick Littlefield said to me that this was going to be like Dick and Jane all over again, and since we had understood Dick and Jane, we would be able to master Latin. In a sense he was right, at least for the first month or two.

We learned eight to ten new words each lesson, and, no doubt to make things easier, there were usually a few English cognates, some more obvious than others. Mr. Fuller (and the text, for that matter) went to some length to mention cognates to help us build our own English vocabulary. There was a heavy emphasis on grammar. Early on we were taught about verbs and how to conjugate them, starting with the first conjugation (*porto, portas, portat,*—to carry, for example). After learning the present and future, we were told about the "perfect" and "imperfect." These were terms we had not learned in English grammar, and I remember Mr. Fuller discussing the distinction in class, illustrated by examples—the difference in this case between "I carried," and "I was carrying." Somewhere along the way we learned the past perfect—"I had carried"; and future perfect—"I will have carried"; but I'm not sure this was in the First Form. I think we did get into passives this year—"I am carried; I was carried." *Porto* was a handy verb—the Romans were merchants and it seemed that they, their ships, their chariots, their wagons, and their litters were always carrying someone or something.

We also soon began to work our way down through the five declensions of nouns and their six cases: nominative, genitive, dative, accusative, ablative, and vocative. It did not take long to understand the first four cases (which had clear counterparts in English usage), but the proper role of the ablative seemed quite elusive, as it should, and as for the vocative, how often did we go around talking to the furniture ("O Desk, thou art a solid place whereon to set a pad of paper...")? The last point was hastily conceded by Mr. Fuller, and he somewhat lamely admitted that this case was used mostly in poetry. Early on we were introduced to gender distinctions in nouns, and I assume we were not the first class to ask Mr. Fuller why sailors were feminine.

---

143 Our text was *Using Latin, Book I,* Chicago: Scott Foresman and Company, 195(?).

We also learned adjectival forms early, and how they were supposed to fit with the nouns. And then there were the pronouns. The nouns we had learned down the column—*nauta, nautae,* etc.—but the pronouns we learned across: *hic, haec, hoc*; *huius, huius, huius*.... All this was a bit confusing, but Mr. Fuller explained it with steady patience and had answers to all our questions—which, no doubt, he had heard many times before. At one point to levitate our task he had us decline *hocus pocus*: including *hoci poci, hocibus pocibus,* etc. He wisely did not explain to us from whence cometh "*hocus pocus*" itself, as it might have given offense.

There were no pyrotechnics in class. Mr. Fuller was not a theatrical person. His instruction was calm and matter-of-fact, point by point. But he did take a great interest in each of us and was willing to work with us outside of class if we needed help. He was a very careful and meticulous person. He explained Latin grammar point by point, patiently going over it several times if we did not understand it. He frequently used examples from English to illustrate his points in Latin. He was fair and even-handed. He appreciated hard work and effort, and patiently took them into account. This was lucky for me since languages were one of my most difficult challenges.

I did have some help at home. My father, who never went to college, had seven years of Latin at Boston Latin School when that institution was the leading grammar school and high school in the country. He knew his Latin and could easily drill me in my exercises. Aunt Amey, who was a linguist, also knew her Latin, and I got encouragement from that quarter as well. I remember that Mr. Littlefield (Bancroft Littlefield, Sr.) was accomplished in Latin, and when I visited the Littlefields during this year (which was frequent), he would speak to us in Latin, use Latin phrases, and generally offer encouragement.

Our text, which I no longer have, started with very simple sentences (*Casa nostra alba est*; *America patria nostra est*), and fairly soon graduated to simple paragraphs and then to simple stories, as vocabulary was added. Most of the tales were about things Roman. I remember we read some stories about the founding of Rome, its gods, its architecture, its lifestyle, and its customs. The short narratives were interspaced with grammar lessons, lists of new vocabulary, and, occasionally, with small topics of interest written in English about life in Rome. The latter were probably to encourage attention to the larger subject matter. The text was well illustrated with black and white and color pictures. Each chapter contained practice exercises.

Our homework was to read and understand the assigned portions of the text, memorize the new vocabulary words, and do the exercises. We were frequently tested on the reading—the vocabulary and the grammar. Our homework and our tests included both translation and composition. Early on, when we did not remember the meaning of a Latin word, we thumbed back in the text to find it. Later on, we began to use the vocabulary list at the rear of the book. Our exams were closed book—and for them we had to remember the vocabulary to do the translations.

Although at the onset the prospect of learning a new language was exciting, the experience itself became a daunting challenge. I kept on top of things for a few months, but the seeming rapidity with which new vocabulary and new declensions, conjugations, tenses, voices, and usages hit me was eventually overwhelming, and I fell behind, never really to recover. My interest in Rome and the ancient world never flagged, but I also never sustained the vocabulary needed to read an advanced text on my own, and I was therefore condemned to use the dictionary for large percentages of words in a given paragraph. Translating Caesar and Cicero (which we did in Second and Third Forms) was therefore a very slow and tedious process. It is interesting how a memory can retain some input very well, and other input hardly at all. Obviously, I never used good mnemonics to master vocabulary or grammatical forms in Latin.

Mr. Fuller also spent time talking about Rome and Roman society. This was not an extensive part of the First-Year Latin course—his diversions were limited in scope and fairly infrequent in number. I do, however, remember him discussing a recent historical novel he had just read—it had "Wine" in the title. He even read us a few passages. One of the characters in it explained why she went to the Roman circus to see gladiators eviscerating each other: because she had been brought up to do this and it was part of her cultural tradition. It was therefore in her opinion all right to have such games and for her to watch them. Mr. Fuller was struck by the passage, and I have never forgotten it either.

First Form (1955-56)

Howard M. Roberts

Mathematics. Mr. Howard Roberts taught us math. His nickname among many students was "Mr. Peepers" from the TV character played by Wally Cox. This appellation was based more on his appearance (especially his glasses) than on his personality. He was, I think, fairly new to Moses Brown, and this was his last year there. He was a graduate of Earlham College in Indiana and had a master's degree in mathematics from Penn. I have it in mind that he was doing some postgraduate work at Brown at that time. He knew his subject matter very well and was clearly interested in teaching. He was also an amateur magician.

I believe that the textbook we used was entitled *Modern Practical Arithmetic*.[144] This was designed for both the Seventh and Eighth Grades, and there was some repetition of our previous year's instruction. In many ways the course was a review of Seventh Grade topics, but at a higher level. As its title implies, the text continued the Lower School tradition of teaching math that would have practical applications. I suspect that it was also used to ensure that students coming into the Upper School from outside of

---

144 By Haynes, I.M., Gibson, C.S., Bodley, G.R., and Watson, B.M.: Boston, D.C. Heath, 1926. The book is divided into "Seventh Grade" and "Eighth Grade" sections. I am almost certain that this was used in First-Form (Eighth Grade) math.

Moses Brown were brought up to the level of those coming from the Lower School, if this was needed.

We had an extensive review of percentages, and learned about discounts, markups and markdowns, interest rates, commissions, tax rates, and the like. We did exercises in rounding. We spent serious time on measurements, sizes, areas, and volumes, including those calculated by basic geometry—the areas of parallelograms and trapezoids, for example, or the volume of solids like cylinders: how much water is there in an eight-inch-tall can with a three-inch diameter that is three-quarters filled? Things like that. We also did conversions—from miles to kilometers (or inches to centimeters), for example, and quite a bit with angles—adding and subtracting degrees and learning how to label parts of a geometric figure. In this context, we spent considerable time on geometric constructions with a straight edge, compass, and protractor. We learned how to label geometric diagrams, and calculate how many degrees there were between the various points on a compass.

We also studied proportion and reviewed once more how to calculate the heights of buildings from the length of shadows. We spent some time on roots and powers, and were showed again how manually to calculate square roots. We also spent some time on how to read and make pie graphs, bar graphs, and line graphs. There were also problem sets. These the text divided into problems for boys and problems for girls—the latter focusing on domestic tasks like measuring cloth, keeping budgets, and counting calories for balanced diets. I assume we were assigned the boys' list—that included calculations mostly relevant to agriculture.

There was not a lot of new mathematics in the First Form, just new practical applications of mathematics we had already been exposed to. I would not argue that the year was wasted in this respect, but looking back, we might have really done some strong preliminary work in algebra that would have advanced things for the following year.

Mr. Roberts was very bright, and he brought some concepts to the classroom that were not in the text. One such concept was that of significant figures, namely that in measurements the answer to a problem could not contain more significant figures than were found in any of the components used to calculate it. This led to an intellectual confrontation. In my literalist approach, I argued with him that if you had a yardstick 36 inches long and you sawed .39682 inches off of it, you then had a stick 35.60418 inches in length, and that was that. Mr. Roberts insisted that for this to be the case, the yardstick had to be 36.00000 inches long to begin with, not 36 inches, or your result was meaningless. I remember asking him how big the difference was between 36 inches and 36.00000 inches. I was looking at numbers themselves as abstractions; he was looking at them in this case as measurements. No doubt he was right, but we used to banter humorously about this for quite some time. Bill Brehm reminds me that Mr. Roberts had an exasperating habit of refusing to answer questions or to clarify ambiguities during exams. On all occasions when you asked him a question under these circumstances he would respond, "Use your own discretion." No doubt we learned some new concepts in this class, but it seemed more like an elaborate review session than an advance to a higher level.

English. First-Form English was taught to us by Mr. William P. Taber, a young instructor, new to Moses Brown. He had graduated from William Penn College and held a master's degree from the University of Pittsburgh. He was an excellent teacher—energetic, enthusiastic, and on top of his subject, with a wonderful sense of humor. There was always a smile on his face, he came to know each of us very well, and he could be directly engaging. As noted, he was a Quaker, as were several other faculty (including Mr. Cole, Mr. Howe, Mr. Roberts, and the St. Johns). He had served time in jail for being a conscientious objector, although he never mentioned it, and I didn't know about it until many years later. There was absolutely no bitterness in his style or persona stemming from this.

First-Form English featured a mix of literature, grammar, and writing, as would be expected in a Moses Brown English class. We had an anthology of both American and English literature entitled *Good Times through Literature*.[145] After a few introductory readings, we spent a lot of October covering the section in the anthology entitled "Neighbors around the World." Some of the stories were about personal neighbors; some were about national

---

[145] Pooley, Poley, Leyda, and Zellhoefer, Chicago: Scott Foresman, 1951.

William P. Taber, Jr.

neighbors and foreign cultures, from Britain to Mexico to China. We also read about the United Nations. Mr. Taber took this opportunity to show us the foreign and sometimes non-European origins of many English words (e.g. bazaar, gingham, typhoon, caravan, macaroon). Each story in this anthology was followed by a section asking us what we thought about the tale and another section discussing the author's craft.

We then proceeded to mystery and adventure stories, such as the Sherlock Holmes thriller "The Speckled Band" (with which I had been familiar for many years), a wonderful story called "A Battle over the Teacups" in which a Chinese general is finessed by an agent into demanding that they reverse teacups during a meal—so he actually ended up drinking from the one with the poison in it—and Poe's "Telltale Heart." Mr. Taber gave us a dramatic rendition of the last in class, with the heart beating louder and louder as he read it to us. He was an excellent performer with a lot of panache, and he gave dramatic readings quite frequently. His class was always interesting and I looked forward to it. We could see how much he enjoyed short stories, drama, and poetry, and as he shared his enjoyment with us, literature came alive and his excitement became contagious.

Fred Schwartz remembered one occasion when a different class was reading Ben Franklin's autobiography (this may have been in the Third Form—some of us had Mr. Taber twice). In any event, there was a sexual allusion in the text (he used the word "venery"). Someone asked what it meant, and Mr. Taber, newly married, and a devout Quaker, blushed beet red and did his best to explain it to the class without actually explaining it to the class. Fred recalled that, "Some of us never understood what he meant until later in life, by which time it was too late."

We read other short stories in First-Form English, and many of these had a moral to them, usually about individuals overcoming adversity, or young people developing character and maturity. For example, we read a story about persistence in winning a track meet. We also read about a public physical fight between father and son during which the son realized that he was representing the morally wrong end of things and let the father win. There was a marvelous story about a Welsh mother unexpectedly standing up and singing in a contest, defeating her husband, so he would agree to send their son to music school. There were stories and poems about American heroes Elizabeth Blackwell, Lou Gehrig, Helen Keller, Father Damien of Molokai, and Booker T. Washington.

A large section in the reader consisted of early chapters from *David Copperfield*, probably about a quarter of the novel—enough, anyway, to introduce us to the Murdstones, Betsy Trotwood and Mr. Dick, Peggoty and Barkus, Wilkins Macawber, and Uriah Heep. I think we were also introduced to Steerforth, but did not get to the later stages of his evolving role. This introduced me seriously to Dickens. For outside reading that year, I remember attempting *Bleak House*, (an exercise that produced a few jeers from my classmates). I later tackled the less daunting *Great Expectations*, *A Tale of Two Cities*, and *Oliver Twist*. I also continued reading the D'Artagnan romances, including *Twenty Years Later, The Vicomte de Bragelonne, Louise de la Villaire*, and *Ten Years After*. I never reached *Man in the Iron Mask*. I remember writing a book review of *Bleak House*, and have found reviews of the first two Musketeer books. In addition, I read Perry Burgess's *We Walk Alone* (about a leper colony).

We read the Pyramis and Thisbe play within a play from *A Midsummer's Night's Dream*. In fact, we acted it out in class. Mr. Taber rearranged the chairs to create a theater in the round, parts were assigned, and we read them out loud. Someone was a wall, a floor, a moonbeam, and so forth. I remember that Frank Abella acted out a part that ended up with him being ceremoniously and eloquently dispatched in true Shakespearean fashion. When we had our next exam, part of it was simply to identify by name something we had studied on the basis of a clue provided by Mr. Taber. "Perched on a bust of Pallas," for example might have been a clue for "The Raven." "Abella on the floor" was the clue for Pyramis.

In this anthology there was a section on literary devices, including limericks, puns, and humor. The famous Lady from Niger who smiled as she rode on the tiger was offered as an example of the first. Another such example was the equally famous Nan taking the bucket. We had an assignment to bring a limerick to class, and my father offered a favorite:

> There once was a man from Crewe
> Who found a mouse in his stew.
> Said the waiter, "Don't shout
> And waft it about,
> Or others will want one too."

The limericks were all quite clean in First-Form English. One had to await a later date to appreciate the full possibilities of the genre.

Puns were described as "coppers on a track" that upset the freight train of a conversation. An example of a pun that was offered in the text was Mercutio's dying words in *Romeo and Juliet* after he had been stabbed: "Tis not as deep as a well or as wide as a church door, but 'tis enough, 'twill serve. Ask for me tomorrow and you will find me a grave man."

There was a section on humor which included Ernest L. Thayer's "Casey at the Bat" (... "But there is no joy in Mudville—Mighty Casey has struck out"), Robert W. Service's "The Cremation of Sam McGee," O. Henry's "Ransom of Red Chief," and Stephen Leacock's "My Financial Career." There was also a ditty, written by Ogden Nash, entitled "The Purist." I memorized it, and have never forgotten it because I have encountered in the academic world many individuals like the hero in the poem:

> I give you now Professor Twist,
> A conscientious scientist.
> The Trustees said, "He never bungles,"
> And sent him off to distant jungles.
>
> Encamped on a tropic riverside,
> He chanced to miss his loving bride.
> She had, a guide informed him later,
> Been eaten by an alligator.
>
> Professor Twist could not but smile:
> "You mean," he said, "a *crocodile*."

Classes themselves were lively and engaging. Mr. Taber often posed questions and sought our opinions in the discussions of the material we had read. We were encouraged to speak and to ask questions. I forget how the topic arose, but on one occasion we asked him what communism was—maybe a follow-through from a session earlier that day with Mr. Odell. In any case, Mr. Taber agreed to hold a special discussion after class to explain it to us—and this led to the formation of the Discussion Club (as described in Volume II) which he agreed to advise, and which often met in his apartment.

We also read poetry in class. I remember Mr. Taber's very dramatic rendition of Vachel Lindsay's "Boomalay, Boomalay, Boomalay, Boom" done in sustained rhythm with much modulation in the level of sound—from a whisper to a shout. It certainly got our attention.

And then we studied grammar. I do not remember the text,[146] but I do have a workbook that accompanied the anthology. Mr. Taber spent a lot of time on grammar and on diagraming sentences. We had diagramed a lot in the Lower School, but now we did it with very complex sentences and with all sorts of participial phrases, gerunds, infinitives, and the like. I can remember how some of these phrases would be put up on lines mounted on top of little posts placed on the main horizontal line of the diagram. Others would be on posts rising from lines hanging underneath the main line. At

---

146 Apparently there was one; I see reference to it on our assignment sheets.

times a symbol, such as a triangle, was placed under the line to identify the grammatical form. Some modifiers went at angles to the main line.[147] Mr. Taber gave us rules for doing this and made a game out of them. I found it to be a lot of fun. I remember on one exam he had us diagram the sentences in Lewis Carroll's "Jabberwocky," much to the amusement of the class. It can easily be done: even though many words are nonsense, the structure of the sentences and the role of each word in those sentences is clear, and hence the whole is diagram-able.

Mr. Taber also gave us direct instruction in participles (and how to avoid dangling ones), participial phrases, prepositional phrases, compound sentences, and complex sentences. We were told how not to split infinitives (today a lost cause), and how not to misplace modifiers. From the assignment for February 3, 1956:

"Today we will study adjective and noun dependent clauses. ... Learn the adjective clause openers. Write five sentences containing adjective clauses. .... Then diagram at least three of those sentences. Next, write five sentences with noun clauses, being sure to use one as a subject, one as the direct object of the verb, one as a predicate noun, one as the object of a participle, and one as the object of a preposition. Finally, diagram three of these."

And for February 6, in anticipation of a test:

> Don't forget to review the definitions of clauses and phrases, the coordinating conjunctions, relative pronouns, adjective clause openers, the use of adverb clauses, the use of adjective and noun clauses, the punctuation of compound sentences, the punctuation of adverb clauses, the punctuation of adjective clauses. Then it should be easy.

He also showed us how to streamline our sentences, but he was not a stickler for parsimony; rather he was a stickler for logic—sentences constructed rationally and according to common sense so the meaning was clear. I am sure that this extensive treatment of grammar was designed not only to strengthen our understanding of English, but also to prepare us to study

---

147 Some of this could have come in the Second Form with Nichols, but I think we did these complicated diagrams with infinitives, etc., in the First Form.

foreign languages, which in those days were taught with extensive reference to grammar.

Our workbook contained many different exercises, some on pronunciation, some on grammar, many designed to build vocabulary, and many designed to build and test comprehension. These were presented in attractive and interesting formats, often using pictures and cartoons. Many could be considered games and puzzles. Mr. Taber used them selectively, but these exercises added to the variety of what we did in class.

We also wrote a lot. We were asked to write reviews (often in response to directed questions) about the stories we read in our anthology. And then there were the usual book reviews. In the Lower School we had been asked to describe our favorite passage in the book we reviewed; now we were asked to discuss "something about the plot..., something about the main character (or a character who interested you), and ... how you felt about the book after you had read it."[148] Sometimes books were assigned; sometimes we could make our own choices. Barry Fain remembered that on one occasion a book review was due the next day and he hadn't read anything. He discovered that Bob Dean and a third classmate were in the same boat. So they decided to improvise. They made up a fictitious book, gave it a title and publisher, and proceeded to review it. Two of them liked it and one of them did not. They wrote their reviews, submitted them, and succeeded in pulling it off. When they got their papers back with different grades, however, they complained to each other, but didn't dare take the matter up with Mr. Taber![149]

I don't remember many details about our First-Form essays (he called them "themes"), but I have found a few: an "Adventure in a Shoe Shine

---

148 From assignment sheet, October 10, 1955.
149 Barry, who joined our Class in the Third Grade, and stayed through Upper School graduation, received his bachelor's degree from the University of Pennsylvania, graduated from Columbia Business School, worked for an advertising firm in New York, and then returned to Providence where he joined and expanded the family retail carpeting business throughout New England. He then founded *The East Side Monthly*, a sophisticated journal of news and commentary for that socially prominent neighborhood, which contains Brown University and the Rhode Island School of Design, and is arguably the intellectual center of Rhode Island. Few, if any, locales in New England have a dedicated newspaper of this quality. Barry remains its editor and publisher in 2020, presiding over an impressive staff of writers. This is one of six regional weeklies in Rhode Island owned by Barry.

Parlor" (a first-person fictional account in which I discovered I had no money with me and could not explain this to the German-speaking proprietor), "A Night to Remember" (a description of the geography class banana party mentioned above—whose title was no doubt cribbed from the movie of that name about the *Titanic*), "A Place I used to Live" (a description of our home in Methuen, Massachusetts), "Better Neighbors make a Better World" (Mr. Tabor, not surprisingly, liked this essay), "Trash Collection on our Street" (in Providence), "My Puppy on a Spree" (about Pluto's antics), "A Rush to the Snack Bar" (at Moses Brown), and "The Farm in Springtime" (a descriptive pastoral). These essays were about 250-400 words in length. Apparently there were a few attempts at fiction, but most were descriptive and recounted real experiences, as the titles suggest. Whether we were mainly limited to descriptive essays or whether it was just my imagination that was limited, I do not recall. My essays were not especially exciting, and received grades in both the "B" and "A" range.

Every so often Mr. Taber took the class to the Upper School library, the domain of Mrs. Helen Paxton, which was located at the back of Alumni Hall. She described the collection to us. We were taught about Dewey and his decimal system, instructed on how to use a card catalogue, and shown how to find books in the stacks. During some of the time we were there, we also read.

Mr. Taber's classes were always enjoyable. Part of this came from personality and willingness to let us participate in discussions, but another important reason was the quality, and especially the variety, of the materials we read. Many were adventure stories, many were humorous, and many were about people our age. All seemed entertaining. Added to the variety found in the reading was the variety we encountered in class: oral reports, discussions, trips to the library, diagramming sentences at the board, listening to well-spoken poetry, reading plays, acting in skits—questions and more questions. Despite the course being well-structured and well thought out, we seldom knew exactly what to expect from Mr. Taber when we came through the door, and that was exciting. Things never dragged. All in all, First-Form English was a very engaging and memorable experience, an excellent example of how an instructor can make a real difference in bringing a subject alive in the classroom. We were sorry that Mr. Taber left Moses Brown a few years later.

Art. We had art once a week with Mr. Cole, whom we knew well from our many years in Lower School shop. His focus this year was on making artifacts. One example was an ashtray. To create this, we placed a copper disc on top of a wooden mold with an appropriately shaped depression and then hammered it down into the mold until it formed a tray with sides bending up. Into this tray we placed a layer of ground glass, and then decorated it in patterns with minute glass pieces of another color. We fired the result with a Bunsen burner to melt the glass into a glaze. It is possible that we ourselves did part of the firing with the Bunsen burner and more was done by Mr. Cole in a kiln, but I am not sure. I do remember our being instructed on how to light and use the Bunsen.

I think we also did ceramic work in First-Form art: monogrammed tiles on which to place hot dishes; vases; and more ashtrays. I don't remember us using a potter's wheel in the First Form, but those who continued with art after this year used one later on. We fashioned these artifacts from clay, coated them with a glaze, and then left them for Mr. Cole to fire in the kiln. I'm sure we made prints using linoleum blocks on which we carved designs with little gouges (I seem to remember making Christmas cards in this fashion). Some of us made jewelry, fashioning a ring from copper or silver that featured a large glass stone. I'm sure there were other projects, but these are the ones I remember. I was not very good at any of this, but soldiered on. Others were indeed very good at art and crafting.

Mr. Cole was very patient with all of us throughout. I remember him for his positive attitude and good sense of humor. In the Second Form we had to choose between art and shop, and I chose the latter. Half the Class, however, chose art. After the Second Form a few gifted classmates were given the opportunity to continue their art work with Mr. Cole on a tutorial basis. Al Crandon[150] from our Class did this and has the highest of praise

---

150 Al Crandon joined our Class in the Fourth Form. He attended Beloit College for two years and then, with the help of Mr. Cole, was admitted to the Columbia School of Architecture in New York, where he earned his bachelor of architecture degree. Joining the Army after graduation, he served in Vietnam where he was a Civil Affairs officer—"which meant doing good deeds in bad places." While in Vietnam, he developed the use of ferro-cement for boat building. He designed and built boats for Vietnamese fishermen that were more rugged and enduring than those made from wood. He built a large boat for himself, which he used to transport refuges from Vietnam to Singapore at the time of Saigon's collapse. After the war, he remained in the area, living in Singapore, where he built an interior design business, designing the interiors of 70 banks and of the Singapore offices of large American corporations, including GE and Raytheon. When relations resumed with Hanoi, he designed the interior spaces for a large number of American corporations who opened offices there. He retired to Duxbury, Massachusetts.

for Mr. Cole's artistic talents and his careful work with these special students.[151] He learned a lot from him and credits Mr. Cole for inspiring him to continue to use his artistic talents beyond high school. As Al remembered, "Leo Cole was a great teacher. His secret was to identify a student's special talent and then amplify it. In my case it was drawing—he encouraged me to draw, gave me the facilities, and offered constructive advice. He would plant a seed and make sure it grew. Drawings I did at Moses Brown helped gain me admission to the art program at Columbia."[152] Al became a naval architect as his life's profession.

Shop. Mr. F. Warren Howe, Jr., taught us shop once a week in the First Form, and this was my initial experience with this marvelous person. I worked with him again in shop in the Second Form and for two years after that as "assistant manager" and then "manager" of the track team, which he coached. "Junie" Howe—a nickname we were told he did not like—also taught Mechanical Drawing, and many took that class with him in the Third Form or later.

He was indeed a wonderful person, almost always with a smile on his face. He and Mr. Odell were good examples of the adage, "The worse the hat, the better the person." As an instructor, he was very patient with us in shop. He worked with us on plans and then on execution. He was well-trained himself, and he was a very careful worker, moving deliberately around the room between the workbenches in his neat smock, carefully reviewing with us how to use the power tools, quietly showing us how to get the results we wanted, and calmly giving us good advice. He allowed our ambitions to define the task, and then showed us how to modulate them to achieve a plausible result. He connected with us quickly and always showed a lot of enthusiasm for our projects. He had an encouraging air about him. You liked him instinctively, and were willing to work hard to achieve his approval.

Mr. Howe also liked chocolate pudding. This was often served at lunch where he presided as the master at one of the tables. Bill Brehm recalled

---
151 Telephone interview, August 16, 2016.
152 *Ibid.*

that when the pudding came, Mr. Howe invariably tried to talk some of the boys out of eating their portion: "Now you don't really want to eat any pudding, today, do you? That pudding really doesn't look all that good today, does it?" And then, when he succeeded in dissuading someone from partaking of the pudding, he would, good-naturedly, with a smile and a chuckle, say that it shouldn't go to waste, and serve the portion to himself.

In shop, we were introduced to power tools in a serious way. We were now permitted to use the old band saw, which must have been a museum piece even in those days. I hope the School still has it—if it does, the Smithsonian might be envious. I'll bet it had been in that shop since the late nineteenth century. Despite its antiquity—or perhaps because of it—this was a very useful machine. We could cut anything on it, and in any shape. It was potentially dangerous, although it had guards. We were instructed in how to use it, and this was a vast improvement over having to saw wood by hand. We were also introduced to the lathe. Again, we were given careful instructions about how and where to hold the tools we used on the lathe to shape the wood (e.g., always place the tool on the horizontal guide bar before letting it touch the wood so it would not fly out of your hand). It had some safety devices, but like the band saw it was a potentially dangerous piece of equipment. We were not supposed to stand near it when others were using it.

We were also shown how to use a power drill, a power sander, and a power jigsaw. Mr. Howe had a router (which hollowed out wood or shaped an edge), but we were not permitted to use this, at least not in the First Form. If we had a project that required its use, Mr. Howe would run it for us.

With these tools, we could now move woodworking to a different level from that we were used to in Lower School. I liked using the lathe. I remember turning a fairly large bowl under Mr. Howe's close instruction. I glued several pieces of wood together, bonding them with a special adhesive. We used clamps to do this and let it sit for at least a week so the glue could fully set. I remember Mr. Howe telling me how important it was to get this right so the pieces would not fly apart when we put it on the lathe. I then sawed the bonded boards into a circle, mounted the wood on the lathe, and shaped the bowl, using several different tools. The first step was to shape the outside into a smooth circle curving inward towards the base.

Then, under his instructions, I shaped the inside, working outward from the center. Finally, I shaped the lip.

I also used the lathe to make a gavel for my mother, first turning the head, and then turning the handle. When these were glued together I stained it and later waxed it. She used this for many years to keep order among the gentle ladies of the Roger Williams Family, the Colonial Daughters, and the DAR. I also turned out a potato masher. I still have all three of these artifacts. Some of my classmates turned out baseball bats. These were one of Mr. Howe's specialties. He had high-quality ash wood set aside for this purpose. I think he also had special birch wood set aside for breadboards and butcher blocks. I enjoyed this class very much in the First Form and looked forward to working with him in the Second.

Music. We had regular instruction in music this year, meeting once a week, I believe. Our instructor was Mr. William Reifsnyder, a graduate of Yale College with a master's degree in music, also from Yale. He was a young guy and a competent lecturer, as I recall, but I really don't remember much more about him. The class met in the Music Room at the Power House. He was very interested in jazz, and he had us purchase a music appreciation book that discussed jazz in a formal way. We read this book and may have been tested on it, although I am not sure of that. I do, however, remember him using the blackboard, and I was interested in his five-piece chalk holder, with which he could draw a staff in one motion.

Part way through the year he was apparently instructed to prepare us better for singing in Chapel. This was a bit distant from jazz, but he responded to the request. I remember we learned to sing a few hymns which subsequently appeared on the Chapel program. These included "God of our Fathers, Whose Almighty Hand....," a hymn that is supposed to begin with a trumpet flourish, which Mr. Fuller imitated on the piano with great gusto. Another was "For all the Saints who from their Labors Rest" whose militant lines seemed at the time oddly out of place at a Quaker school—although we also sang "Onward Christian Soldiers" in Chapel. We also learned "Once to Every Man and Nation Comes the Moment to Decide." I don't think I had ever heard this in church before, but have since, and

First Form (1955-56)

it reminds me of Mr. Reifsnyder and Moses Brown Chapel. I think there were several other hymns we learned with him, but I do not remember which ones.

Some of us tried out for Glee Club, which I think was still directed by Mr. Kennedy, but I did not. I do remember an excellent concert they gave at Alumni Hall, and I think it was this year.

Bible. We had a class featuring the *Bible* with Mr. and Mrs. St. John. I think she taught the fall session and he taught the spring session. This met once a week in Alumni Hall. We learned about the *Bible* itself—its origins, authors, and translations (ancient and modern). We were taught about its historicity, given some sense of chronology and dates, and introduced to the *Bible* as poetry and genealogy. But the main focus was on the *Bible* as the source of lesson. We read portions of the Old Testament through the beginning of Kings, concentrating on Genesis, Exodus, and both Samuels, with a few stories from Numbers, Deuteronomy, Judges, and Daniel. For the New Testament, we read the Book of Matthew.

This meant that we covered the Creation; Adam and Eve; Noah; the Tower of Babel; Abraham, Isaac, Jacob, and Joseph; Moses, the Passover, and the escape from Egypt; the Ten Commandments and the Golden Calf; the death of Moses; Joshua and the fall of Jericho; Samuel, Saul, David, and Solomon. Also, we read the stories of Daniel in the lion's den and of Shadrach, Meshach, and Abednego in the fiery furnace. We were also given a brief history of the Jewish people after the death of Solomon down to the Roman conquest. Finally, we studied the ministry of Jesus as presented in the first Gospel, with an emphasis on the Nativity, the early ministry, and especially the Sermon on the Mount. About three-quarters of the course was on the Old Testament and about a quarter on the New.

Mrs. St. John was a tall, attractive woman, plainly dressed, probably in her late forties at the time. She was articulate, yet soft-spoken. A graduate of Radcliffe, she was obviously quite intelligent and well-read. I got the sense that she was a very cultivated person and a strong one. We were supposed to read passages for each session, but often we didn't, and she would have

The St. Johns and Thomases

Mrs. Nancy St. John at lunch with (L–R at top) Fred Schwartz, Herb Sawyer, and Vin Buonnano

to teach the passages without much comment from us.[153] This did not seem to daunt her. She was always well-prepared, certainly controlled the class well, and was fully in command of the proceedings.

Mr. St. John was more easygoing. He seemed to be an excellent scholar: he was a Harvard graduate with a master's degree in education; he had also studied at Corpus Christi College at Cambridge University in England; he came from a family of educators. He was a calm and quiet person, a subscriber to Quaker values. He was intellectually sophisticated and thoughtful. His presentations were more tentative than those of his wife, but clearly based on erudition. I remember him talking quite a bit about David, whom he described in an attractive light. During one of these sessions, I launched a full-scale attack on David, either in a presentation or in response to a question. David strayed quite a bit at times—the Uriah episode, Bathsheba generally, his handling of Absalom—and all this gave me the opportunity to make the iconoclastic point that David was not all that he had been cracked up to be by his admirers. Mr. St. John listened carefully and respectfully to my points, scratched his head (literally) as if all this was something that had not occurred to him before (although I'm sure it had), and gently responded that perhaps there was something to what I had said, but that I must not forget David's virtues as well. Having made my case, I did not press the matter, and adopting Mr. St. John's own approach, conceded that he, too, might have a point. So things passed off pleasantly. Mr. St. John really did seem like a very nice person.

Was this *Bible* course taught from a "Quaker" standpoint? If so, it was done very gently, as appropriate. In the Quaker tradition, as I understand it, religious truth is sought in scripture, in contemplation, and in an understanding of the perspectives and values of others, and not in the fiats of human authority. It is reverently sought, often in silence, and the journey itself is part of the lesson. Those truths are strongest that one finds on one's own. Teaching the *Bible* in the Quaker tradition, therefore, was an exercise in acquainting students with the scriptural building blocks from which they could eventually develop their own understandings and convictions.

---

153 Our negligence probably stemmed from the fact that the course was not supposed to count for much, if anything, to our overall average, but we did receive grades on our papers. Whether the course itself was pass/fail or ungraded, I do not remember.

In the Old Testament section of the course, the Creation, including the story of Adam and Eve, was respectfully treated as important legend; not as a strictly literal account, but as legend still containing inspired lessons for us. The stories from Abraham on down were treated as fully real—these were real people living in real time through real events—but their significance was presented in terms of what their lives and choices told us about God and what God expects of us. With the exception of the Ten Commandments themselves, to which we were powerfully introduced (and which we were asked to memorize),[154] we were not taught the "answers," but how to explore the questions to find answers for ourselves. The St. Johns were not there to lay down the law, but to let us explore and identify on our own what was, nevertheless, still the law. By the time we had finished the Old Testament portion of the course, we were expected to know the major figures and the generally recognized main events of the *Bible* through Solomon. Although most of this was taught as history, it was didactic history respectfully taught from a sacred text. We did not study Job, Psalms, Ecclesiastes, or the major prophets in *Bible*—although we were introduced to many of them and their sayings throughout our years at Moses Brown, sometimes at Chapel, sometimes by speakers, sometimes in ceremonies.

The New Testament portion of the course was from Matthew. We began by studying the Christmas Story and the story of John the Baptist. We then studied Jesus's early ministry, including the temptations and the recruitment of the Disciples. The main part of our study of Matthew centered on the Sermon on the Mount, which we explored in some detail. The following are examples (from the course outline) of questions to be raised in class about the Sermon:

- What sort of people does Jesus call "Blessed" in the Beatitudes—the strong, the successful, the cheery, the ambitious, the rich, the poor, the good?

- What does Jesus say about following Jewish law? Does this conflict with his attitude towards the Pharisees at other times?

---

154 I find two quizzes on the Ten Commandments in my papers—on one of these I listed eight, forgetting taking the name of the Lord in vain and honoring thy father and mother; on the other (hopefully subsequent) one, I listed nine, forgetting only the graven images.

First Form (1955-56)

- What does Jesus say about anger? What are good ways of managing our own anger?

- What does Jesus consider more important than the offering of a gift at the altar?

- Quakers have often refused to take legal oaths. Why have they refused?

- Do you think "turning the other cheek" makes a friend out of the attacker?

- Do you know examples of people who have "loved their enemies" and been able to turn enemies into friends?

- What kind of treasure is safe from moths and rust?

- How does Matthew phrase the Golden Rule?

- What do we learn about Jesus from the report that "he taught them as one who had authority"?

I do not recall in any detail the discussions in class resulting from questions such as these, but I do recall Mr. St. John's moderate and deliberate style in leading those discussions, and I therefore expect that such issues were explored, gently, but perhaps systematically, by letting our opinions unfold. This would certainly have been the Quaker approach. As a church-owned religious school, Moses Brown aimed to teach students by exposing them to religious ideas and beliefs, but it was committed not to indoctrinate them, a commitment appreciated by the parents of many faiths whose children attended the School.

We had exams in this class, but most of the questions were factual, not interpretive. We also wrote a few biographies of Old Testament figures.

Study Hall. A discussion of the Upper School learning experience would be incomplete without a description of study hall. The study hall space itself contained about 150 desks, with eighth graders seated in the front rows. We migrated back, year by year until, as seniors, our desks were in the rear. The boarding students studied in their rooms and sat on benches in study hall during morning Chapel exercises. This large chamber occupied the west half of the second floor of the large wing west of Middle House. It had tall windows on three sides and there was a lot of light. There was an elevated desk near the middle of the north wall where the study hall master or proctor sat and kept order. The student desks faced east, and in front of them next to the east wall was an elevated podium from which speakers could address the assembly of students, typically during Chapel each morning. Separating study hall from Middle House itself were classrooms, a stairwell, and a lounge area. For a more detailed description of study hall and the Upper School classrooms, see Appendix I.

As in Lower School, we had our individual desks, and they were crammed with books, papers, pens, and pencils. Some pasted pictures on the lid. We spent about a third of our hours in what was called "study hall," a designated part of the daily schedule. Supposedly this was to do homework, but it was free time for any purpose, and we could read or work on projects, or carry on surreptitious conversations with our neighbors either by directed whisper or by passing notes. In the First Form, Peter Sanderson sat in front of me, and until the room settled down into a study mode, we frequently played a game in which we locked hands and tried to pin the other person's thumb down with our own.[155]

Study hall time for the day students took place in the study hall chamber itself. Boarders did their study hall time in their own rooms during the day. Time was also set aside for study hall sessions in the evening. In the early years, there was always a master presiding over the room; by our senior year, students were allowed to do this. Each person presiding had his own style. I remember Mr. Herman walking down from the front of the room in that funny gait of his, mounting the desk, and sitting there like an oriental pasha. He was always a presence. From time to time he would spot non-permitted behavior and bellow out, "Sydlowski ['59], you dizzy ape, stop that this instant." If the intended result was not produced, he would come down and deal with matters more directly, at times humorously

---

155 Peter Sanderson left Moses Brown after the Second Form.

shaking his fist in someone's face, or faking a swipe at them, but always with a twinkle in his eye. Everyone liked him and his gruff manners, but no one would cross him, and so with such occasional forays he was able to control things very well.

Mr. Raines, head of the History Department, who in our Second-Form year was given the title of Dean and put in charge of discipline, also could control us. His manner was very different—he wouldn't yell out, he would just walk down to where he needed to be and with an impatient smile on his face tell the miscreant (in a deep "Come on children, why don't you grow up?" tone of voice) that indeed we had a PROB-LEM that needed to be dealt with (which invariably produced a quick solution). Some of the more junior faculty, less sure of themselves, were on occasion less able to control things. Adolescent boys can hone in on insecurities like heat-seeking missiles.

The study hall chamber itself, in addition to providing space for the daily Chapel exercises, was used to administer well-proctored final exams and, occasionally, standardized tests, such as those to determine National Merit Finalist awards, but its main purpose was to provide a venue where we could study before, between, and occasionally after classes. And there were indeed occasions when we actually did study in study hall time. The time was useful to dispatch the shorter homework assignments, especially those that did not involve research or sources outside our texts. It was, however, a bad strategy to leave homework undone, counting on time in study hall to complete it the next day before class. Somehow when that occurred, it always seemed that the time proved too short and the distractions too diverting. Over the years, I never could concentrate enough to write essays there, or focus on Latin or German vocabulary. Even serious math problems that required new procedures needed more concentration than was afforded in study hall time. However, I did find it a good time to read a history text or a short story from an English class anthology, or diagram sentences, or complete exercises of a workbook variety, or fill in blanks on take-home science exercises, or do the final version of lab reports. I don't remember doing much recreational reading during study hall either, but for some this was an appropriate use of their time. The whole study hall experience was new and quite different from the Lower School, but it soon became very much part of our daily lives.

XI

Second Form
(1956-57)

Second Form was the last year during which Nick Littlefield, Tommy Clark, Bill Fischer, and Harrison Huntoon—mainstays of the Lower School East Side "old guard"—were still at Moses Brown. They were to leave at the end of the school year for Milton, Choate (followed by Belmont Hill), Exeter, and Taft, respectively, and were making plans to do so throughout the year. Bill Goddard (at St. George's), Derric Chesebrough (at Milton), and Chad Gifford (at St. George's) had already left after completing Lower School. In addition, Alan Volkman, a classmate and good friend with whom I had spent many hours playing chess and Monopoly, left after the Second Form for Warwick High.

In Second Form we had five full courses that met daily and only one mini-class that met once a week. In Second Form most of us had First-Year Algebra with Mr. Joseph Tinker, Ancient History with Mr. William Westland, English with Mr. Paul Nichols, Second-Year Latin with Mr. Fuller, and General Science with Mrs. Ada Full. Throughout our entire Moses Brown experience, we had had both Art and Shop every year. Now, however, we had to choose between them (for our mini-course), and I chose Shop with Mr. Howe. There was no formal instruction in music or *Bible* this year. Some of my classmates took First-Year French with Mr. Detlefsen, as I recall (Nick Littlefield used to refer to him as Mr. Dettel-fetsen). This may have been in preparation for transferring to other schools, and probably replaced Ancient History or General Science.

Math. First-Year Algebra was taught by a memorable iconoclast—Mr. Joseph Tinker, whose normal means of transportation to School was a hearse he had painted green after buying it, no doubt, on the cheap. He was a stolid Hampshireman with his BA from the University of New Hampshire at Durham. He had also done graduate work at Boston University and at the University of Vermont. He was a very nice guy with a wry Yankee sense of humor. He liked me and I liked him. I had known his nephew Tommy Tinker in class during my first months at Moses Brown several years before. Still, I must say that First-Year Algebra, as he taught it, was not one of the better classes I had in Upper School.

After a bit of review, we started with the basic rules for adding, subtracting, multiplying, and dividing algebraic expressions, and then for manipulating equations to solve them. We went on to learn how to solve a pair of two equations with two unknowns. We were introduced to the difference between monomials and polynomials and how to add sets of the latter.

This was straightforward, but I had difficulties with the actual manipulation of the equations, especially when the exercise involved squares and other exponents. I had lots of trouble with simple multiplications such as: 3X squared plus 2x, times 5X squared plus 8. I remember on one exam doing such a computation, getting an answer I deemed unsatisfactory, crossing out the result, and proceeding to the next question. When I got the exam back, Mr. Tinker noted that my crossed-out answer was actually correct, and that he was giving me credit for it. He was a nice guy, and I was grateful for the points, but the calculation itself remained an even greater mystery: at least before this episode I had thought I knew what I didn't know—now I wasn't even sure of that.

We also reviewed square roots and powers, proportion, and negative numbers; and we learned simple factoring. I understood these exercises better, and that understanding probably helped me get a passing grade for the class. In addition to all this, we were taught a few basic formulae—such

Joseph W. Tinker

as D = RT and I = PRT.[156] Using such formulae, we began to think about the "problems" we had had since the Fifth or Sixth Grade in terms of formal algebraic notation. Instead of figuring out how to solve problems in our head, we reduced them to algebraic equations and then manipulated the equations to find a solution. This was all very well and good, but if I couldn't manipulate the equation properly, I couldn't get the right answer. Sometimes it was easier to consider the questions as thought problems and solve them independently (the old way), either in one's head, with simple arithmetical methods, or by trial and error. This, however, was frowned upon—unless you got the proper result by means of proper algebra, it did not count. Mr. Tinker did not go over these concepts enough in class for me to catch on easily. Others may have fared better, but I fared not well at all. Perhaps it was carelessness on my part, but I had problems with the computations. It is possible that the concepts and procedures he taught were so obvious to Mr. Tinker himself that he assumed they were obvious to everyone. I have encountered mathematicians and physicists who understand concepts so well intuitively that they can't relate to those who

---

156 Distance=Rate x Time; Interest = Principal x Rate (interest) x Time.

do not—and find it difficult to explain to others what is intuitively obvious to themselves.

Tinker knew his subject matter well. When explaining something, he was direct and matter-of-fact. At times he could be abrupt. Strangely, he seemed a bit shy, and his crisp explanations—or responses—may have been a way of masking that shyness. He could unwind, set aside the New Hampshire granite, and be quite friendly, but he seldom unwound when giving instruction. He was a minimalist when it came to teaching. It is unfair to say that he never taught anything. He would occasionally give us a demonstration of some algebraic principle, but then he would not take the time to see if we had understood it. Basically, he told us to read the book and do the exercises. The book to me was often not self-explanatory, and, quite frankly, I didn't learn a lot from it or from class. There was neither extensive class instruction in formulaic ways to achieve a result, nor instruction in conceptual ways to examine a problem and work out the method of solution by ourselves. Mr. Herman in subsequent courses also challenged us to work things out for ourselves, but he took an intense interest in whether or not we had succeeded in doing so. Mr. Tinker had a laid-back approach to the whole learning process and did not press us. This, in my case at any rate, made a world of difference.

Part of this was my own fault. In Lower School math we were used to instruction from teachers, supplemented by books. Here we were to receive instruction from a book, supplemented by the teacher. This was an important transition, but I didn't fully recognize it as such and blamed the teacher for abdicating his role. In addition, I was not a model student in this class. I forget whom I sat next to, but I sat right in front of Mr. Tinker on the right side of the classroom next to the wall as we faced his desk, and I used to talk fairly frequently to the person next to me on the left—I truly don't remember who it was. One day, Mr. Tinker had enough of this and ordered me out of the room. I stood in the hall outside, wondering what would happen next. Within a few minutes, Mr. St. John, of all people, came up the stairs from the chemistry lab below. He looked back at me, but said nothing, and went his way. Mr. Tinker never mentioned the episode afterwards, and there were no formal consequences. After this, I became a bit more tractable.

Mr. Tinker spent much of the second half of the year reading Damon Runyon stories to the class (at least it seems in retrospect that this is how we spent most of our time). It was one way in which he unwound. They were fun. I certainly remember Harry the Horse and several other Runyon characters who later formed the basis of *Guys and Dolls*. I also remember Mr. Tinker in this context complaining about dime novels whose covers had "babes with no clothes on," but which, regrettably, contained few, if any, stories about babes with no clothes on in the text. What all this had to do with First-Year Algebra was not clear, but since we all enjoyed it, none of us complained. In fact classmates recall making a game of trying to get Mr. Tinker to go through the entire class period without mentioning any math at all. Occasionally they were successful.

I guess this ultimately may have caught up with Tinker, because he was dismissed a couple of years later. I am not privy to the reasons or the details. It may have been a decision on the Headmaster's part that had nothing to do with Tinker's teaching foibles. At any rate he left at the end of our Fourth-Form year.

Let me reiterate that he was a very nice guy, and on a personal level he could be a lot of fun to be around. He was advisor to the *Mosaic* and I sat down with him at the end of the Fourth Form, as the next year's editor, to go over how the staff should deal with the publisher and handle any other details he thought we should know about. He was very friendly and very helpful, and had he stayed, I'm sure I would have enjoyed working with him. He was smart and I think he liked being at Moses Brown a lot. With some mature supervision of him, including some friendly guidance, things might have turned out very differently for him and for us.

Ancient History. Mr. Westland, our instructor in Ancient History, was physically a large person, a bit lethargic in style, who lumbered along like a slow, but civilized, bear. His classes matched his ambulatory style. At times it seemed that he was not particularly engaged in the topic he was teaching and was just going through the motions. His main problem may have been that ancient history was not his primary field of expertise, and he was not fully on top of the subject he was teaching. As a graduate of Brown, with a

William R. Westland

master's degree from Boston University and some coursework at Harvard, he was not lacking in intelligence or experience with history, but he had probably been trained to teach some other historical period.

He was also new to Moses Brown. I don't know the full story here, but it may have been that when Mr. Raines was appointed Dean (perhaps at the last minute) the School had to hire someone quickly to teach his courses— just before the term began—and Mr. Westland arrived under those circumstances. Rumor had it—perhaps a false unfair rumor—that every morning Westland went into Raines's office and was prepped on what to say and do in class, and then went down and taught. This procedure by itself might have worked had the class consisted entirely of lectures, but when questions were permitted, deficiencies would quickly appear. Don't misunderstand me here; I liked Mr. Westland as a person. He was a nice guy, and he was certainly trying to make the class happen, but frankly, I found much of the course duller than dishwater. This was the only history course I took in ten years at Moses Brown that would even remotely deserve that description.

Others in the class sometimes felt the same frustrations. Bill Brehm used to sit next to Hernan Franco and they would on occasion get into an altercation to relieve the monotony. Bill remembered once punching Hernan in the stomach during one of Mr. Westland's lectures.[157] Westland halted his instruction and ordered Bill out of the classroom. As Bill was standing up to leave, Bill Fischer piped up and asked, "Bill, where are you going?" Westland then told Bill Fischer that unless he shut up he could join Bill Brehm. And so forth.[158]

Our text was Morey's *Ancient Peoples*, which I cannot find, so my comments on it are from memory. The previous year they had used the massive *Ancient History*[159] by Brown University's formidable Charles Alexander Robinson (whose son Frank went to Moses Brown during our time there), and which I had bought secondhand at some expense the previous year, assuming we would use it in Second Form. When the texts were switched, I was stuck with it, although in later years I was glad to have it as a reference. Comparing the two at the time, I quickly concluded that the Robinson text was much more advanced and much better written. I wish we had used it for both scholarly and pecuniary reasons, and on both grounds felt a bit cheated!

Morey's *Ancient Peoples* was sadly out of date and inappropriate in some ways, certainly by today's standards. I remember it making cross-cultural comparisons with overtones that you would rightly not see in a modern text. None of that, however, was repeated or in any way endorsed in class. The book started with the Fertile Crescent, and starred such people as the marvelously euphonious Tiglath Pileser the Third, the more prosaic Hammurabi (with his laws), the snarling Sennacherib, the majestic Ashurbanipal, and the biblical Nebuchadnezzar, who ended up eating grass, as

---

157 Hernan Franco joined our Class in the First Form. He became a successful lawyer, practicing in Chicago and Puerto Rico.
158 Bill Brehm, who came to Moses Brown in the First Form and graduated with us in 1960, got his AB at Cornell and his MBA at Stamford Graduate School of Business. He served four years in the Air Force. Stationed in California full time as an administrator of contract aircraft, he rode around the Pacific in contract airplanes. Returning to Rhode Island in 1970, he joined his father's jewelry importing business and later ran it, selling out in 2011. A resident of Chestnut Hill, Massachusetts, since 1986, he also has a vacation home in Vermont, handy to the ski slopes. He and his wife, Gerri, enjoy traveling throughout the USA and Europe.
159 New York: Macmillan, 1951.

I recall. And then there was the much more pronounceable (and spellable) Sargon I. We encountered the Sumarians, the Hittites, the Assyrians (Ninevah rose and fell), then the Lydians, and finally the Babylonians—First and Second, the latter of which went by the name of Chaldeans, as we were told. Why they were not simply called the Chaldeans instead of the Second Babylonians, we were not told. Most of them seemed to live between the Tigris and Euphrates, and were always fighting each other. Some things don't change.

We then moved on to the Egyptians, whose empire had been a contemporary of most of the above, and with whom we were much more familiar from Lower School. Morey's contained maps of the various ancient empires (colored in impressive greens, yellows, and purples), and we were asked to make our own maps showing their extent. Whether the maps were valid in the sense that the empires had real boundaries in the modern meaning of the term is subject to debate, but the maps at least attempted to define the extent of the political influence that these empires exercised. Besides, they were fun to make and color in.

From the Egyptians we graduated to the Medes and the Persians, and made the acquaintance of Darius, Xerxes, Artaxerxes, the Royal Road from Sardis to Susa, and how messengers traveling that road who brought bad news would be executed upon delivery of their message. Mr. Westland pronounced "Darius" with the accent on the first syllable; my father told me that he had been taught that the accent really should fall upon the second, but advised me that it would not be diplomatic to make a point of this with Mr. Westland.

From the Persians we advanced to the fifth century (BC) Greeks (who were fighting with Persia during that time at Marathon and Salamis). We then spent serious time on the Peloponnesian War between Athens and Sparta. Since Athens was the more famous city, the presumption was that Athens would win this war—indeed Athens at the time was often compared to Britain or America, and Sparta to the Russians—so it was obvious who should win. I can remember standing in study hall talking with someone who had not yet finished the week's reading. As he departed, he made a comment about the Athenian victory. Bill Brehm (who was also standing there) and I exchanged glances, and we remarked to each other, "Boy, is he in for a surprise!" We also spent a lot of time on Greek culture—architecture, literature, philosophy, and government. There was a lot of memorization even here in an Upper School class.

Then it was on to Alexander, the Alexandrian Greeks, and the beginnings of Rome. We studied the clash between Greeks and Romans in southern Italy involving Pyrrhus and his famous victory. We revisited the Punic Wars between Rome and Carthage which we had studied with Mrs. Bluhm in Sixth Grade. The text covered the development of the Roman Empire more broadly, and here our experience with Mr. Fuller helped. Mr. Westland spent a lot of time on the last decades of the Republic, the rise of Caesar, and the Triumvirates. We got solidly as far as the Antonines, with a hasty epilogue about the invasions, 476 fall, and rescue under Justinian. Again, the text was full of maps tracing the expansion, consolidation, and contraction of the Roman Empire—which was colored light red in all of them, as I recall.

In terms of content, this was a reasonably solid factual history course. I found it very dry, however. We covered more than we had in the Sixth Grade, but I was very happy to have had the Sixth Grade background. Mr. Westland's course seemed less engaging. It consisted mainly of memorizing names, dates, and battles—and also Greek cultural icons like Pheidippides, Phidias, and Praxiteles (or political leaders like Themistocles, Pericles, and Demosthenes). Unlike our experience with Mrs. Monahon, we heard few anecdotes or stories to bring the historical data alive. We were told a little about the political system (with its archons, ephors, and ostracisms), but not how it really worked. Aside from a few diagrams in the text, we were told little about the strategies by which battles were won; there was certainly nothing extensive taught about them in class. Although we were introduced to lots of sculptors, architects, artists, and even a few athletes, there was little of interest that tied us to them. We read no plays of (or even excerpts from) Sophocles, Euripides, or Aristophanes, nor were we introduced to their plot lines or anything in depth about their literary, philosophical, or political significance; at least not anything I remember. A more in-depth introduction to these people might have been interesting, depending, of course, on how it was presented. Again, Socrates, Plato, and Aristotle were mentioned, but their historical significance to Western culture was not explored in any depth.

Mr. Westland's style, like that of Mr. Raines later, was to give us organized notes listing and cataloging the basic data he considered important. We were also more or less given instruction in how to transcribe them: with headings and subheadings. I suppose the idea was to get us to know how to take notes—or at least to ensure that we departed the classroom with a written record of what was considered important—but in fact the whole exercise seemed to turn into a rote procedure, and we didn't really engage with these notes. To me they served more as barriers than as aids. Despite similarities in format, the experience was very different from that with Mr. Raines three years later. Raines could make facts and dates glow in the dark, but Westland couldn't. Raines's notes without Raines fell flat on the floor. So, if I may continue to mix the metaphors, we just plowed ahead.

There were frequent quizzes and recurrent attempts at class interaction— Mr. Westland would ask us questions about the text to see if we had read it. But because we never quite understood just why all this was important to learn, the class grew restless, and at times sarcastic. I remember on one occasion Mr. Westland asked us who Archimedes was. Jack Nixon spoke up and said, "Wasn't he the guy who invented the screw machine?" The class thought this hilarious, but poor Westland, I'm afraid, did not.

English. Our Second-Form English instructor was Mr. Paul Nichols, a memorable character who was at Moses Brown for only one year.[160] He was a very intense guy. A lot of people liked him; a lot did not. Those who did not referred to him as "Pig Eyes." The sobriquet caught on, and students in study hall at times would oink at him.

I was among those who liked him. He was very outspoken, and you never quite knew what to expect from him. He would breeze into class and begin a subject on the fly. It might bear little resemblance to the subject of the previous session. There was indeed an arbitrary quality to him (which may have led to many of the criticisms), but there was never a dull moment in class. He was involved. He made the subject matter interesting. He was the

---

160 He was a graduate of Bates College.

Paul A. Nichols

drama coach and he had a sense of the dramatic; he was also the debate coach and he loved to argue.

I remember many years later a conversation at Harvard between a young faculty member and the legendary John Finley, the formidable Eliot Professor of Greek Literature, concerning someone that the Classics Department was considering hiring. The younger prof, with some emotion, expostulated to Finley, "You just can't hire him ... put simply, the man is certifiably mad." Finley paused a minute, cleared his throat thoughtfully, and responded, "Yes, you are right. He is undoubtedly mad.... But he has *flair*." Nichols, though not mad, had flair. For this and other reasons, I always thought that his dismissal by St. John after one year was a big loss for Moses Brown, but I never knew the full story.

Mr. Taber had grilled us extensively on grammar and sentence structure. Mr. Nichols, building on this, taught us usage. For example, Taber had concentrated on telling us what a participle was and how to use one properly; Nichols concentrated on telling us how to use one effectively. He taught sentence structure, proper expressions, when to use and when not to use complex modifiers, and so forth. He drilled us on the proper use of contrary-to-fact subjunctives: "If I *were* going home tomorrow, which I am not, I would take the train"; but "If I *was* to find a hole in my pocket, which someday I might, then I would have it mended." This was good grounding. I can remember trumping copy editors at prestige publishing houses with such proper usages.

We had no grammar text, but Mr. Nichols handed out sheets with complex sentences on them containing (often subtle) errors that we had to correct. These probably came from some source like the Modern Language Association. They were real challenges, and I remember at times puzzling over them at some length. Understandably Nichols occasionally got confused himself, but he found us the answers. We did not revisit usage at this level until we had Mr. Paxton in the Fifth Form.

For literature, we had an anthology, and in addition we were required to read a lot of books other than those in the class curriculum. The outside reading in my case was largely from non-American non-English authors in translation. I do not know if this was a requirement or simply a coincidence. I remember reading four novels by Victor Hugo that year: *Hunchback of Notre Dame*, *Les Miserables*, *Ninety-Three*, and *Toilers of the Sea*. Mr. Nichols asked me to do a book review that would compare all of them—their similarities and differences—as a combined exercise. This was the first time I remember being asked to have a crack at literary criticism, and I enjoyed the exercise. Before this a book review was basically a summary of what the book had said and what it meant to us personally. Now we were being asked to evaluate the book and compare it to other books. Nichols was treating us as adults, and this was flattering.

I remember that he also had us read *Crime and Punishment*, telling us in advance that the axe scene was one of the grimmest in all literature. Of course, after that observation, all of us just had to read it. I also remember getting a severe case of poison ivy late that fall out at the farm, and being laid up at home for a week in early December with my feet propped up on a stool. While immobilized, I read *War and Peace* to the tune of

Christmas carols—an interesting combination.[161] Whether *War and Peace* was a class assignment, a suggestion from Nichols (Read another Russian novel!), a suggestion from home, or the by-product of a movie (starring Marlon Brando) which came out about that time, I don't remember. But after reading these two, I had had my fill of Russian novels for quite a while, despite my father's facetious promptings that if I was so taken with the Russians, I really should read *Anna Karenina*.

The anthology we used in Second-Form English contained both American and English authors.[162] It opened with mystery stories—including a familiar Sherlock Holmes tale, "The Adventure of the Six Napoleons," and Richard Connell's marvelous "The Most Dangerous Game," which I had read before in Lower School. Nichols supplemented these with an adventure tale about a bet between two strong-willed persons that ran along the following lines:[163] one volunteered to be locked in a room for twenty-four hours and bet a large sum of money that he could make the other open the door and let him out before the time had expired. He was duly incarcerated. After a few hours, the one locked in the room began to show signs of serious, escalating sickness. Claiming to be deathly ill and in need of immediate medical attention, he begged to be released from the room and rushed to the hospital. Was he faking it to win the bet? Or was his life truly in danger? How to tell? What were the moral obligations, if any, of the other party to the bet? The dilemma was marvelously and convincingly set up. It was so well done that I will not share the ending.

There was a section of stories about adolescents our age forging relationships with each other and wrestling with incipient adulthood—and the responsibilities it entailed. There was a biographical section designed to inspire.

In addition, there was also a very long section containing an edited version of *Silas Marner*—one of the dullest books ever penned—which we dutifully tried to read. I made a map of Raveloe for homework, and this cartographical exercise was the only thing I enjoyed about *Marner*.

---

161 I guess the common denominators involved winter and sleigh rides.
162 The list of authors evoked the image of a law firm: Pooley, Poley, Leyda, and Zellhoefer, *Exploring Life through Literature*, Chicago: Scott Foresman, 1951.
163 It was not in the anthology—I forget the title and author.

Another major part of the anthology was *Julius Caesar*. We had to memorize parts of this and we did a reading in class. I read Cassius—the dangerous one (with the lean and hungry look) who thought too much. Mr. Nichols told us a lot about this play and argued that Brutus was really the main character. He discussed how it was staged, and he did some readings himself, with an emphasis on explaining the meter. I remember writing an assignment for him on *Julius Caesar* in iambic pentameter, an unanticipated approach to a paper that got his attention in a positive way. We also were asked to select and read another Shakespearian play. I chose *Henry IV, Part I*, and wrote a lengthy treatise on it, largely on its plot line, but also on Hal's motivations and the development of his character.

Drama was Mr. Nichols's first love. He was the drama coach and he produced three challenging classic plays that year, starting with Moliere's *The Miser* in the fall. His second production, which I remember very well, was *The Caine Mutiny Court Martial*, which was given during the winter. This was a serious contemporary Broadway drama. Dan Segal played Queeg. The third was the *Medea*. All three of these plays were demanding, but the cast rose to the challenge of Nichols's exacting requirements and all three productions were memorable. Whatever else might be said about Nichols, he knew his theater and was a superb drama coach.

Not surprisingly, Mr. Nichols emphasized oral skills in class. Not only did we read the excerpts from *Julius Caesar*, but we also were asked to make oral reports. I remember speaking on the poet Oliver Wendall Holmes, Sr., whom Nichols contemptuously referred to as a "mere versifier." I felt this was unfair to Holmes, but it did provide a good opportunity to debate Mr. Nichols. He also used to have sessions where he would give us a topic and we were supposed to speak about it on thirty seconds' notice. He selected a victim, announced the topic, and we stood up and spoke. In this format, I defended the teaching of Latin in high school, and Nick Littlefield defended mandatory sports. Nick's defense was much more colorful than mine. He responded with an appropriately passionate defense, whose punch line was that if you were standing next to a car and someone drove down the street right at you, then your sports training would enable you to jump up onto the roof of the car and save your life. Nick could be a master of the absurd, and on this occasion, I think, he scored well on Nichols.

Second Form (1956-57)

We also read Coleridge's *Rime of the Ancient Mariner*, and, as I recall, we took turns reading parts of it out loud. The emphasis in class on the spoken word may have been part of Nichols's attempt to identify good potential for the Proscenium Club and especially for the Debate Team. Mr. Odell had formed the debating club the previous year, although competition was on intramural lines. Mr. Nichols became its coach after Odell left, and he started interscholastic competition. One of the major School events of that period was the annual declamation contest, which had endowed prizes. In 1957, Nichols's debaters—Russ Carpenter ('59), Bruce Pansey ('59), and Dan DeVleig from our Class—swept the event.

The School continued to hold the Book Fair throughout the Upper School, and it gave strong support to our English class and our reading program. We were encouraged to participate. It was sponsored by the Parents Council, and parents worked the tables. My mother was still active in it, and during Second Form, she was in charge of recruiting parents to help her run the "Junior High" Department. Her records show the great extent to which Second-Form mothers volunteered to assist in this enterprise: On Thursday, November 1, Mrs. Marshall worked from 2:00 p.m. to 3:00 p.m.; Mrs. Forman, from 3:00 p.m. to 4:00 p.m.; Mrs. Saklad, from 4:00 p.m. to 5:00 p.m.; Mrs. Criss, from 5:00 p.m. to 6:00 p.m.; Mrs. Sanderson, from 6:00 p.m. to 7:00 p.m.; Mrs. Corris, from 7:00 p.m. to 8:00 p.m.; and Mrs. Littlefield, from 8:00 p.m. to 9:00 p.m. On Friday, November 2, Mrs. Barrett worked from 10:00 a.m. to 11:00 a.m.; Mrs. Fischer, from 11:00 a.m. to 12:15 p.m.; Mrs. Huntoon, from 12:15 p.m. to 1:30 p.m.; Mrs. DiLibero, from 1:30 p.m. to 2:30 p.m.;[164] Mrs. Kilton, from 2:30 p.m. to 3:30 p.m.; Mrs. Saywell, from 3:30 p.m. to 4:30 p.m.; and Mrs. Clark from 4:30 p.m. to 5:00 p.m., and no doubt afterwards to help pack up. My mother was there for the whole period, and in charge of setting up, record keeping, and picking up afterwards.

---

164 Mrs. DiLibero was Ralph DiLibero's mother. Ralph joined our Class in the First Form. After graduating from the University of Pennsylvania, he went to medical school, graduating from Hahnemann University Medical School, later part of Drexel University. He became an orthopedic surgeon, specializing in neuromusculoskeletal medicine. He has practiced in California most of his professional career, is highly acclaimed in his profession, and is the author of a recently published book on medical economics, entitled *Man, Money, and Medicine*.

Latin. In Mr. Fuller's Second-Year Latin course we had a textbook from a different series than the text we had had in First-Year Latin.[165] It had a much more modern appearance, and was aimed directly at American students, but I did not like it as well, and there were confusions since the second book did not begin exactly where the first left off. For the third year, incidentally, we went back to the original series.

We started with some review of the previous year and read materials about Athens designed to reinforce our commitment to democracy. We then read a bit of Livy and went on to Caesar, whose Gallic Wars constituted the main focus of our readings.

I did like Caesar: *Gallia est omnis divisa in partes tres...*, or whatever.[166] We did not read the whole text. Our book interspaced actual passages from Caesar for us to translate with summaries of the omitted passages so the story line was complete. It would tell you about the bridge over the Rhine, but did not ask you to translate the passage about its engineering.

As we advanced through the year, I fell more and more behind in terms of keeping up with the new vocabulary and especially with the grammar. With respect to the vocabulary, I probably did not spend enough time on it. We certainly did not do the repetitions we had done with math and spelling, for example, in the Lower School. Also, I had not developed any effective cognitive matrix or other mnemonic device to help remember the new words—and, in this regard, we seemed to be running out of cognates with which I was familiar. Cold memory and repetition were all I knew, and, to lock in the words retentively, I lacked the discipline for the one and the patience for the other. The expanding vocabulary demands of our ever-advancing text became more insurmountable week by week, and translating anything successfully became increasingly an exercise in continuous dictionary or glossary page-flipping. I was not alone in this regard, but many others had far less difficulty than I did.

---

165 Ullman, B., and Henry, Norman, *Latin for Americans, Second Book*, New York: The Macmillan Company, 1950.
166 My father had always said, "*Omnia Gallia in tres partes divisa est*," probably from his high school text—which may have originated in a different manuscript than our text did. I remember we were told that "Omnia" meant "Greater," not "All," and hence referred to "Greater Gaul," not "All Gaul."

In addition, by now we were being exposed to advanced tenses, grammatical forms, and usages, such as the future perfect, subjunctives, participles, etc. I could handle these concepts in English, but was overwhelmed by them in Latin. Again, I fell behind cumulatively and exponentially. It seemed that every day there was a new grammatical concept. I could temporarily master a lesson and successfully do a few exercises based on it, but soon it would be eclipsed by a new lesson and fade out of memory into unrecognizability. Mr. Fuller always explained things clearly and employed good examples from English usage to illustrate his points. I understood his lessons well. I just couldn't seem to retain them and fit them into a larger matrix of understanding.

We swam slowly through all this, and I'm not sure that I would have survived but for the extra credit we got for outside reading in Roman history. Mr. Fuller had a large collection of books, fiction and nonfiction, about Rome and the ancient world. He would lend these to us and we got extra credit for reading them. I think we had to submit a short book review, but maybe not.

In any event, I did a lot of this kind of reading. I really enjoyed it. I remember many adventures, one regarding the destruction of the Roman Army under Cotta, one about Caesar's victory over Vercingetorix, one about gladiators, others about life in Rome. Many of these were novels in the first person, and I remember liking them more than the third-person presentations. There was one book we read about Pompeii and its destruction; this the whole class may have read. I suppose that in terms of learning Latin, my time would have been better spent on conjugating the future perfect, but reading novels was a lot more enjoyable, and I did get some credit for it. By and large, however, I was never fully able to keep up with the level of Latin we were attempting, and as the year progressed, my hold on what was going on, especially in terms of composition, became more tenuous. This problem was to increase even more in Third-Year Latin.

General Science. In Second Form we had a class called "General Science." I liked it a lot and learned a lot in it. It was a very basic course in how things worked in both the natural world and the man-made world.

Although we occasionally did use some math, it was mainly descriptive.[167] Taught by Mrs. Ada Full, the course attempted to cover a very wide range of scientific and engineering phenomena. Mrs. Full was a quiet, competent, no-nonsense instructor who was both friendly and professional. She held our attention by making the subject hold our attention. I remember this course as being very well taught. She was a graduate of Pembroke College at Brown University, and the only woman instructor we had in a regular course in the Upper School.[168] Her own field of expertise was biology, and naturally we got a reasonable amount of biology in this class, but she went into many other topics with enthusiasm and understanding.

Part of the course was in mechanics—starting with the six simple machines and the principle of mechanical advantage. We quickly went on to the conversion of chemical to mechanical energy, learned how the four-stroke internal combustion automobile engine worked, and saw how the rotary combustion "Wankel" engine (then being pioneered) might be an interesting alternative. We learned how standard and automatic transmissions worked. We also were taught how steam piston engines worked on locomotives, and the basic principle behind the diesel electric locomotive.

We learned about turbines, traditional and modern, and also how dynamos, generators, and motors worked—and the basic phenomena of magnetism. We learned the difference between an incandescent, fluorescent, and neon light—I wrote a paper on this, complete with diagrams. We learned the difference between direct and alternating current, how transformers worked, and the principles behind transmission lines. In this regard, we also learned about batteries—dry cell and wet cell and their differing characteristics. As I recall, we learned how to diagram a simple electric circuit with switches—and also how to wire lights in parallel or in series. In a more theoretical way, we learned a bit about electricity itself, including positive and negative charges and the flow of electrons. In this regard, we were taught some chemistry, including the difference between an atom and a molecule, but the focus here was mostly on industrial processes, where we

---

167 Our text was Paul Brandwein, Alfred Beck, Leland Hollingsworth, and Anna Burgess, *You and Science*, New York: Harcourt Brace, 1955. The authors, principally, were high school teachers and science program supervisors, at least one teaching jointly at the college level.

168 Miss Sadlier taught us speed-reading and comprehension in a special once-a-week "remedial" class that everyone took.

reviewed some familiar acquaintances from the Lower School, including vulcanizing rubber and the various different methods of steel making and oil refining. In addition, we were taught how a jet engine operates and how a nuclear submarine was propelled. I remember Mrs. Full carefully demonstrating many of these principles with diagrams on the board. All this was very introductory and simplified, but we were taught the basic ideas behind machines, and it did give us a good introduction to how the mechanical, chemical, and electrical worlds operated. In many respects this course continued the tradition of exposing us to "practical" knowledge that we had periodically encountered in Lower School English, math, and social science classes. Some of this emphasis may have been motivational—to stimulate interest in a topic by showing why it was "relevant"—but it was also developmental in terms of building our ability to understand and relate to the adult environment, especially the artificial (designed) environment, in which we were to live.

I don't remember any labs in General Science; if we had any, there were only a few, and I don't recall anything we might have done in them. This course, however, was a very important one for getting us to understand how things worked so that we were conversant in a modest way about the world of technology. Whether or not we went on to become engineers or scientists, this was very useful information when it came to understanding the world around us. Also, showing how something works and why things in the artificial environment behave as they do is an important intellectual exercise. A well-taught class about how things work (and this class was well-taught) can stimulate curiosity in general—and may motivate, for example, the curious to ask why things in the social environment work the way they do. Moreover, in my case (and I expect in the case of many classmates) it was easier to understand these simple mechanical principles than it was to understand the more abstract principles we were about to be taught in mathematics.

I am sure this focus at Moses Brown on what makes things tick was deeply grounded in the New England nineteenth century intellectual and cultural tradition, both at home and in its diaspora—as well illustrated in works of such variegated thinkers as Franklin, Emerson, Bowditch, Holmes, Jr., US Grant, Twain, Addams, Dewey, and James. Even Verne in his American-oriented *Mysterious Island* recognized and evoked this tradition. It is a tradition that loves to explain things and share useful knowledge. Few adults in my family ever refused to answer the question: "Why?" There is a tendency in the liberal arts tradition to focus on more abstract concerns, but I think exposure to some basic principles and constructs of the artificial environment is just as important for a student as exposure to the basic principles of the natural environment (which for centuries has constituted a solidly recognized part of the liberal arts). I'm very glad that Moses Brown did provide that exposure in my day, and I hope it still does. I wish other schools did as well.

In addition to the artificial environment, we were also taught about the natural world in our course on General Science. There was a section on astronomy—the planets, eclipses, gravity, galaxies, super novae, distances, and the cosmological understanding at that time of the origins of the universe. Given my father's shared interest in this topic, elementary astronomy was very easy for me. Bill Barrett remembered that in the astronomy section one of the exam questions was why the full moon appears larger when near the horizon than when high in the sky. He did not remember this being covered in the book or in class, and tried at the time (without success) to come up with a reasonable-sounding answer. The correct answer was that this phenomenon is merely an optical illusion. He says that since then he has never observed a rising full moon without thinking of that exam question.

I believe we had some elementary geology, building on that we had learned from Mrs. Monahon in the Lower School. We also had a section on weather and climate—cold fronts, warm fronts, occluded fronts, the Coriolis force, and how it all applied to hurricanes and tornadoes. This enabled us to improve our understanding of the daily weather map in the newspaper. We learned about isobars and how Fahrenheit and Centigrade were calculated—and we reviewed how to convert one to the other. We may have learned about Kelvin and absolute zero, but this I am not sure. We certainly learned about thermometers and hydrometers.

Mrs. Full, of course, did not neglect her own field of biology, but in this class (since she expected to have most of us the following year in her formal biology class) she did not go into great detail. Following the text, her focus was on health science. We learned a bit about metabolism, quite a bit about

Second Form (1956-57)

F. Warren Howe, Jr.

the circulatory system, and a few things about diseases and medicines, but this was all fairly basic; we didn't study life forms other than humans, and we only studied humans from this practical viewpoint.

Shop. In Shop we were encouraged to undertake special projects, some of our own design. More baseball bats were made this year. Some classmates made nice bookcases and tables. I seem to remember wooden vessels (perhaps vases) being turned. Products built under Mr. Howe's supervision were of high quality, and I expect that many of these are still in use. I chose to build a corner cupboard. I do not remember why I decided to do this, but I certainly had seen corner cupboards in historic houses, and we didn't have one at Brown Street. Unfortunately, we didn't have many appropriate corners in which to place one either, but I somehow neglected to remember this potentially important consideration. It was a major project, and it took most of the year. Mr. Howe and I designed it in the fall, and it was a more complicated project than at first it appeared to be, involving very careful

Mechanical drawing

measurements and precise woodworking to make things fit, together with recurrent improvisation when things did not work out fully as planned.

I built it in two sections. As I remember it, the top section was built first, and it gave me more trouble than the bottom section. It was basically a three-dimensional triangle, but instead of joining the sides together directly at the back (with each row of side boards meeting at a right angle), I decided to have a spine consisting of a fairly narrow board, with the side boards meeting it at the appropriate 135-degree angle. I do not remember why I did this—perhaps the design was based on those for other corner cupboards I had seen. It proved, however, to be a very fussy design feature, and I had a lot of trouble shaping the spine accurately and fashioning shelves to fit against it precisely so that when the two rows of side boards were attached to the shelves the whole thing would fit together tightly. I used corrugated fasteners to bond the boards together to make the shelves. When the spine, sides, and shelves were complete, which included precise planing and sanding, then everything had to be fitted carefully together, and that was no small undertaking either.

Mr. Howe was very helpful working through all this with me. Often we would have to plane a bit more to make things fit. My design for the basic

Second Form (1956-57)

top section called for a segmented pediment on top of it. This required bonding a couple of thick boards together to form a triangle, cutting it to shape with the jigsaw, and then routing the exposed edges to form a patterned edge. Again, Mr. Howe helped with this, especially the routing. I then turned a "pineapple" spindle on the lathe to go on top of the pediment (I kept it plain). When all this wood was nailed, fastened, and glued together, the top was complete.

The bottom was easier. I suppose it was basically a duplicate of the top, although marginally larger, and the experiences making the top helped for the bottom. When it was all finished, we put it together and it stood a good seven feet high. By then, it was the end of the Spring Term, and there was no time left to stain and finish it.

I remember my father coming over to the shop and he, Mr. Howe, and I loaded the bottom section into the back seat of the car—turned on its side, the triangular shape just fit. We then returned for the top, a slightly easier fit, but, with the pineapple, a more delicate proposition. All went well. When we got it home and assembled it in a corner of the kitchen (the only real corner in the house where it would fit appropriately), it looked fine. How to stain and finish it? I might have done it in the basement, but my folks suggested that they send it out and have this done professionally. I quickly agreed, and our upholsterer, Mr. Kilgus, did a splendid job. It is still in use.

The end of the brief St. John era. The school year 1956-57 was a turning point for our class and for the School, culminating with the departure of Mr. St. John. As noted above, many of my close friends left Moses Brown at the end of the Second Form. This exodus may have had nothing to do with Moses Brown itself—many would have left under any circumstances to attend boarding school—and I believe most found that Moses Brown had prepared them well for their new schools. Still, given the Second-Form experiences with Tinker, the mercurial unpredictability of Nichols (which some parents may have found unsettling), and the semi-disaster with Westland, many parents of Second Formers might have asked whether or not a change in venue would improve their sons' educational prospects.

Moreover, there were questions of prestige—in the prep school pecking order at that time there were other academies that stood above Moses Brown, with all the implications their standing held for social prestige and perceived chances for admission to the Ivies. I asked Nick Littlefield a long time later if he had ever regretted leaving Moses Brown for Milton Academy, and he replied that he had not. We met again at Harvard.

With respect to intrinsic academic quality, my parents concluded, I believe correctly, that most instructors we were about to have at Moses Brown during our next three years of Upper School could have easily held their own with the best teachers at Choate, Groton, or Milton. Certainly Messrs. Cate, Whitford, Paxton, Raines, Fuller, Herman, Howe, and Mrs. Full were instructors of great erudition and teaching experience; many of the more junior faculty, such as Messrs. Taber, Corbett, Pratt, Jeffers, and Bixby, were also identifiably superb apprentices. We had indeed lost Odell to a doctoral program, but his decision to return to Moses Brown, when he obviously could have had many other options, was itself an endorsement of the School's intellectual quality by one who was in a position to know. In addition, college placement under Mr. St. John had been strong: nearly half of the Class of 1956 had gone to an Ivy League College; if you add the "Little Ivies" (such as Amherst, Wesleyan, Colby, and so forth) and major non-Ivy prestigious universities (such as Johns Hopkins, University of Chicago, MIT, Tufts, etc.), the percentage rises to two-thirds. In 1957, the year he left, the percentages were 58 percent and 74 percent, respectively. By other measures of academic achievement the School was doing well. The May 1957 issue of the *Moses Brown Bulletin*, perhaps in response to questions regarding the School's academic standing, cited statistics from standardized tests that placed Moses Brown considerably above the median levels for independent schools.

The School itself, however, was having problems at this time with restiveness in the student body outside of the classroom. This largely involved disciplinary issues with the upperclassmen and a growing attitude of disrespect among many students for the administration—and even for the School in general. The appointment of Mr. Raines as a Dean with disciplinary duties at the end of Mr. St. John's first year was presumably in recognition of these issues. Raines addressed them well, but some of the underlying discord persisted, and study halls were still unruly at times.

Moreover, some on the faculty were also restive and said so in class. Such news gets out. Criticisms cumulate. These factors collectively may have contributed to the student exodus. In addition, there also was active recruitment by other preparatory schools targeted at Moses Brown students. My parents were contacted and urged from several quarters to send me away. They decided not to, and personally I never regretted their choice, but certainly the attempt was made.[169]

With respect to Mr. St. John's departure itself, there may have been administrative issues of which I am not aware. Also, Mr. Thomas's stewardship was a hard act to follow, and would have been for anyone. Mr. St. John was certainly hurt by the failure of a much-touted capital campaign launched with great fanfare at a dinner featuring President Barnaby Keeney of Brown and Headmaster Bill Saltonstall of Exeter Academy as the principal speakers, but which raised little more than half its initial goal. I believe that there were also concerns about Mr. St. John's leadership arising directly from the faculty. The student exodus mentioned above may indeed have played a role. He was a very nice person and a good scholar. He came from a famous family of largely Episcopalian New England educators. A convert to the Society of Friends, he held many solid Quaker values. But gentleness may not always be the best approach to handling unruly students or skeptical faculty looking for leadership. Mr. Thomas was also a Quaker, but he was a much more muscular one.

I am not privy to the relationship between Mr. St. John and the boards above him, nor to the details of what happened, but I gather that there was eventually a revolt in the School Committee or in the Board of Trustees that proved decisive, and Mr. St. John, much to the surprise of a lot of people, departed Moses Brown in the summer of 1957. With the '60s and '70s not far away, his was to be the first of four consecutive headmasterships that ended abruptly or in controversy.

---

[169] My parents were invited to meetings and social events where representatives from other preparatory schools spoke and promoted their academies. I remember them attending a meeting on Prospect Street where representatives from St. George's urged them and other parents to send their children to Middletown. I recall that there were several other such meetings.

XII

Third Form

(1957-58)

The Third Form was academically my worst year in the Upper School. With some exceptions, I didn't enjoy the courses I was taking then as much as I had enjoyed most of the courses I took in previous years. Also, with the textile industry in the North increasingly under challenge from Southern competition, the Wanskuck Company, which my father managed, was sold by the Metcalfs, and the new owners basically bought it to liquidate it for tax purposes, despite the fact that it was still operating at a good profit. It closed in 1956, and my father changed jobs. His new job took him South for extended periods of time, and things at home were therefore a bit uncertain and confused. Looking back, this change and the attendant uncertainties may have contributed to my travails.

In addition, the departure of many old friends for other schools may also have taken a toll.[170] I still had friends at Moses Brown, and I was to form friendships among new classmates, but a lot of what had been life's constants no longer were. Some classmates, like Ed Corris,[171] Herb Sawyer,

---

170 I may not have been fully aware of the psychological impact of this at the time.
171 Ed Corris joined our Class in the Sixth Grade. He went to Trinity College after graduation, thence to Ohio Wesleyan and Ohio State, and then to Harvard Business School, where he earned his MBA. He settled in the Boston area, where he still resides. Ed spent his life in the business world, principally as an entrepreneur. After working for a firm that manufactured college jewelry items (class rings, etc.), he set out on his own, organizing a temporary help business "Corris Girls" (like Kelly Girls), which he expanded to include a typewriter rental business. He pioneered video rentals at the dawn of that industry, and built a chain of video stores in the Boston area. Later he entered the highly creative field of making board games, and then computer games as technology advanced. Many of his games were designed to be educational.

Frank Abella, and Steve Koffler,[172] had been with us a couple of years in the Lower School and were now old hands at Moses Brown, but Bill Barrett, Bob Dean, Barry Fain, Vin Marcello, Jack Nixon, Mark Saklad, and I were all that remained of those who had gone through at least four years of Lower School.

1957-58 marked Robert N. Cunningham's arrival as Headmaster. He was a Phi Beta Kappa graduate from Princeton and a Rhodes Scholar at Oxford. He was the first non-Quaker Head of School in Moses Brown history. He had close professional ties to the New England prep school culture centering around Exeter and Andover—and these tended to shape his ideas of what a prep school should be. Initially he was generally well-liked. He was decisive, willing to make decisions, willing to impose discipline, and, in this regard, willing to expel. Order returned. Mr. Raines remained in the position of Dean for a couple of years, and he may have been as responsible as Mr. Cunningham for the results, but Mr. Cunningham got the credit. There were also administrative changes and major curriculum revisions. To many, the contrast with Mr. St. John was welcome. Cunningham was careful to be on his best behavior during his first year, and at its end he went from being "Acting Headmaster" to full Headmaster in his own right. My father (who was on the Parents Council) commented favorably at the time on Cunningham's deportment and fair treatment with respect to the various other candidates brought to School for interviews.

As things turned out, however, Mr. Cunningham also had insecurities, engaged in favoritism, recruited informants among the student body, and was willing to intervene at times in what appeared to many as an arbitrary fashion. He ordered the Lower School reorganized, and this eventually led

---

[172] Steve Koffler, whose family had owned American Tourister, joined our Class in the Sixth Grade. He graduated from Rensselaer Polytechnic Institute, where he earned his PhD in solid-state and material science engineering. Entering the field of finance, he worked on Wall Street, and then moved to California where he became a senior financial executive of Mattel Inc. According to his obituary in the *Los Angeles Times*, he started his own investment firm, Koffler & Co., which handled the sale of Jenny Craig to Deutsche Bank. He also served as managing director of the Los Angeles office of Merrill Lynch & Co., where he arranged Disney's $100 million rescue of L.A. Gear. He was also managing director of the Los Angeles offices of Smith Barney, Sutro & Co., and of Barrington Associates. He served on the boards of the Greater Los Angeles Zoo, the Los Angeles Opera, and the St. John's Health Center Foundation. Tragically, he died of cancer, age 62.

Robert N. Cunningham

to Mrs. Cullen leaving for Warwick High School when she was no longer permitted at Moses Brown to teach her beloved English—and the School lost one of its best Lower School teachers. He also eventually sent Mr. Allen back to the classroom—and, although I'm sure he was an excellent teacher, the School lost the talents of one of its most effective administrators. All this was done as part of a reorganization not long after the creation of the Middle School. As time passed, Cunningham became defensive, and that did not help matters. When Mr. Paxton in a jovial forum tried to make light of Mr. Cunningham's installation of speed bumps on the School driveway by referring to them as "Bob's Bumps," Cunningham rounded on Paxton and turned a light moment into embarrassing one.

I can remember an episode in the Third Form. One day I was summoned to Mr. Cunningham's office and was asked the question, point blank, had I ever been asked by a student to lend him some money? I saw nothing particularly wrong with being approached for this purpose, and truthfully responded that, yes, in fact I had been asked. Cunningham then asked me if I had lent any, and I truthfully said that I had not. He then produced a written note to me from a fellow student asking for money. How he got this, I never knew. I certainly had never shown it to anyone. Perhaps I had stuck it in my desk and the desk had been searched. Perhaps it had fallen into another student's hands and they had brought it to him. In any event, he had this note, and he seemed to be in possession of other student notes. I had been truthful in my responses to him, and also had lent no money. There were no further consequences to me, but apparently the student involved had sought to borrow from several others. I knew him fairly well, but was unaware of why he was soliciting money. Anyway, this was deemed inappropriate behavior, and he was dismissed. There may have been other factors involved that I never became aware of, but I always felt that this was an unjust outcome. Hernan Franco at a much later date also nearly became a victim, but thankfully he was saved through the intervention of the faculty, most notably Mr. Whitford.

On this same occasion in Mr. Cunningham's office, he asked me if I would be willing to report back to him on the goings-on among the student body. It was pretty clear he wanted me to be some sort of informant. I gathered from him that should I do this, I would not be alone in that capacity. I remember telling him that if I heard anything interesting I would pass it along—but I was frankly appalled by the prospect of spying on my classmates, and I never told him anything. Nor did he ever ask me to again. Since there was no repeat performance, the episode faded into memory, but from my perspective the Cunningham bloom had begun to come off the proverbial rose.

His wife, Griselda, was a Higginson and therefore a person of means. I believe that the Cunninghams donated generously to the School. Mrs. Cunningham was an excellent hostess for School events, and took her role seriously. Personally, I never had an unpleasant passage with her. She mobilized members of the staff to form small groups to go about the campus picking up shards of glass and other unwelcome objects that detracted from appearances and harmed the environment. Although she hosted dinners for students at the Headmaster's apartment, she was generally at some distance from the student body—unlike the three previous headmasters' wives, all of whom taught in the classroom, with the most recent two having taught music and *Bible*, respectively, to the Class of 1960. According to a reliable (and supportive) witness from that time, the

Griselda H. Cunningham

marriage was rocky, with Mrs. Cunningham addressing her circumstances stoically and with dignity. By the time Mr. Cunningham departed in 1964, in the middle of the school year,[173] he had become the focus of social gossip and had acquired a number of antagonists among the faculty.

Allan Cokin saw some of Mr. Cunningham's negative aspects early on—much sooner than I did. Unfortunately for Allan, he made no secret of it, and with Cunningham's information sources, Allan's opinions probably reached the highest level. Allan always felt that the School had not

---

[173] I am unaware of the precise details surrounding his departure in January, 1964. The general assumption is that he was dismissed. Jerry Zeoli, however, recalled a phone call from Mr. Cunningham telling Jerry that he had resigned on his own initiative due to a dispute with Board members that frustrated his plans. In this regard, Mr. Cunningham soon received a good offer from the Smithsonian. Mr. Paxton's book, *Moses Brown School, A History of its Third Half Century*, is delicately vague beyond hinting at disagreements between Cunningham and the Boards. The paragraph devoted to the episode comes at you so abruptly that you wonder if some more extensive material from a previous draft was edited out to avoid opening old wounds. Most, if not all, of the key players are now gone, and since all this happened nearly four years after we graduated, perhaps we, at any rate, should let it go without further speculation at this point.

supported him fully in his college applications, and that as a result, he did not get into the colleges he wanted to. I know no details here, but looking back, there may have been something to his suspicions. I do remember Allan criticizing the Administration in Chapel, with Mr. Cunningham sitting right next to him, for its lack of support for our East Coast Model UN expedition to New York (when we tied for first prize in a competition involving about a hundred schools). I'm sure this public criticism by Allan won him no points with Cunningham. Allan also worked behind the scenes to ensure that our Class did not vote to dedicate the yearbook to Mr. Cunningham (who may have expected this honor), as detailed in Volume II. I doubt, however, that an account of this ever reached the Headmaster.

In all fairness, however, the photogenic Mr. Cunningham was at that time (and still is) well regarded by many supporters. As one classmate observes today, "He had his favorites, and I was one of them," citing Mr. Cunningham's frequent notes of recognition and encouragement, personal interest in his future, and help with getting him accepted to college. The Headmaster became supportively involved with student activities such as the SAC and the Rod and Gun Club (which was basically his idea). He was an ardent fan of the sports program (which saw a true renaissance during this time), and a regular presence at sports events. In my case, he took time to urge me in person to go to Harvard instead of to Brown, and I never regretted the advice. Doc Odell pointed out to me that Cunningham was the first Headmaster in modern times to raise serious money for the School and that in his relatively short tenure he increased faculty salaries by substantial amounts. He also instituted and funded other benefits for the faculty, such as sabbaticals and a firmer pension system. Building on Mr. St. John's beginnings, he developed and set in permanent place a professional Alumni Relations and fundraising staff. These were solid and important achievements with long-term benefits.

Most of all, Mr. Cunningham left a large set of footprints on the physical campus, as Mr. Paxton's School history recounts.[174] He was an initiating (and then an energizing) force behind the creation of Friends Hall; the Waughtel-Howe Field House; the Campanella Football Field (which also brought with it a quarter-mile track—with a 220-yard straightaway—to

---

174 See Paxton, Chapter XI, *passim*.

replace the five-laps-to-a-mile track near the tennis courts); the reconfiguration and landscaping of the old playing fields north and west of the main buildings; the renovation of the Hawes Gymnasium; new tennis courts; and the creation of enhanced quality space for the Lower and Middle Schools—a truly impressive record. Much of this was funded through a "Program for Progress" which brought nearly $1 million to the School in the 1960s, with $300,000 coming from the New England Yearly Meeting of Friends, and the rest from private contributions. He left much to build on. Whatever else may be said of him, good or bad, he did cut a wide swath during his seven-year tenure, and he was an important link in our chain of causation during the last three years we were at the School.

In Third Form, I had math with Mr. Marion L. Herman; biology with Mrs. Full; English with Mr. Kenneth Bennett; Third-Year Latin with Mr. Fuller; and German with Mr. Arthur Cate. Formal classes in art, music, and shop were behind us by now. This five-course schedule was similar to that of most classmates, except that a majority of them took French, not German.

Math. Mr. Herman was one of the most memorable figures in the Upper School. He held forth in Room 11 on the first floor, directly under study hall, in the northwest corner of the building. This room, both at the back and along the window ledges, was cluttered with old papers and (in our time) seldom-used instructional tools—pyramids, icosahedrons, cubes, and the like. This was the famous Ape Den—he called us monkeys when he was not calling us crumb bums—and I'm sure we often deserved the designations. There was never a dull moment in his class, and that was the whole point. Mr. Herman was entertaining as well as challenging.

Everyone called him the "Babe" behind his back—either from baseball's Babe Herman or from baseball's George Herman ("Babe") Ruth (whom, in the face, he resembled to some degree).[175] He was from Pennsylvania, a Dickinson graduate, with a master's degree from Columbia. At first glance, he appeared to be a very fierce character, but he actually was a marvelous person with a wonderful sense of humor and a twinkle in his eye—a person

---

175 These were two different players. Paxton, p. 163, asserts the nickname came from George Herman Ruth (Babe Ruth); others insist it came from "Babe" Herman.

Marion L. Herman

of many strongly held opinions which he would express unreservedly. His standard dress included a US Lawn Tennis Association green blazer and orthopedic shoes.[176] In addition to his classroom duties, he was Director of Testing, the varsity tennis coach, and advisor to the Chess Club. I remember that he became my advisor and wrote me recommendations to accompany my applications to colleges; I still remain grateful to him for this. His trademark was a rubber stamp with his initials on it surrounded by an oval. This M.L.H. designation appeared not only on returned math papers, but on official communications from the School that he sent out in his various administrative capacities.

He was as intellectually and personally honest as anyone you would ever meet. What you saw was what you got—there was no hidden agenda. There was never any instance of his saying one thing and doing another

---

[176] I am grateful to Bill Barrett for this recollection.

Third Form (1957-58)

(commendably, this could be said for most of the Moses Brown teaching staff). He would often hold forth in high dudgeon at the beginning of class on just about any topic, from politics to the latest medical discoveries. I remember he once told us in great solemnity that for each extra pound of weight we acquired, the heart would have to pump blood through another mile of blood vessels—so we should keep trim. He would not take a lot of class time on this, but it was intense time, and it was not unknown for him to take a few minutes at the beginning of class to expound on the defects of the Democratic Party and the virtues of the Republican Party. One of his favorite expressions when holding forth on political (or even School) issues was, "No matter how you slice it, it's still baloney."

He was indeed a Republican—an old Republican, from the Taft wing of the party. He was even more conservative (in the old meaning of the word) than Mr. Raines, and that was going some. I remember the morning after the election of 1958 Mr. Herman bemoaning the fact that the US Senate not only had been captured by the Democrats, but that it would be held by them for at least four years, given the prospects for 1960. In fact, they held it for twenty-four years. I don't remember when Mr. Herman passed away, but he may never have seen a Republican Senate again.

He was an excellent teacher, but with an interesting teaching method. He would seldom explain anything, but insist that each person in the class figure it out for himself. This would take place in repeated trials, until finally a solution was obtained. It could be very exasperating, but also very instructive in terms of finding out how one should approach the solution of problems. Only on rare occasions would he actually explain what was needed or what should be done—and this after the class had worked hard and still failed to find out what was required. He wanted us to think for ourselves and figure things out for ourselves, and this was to him more important than the specific solutions to any mathematical problem—or really any specific level of mathematical competency. He probably understood very well that those who figure out how to solve problems on their own will remember how to solve them much better than those who had it explained to them. Therefore, when we asked him for a solution to a problem, he would often respond, "Why should I have to snow, just so you can get the drift?"[177]

---

[177] He used many variations of "snow...get the drift."

Even when he explained something, he still tried to get us to think things through on our own. I remember once in Fourth-Form Geometry he was trying to get Bill Barrett, who was standing at the blackboard, to use a certain Euclidian axiom in his proof. Bill, who was very good at math and geometry, was having a temporary lapse, and Mr. Herman just couldn't get him to state the rather fundamental Euclidean building block that the proof required. So he took a wooden yardstick, held it up dramatically in front of Bill (and the class), then broke it in two over his knee, raised the two parts up in the air at a distance from each other, made a face that would have excited envy in W.C. Fields (whom he resembled), and finally brought the pieces slowly together, looking in Bill's direction. A light flashed, and Bill quickly stated, "The whole is equal to the sum of its parts." Mr. Herman, you see, never actually gave the answer.

He was very interested in the character development of his students. The "monkey" (or "ape") designation was a humorous way to put us in our place and counteract the high opinion we had of ourselves. If he heard nonsense from us, he called it that to our faces, often using the expression "horse feathers" (or "hogwash") in response to one of our points. He never ceased to remind us, usually also in a humorous way, that we had much to learn. If one of us recited at too great a length or with a hollow argument, he would admonish us, "Sit down, sailor, you're rocking the boat," or "You're full of coke."[178]

He took a great deal of interest in us as individuals, and was constantly joking with us and singling us out for comment or attention. For example, he repeatedly chided Barry Fain about "You have the floor, Fain has the floor covering"—a line from his family company's ad on TV. There was an intensity to his locutions, even his jokes. He never yelled, but always spoke authoritatively at a decibel level that commanded attention. If he briefly left the room, decorum would always prevail.[179] He might even shake his fist in your face in mock anger, but always with a bit of a grin and a facial gesture right out of vaudeville. He was forever exhorting us to achieve, to better our performances, to stretch ourselves as far as we could—trying to motivate us, and not only in math. He emphasized our potential, as well as our responsibility to achieve it. One of his favorite expressions was the

---
178 Taped interview with Ted Armstrong, March 27, 2014.
179 Bob Smith ('58); taped interview, March 26, 2014.

Biblical, "To whom much is given, of him shall much be expected." (For unto whomever much is given, of him shall much be required... —Luke 12:48). The implication was that anyone at Moses Brown, and certainly anyone sitting in Room 11, qualified for membership in the group of those to whom indeed much had been given—and hence from us much should be expected. Another expression he used frequently was the more portentous, "the mills of the gods grind slowly, but they grind."

He was a fascinating personality who cut a large swath in our consciousness. Few knew that his wife was an invalid, and that this ebullient man, so alive and engaging in the classroom, returned upstairs each afternoon to confront unceasing personal tragedy. She passed away during the summer before our senior year.

From our textbook in Second-Year Algebra,[180] we were given instruction in number theory (including negative numbers and irrational numbers); roots, primes, and factoring; polynomials (which by now were a bit less daunting than the name); radicals (which were actually rather tame); absolute values (easy); quadratic equations (hard: these gave me real difficulty, and they were very important); proportion (enjoyed it); geometric series and binomial expansions (again, daunting in their calculations); and logarithms (which were supposed to make calculations simple, but made things worse for me). We also had a bit of coordinate geometry somewhere along the way (although there was a lot more of this in the Fifth Form). Some of the new concepts I understood; some of the old ones I still had difficulty with, especially given my experiences in Mr. Tinker's First-Year Algebra class. Algebra was cumulative, and I had a lot of cumulating to do.

But there was more than the above. In addition to our text, Mr. Herman had us buy our old nemesis from Lower School, *Learning to Compute*. Apparently some of us still couldn't, and needed remedial attention. The exercises in that little volume were predictably boring, but manageable. Herman also had us buy a thin green exercise book called *Reviews and Examinations in Algebra*, written by two mathematics instructors, both from the Math Department at Phillips Andover: Messrs. Oswald Tower and Winfield Sides.[181] This was a no-nonsense volume, quite consistent with

---

180 Fehr, Carnahan, and Beberman, *Algebra Course 2*, New York: D.C. Heath, 1955.
181 Oswald Tower and Winfield Sides, *Reviews and Examinations in Algebra*, Second edition, D.C. Heath and Company, Boston, 1953.

Andover's North Shore Calvinist heritage. I'm sure its original purpose was to divide the elect from the damned, and in the first year, I was among the damned. It was filled both with exercises and problems, starting with factoring and proceeding through simple algebra to quadratics. We used it during all three years I had Mr. Herman.

Both the exercises and the problems grew exponentially in difficulty from simple to challenging to diabolical. Most problems seemed to involve railroad trains going in different directions at different speeds, sprinters running around tracks lapping each other, tanks being filled and emptied simultaneously, or interest rates on loans with complex terms negotiated by crafty bankers. Bill Barrett remembered a question asking what time it would be when the hands on a clock were at a certain specified angle with each other, and then, so many minutes later, they were at a different specified angle with each other.

The book was published in 1953, but it was a second edition, and the problems themselves seemed to come from a much more distant era—where freight trains went about 10 miles an hour and passenger trains went about 30 miles an hour—although I must admit that the speed of the Boston and Maine Railroad, which went through Andover (and on which I rode in wooden cars pulled by steam engines as a child) may have been accurately portrayed in these exercises.[182]

Here is a typical problem from Tower and Sides: "A Ferris wheel at a carnival can carry four passengers in each car. On the first trip of an evening, the passengers were seated four in the first car, two in the second car, and one in the third car; the same arrangement then continued all around the Ferris wheel. When the first trip was over, two-thirds of the passengers remained for the second trip, and three times as many got on as got off, leaving half a car vacant. How many passengers could the Ferris wheel carry?"[183]

And another: "Two steamers, S and T, have total crews of 20 and 15 men, respectively. S needs five days to complete her voyage and T needs ten days

---

182 One question did indeed involve the Boston and Maine—although the carrier was not identified as such. It begins: "A train leaves Portland for Boston at 8:00 A.M. and arrives in Boston at 12:30 P.M. ...." I'm not sure of the distance between Portland and Boston, but you can drive it today in less than two hours. This train was presumably not the Pine Tree Limited!
183 Page 170.

Third Form (1957-58)   253

to complete her voyage when it becomes necessary to rescue 56 persons from a sinking ship. How should these people be divided between S and T so that if S and T proceed to their respective ports, the same daily share of food shall be possible for everyone? Assume that S and T had just enough provisions for their voyages when they went to the rescue of the third ship."[184]

And a third: "Three cans are partly filled with water. If 3 quarts are poured from the second into the first, the first will then contain as many quarts as the other two together. However, if instead 5 quarts had been poured from the first into the third, the third would have had as many quarts as the second, and the first would still have had 2 quarts more than the second. How many quarts were in each can originally?"[185]

And a fourth: "A tank can be filled in three hours less time by one pipe than by a second pipe. If the water is flowing from both pipes the entire time, then the tank is filled in two hours. On one occasion the water was turned on from both pipes, and at the end of two hours the tank was found to be half full. Water from one of the pipes had stopped flowing. Which pipe was it, and for what length of time was the water flowing from it?"[186]

And finally: "One tank is filled with g gallons of wine and another tank with w gallons of water; m gallons are taken out of each tank—that from the first tank transferred to the second tank, and that from the second tank transferred to the first tank. This operation is repeated. Find the quantity of wine in the second tank after the second operation of transfers."[187] I think a much more relevant question might have involved the *quality* of the wine in the first tank after this double watering down had occurred, but that was not asked. Incidentally, problems involving vessels filled with wine and water were an obsession with Messrs. Tower and Sides. Perhaps Andover in those days was less stringent regarding alcohol than Moses Brown—or perhaps it cleverly dealt with the problem through adulteration.[188]

---

184 Page 115.
185 Page 124.
186 Page 159.
187 Page 169.
188 Alternatively, Tower and Sides may have been poking hidden fun at the late 19th Century Ritualist flap in British Anglican circles where the mixing of wine and water in the chalice had occasioned controversy and legislation forbidding the practice. Hidden jests are not alien to New England humor.

I'm not sure the following example came from Tower and Sides, but Mr. Herman once gave us a marvelous problem involving a swimming pool with three pipes of different sizes pouring into it with different rates of flow. We had to calculate how long it would take to fill. That by itself would have been negotiable, but the drain also was open at the same time, so we had to account for the fact that water was flowing out as well as in. Somewhere along the way leaves clogged the drain to retard the rate at which it let the water out, and someone at some point turned off the water from one of the pipes. We were to calculate when the pool was full, and express it as a single number of minutes.

We were actually supposed to solve these—and thereby develop our reasoning skills and ability to conceptualize in symbolic notation. In many cases, of course, there were no practical applicable skills being developed—unless one were to become a railroad dispatcher, swimming pool manager, ship's purser, vintner, or carnival operator. But the point was to develop the ability to meet a wide range of either theoretical or practical problems with some skills to solve them. In the Third Form, I had real difficulties, both with straight exercises (involving, for example, solving equations, factoring, or simplifying complex expressions), and especially with the problems. Only when I got to geometry did I begin to understand Second-Year Algebra, and by the end of the Fourth Form, I could run through the Tower and Sides problems like a hot knife through butter (although I probably no longer could). But that was in the future. Second-Year Algebra was a real rough grind. I got a "C" in the Fall Term, and had to come in on Saturdays. Somehow, I managed to eke out a "B-" for the year, but it was not easy.

English. For English, we had Mr. Kenneth Bennett, new to Moses Brown that year as I recall. He came from California and was a graduate of the University of California. He was a person whom I could never quite figure out. I didn't care too much for him, but it would be hard to say why. I never had an unpleasant passage with him; he was never unfair to me. His classes were often engaging, and he took an interest in us as students. But somehow, I never quite felt comfortable with him the way I had with teachers like Odell, Fuller, Taber, Full, or Herman—or later with Pratt,

E. Kenneth Bennett

Jeffers, and Raines. In their classes you could say what you thought and not have to guard yourself. There was a sense of rapport with them that I never seemed to have with Bennett. There was a slight air of superiority about him, and this may have been a bit distancing.

I later worked with him on the Model UN in the Fourth Form when we hosted it at Brown, but in a minor capacity, and there was not much interaction. He was also advisor to the yearbook (which I edited), but in that case the staff did most of the work, and Mr. Bennett's role was simply to make sure that something was happening. So again, I did not spend a lot of time working with him in this capacity either.

Perhaps I am being unfair, but there were others who had hesitations about him, or just didn't like him, and they called him "Buzzy Bennett"—perhaps because he had a buzz haircut. He lived on corridor, and I think that some boarders had reservations. On the other hand Allan Cokin did very well in this class and thought highly of Mr. Bennett, as did Dave London, who styled him "first-rate"—an especially important evaluation since Dave had just joined us from another school and had good grounds for comparison. I guess it was just a matter of personality and it remains difficult to pin down.[189]

During the Fall Term, Third-Form English met in Room 4 on the north corridor—where we had had math with Mr. Roberts. It then moved into the old biology lab on the same corridor when we returned from Christmas break and Mrs. Full moved with her class into the new Thomas Science Building. Mr. Bennett taught a good course. As Dave London recalled, "he was business-like in class, and knew his stuff."[190] That was certainly true. I recall his teaching style as matter-of-fact commentary interspaced with a few humorous asides. He focused on a text, often read parts of it, and then explained the author's purposes. He enjoyed humor, but presented it with a knowing smile more often than with a laugh.

The entire course focused on American literature. We had a large anthology from the same series used in the First and Second Forms.[191] It opened with a set of essays in a section called "A Modern Sampler," paralleling the introductory essays in the earlier anthologies from this series. These essays, however, with some exceptions, were less aimed at adolescents, and more at a mature reader, many being "realistic" in the literary sense of the word. There was a section on American political writings, some iconic (like the Declaration of Independence and Lincoln's Second Inaugural), others illustrating democratic practices. I do remember that we had to memorize the Declaration of Independence (except for the Bill of Particulars), and recite it in class. Allan Cokin did a great job with this. I memorized it accurately, but when asked to recite, I did so at lightning speed and spoiled the effect. Although this was not my intention, it may have seemed a parody.

---

[189] Allan Cokin joined our Class in the Second Form, and soon became an academic superstar and later Captain of the basketball team. He graduated from Cornell University, and eventually became a professional bridge player. He was forced to step down from the American Contract Bridge League as the result of an incident in 1979, but was reinstated a few years later. He made amends, and upon his passing, the president of the ACBL, quoted on the internet, stated that "He was a fabulous teacher and a fabulous coach. There are [countless] women in Palm Beach County whom he taught to play bridge. He was a model citizen, very helpful, and supportive of bridge."
[190] Interview, 2010.
[191] Pooley, R. C., Blair, W., Hornberger, T., and Farmer, P., *The United States in Literature*, Chicago: Scott Foresman and Company, 1957.

In any case, Mr. Bennett did not appreciate my manner of presentation, and he was right.

The part of the anthology on which we spent the most time in class was a section that provided quality examples from a set of major American authors, chronologically arranged, beginning with the colonial period and going tentatively into the twentieth century: Franklin, Irving, Thoreau, Whitman, Twain, and Stephen Vincent Benet. The selections included prose and poetry, fiction and nonfiction. For each part, there was a discussion of the period and its special literary styles, and mention was made of other authors and poets not anthologized in the book.

The colonial period featured Franklin (with serious excerpts from the *Autobiography* and from some of his later writings), but also contained some early American poets. The second (post-Revolutionary) period contained several selections from Washington Irving—including an essay about an English Christmas. Thoreau represented the Transcendentalists; we read passages from *Walden* (including the battle of the ants), and *Civil Disobedience*. There was a section on Whitman—I remember reading "When Lilacs Last in the Dooryard Bloomed" for the first time in this class.

It is strange how poetry can be evocative in unpredictable ways. The association of lilacs with the Civil War in this poem reinforced an earlier association between the two in my consciousness. The folks always took me with them when they drove to Webster, Massachusetts, around Memorial Day to decorate my grandfather's stone. In the same plot was the headstone of Great Uncle Lo,[192] who had been a Civil War veteran, some of whose stories about the war had been retold to me by my father. The Civil War was thus in our family's oral tradition. In addition, that section of the cemetery contained the graves of many other Civil War veterans.

After putting the geraniums in their proper places, we would repair to the nearby home of Cousin Fritz (my father's first cousin), a landscape architect who had surrounded the federal mansion where he lived with every conceivable variety and color of lilac—which were usually in full bloom at that time of year. We would wander around admiring them and smelling

---

[192] Loring Davis Waters

their rich fragrance. To complete the "association loop," Cousin Fritz on Memorial Day always flew the very same American flag over his front door that had flown there during the Civil War. Webster, lilacs, and Memorial Day had always meant the Civil War to me, and Whitman's poem put it all together in a very new and striking way.

The anthology also contained a section on Twain, including "Huck Visits the Grangerfords" from *Huck Finn* and some humorous short stories (including the famous "...*Jumping Frog*..."). Bennett liked Twain, and I remember him reading us the Grangerford piece and then discussing it, pointing out its use of satire to lampoon romanticism. Although it was not in the anthology, Bennett also read out loud Twain's steamboat landing passage from *Life on the Mississippi*, illustrating his extraordinary ability to write descriptive prose. Dave London, too, remembered Mr. Bennett walking around reading out loud to the class. In other English classes, the students often read; in Mr. Bennett's and Mr. Taber's, they themselves often read. Crane's "A Mystery of Heroism" was included in the anthology, and someone did a book report on *Red Badge of Courage*. We also read Bret Hart's *Luck of Roaring Camp*.

Steven Vincent Benet represented the twentieth century in this collection. We read, among other works, "The Devil and Daniel Webster" and "Listen to the People"—a World War II-era epic poem affirming democracy. Mr. Bennett also shared portions of *John Brown's Body* with us. Bennett supplemented Benet with other twentieth century authors.

In a subsequent part of the anthology, we read quite a bit of American poetry, including Bryant's "Thanatopsis," Poe's "The Raven," poems from the Concord/Cambridge set—Longfellow's "A Boy's Will," Lowell's "The Courtin'" (I remember Bennett laughing over "His heart kep' goin' pity-pat, But hern went pity Zekle"), Whittier's "Dear Lord and Father..." (which we already knew), and Emerson's "Rhodora". We also read some Dickinson, and a few moderns (Frost, E.A. Robinson, Sandburg, MacLeish). There was a section on humor with a hilarious Thurber piece on his college days illustrated with a couple of his drawings.

We did not read the entire anthology, and there was much more to the course than works contained in it. First, Bennett required us to select an author, read his or her major works, and then write a serious report on the corpus. Bill Barrett and Bill Brehm each chose Herman Wouk. Al Cokin picked Steinbeck. I picked Melville. I did so because Bennett said he admired him. This was a very bad strategy on my part because Bennett obviously knew a lot more about Melville than I ever did or could at that time, and so he was very critical in an informed way of my efforts. I reread *Moby Dick*, of course, but also the romances *Typee* and *Omoo*, and some short stories, including "Bartleby the Scrivener" and "Billy Budd." I also read a little secondary literature on Melville—Lewis Mumford, as I recall. My eventual treatise on Melville was not a very distinguished effort, but the assignment gave me an opportunity to write a major paper based on extensive reading and some secondary research. It was also a project that took place over a large part of one term.

In addition to this project, Bennett had the whole class read Miller's *The Crucible*, and we discussed it in some detail. We also discussed specific passages from it in class. We found it to be a powerful play highlighting one of the worst troughs in the New England story. It portrays many human qualities, from hypocrisy to heroism, and we explored such values in class. We read this play only a few years after the political demise of Joe McCarthy and less than a year after his actual demise. Its significance in the McCarthy context was made clear to us.

Bennett was much taken with Faulkner, and we read *Intruder in the Dust*—one of the more user-friendly of the Faulkner novels. It was entertaining and amusing, with an exciting plot and some real drama. You could read it at several levels, and it needed some explaining for high school sophomores, but I do remember enjoying it.

We read Steinbeck. Allan Cokin, who chose Steinbeck as his special author, spoke to the class about him. I remember his description of "Bus Stop." I also remember reading *Of Mice and Men* at about this time. I don't think we read *Grapes of Wrath*, but Mr. Bennett read passages from it to us in class. I remember him discussing "realism" in this context and making the point that "realism" was a special literary term and was not actually "realism" in the dictionary sense of the word. If you wanted the latter, he argued, then you should read Thornton Wilder's little farce, "The Happy Journey to Trenton and Camden," also in our anthology, which reflected with little elaboration what most ordinary people's lives were about. We also were introduced to Hemingway. Somewhere along the way we read *The Old Man and the Sea*, but I'm not sure it was this year.

Allan Cokin was really a star performer in this class. He was very interested in twentieth century literature, very engaged with what was unfolding in class, and an inspiration to many of us.

I think it is fair to say that the entire course focused on literature. We had some exercises in reading comprehension, but we did not spend much time, if any, on grammar or writing style. We wrote a lot, but were assessed more on content and argument than on style, although we were marked down for obvious mistakes in grammar, punctuation, and even penmanship. It is not that we had reached an age where teaching grammar, usage, and good writing style were no longer necessary—we certainly revisited them with a vengeance in Mr. Paxton's class two years later—but Mr. Bennett was really teaching a low-level college literature course, and with this, he did a good job. I'm sure that young instructors, such as Bennett, Pratt, Justin, Jeffers, and others, coming to Moses Brown from recent college or graduate work, brought their experiences and newly formed intellectual and pedagogical perspectives directly to the classroom. We were the immediate beneficiaries.

Mr. Bennett gave each of us an oral exam near the end of the course. I recall him asking me at the start of this who Alexis de Toqueville was. The name was familiar—I had some vague memory of Bennett's having mentioned him early on (in the colonial period, I erroneously thought)—but as to who he was, what he had written, or why he was important, I had no recollection. The name was obviously French, however, and I had some vague memory that de Toqueville had come to America and had written about it, and all this triggered the memory of another French name: Eugene de Crevecour whom Bennett had also discussed in the distant past.

So, perhaps to show that I was not drawing a total blank, I naively asked Mr. Bennett if de Toqueville was in any way connected to de Crevecour. He brightened up a bit, replied (no doubt to be helpful) that there were indeed some similarities, and generously asked if I would prefer to discuss de Crevecour instead of de Toqueville. The problem was that I really

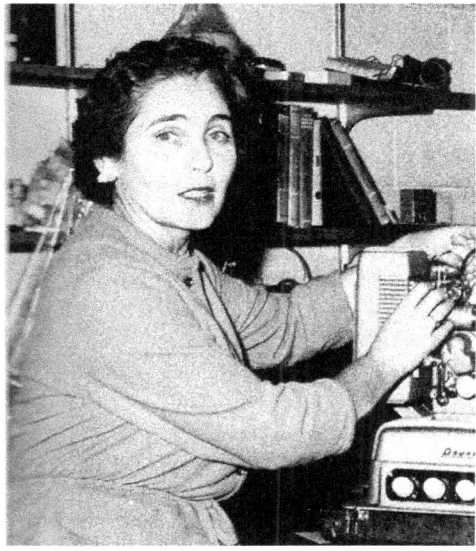
Ada T. Full

hadn't the faintest idea who de Crevecour was either. All I had remembered was the name. This further admission led to an awkward silence. To get things back on track, Bennett then asked me a question concerning Melville, with whom he knew I was familiar, and I was able to recover a small amount of the considerable ground lost with de Toqueville and de Crevecour. My introduction to oral exams was not auspicious, and I never broke into the "A" range in this class.

Biology. Mrs. Full's biology course was the class I enjoyed the most in the Third Form. In the Fall Term, we met in Room 7, the classroom we had used for General Science, which was also the old biology lab. In January, when we returned from Christmas vacation, all the lab materials and equipment had been moved to the new biology room on the south end of the L. Ralston Thomas Science Building where we met for the rest of the year.

Mrs. Full, who used a model of a human skeleton as a coatrack, was a very good teacher, and we were familiar with her from General Science the previous year. She knew her subject thoroughly and seemed to be on top of new developments, including the early stages of RNA and DNA research. Her lectures were straightforward and clear. She had a good sense of humor and a relaxed, but no-nonsense, manner. She would arrive at the beginning of class, set forth the agenda for the day, and proceed to teach. She was very adept at using visual aids, and she had a new machine, of which she was very proud, that would project images onto a screen directly from a microscopic slide. She was very willing to answer questions and go over material a second time. She did not view her role as providing inspiration, but instruction. She was friendly and fair with everyone, and a calm presence in the classroom. She was willing to work with us individually. For example, towards the end of the year she encouraged us on an individual basis to develop experiments and demonstrations so that we might participate in the Rhode Island Science Fair. Several did this. I remember fashioning a model of the ear, but it was a fairly clumsy one—a disappointment to her—and I did not enter it.

The late Bob Smith ('58) recalled once being bored during biology lab and asking Mrs. Full, "Why are we learning this stuff? Why are we cutting up frogs?" She had responded by saying, "Look, you may never be in a lab ever again in your life, but I'm trying to teach you a way of thinking—so that you can analyze things when you get older." According to Bob, "That stuck with me. That was very powerful: don't worry about the contents—it's the way of thinking I'm trying to teach you."[193]

Although our text, *Modern Biology*, by Moon, Mann, and Otto,[194] was quite new, it was probably based on very classical biological forms of instruction. This book, indeed the whole course, was built around the identification and classification of various organisms, from very simple ones to very complex ones, together with an analysis of their structure, the functions of their component parts, and their interaction with their environment. The course itself was built around the reading, and especially around Mrs. Full's lectures and her own handouts. All this was augmented by labs in which we saw firsthand what both the text and Mrs. Full were describing. Memorizing the names and functions of specific components of each organism was a central requirement of the course.

---

193 Taped interview with Bob Smith at his Providence home, March 26, 2014.
194 New York: Henry Holt and Company, 1956.

The course began with a brief discussion of the environment itself and the physical and chemical bases of life. Then there was a major section on botany, followed by an even larger section on animal life. The course ended with some genetics and speculations by Mrs. Full regarding the future direction of biological research.

We started with some basic building blocks of biology, such as proteins and amino acids, starches, the nitrogen cycle, and so forth. We then studied plant life, looking at the roots, stems, and leaves of plants that had seeds, and then at seedless plants, mushrooms and the like. We learned the difference between the monocot, the herbaceous dicot, and the woody dicot—and drew cross sections of them. From this we then proceeded to the animal kingdom, starting with the simplest species and then moving up finally to humans. We had to learn the phyla, many of the classes and orders, and what characteristics separated them. I remember sponges and worms and then arthropods, which included lobsters, spiders, and insects. Using the text and handouts, Mrs. Full carefully presented the various parts of the organism and discussed their functions as we went up the scale of complexity.

This was the first course we had at Moses Brown with serious, well-structured labs. I think they were held once a week, although during some weeks they may have been more frequent. The purpose of the labs in almost all cases was to produce a systematic examination of a life-form, either under the microscope or as the result of dissection, followed by a careful drawing of it. Each of us had his own jar filled with formaldehyde containing the various specimens we were to examine or dissect.

Our first labs were basically to acquaint us with the equipment and to do simple microscopic exercises with preexisting slides. We then, as our first real application, went on to examine and draw the euglena, a one-cell phenomenon that is considered both a plant and an animal. We put the euglena specimens in a matrix of cotton to stop them swimming around, looked at them though the microscope, and then drew one of them, labeling all the parts of the cell we had seen.

We then graduated to amoebae, which moved too slowly to create motion problems for the microscope; they were not exactly riveting actors, but if you had enough patience you might see one divide in very slow motion.

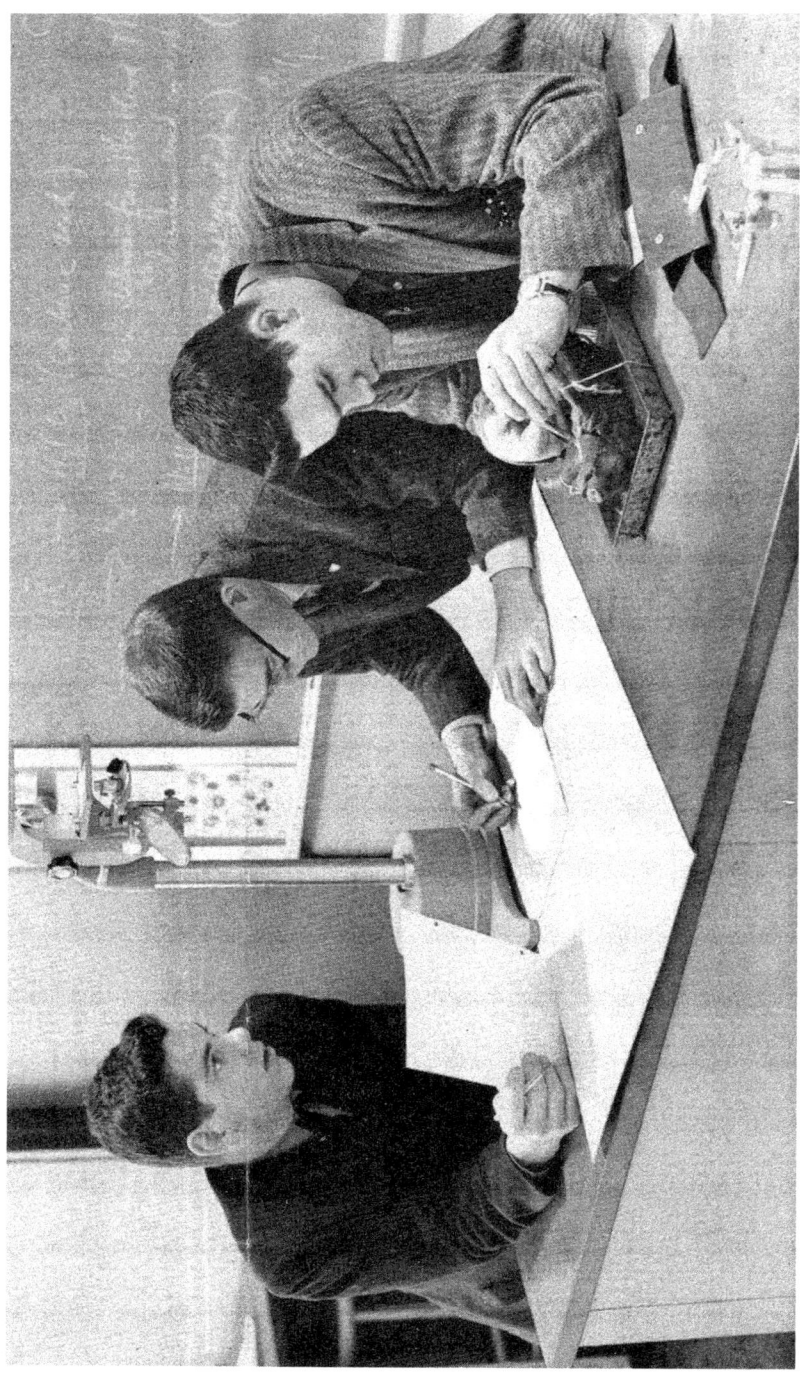

Bob Marshall, Ned Young, and Al Brenner in biology lab.

Thence to hydra, which I believe were dead and could be looked at with leisure. From them we passed on to worms—I remember seeing a liver fluke under the microscope. I don't remember doing anything with sponges in lab (other than mop things up)—although Mrs. Full talked about them in class and we had to identify their various parts—but we did dissect an earthworm and a clam. I don't think we dissected any arthropods, although someone may have cut up a crayfish, and I seem to remember seeing a millipede at some point along the way.

We spent the rest of the year on vertebrates, starting with fish. From there we went to amphibians and thence to reptiles and birds. As each succeeding specimen became more complex, Mrs. Full spent more time on showing us how to dissect it. We had scalpels and other instruments to cut, pin, and hold the pieces in place. Our drawings became more complex. I think we dissected a fish and a frog. Our text had a drawing of a frog with plastic overlays showing the various organs layered over each other—as you turned the overlay new organs were placed on top of the ones previously displayed in a sort of three-dimensional demonstration.

The course culminated with mammals, including humans, on which we spent a fair amount of time. At this level of complexity, identifying the various organs, including the bones (we had to memorize the names of countless bones), was only the first step. Mrs. Full, supported by the text, went into great detail in class about the functions of each mammalian organ and how the whole organism functioned interdependently. She explained the heart, the lungs, and the circulation of the blood. She explained the lymph system and the immune system (and their functions). She explained the digestive system. She explained the nervous system and the brain, together with eyes, ears, and nose. She explained how the kidneys and the liver worked. She discussed hormones, their functions, and the organs that produced them. She explained muscles and the chemical process that made them contract in order to move the limbs. She did not go into great detail, as I recall, regarding the human reproductive system, but she did spend some serious time on genetics at the end of the spring. We carefully drew most of the major human organs, labeling their various parts.

To illustrate her points, Mrs. Full had either pictures or models of the organs she was discussing, like the heart or the eye. Again, in the text, there was an overlay like the one for the frog showing the various human organs in layers.

In lab, we each dissected a fetal pig (due to its anatomical similarity to the human body). This was a major undertaking. Mrs. Full provided us with detailed written instructions for these dissections. There was obviously no dissection of the human body, but, as I recall, a classmate arrived one day with some sperm which he put on a slide and thence under the microscope. We were not informed as to how this specimen was obtained. Mrs. Full was not at all amused. As Bob Smith recalled, some students gave her a hard time.[195] After all, she was one of the very few female instructors in Upper School—and she was teaching biology to adolescent boys. Still, she always managed to maintain control of the class, held its attention, and earned the respect of just about everyone there.

Diversions aside, this was a very solid course, and a credible introduction to good science. It relied heavily on memorization and emphasized the ability to identify. We memorized countless cell parts and organs. We memorized the major bones in the human skeleton, keeping our tibias conceptually apart from our fibulas. We memorized the phyla, subphyla, and in the case of vertebrata, the classes. For the class *mammalia*, in turn, we memorized many of the orders. With all this memorization, it was a course designed to build a basic vocabulary of biology and to give a good overview of how organisms function. I imagine it was very good grounding for college botany and anatomy courses, and ultimately for pre-med classes and medical school itself. At a deeper conceptual level, it developed the concepts of structure, function, system, and interactivity in a relatively sophisticated way. As Bob Smith noted, it introduced us to a new way of thinking—in this case a less linear way than much of what we had learned before in math classes and General Science. The course also introduced us to laboratory work with its emphasis on careful observation, careful procedure, and careful portrayal of the results. Despite the fact that it came at the very dawn of the RNA and DNA revolution, and that there have been enormous advances in biology, genetics, medicine, biochemistry, and bioengineering since, this same course, if taught today with a little modification, would still provide a useful introduction to the vocabulary

---

195 Taped interview, March 26, 2014.

of biology and to a basic understanding of how organisms and their components function.

Looking back on all this, it seems that I found it much easier to memorize the vocabulary of biology than the vocabulary of a foreign language. I think this was the case for others as well. I am not sure why it was the case, but I suspect that it had something to do with the help afforded to memory by visual, spatial, and functional factors. Having a drawing or a picture of something and associating it with a location in a larger matrix seemed to make it easier to remember its name and especially its function.

Our textbook, in addition to its main focus on botany and zoology, also discussed the environment and environmental concerns—natural resources, conservation, preserving native habitats, and what today would be called sustainability. This was an important subtheme throughout. Mrs. Full did not emphasize these objectives at length in class, but she did mention them and certainly endorsed them. In this sense, Moon, Mann, and Otto anticipated many contemporary developments in what today would be called environmental science. For me, Third-Form Biology was one bright spot in an otherwise fairly drab year.

Mechanical Drawing. In the Third Form we were offered the option of taking Mechanical Drawing with Mr. Howe as an alternative to Third-Year Latin. About a dozen or so of us did. Bill Brehm was one, and the following is based on his recollections.

The Mechanical Drawing class met in a small room carved out of the Shop area in the basement of the Studio directly on the left as you entered from outdoors. The room no longer exists. It was on the south side of the building and was created by two partitions (forming the north and east sides of the room) meeting at a right angle. These had metal bottoms rising about four feet up from the floor with glass above them rising to the ceiling. The glass in all probability was used in the walls to let light pass from the windows of this room out into the Shop area, and from the windows of the Shop area into this room. It enabled people in the Shop area to observe Mechanical Drawing students at work, and vice versa. The door was in the shorter (east) partition near the door leading to the outside of the building.

There were a dozen or so drafting tables in this room and tall chairs which could tip over backwards if you were not careful. As I recall, lights with conical shades hung from the ceiling over each table in the early days, and were replaced by fluorescent lights by the time we were in the Upper School. The area had maps and drawings on two walls, with the glass partitions largely left clear. One of these drawings was a plan for dividing up the acreage in nearby Dexter Asylum into house lots—which never happened because Brown University bought the land to use for its athletic facilities.

Mr. Howe was a graduate of the Rhode Island School of Design. As Bill Brehm remembered it, he did not use a textbook. His Mechanical Drawing classes began by introducing students to front, side, and top representations of objects. Initially, these were very simple objects, regular and easy to draw, but in a short time the objects became irregular and the views were no longer straight-on; the representations were from different angles. Along the way he introduced the students to the concepts underlying perspective, and then to two-point perspective.[196]

Mr. Howe used wooden pieces as models. Initially these were simple cubes, pyramids, and other common geometric figures, but he soon introduced complex wooden pieces, often with holes cut into them. Bill remembered an object with a fairly sharp bowl-shaped depression in it. Students were required to draw each object from different angles, often using perspective. As the course advanced, mechanical objects, such as screws, bolts, shafts, cams, and gears, were drawn. Finally, near the end of the course, students were given some instruction in architectural drawing, including floor plans, simple elevations, and simple landscape designs.

Each student had a mechanical drawing set, including straight edge, compass, and a range of templates with different angles and curves. At the beginning, all work was done in pencil; later on the class graduated to ink. By the end of the course, they were actually doing blueprints.

Mr. Howe would explain the day's task and then would walk around to each drafting table and comment on each student's progress. If something

---

196 As Bill notes, that is what we are doing now—viewing Moses Brown from two perspectives separated by 50 years.

was wrong, he would point it out, and you were often left to figure out how to fix it. All drawings had to be labeled in precise fashion with an appropriately lettered name in simple, but bold, calligraphy identifying the student who had executed it. There had to be a title and date on each. As the drawings became more complicated and more mechanical, parts were labeled and measurements included with attributive arrows appropriately drawn to the relevant parts of the object portrayed. There was a premium on neatness, clarity, and precision.[197]

This was very much an introductory course, but in it Mr. Howe taught students some fundamental rudiments of art, engineering, and architecture—as well as how to think with clarity, and to execute designs with care and precision. It was excellent training (or at least an excellent beginning) for anyone who wished to enter the creative arts, broadly defined. It taught one to think structurally, and this by itself was potentially as important as the specific skills acquired at the drafting table.

Bill remembered Mr. Howe as a very nice person—whom he would have described at the time as "a kindly old man," although he resists this appellation today since Mr. Howe in the 1950s was decades younger than we are now. He says that if he was forced to choose one adjective to describe Mr. Howe's style, it would be "encouraging." He "did not get 'in your face.' If you were not performing well, he would try to correct your errors."

Mr. Howe was patient and he took a great deal of time with you on an individual basis. Bill recalled, "As my advisor, he monitored my academic progress or lack thereof. He encouraged and congratulated. In the days when doctors still made house calls, Mr. Howe came to my home to see me after my appendectomy and to talk to my parents about my college applications."

He was a Quaker and always had a very positive outlook on life (which may have contributed to his living to be ninety-nine—Mrs. Howe made one hundred). There was usually a smile on his face. He often greeted you with jocular enthusiasm. He laughed a lot, and could see humor in most situations. He frequently kidded around with you and occasionally used his very

---

[197] Bill remembered, (note to me, June 11, 2010), that one student, Halsey Herreshoff ('51), turned in a perfect drawing, but had points taken off because he spelled his own name wrong!

disreputable felt hat to strike a theatrical pose. But in his presence, there was never any question about who was quietly in command—whether it was in Shop, in Mechanical Drawing, or out on the track. Underneath all the good humor, there was a very strong person who knew how to handle us kids, and knew how to earn our respect.

Third-Year Latin. I entered Third-Year Latin with some trepidation, since Second-Year Latin had been an increasing challenge. I didn't have to take it, but I was encouraged to do so by parents and advisors. Our instructor again was Mr. Fuller (Mr. Herman was the only other instructor I had three times in Upper School). Although we did do some composition (and had a special little workbook for this purpose), most of the course concentrated on translation—and for this I was grateful. The routine was for us to be assigned passages for homework, and then translate them in class. This I could keep up with by using a dictionary the night before to try to get on top of the vocabulary. This practice was encouraged.

At the beginning, our principal author was Cicero, and I liked Cicero. We read his signature philippic against Catiline ("*O Tempora! O Mores!*"), as well as other speeches of his. The political circumstances and significance would be explained to us to contextualize the oration. Although these were in a textbook, and presumably edited to some degree, I think we translated a large percentage of each original speech. Later in the year, we read some of Virgil's *Aeneid* (selections from the first, third, and fourth books, through Dido, as I recall), and a few poems of Ovid.[198]

With respect to grammar and composition, by now we were in the big leagues: subjunctives, contrary-to-fact usages, indirect discourse, supines, deponents, gerunds, and lots of new ablatives.[199] We were supposed to use these forms in writing Latin sentences. Mercifully, we were not assigned a lot of them. Still, they reminded me that somehow I had let things get so far ahead of me that I could never catch up—without going back to the middle of the first-year text and, effectively, starting all over. I remember meeting

---

198 For the poetry, we used Wilbert Lester Carr and Harry E. Wedeck, *Latin Poetry*, Boston: Heath and Company, 1940.
199 See *Exercises in Writing Latin to Accompany Using Latin III*, Chicago: Scott Foresman, 1957.

Third Form (1957-58)

Harrison Huntoon, one of my former classmates, then at Taft, when he came home for a visit. He engaged in a humorous exercise of one-upmanship by asking me if we had reached the past periphrastic in Latin class.[200] I had to admit that we had not. I did turn the tables on him a bit by asking him to explain it to me. He was somewhat vague in his response, which was self-referentially appropriate since the periphrastic (I subsequently learned) refers to vague (perhaps redundant or unnecessary) speech. The problem for me was that by this time everything in Latin was periphrastic.

Returning to the lifeline used in Second-Form Latin, I earned extra credit by supplementing the Latin itself with more outside readings from Mr. Fuller's book collection, which, combined with successful in-class translations, kept my grade marginally respectable, but the Latin itself was still daunting. Again, vocabulary was a stumbling block. If you knew what the words meant, you could often piece together the tenses, cases, etc., from the context, but by now vocabulary itself was almost totally an exercise in dictionary thumbing.

German. This was the year that Moses Brown expected us to begin learning a modern language. I took First-Year German with Mr. Cate—a grand person and a very erudite scholar. He easily could have taught at the college level, indeed at the graduate level, but he clearly had devoted his life to Moses Brown. We were among the last classes to have him—he retired at the end of this academic year, receiving much acclaim, although he did return from time to time to teach special classes. He was fully fluent in Greek and Latin, both of which he had taught at Moses Brown. He occasionally quoted to us from both. On more than one occasion when I went to his office hours to ask a question he would be sitting there reading a text in Greek. Once he read a passage to me and translated it. I forget where the passage was from, but it was about drinking and its perils, and it culminated with the line, "water is best." Homer was decidedly his favorite Greek text.[201]

---

200 Harrison Huntoon joined our Class in the early years of Lower School, leaving us for Taft at the end of the Second Form. After a long and fruitful career with NASA in Houston, Texas, he returned to Rhode Island to help manage his family's successful textile business—one of the few remaining today in New England. He passed away in 2021.

201 *Quaker*, June 3, 1958.

On another occasion, when I entered Mr. Cate's classroom, he and Mr. Whitford were standing there, and on the desk was a handwritten illuminated medieval manuscript (I think it was a reproduction; it could possibly have been an original, I'm not sure). They were busy, and I did not interrupt, but did follow the conversation from a respectful distance. Mr. Cate was translating the manuscript for Mr. Whitford, who understood Latin, but was apparently having some difficulties with the dialect of this particular passage and the frequent use of abbreviations in the text. I remember Mr. Cate pointing out to Mr. Whitford that "p" in the manuscript meant "per." I don't remember any of the other abbreviations, but I do remember Mr. Cate's finger slowly passing over the manuscript line by line as he read the Latin and translated it carefully, looking up at Mr. Whitford from time to time, while Mr. Whitford followed along and nodded recurrently with very engaged understanding.

Mr. Cate was well-traveled, having visited ten foreign countries before the age of jet aircraft (Switzerland was his favorite country, and Bächistock in the Glärnisch Alps just southwest of Zurich was the highest mountain he climbed). French was Mr. Cate's favorite modern language—he liked its clarity—and he frequently taught it.[202] He also spoke Spanish and Italian—he once told us that Colpit's Travel Agency called him occasionally when someone arrived in town who didn't speak English, and he would go downtown to their rescue, translating from almost any modern language. He spoke Dutch fluently, and I think one of the Scandinavian languages, probably Swedish. I'm nearly certain that he was also fluent in Russian because when Sputnik was launched he told us with authority how to pronounce it [spootnik], and what it meant [little traveler]. I don't know if he spoke any oriental language, but he may have, since, according to the *Quaker*, he was fluent in thirteen languages.[203] He occasionally taught Spanish at Moses Brown. One of my classmates humorously recounted his travails being in a small Spanish class taught by Mr. Cate—the other two members being native Spanish speakers Joe Abella and Hernan Franco!

Mr. Cate was a person of great intellectual curiosity, and not just in his beloved humanities (which he defined as history, literature, and human

---

202 *Ibid.*
203 *Ibid.*

Arthur W. Cate

thought).[204] I remember once coming to his office before class and he was discussing relativity with two or three people standing around the desk. "Can you tell me," he asked, "taking into consideration the motion of the earth, the sun, and the galaxy, exactly how fast this point on my desk here moves in some absolute way? Or can you only tell me how fast it moves with respect to something else?"

When Mr. Cate taught us German, he was on the verge of retirement. He was not too well physically. He had lost the use of one eye some years before. The story went that he had stepped on the upright tines of an iron rake left carelessly on the ground—and the handle had sprung up and hit him in the eye. He was having other health problems. I remember that he had to have a serious operation the year after he retired. On that occasion he adopted the strategy of telling his surgeons a series of riddles before the operation, informing them that he would reveal the answers

---

204 *Ibid.*

afterwards—so if they were really curious about knowing those answers, they had better do a good job. One was "What is a "psycho-ceramic"? Answer: "a crack-pot."

In addition to being a scholar, Mr. Cate came across in class as a very warm, friendly, and understanding human being. He always seemed upbeat and engaged. Every point he made seemed to come across as a piece of good news he had just heard and was very anxious to share with us. He enjoyed his subject and wanted us to feel this same enjoyment. In his enthusiasm, he would step forward and backwards, and occasionally, in the latter case, bump his head against the blackboard—which did not seem to bother him at all. He shared experiences. He also used linguistic analogies. I remember once he was discussing how in German the infinitive form could in certain circumstances be used as a substitute for the indicative, and he asked us if we had ever been up to New Hampshire and heard people from the backwoods greeting each other with a "How be you?" He said this was an ancient usage going way back in Old English with its German roots and was directly related to an analogous usage in modern German.

Mr. Cate's German course was clearly taught in the classical manner—probably going back to the methods of the nineteenth century. This was not Berlitz or the intense method of the language lab so much in use today. Nor was it in any sense a course with total immersion; he taught in English, although he often spoke to us or read to us in German to illustrate his points. It was, however, good grounding and the class was always interesting. This course had one common feature with other language courses at Moses Brown: an early emphasis on proper pronunciation. We were to learn *Hochdeutsch*, just as our classmates were learning Parisian French and Castilian Spanish. In German, given its phonetic spelling, after you mastered "*Ich*" the rest of pronunciation seemed easy. This focus on pronunciation may simply have been driven by college standards (or by what was considered appropriate throughout the modern language teaching culture in America), but I think there was more going on here. We were being taught to enunciate in the style and manner of the most educated people in each country. We were being given a basic foundation which, if fully built upon, would eventually enable us to circulate abroad at high social levels without being looked down upon by native speakers; that, at least, seemed to be the aim. We were not being taught business, tourist, or entertainment

German, French, or Spanish, but literary German, French, or Spanish. We were being taught by instructors educated before World War II (in Mr. Cate's case, before World War I), part of an academic generation that had been brought up in a world where Americans were regarded as somewhat culturally inferior to many educated Europeans. With lessons in quality pronunciation, we were being given a capability without which we could never mingle with European social elites on equal cultural terms. It was an absolutely necessary condition, although obviously not a sufficient one, for such a mingling. As we built vocabulary and usage, we would not have to be restyled by a German, French, or Spanish Henry Higgins. Interestingly in this regard, however, pride in the independent American linguistic tradition, as recognized and affirmed by Noah Webster, was sufficiently strong that no one at Moses Brown would have dreamed of teaching us the accents of Queen's or Oxford English—and few of us would have felt at a cultural disadvantage in the presence of one who spoke them.

The text Mr. Cate used was *A First Course in German*, by Huebener and Newmark.[205] He also used *A Basic German Reader* written by Hagboldt and Kaufmann.[206] Both featured the old script. The main text began with pronunciation, largely cognate vocabulary, and simple usages. From there it worked itself up. Each section had explanations, readings, and exercises at the end. There were simple stories, each building on the vocabulary of the previous ones. We were taught rudimentary grammar: pronouns, prepositions, and verb tenses. We learned common phrases. The emphasis was on reading, and as we advanced, we also began to decipher the stories in our reader. For homework, typically we had easy compositions. Many exercises consisted of sequences of simple sentences with slight variations:

> The chalk is here
> The eraser is here
> The pointer is here....
>
> I have the chalk
> I have the eraser
> I have the pointer....

---

205 Boston: D.C. Heath, 1952.
206 Boston: D.C. Heath and Company, 1943.

A chalk is here
An eraser is here
A pointer is here....

I have a chalk
I have an eraser
I have a pointer....

Vocabulary was only a bit easier for me in German than in Latin, although having randomly gendered nouns was always a problem. Still, by the time we reached Third-Year German in our senior year, I had the hang of sentence structure, tenses, and cases, and could use common idioms. Vocabulary, however, was always somewhat of a barrier—this in a language with lots of cognates and freight-train words composed of other words hitched together. Mr. Cate, with gentle humor, at times gave us marvelous examples of German compound words, quipping that Germans would prefer to use as a single compound word such as that-piece-of-cloth-useful-when-necessary-to-blow-air-out-of-a-facially-protruding-appendage" rather than a "handkerchief."

An early disaster with vocabulary came in our first comprehensive exam at the end of the Fall Term. One of the questions was: *"Nennen sie die Haustiere."* I knew that *"nennen"* meant "name"—so we were supposed to name something. So far, so good. *"Haus"* plainly meant "house"—so we were to name something to do with a house—something domestic. But what were *"Tiere"*? I drew a total blank. I could not remember that it meant "animals"—in this case, combined with "house" it meant "domestic animals" and we were being asked to name some: dogs and cats, *Hunde* and *Katzen*, presumably. "Animal," however, did not come to mind. So I tried to figure out what *Tiere* might mean. It was easy to dismiss lots of things I knew it wasn't—clocks, stoves, tables, etc. Desperately, I concluded that *"Tier"* might have an English cognate. What could it be? Well, "tier" was an obvious candidate, so, all other routes failing, I responded hopefully, "The first floor, the second floor, and the third floor." Nice try.

Near the end of our first year, we all learned to recite the opening stanza of *"Die Lorelei"*: *"Ich weiss nicht was soll es bedeuten, Dass Ich so traurig bin; Ein Marchen aus alten Zeiten dass kommt mir nicht aus den Sinn; die Luft is kuhl und es dunkelt; and ruhig fleisst der Rhein; der Gipfel des Berges funkelt in Abensonnenschein* ..... I remember we had to write this out on our final exam.

We were taking this class not much more than a decade after the end of the Second World War. The textbooks went nowhere near that war or its predecessor, nor in any way portrayed German history critically. They presented a Germany of happy people engaged in traditional activities, with their farms and animals and festivals, together with semi-humorous characterizations of people like professors and bakers and policemen. Humor, in fact, was frequently used in many of the stories. It was almost like a series of modern fairy tales in a gentle fantasy land. I suppose this text might also have been available for use with students at a much younger age, and so anything dissonant would not have been appropriate. And I also suppose, on reflection, if you employ very simple vocabulary words, you are limited initially to presenting a "Dick and Jane" kind of atmosphere with *Vatter* und *Mutter* und *Kinder* und *Hunde*, and that may be part of what was going on here. Still, we were fifteen years old and it all seemed to be part of a gentle lost fairyland that might have had some reality in the Germany of 1890. Although I would not have used the word at that time, these books really were more than a bit patronizing in their attempt to be nice to Germany and the Germans. I'm not being critical of Mr. Cate here, but I will say that when we got to Second-Year German, Mr. Justin, our instructor, a former GI with a German wife, not long out of the American occupation zone, introduced us to a very different Germany and a very different idiom than that of Goethe with his castles and his gently flowing Rhine. It was a bit of a jolt, a real disconnect.

French. I did not take French, and therefore never had the opportunity to take a class with either Mr. Pezet or Mr. Whitford. The former was a newcomer to Moses Brown in our Second Form, the latter a Moses Brown institution. Some members of our class had Mr. Pezet in the Third Form and later. Dave London recalled that Pezet, a graduate of the University of Dijon, came from a very wealthy industrial family in France and that they had found a sinecure for him as Deputy French New England Consul for Rhode Island, a job with few duties, almost an honorary position, one that looked good on a résumé. This circumstance enabled him to teach

Maurice L. Pezet

his native tongue at Moses Brown without serious interference from his consular duties. Most remember him as a nice guy with oddities. He was in his early twenties, not much older than we were, and according to Fred Schwartz's dry humor, even more French than Mr. Whitford. He married an attractive and interesting woman from Michigan who wed against her father's advice. Dave London remembered him as a man who sweated a lot, always looked like he needed a shave, and wore aromatic nylon dress shirts. He also smoked frequently—while we were forbidden to smoke at all.

Pezet had a unique car of which he was very proud—and which was the object of some ridicule among the upperclassmen. According to Bill Barrett and others, on one occasion, when Pezet was parked in front of the Studio, a member of the Class of 1958 drove his own car up to Pezet's (touching bumper-to-bumper) and challenged him to a pushing duel. Perhaps inappropriately, Pezet accepted. There was much revving of engines, clouds of exhaust, spinning of wheels, and smell of burning of rubber, but neither car was able to push the other back. In the process, the bumpers became locked, and there was subsequent difficulty in unlocking them.

Third Form (1957-58)

Accounts of the acrobatic means of disentangling this predicament became a source of much merriment on campus.

This young, dynamic, extroverted Frenchman was a lively presence in the classroom, and he often regaled students with stories of his encounters with American culture and practices. On one occasion, he was arrested for speeding down Blackstone Boulevard at a rate considerably higher than the law allowed. Apparently he had informed the officer that he couldn't imagine adhering to a speed limit of twenty-five miles per hour—why he couldn't even stay awake at that speed! The officer apparently was not impressed by the argument. Pezet had a *joie d' vive* which he brought to French instruction. One routine assignment was to learn the cities of France, and one of these cities was Brest on the Brittany Peninsula. Pointing out the shape of that peninsula and the location of the city on it, Pezet told his classes that it was certainly easy to remember the name and site. He was very active on campus. He took some class members on a trip to France, possibly in connection with the *Alliance Francaise*. He was also an advisor to the Moses Brown delegation to the East Coast Model UN in 1958 when it represented France and had to defend its Algerian policy. Mr. Pezet himself was drafted while at Moses Brown and actually spent time in Algeria. He returned to Moses Brown afterwards and stayed there into the 1970s. He later became Headmaster of the UN school in New York City.[207]

Mr. Pezet struck Dave London as a bit strange: an instructor who had problems with some of the more creative responders in class, such as Alan Holoff, who was a constant punster and jokester.[208] On one occasion, Al quipped something and Pezet got in his face and told him he was going to kick him out of the class if he did anything like that again, whereupon Al said, "if you kick me out of class, I'll push the down button on your elevator shoes." Pezet marched him right out of the room in person.[209]

---

207 Taping session at the 50th Class Reunion. May 8, 2010.
208 Al Holoff joined our Class in the Second Form. A graduate of Tufts University, he built upon his experiences in playing tennis at both Moses Brown and Tufts to spend an enjoyable life as a tennis instructor in both Florida and Rhode Island. He served many years as the Tennis Director at the Kirk Brae Country Club in Lincoln, as well as the Summer Tennis Director at the High Ridge Swimming and Tennis Club, also in Lincoln. In addition, he coached indoor tennis at Tennis Rhode Island in East Providence. Al has coached tennis to students of all ages, from young children to adults, and still enjoys keeping active in this exciting and challenging profession.
209 Interview with Dave London, August 29, 2010.

The late Russ Carpenter ('59), who took a class with Mr. Pezet during his senior year when Mr. Whitford was on sabbatical, was a bit more generous. In fact, his recollections were quite positive. According to Russ, Pezet emphasized both reading and conversation in his classes. He talked a lot about France. Despite being a native speaker, he was not on top of French grammar as much as Mr. Whitford was, but he emphasized conversation more, and he assigned a lot of reading, including novels. Russ remembered reading Antoine de Saint Exupery's *Vol de Nuit* (which he enjoyed a lot) in Pezet's course. After graduation, when Russ was in Paris, he remembered that a French student he met was quite impressed that he had read this novel in an American high school class.[210] When Russ was in France, Mr. Pezet's parents and his new wife (who had taught at Lincoln) entertained him in Tours and showed him the chateaux and beautiful countryside in that vicinity while Mr. Pezet himself was in the French army.

Although Mr. Pezet was memorable in his own way, Theodore S. Whitford was one of the great teachers at Moses Brown, one who holds a special place in the memories of the Class of 1960 as the man to whom we dedicated our yearbook. Even though I never took French, I knew him fairly well from other School activities, and I was the assistant manager of the swimming team that he coached during the Winter Term of my senior year. The story of Moses Brown in the 1950s would be sadly incomplete without a serious mention of both Ted Whitford and his methods of teaching French, which a majority of my classmates encountered.

He was a major presence on campus, an elegantly articulate and cultured gentleman who was at the same time compassionate, approachable, humorous, often down-to-earth, and very engaged with his students. His compassion was memorable. Alumnus Bob Krause ('63) described Mr. Whitford "... as one of the most caring persons I ever met. His sense of caring and solicitude extended well beyond the classroom walls. After his students completed their French courses and moved on to other courses and different academic interests, Ted kept track of them. He remained vitally interested in their progress, because he cared."[211] I could say the same about his lasting interest in those of us who never took a class with him.

---

210 Telephone interview, May 23, 2011.
211 The quotations from Krause in this section come from the *Cupola*, Fall, 1992, p. 22. They are excerpts from Bob's eulogy delivered at Mr. Whitford's memorial service that fall.

Third Form (1957-58)

Theodore S. Whitford

Pete Parker recalled Mr. Whitford as a man of tremendous dignity.[212] "Because I was a boarder, I was occasionally required to go to Sunday Quaker Meetings. Mr. Whitford usually spoke. He would never speak first. He would always wait until things had a chance to develop, and then step in. When he started speaking, everyone else stopped, paid attention, and listened to what he had to say. And what I always noticed was that he spoke very moderately, very slowly, very quietly, and very pointedly. And then it would be over, and he would say thank you, and that was the end of it. That was pretty much the way he conducted his entire life."[213]

He was a man of sterling character who did not flaunt that character. He was highly cultured, but wore this attribute so easily that it always seemed

---

212 Pete Parker joined our Class in the Second Form. He received his master's degree in finance and accounting from the University of Chicago and went to work in the Albany, NY, area where he became a top executive in the finance department of the region's largest health insurance company—CDPHP. A star of our swimming team, he still swims and is active in civic and service organizations.
213 Taping session at the 50th Class Reunion. May 8, 2010.

a natural part of him—never affected, never artificial, and never an assertion of superiority. Krause puts it well, "... his manner was refreshingly unvarnished and unembellished. There were no airs or affectations about Ted. He was totally without pretense."

He played no games with you and you never felt that you needed to look for a secret agenda. You knew he was a straight shooter. And if his objective was to change you by cultivating your talents, it was never to manipulate you in any hidden way for some hidden purpose: "The essence of Ted Whitford was his underlying fairness, his decency, and his unyielding moral convictions. He was in every sense one of nature's true gentlemen."[214]

His honesty and sense of fairness were appreciated beyond the campus. When I was an assistant manager of the swimming team we had a meet in Pawtucket. Mr. Whitford and a couple of other coaches judged the various dives. He would watch the diver carefully, then turn his head away (presumably so he would not see the scores from the other judges) and then hold up a card with his score on it. From the intent look on his face, you could tell he was taking this task very seriously. As the diving event proceeded, I stood on the edge of the pool watching. Next to me stood a man in his sixties, who turned out to be a retired coach from another school. He deduced that I was from Moses Brown, and he struck up a conversation which soon turned to the topic of Mr. Whitford. He told me that Ted Whitford, in his opinion, was the best judge of diving in Rhode Island, keenly observant and scrupulously honest—one with a statewide reputation for never unfairly favoring his own divers in competition. He said, "Let me show you why he is such a good judge." After each dive, and before the judges revealed their scores, this coach predicted what rating Mr. Whitford would give, adding commentary about the dive. His predictions were extremely accurate. In one case, right after the diver hit the water, the coach pointed out to me that the dive had been defective in some subtle way that had not been very obvious—and that the defect should lead to a loss of points. He said, "Now you watch, Ted Whitford will notice what happened and the other judges probably will not—expect to see him scoring the dive a point or two lower than they do." And that was exactly what happened. I was very impressed.

---

214 Krause, *Cupola*, Fall 1992.

Russell Carpenter also remembered Mr. Whitford's sense of fair play. Their first major encounter came when Russ competed in the Upper School Declamation Contest in the First or Second Form—long before he had taken a class with Whitford. In this contest, he recited the famous soliloquy from the opening scene of Act II in Shakespeare's *Richard II*:

> This royal throne of kings, this sceptered isle,
> This earth of majesty, this seat of Mars,
> This other Eden, demi-paradise,....
> This blessed plot, this earth, this realm, this England.

Russ did not win the contest. Mr. Jansen, one of the judges, explained (although not directly to him) that during the presentation he had clutched the edge of his jacket in nervousness and had thereby somehow spoiled the effect. Russ accepted this as a legitimate criticism, but Mr. Whitford, also a judge, apparently dissented, and without saying so directly, complimented Russ in terms that clearly indicated his disagreement with the result, stating that his excellent diction during the recitation had been "almost Elizabethan."

Like so many other cultured New Englanders, Mr. Whitford was not ashamed of menial labor, and embraced its dignities and refreshing qualities, even under undignified and unrefreshing circumstances. During the height of the Great New England Hurricane of 1938, he rushed to the top of Middle House and helped save the cupola; School photographs of the damage done by that storm show Ted Whitford out on the grounds leading the cleanup effort. In addition, Fred Schwartz recalled, "Mr. Whitford ... taught all summer in Maine, which meant that he taught year around. I was there for one of these summers ('Remedial' was my middle name). I remember the camp had a very antiquated sewage system, and on one occasion Mr. Whitford, appropriately attired in hip boots, was literally up to his waist in what the French would call '*merde*.' I remember watching him for a while and thinking, 'I'll have to bring this up in class.'"[215]

He was one of the few members of the Upper School faculty who were really native Rhode Islanders (Doc Odell was another). Although born in

---

[215] Taping session at the 50th Class Reunion. May 8, 2010.

Pawkatuck, Connecticut, Mr. Whitford grew up in Westerly and attended Westerly High School.[216] According to his wife, Mrs. Ruth Whitford, he went to Amherst College with the idea of becoming a physician (his uncle, who was very fond of him, was a doctor), but a French teacher recommended that he apply to spend his junior year in France. Amherst gave him this opportunity, which both fanned his enthusiasm for the language and offered him the chance to study it with intensity. When he graduated from Amherst, his father was sick and Mr. Whitford did not want to burden him with the cost of medical school. He thought he would teach for a few years first, and then, perhaps, revisit the idea, but the Second World War came along, he loved French, and the medical path was the one not taken. He taught briefly at Manlius Military Academy in upstate New York and then, wanting to be closer to home, successfully applied for a position at Moses Brown.[217]

After Pearl Harbor, he tried to enlist, but he had a dislocated shoulder and the Army would not take him. Later on they needed more manpower, became less fastidious, and drafted him. After basic training at Fort Devens, he was sent to the University of Pennsylvania to take a course in the "villages of northern Africa," and to learn Arabic. The idea was that the US would need the personnel to run villages in North Africa after the "Torch" invasion in 1942. De Gaulle, however, assumed that responsibility, and the program was cancelled. So Mr. Whitford soon found himself in a troop ship steaming east in convoy. Somewhere in mid-Atlantic the convoy split. Half went north to England; Mr. Whitford's half went south into the Mediterranean, and he eventually found himself in Cairo. He was soon moved to Tehran, and ultimately to Abadan at the head of the Persian Gulf on the Iranian border with Iraq. By then he could speak Arabic fluently, and he spent much of the rest of the war there in Persia as a translator and cryptologist.[218]

---

216 His son lived there in the family homestead until his death in 2017.
217 Interview with Ruth Whitford, June 20, 2011.
218 These personal details were given me by Ruth Whitford (taped interview, June 20, 2011). According to Mrs. Whitford, during the Second World War he also was an inspector of outposts, including British outposts, stationed around Africa. She recalled that even years after the war, he was scrupulous about not revealing classified information, and his wartime recollections were therefore cautiously vague, even with her. I am deeply indebted to her for sharing her recollections and also for sharing with me the poems by Mr. Whitford reproduced here.

According to Mrs. Whitford, he was very close to his parents, and his love of family was considerable. For Thanksgiving, 1944, he sent the following poem home to them from Abadan:

> This season like the others calls us back
> To hearth and town we know so well:
> Those there we left across the swell
> Of seas are our Thanksgiving; there's no lack of
> Gratitude within us.
>
> In memory the strands of life hold fast
> Their cherished moorings; tides of war
> May shift our vessel straight before
> The winds of death; yet calm our mind, the blast
> Can strike no fear within us.
>
> In hope the present fades away, the thought
> Of turning home fills up the heart,
> Our loved one's face, our sons' whose part
> It will not be to fight, for they'll be taught
> The error once within us.
>
> In love the meanness of our struggle dies—
> The kindness that we've known supplants
> The bitterness which love recants;
> In sober moments blessings past arise
> To bring a peace within us.
>
> Almighty God, teach us to see thy love—
> If not in bounty counted, still
> In strength thou lendest to our will,
> Whose confidence is born of things above
> The commonplace within us.[219]

In the classroom, French was Mr. Whitford's first love, although he also taught Latin. He had an enormous attachment to France and French

---

[219] November 23, 1944. Reprinted in the *Westerly Sun*.

culture, and was widely read in European history and literature from the Renaissance through modern times. He was also a devotee of classical music. All of this rubbed off in varying degrees on his students (and even on some of us nonstudents). As Jack Nixon observed, "What do we remember most about Moses Brown? Most of us remember a person: a teacher or a coach who taught us values, feelings, and appreciation for some of the nice things of life. These were the Grandmasters, and Ted Whitford was one of them."

Russ Carpenter remembered that Mr. Whitford was a person who controlled his class totally. He was always in charge, covered what he wanted to cover, and was a dominant presence in the classroom. He did not control by aggressiveness or strong expression, but by a quiet sense of authority. When he entered the room, order prevailed. Russ recalled that on one occasion Mr. Whitford was late to class and the students awaiting him were loud and rambunctious. As he entered (and the decibels plummeted), he looked at Russ and said with a small smile, "Do you know that your voice carries a long way?"[220]

Dan DeVleig remembered that Mr. Whitford had a serious physical affliction—a lot of nasal congestion, and he always carried a handkerchief around. "I used to watch him manage it and wonder how he could take care of that problem without exciting derision. But derision never happened. ... He had this handkerchief about the size of a baby's blanket and he would cough into it, clear his throat, come back, speak some more, and about five minutes later have the need to use it again. I thought at the time that it must be really difficult for a teacher who is trying to hold attention and maintain your respect to handle a problem like that on a day-in and day-out basis for years and years and years, but Mr. Whitford commanded enough respect to succeed."[221]

Russ recalled that in teaching French, Mr. Whitford gave special emphasis to accent, vocabulary, and grammar. The class also read a reasonable amount of French and thereby developed a solid reading capability. They had a lot of practice writing. Students, however, were not exposed to a lot of conversation, and they were less than fully comfortable with conversational

---

220 Phone interview, May 23, 2011.
221 Taping session at the 50th Class Reunion. May 8, 2010.

French. It was practiced much less, and was the language skill most in need of cultivation in later years. Russ did, however, remember that Moses Brown prepared him well for French literature courses at Princeton for which he had to write essays and take exams in French—and do so in classes with other students who came from even more prestigious schools.

By all accounts, Mr. Whitford spoke with a perfect Parisian accent which he passionately wanted to teach to his students. Mark Saklad heard that when Mr. Whitford attended the Sorbonne, his accent was purer than that of most native Parisians.[222] He wanted his students to distinguish themselves by mastering that accent. In a highly stratified and culturally aware society such as that of France, quality of accent and expression would facilitate entry to cultural and social strata that might be denied to those who could not employ the French equivalent of the Queen's English (*Pygmalian* could have been set in Paris just as well as in London). Also, an emphasis upon quality of accent was fully consistent with an emphasis on excellence, on doing one's best, and on developing a sense of pride in accomplishment: "In his elegantly understated way, Ted somehow managed to instill in all of his students a sense of pride in whatever they undertook, and he did it with such grace and skill that you actually felt honored that he would even be interested. But you see, that was Ted's nature; he cared."[223]

Whatever his motives, Mr. Whitford unmistakably held his students meticulously to the highest standards of French pronunciation. Bob Krause provides us with a marvelous autobiographical excerpt that underscores that point, and is very revealing of how much Ted Whitford cared both about accent and about his students:

> In 1965, I spent the summer working in France. At the end of summer I went up to the Moses Brown campus, and prowling around in search of old friends, I was delighted to find Ted. After three months in France, I couldn't wait to demonstrate for him my French proficiency, and I immediately began to chatter away in this foreign language. Apparently, this language was considerably more foreign than I thought. A rather puzzled look came over Ted's face. He cocked his head to one side, wrinkled his patrician nose, and demanded, "Just where in France have you been?"

---
222 *Ibid.*
223 Kraus, *Cupola*, Fall 1992, p. 22.

"In the southern part," I happily replied, "Near Nice and Marseille." ....
"Robert!" he exclaimed, stabbing me with a piercing glare through his ever-present rimless spectacles, "you have developed the worst French accent that I have ever heard! You have ruined that good classical Parisian French that took me four years to drum into your head. Your French sounds like a bowl of bouillabaisse!"

Whereupon, Ted led me to his house (he lived on campus at the time) and produced a tape cassette for elementary French elocution. "Here," he said, thrusting that cassette at me, "take this home, put it in your tape machine, and repeat the phrases continuously until you have rid yourself of that horrible accent! Or else I shall personally call the Amherst French Department and forewarn them that you should not be permitted to enroll in your French class this fall until you have spent at least two intensive weeks in the language laboratory."[224]

Russ Carpenter agreed that Mr. Whitford's emphasis on accent was well-placed. It came with a lot of practice. He remembered especially those class exercises in which there were numerous repetitions of French nasal sounds—*an, in, on, un*—until students were able to pronounce them to Mr. Whitford's satisfaction. Repeated rapidly, these four vocalizations (used extensively throughout the language) resembled the grunts of a (perhaps highly cultured) pig, and were so described by Mr. Whitford.

He taught language in the very traditional way of that period—with lots of emphasis on grammar and structure. You built the edifice from the bottom, piece by piece, putting each part solidly and logically in place: tense, voice, number, mood, case. Mark Saklad and Bill Barrett remembered, for example, that Mr. Whitford taught his classes to repeat all the French pronouns in three seconds flat, and he brought a stopwatch to class to time them (the record for their crisp pronunciation was claimed to be an unbelievable 1.5 seconds).[225] As vocabulary expanded, the new additions fit into the existing structure, and the edifice slowly grew. Memory was the servant of logic and rational arrangement. Each new word, each new tense, each new case was fitted into (or added to) the evolving structure. Today, a lot of language

---

224 *Ibid.*
225 No doubt the one he used for swimming practice. Taping session at the 50th Class Reunion. May 8, 2010.

is taught with memory as the servant of association—rapid immersion into hearing the spoken language that links together in memory the sequenced phraseologies of the speaker until the listener becomes familiar with what sounds correct from the repetitive flow of words. This can be viewed as developing from the surface down or inward. The first method emphasizes logic and structure, the second, associative sequence. There are things to be said for both approaches (perhaps some people learn better one way, some the other), but languages taught at Moses Brown during the 1950s relied much more heavily on the former method than on the latter. In this respect, Mr. Whitford taught primarily in English, but occasionally in French, and he sometimes presented his points in both. He tried to *teach* French, but not impose it (as might be the case in the more modern method): students were not forced to conduct dialogues in French.[226]

As the edifice grew and became more sophisticated, Mr. Whitford introduced more and more idiomatic French to the mix. Bill Barrett and others remembered that in one instance (when he tried to teach how certain English idioms could be translated into French) he broke up the class when he posited the invitation, "Will you join me in a cup of tea?"—and translated it literally, producing an image of a couple bathing in a teacup.[227]

Russ Carpenter recalled that another feature of Mr. Whitford's instruction was memorization of classic passages in French: the *Marseillaise*, of course, but also the Lord's Prayer and the Nativity Story from the Gospel according to Luke. The class also learned a lot of French songs and their tunes. They must have sung them, although Russ did not remember actually doing this.

Fred Schwartz also recalled that Mr. Whitford introduced him to "something called the precis," stating that it was probably the most important Moses Brown influence on him in terms of his being a lawyer: "It was an exercise of turning four to six paragraphs into eight or nine sentences. Having spent an entire summer doing this, I found it really easy to do when I became a lawyer—particularly in Washington."[228]

---

226 Taping session at the 50th Class Reunion. May 8, 2010.
227 *Ibid.*
228 *Ibid.*

When you are teaching necessary materials that some (or all) might find dull or boring, it is often useful to enliven things. Bob Krause in his eulogy recalled that "no student ever left Ted's classroom unless Ted was convinced that the student clearly understood the day's lesson. I particularly recall an instance when one of my classmates was having difficulty understanding the French expression for the term 'upside down,' Having tried at some length, but unsuccessfully, to explain the idiom, Ted leaped upon his desk and, to the amazement of the entire class, proceeded to execute a perfect handstand. To this day, I can still hear the jangling and clatter of nickels and dimes falling from Ted's pockets onto his big wooden desk and rolling in every direction all over those old hardwood floors."[229] Whitford, like Herman with the broken yardstick, cared enough to put his point across in memorable ways.

Fred Schwartz recalled that Mr. Whitford had a lot of patience with his students: "He was not mean to those of us who were not good at French," and Fred illustrated his difficulties with the language by means of an anecdote. He took a trip to Paris after graduation and attempted to use the French he had learned at Moses Brown as he went through customs. While his passport was being stamped, the passport officer turned to him and asked, "Did you take French in high school?"

"Mais oui"

"It was a waste," the man responded.[230]

Fred does not blame Mr. Whitford!

The pig grunts, the teacup humor, the stopwatch, the handstands—all these were entertaining means of holding attention and fixing points in students' minds. But a more important objective aim was to embed a study of the language in an appreciation of the culture it represented. Mr. Whitford could *locate* French in France. Sometimes his locating was humorous. As Bill Barrett stated, "I have never been to Paris—yet. But Mr. Whitford described very vividly for us what it was like to drive your car in Paris—especially driving around the Arc d'Triomphe which is a rotary with about

---
229 *Cupola*, Fall 1992, p. 22.
230 Taping session at the 50th Class Reunion. May 8, 2010.

eight lanes of traffic. You can imagine that if you got into the inside lane, you might never get out of it. He described perfectly what you should do to negotiate traffic around the Arc de Triomphe, and generally in Paris."[231]

Most of the time his locating and embedding was deeper. Language and culture go together in every country, but a case can be made that nowhere do they conjoin more than in France—and, in this French conjunction, sentiment and emotion play a sovereign role. Mr. Whitford's love for France was legendary and deeply emotional and he easily conveyed this to his students. Jack Nixon recalled:

> I was not a great French student, but, boy, I remember Ted Whitford real well—and the kind of impact he had on me as an individual in his class. What I remember is not so much the iterations and the French, but the way he presented things in class. Ted Whitford wrote French, spoke French, and loved France. He would talk about Paris. He would talk about the buildings in Paris. He would talk in a way that put you right there—in your mind's eye you were there with him in his love, his passion, the way he would share them with you. Like most effective people do, he allowed his emotions to come through when he attempted to convey a message. Ted Whitford had emotions and feelings for France, for the French people, its history, its culture, and for the City of Paris itself. He carried it in the suits that he wore to class. He was France. I had no problem remembering the words of *La Marseillaise*. He had it inculcated into us that if we had a class with him, we became lovers of France, lovers of the French people, lovers of French history, lovers of French culture—lovers of the proper things that Ted Whitford represented to us.[232]

Russ Carpenter strongly concurred with Jack's observations on Mr. Whitford's deeply emotional qualities and their relevance to his subject matter:

---

231 *Ibid*.
232 Taping session at the 50th Class Reunion. May 8, 2010. Jack is being modest about his French proficiency. Although he just missed achieving the college "proficiency" level in the SAT French Achievement exam, when he entered Brown University after a bit of summer review, he passed his Placement Achievement there with much room to spare—one of only a handful of students (out of a hundred) who succeeded on this exam. He gives full credit to Mr. Whitford for his success in this accomplishment (Letter from Jack Nixon to Ted Whitford, September 16, 1960).

In many ways an emotional man himself, he could easily relate to the many emotional dimensions of French culture. He once described going to a Christmas Eve service in Notre Dame, where he sat high above the mass of people on the floor below, and later recounted this experience as being "the closest to heaven" that he had ever been. He was so emotionally caught up in the spirit of the night that he afterwards went to a local bar for a stiff drink to unwind![233]

I remember seeing his emotions voiced graphically in Chapel one morning on the occasion of the death of Madame Warge. Mr. Whitford gave the eulogy. There were tears in his eyes. His hands, his head, his tall figure were all in passionate, but dignified, motion. His voice quivered, but still resonated with emphasis and authority. He described her life and what it had meant to her students, to her friends at the School, and to himself personally. The emotion expressed commanded attention and respect since it was so clearly genuine and, to many of us, so rare in a formal setting. The talk was brief (as Chapel talks always were), but so arresting that even to this day I remember it clearly; not so much the words of remembrance and praise (in elegant English accented by a few words in French), but rather the tone and level of dignified emotion which conveyed the message more accurately and immediately than any words by themselves could have done—and thereby left a more lasting remembrance.

His was the soft, controlled, dignified, yet strong, emotion of the poet. The following untitled pastoral reveals these qualities as well as a love of his native New England which stood alongside his love for France:

> Warm summer sun, the laugh of voices through the open door;
> The playful sound of splashes in the swimming pool nearby;
> A katydid communicating joy in rasping cry;
> Two children run about exploring nature's verdant store.
>
> Red boughs of apples bending under rays of slanting sun;
> Bold crows proclaiming rich discovery of golden corn:
> Quick little feet have left the water's edge where willows mourn,
> For now the cold spring stream is still, its laughing murmur done.

---

233 Interview with Russ Carpenter, May 23, 2011.

Yet summer's long green days and ruddy autumn's full bequest
Together blend their varied wealth, an offering to those
Whose home no dearth of laughter knows, for God such servants chose
To guard the precious gifts of welcome, love, and rest.

—Theodore S. Whitford

Beyond the classroom, Mr. Whitford was a very active citizen of the School and the local academic community. He was the swimming coach, and during Christmas break, routinely took team members on a trip to Fort Lauderdale. Bill Barrett and I remember him presiding at a Cum Laude Society dinner event where the main speaker was Edward Winsor, Chair of the Providence Planning Commission, who shared with us the new Master Plan for Providence before it was made public.[234] He also did corridor duty when he was new to Moses Brown, alternating nights and weekends with Mr. Fuller. As Mrs. Whitford quipped, "Ted married me to get out of corridor duty; I married him to get out of hot summers in Providence—when he fled to Maine."[235] He took a great interest in Moses Brown events, including the Book Fair, and he religiously attended the School's plays and concerts. At Amherst, he had sung in the Glee Club with John Coolidge, son of President Calvin Coolidge. They gave a concert at the White House and were entertained by John's father, also an Amherst alum. While at Amherst, Ted worked at Davenport's Inn where the president and two other men stayed during an alumni event. At the end of the stay, one of the men left a reasonable tip; the second man left a modest tip; Calvin Coolidge, a notorious skinflint, left ten cents.

Mr. Whitford continually promoted French language and culture outside of the classroom. For example, he took a group of seniors to Sanders Theater at Harvard to hear a production of Moliere's *Le Misanthrope* presented

---

[234] Taping session at the 50th Class Reunion. May 8, 2010. The plan shared with us by Mr. Winsor included, among other innovations, the relocation of the railroad tracks from the old Union Station, and the building of the new station. The plan was announced in the *Providence Journal* a few days later. For details of this event, see the *Moses Brown Bulletin*, May 1960, p. 3.

[235] She also quips that Mr. Whitford had three qualities he wanted in a wife: 1) that she be able to speak French fluently (which Mrs. Whitford could not); 2) that she be able to sing (which Mrs. Whitford could not); and that she be able to cook (a task at which Mrs. Whitford says she therefore had worked hard!).

by the Renaud-Barrault Company from Paris.[236] He took boys on trips to France. He was a very active officer of the Rhode Island Chapter of the *Alliance Francaise*, and when that organization held events at Moses Brown, as it frequently did, he organized and hosted them.

The *Alliance* sponsored annual competitive student contests that provided winners with scholarships and summers in Paris. Russ Carpenter won the award for 1959. The Whitfords were in Paris that summer on a sabbatical leave, and Mr. Whitford came to meet Russ at the station upon his arrival. Russ remembered spotting him from the train window as they pulled in. It was the boat-train, and Russ had shared a seat with a girl who had become seasick during the Channel crossing. He offered to help her with her luggage, and Mr. Whitford also rendered assistance. In the course of all this, a piece of Russ's own luggage was somehow left on the train, and Russ remembered that Mr. Whitford subsequently helped him deal successfully with the French bureaucracy to recover it. The Whitfords were gracious hosts at the onset of Russ's time in Paris, showing him around the city, introducing him to the Metro, taking him to the Paris headquarters of the *Alliance Francaise*, taking him to Versailles, and inviting him to share special artichokes during Sunday dinner at their temporary home in the suburbs.[237] Russ's experience was indeed typical of the graciousness and concern that Mr. Whitford showed for his students—and, as in this case, his former students.

He served as advisor to many, and this was one of his most notable contributions. He took the advising role very seriously and took it far beyond the filling out of course schedules. "Somehow Ted always knew if you were struggling or had a problem. He was always there when you needed him, and he was even there when you foolishly thought you didn't need him. ... There was something very comforting about being with him. Simply by his presence, his advice, his wise counsel, and by his easy good humor, Ted had a remarkable ability to make you feel better about things and good about yourself."[238] He had an "uncommon ability to listen, rather than just hear; and therein, I think, may lie the secret of his influence on so many of

---

236 *Moses Brown Bulletin*, April 1957.
237 Phone interview with Russ Carpenter, May 23, 2011; personal interview with Mrs. Ruth Whitford, Providence, RI, June 20, 2011.
238 Bob Krause, *Cupola*, Fall 1992, p. 22.

Third Form (1957-58)

us."[239] This willingness to understand, to empathize, established a strong personal bond between Ted Whitford and those who came to know him. As Dave Burnham stated in a letter to the alumni on the occasion of Mr. Whitford's death, "While many of the old guard were deeply respected and admired, Ted Whitford was profoundly loved."[240]

Bob Krause remembered that "my classmates eventually, and more often sooner than later, came to realize that in Ted Whitford they had an uncommonly strong shoulder to lean on." One of our classmates, Hernan Franco, would certainly agree. As he tells the story, Ted on one occasion strongly went to bat for him. During the spring of our junior year, Hernan (for reasons of discipline) had been given the options of: 1) take a leave of absence for the rest of the Spring Term and return in the fall, or 2) complete the junior year and not return in the fall. He chose the former. According to Hernan, Mr. Cunningham then tried to renege on the agreement by preventing his return and having him dismissed. When he received this news, Hernan went to Mr. Whitford, who was his advisor. He promised to take the matter up at a faculty meeting, and because of his advocacy, the faculty by a narrow margin voted to let Hernan remain at Moses Brown, and the administration went along with this.[241] As a result, Hernan, I am happy to say, was able to graduate with us in 1960.

I am also aware that Mr. Whitford went to bat for a former colleague of his at Moses Brown whose political views (which Mr. Whitford did not share) had rendered him an outcast in the profession, and as a result, had made it difficult for him to land a job.

Ted Whitford could be critical of personal conduct if he felt that conduct warranted it. His criticisms were always controlled, never rendered in anger, and certainly not vindictive. Our classmate Bruce Perry recalled, "I had been elected co-captain of the swimming team, but I talked to Junie Howe and he convinced me to go out for winter track—so I signed up with him. I neglected to tell this to Mr. Whitford. When he found out about it, he came to me and told me how disappointed he was that I had not come and told him, especially since I had been elected Co-Captain. He said that

---

239 *Ibid.*
240 September 1992.
241 Taping session at the 50th Class Reunion. May 8, 2010.

I should consider everybody involved when I made a decision. He spoke in a nice way—there was no hint of malice, but he did make me feel guilty. I still feel guilty, and I have never forgotten this."[242]

I myself remember that on one occasion (when I was fairly new to Upper School) a schoolmate (not a classmate) misbehaved. As I recall, he was just "hacking around," causing noise and trouble, and conducting himself in a loud and inappropriate way. Mr. Whitford came walking along and saw him. In front of me (perhaps he intended to speak indirectly to me as well), he calmly, but severely, addressed this boy in a serious and authoritative (yet quiet) voice, reminding him that his family had been attending the School for several generations (and that he, Mr. Whitford, had had his father in class), that he had a younger brother (whose first name Mr. Whitford mentioned) in the Lower School, that he had a family reputation to uphold, that he needed to be an example for his brother, and that he should be ashamed to be behaving the way he was. At the end of Mr. Whitford's reprimand, which invoked both shame and pride, the chastened boy apologized convincingly. I think he grew a bit towards adulthood in those few minutes, and I suspect in the future he thought twice about acting in similar ways. I can envision other reprimands from other people in similar circumstances being greeted with contempt, postponed derision, or resentment, but it is difficult to envision such reactions to a reprimand from Mr. Whitford.

The Class of 1960 is still proud that we dedicated the *Mosaic*, our yearbook, to Ted Whitford. During the Second World War, across a great divide of space, he sent the following greeting to his family; across the great divide of time, it may speak to us today:

> This week or next — I cannot tell
> For days slip by like grains of sand
> Between one's fingers
> Here in Persia's wastes —
> The fourteenth day of brown October
> That I know
> We called it "sweetest day,"
> When what I could not say found token
> In some gift.

---

242 *Ibid.*

Once more my wish to you is happiness,
The word unspoken is not wrapped
In ribbons, or hidden in the heart
Of full Chrysanthemums.
I send my love
And pray for sunshine in your life:
Not the glare that we know here,
Closing eyes, and withering blade and soul alike,
Parching ground;
Sunshine rather that I used to know,
Sifted through the green of maple leaves,
Sunshine in the smile of friends,
Or caught on tawny heads of children
Playing on the beach,
Sunshine arrested in the frost
Of early morning,
Sunshine of laughter.

This I wish for you —
There is a difference.

—Theodore S. Whitford

XIII

Fourth Form (1958-59)

In the Fourth Form I had math with Mr. Herman, English with Mr. Corbett, Modern European History with Mr. Pratt, chemistry with Mr. Jeffers, and German with Mr. Justin. In the spring we also had a specialized reading course with Miss Helen Sadlier.[243] Academically, it was my strongest year at Moses Brown.

Math. Fourth-Form Math—plane geometry—was one of the most enjoyable courses I ever took. Mr. Herman was in full fettle as always, and this was the year when symbolic math finally began to make sense to me across the board. The class was much more enjoyable than either First- or Second-Year Algebra, and the disasters of those two years quickly faded into the past.

I remember taking an exam a few weeks into the term, probably our first in plane geometry. A proof was called for, and I sat there in class with nothing on paper trying to figure it out. It involved a set of triangles inscribed in a circle—I don't remember exactly what we were to prove. I kept going over it, with the clock ticking. Then suddenly, near the end of class, there was a eureka moment, everything fell into place, and I hastily wrote out the proof just before the exam was over. This seemed a triumph, and from then on, geometry was fun and a challenge.

---

[243] At the suggestion of my parents, I tried to do a little Fourth-Year Latin reading with Mr. Fuller, but was not enthusiastic about doing so, and couldn't swing it. We read some Pliny, but didn't get too far.

We started with triangles, rectangles and squares, then added circles to the above, and finally branched out into more complex polygons. We became very familiar with the proportions of the isosceles right triangle and the 30-60-90 right triangle—and the usefulness of both in calculations and proofs. We explored the concept of tangents and the right angles drawn to them. Although it was not in the text, we did do a little solid geometry. We made a few formal constructions. We also spent a lot of time that year reviewing algebra.

The whole world of axiomatic proof was new to me, and was greatly appealing. Exercises became puzzles and games, and I spent lots of time on them, sometimes late into the evening, determined to figure out every problem in a chapter. Solutions built on each other, and you cumulated a repertoire of many remembered axioms and proofs that could be drawn upon to build proofs at the next level.

Again, Mr. Herman would almost never explain anything. In class, he would throw out a problem and the first one to get the proof would go up to the board and present it. Homework was also handled in this same way, and we became the instructors of each other.

Collaboration was encouraged. Jeff Forman used to call me up almost every night, and we would go over the homework for the next day. I remember on one occasion that he had developed a proof of a particularly complex problem that I had not yet looked at. His proof seemed great, and I told him so. Next day in class, he presented it at the blackboard. I remember sitting there watching as he did this. Suddenly I spotted a flaw in the proof that I had not noticed the night before. It had something to do with the need to prove, not just assume, that line A-B-C was, indeed, a straight line. What to do? If I pointed it out, Jeff would think I had set him up. Mr. Herman said nothing, so I kept my mouth shut and showed it to Jeff afterwards—to the great amusement of us both.[244]

---

244 Jeff Forman joined our Class in the First Form. After graduating from the University of Southern California, he worked nearly three decades for IBM in marketing and sales, where he was involved in the marketing of mainframe computers and later in personal computers, based in Palo Alto. Later, he worked in their software development lab in San Jose. While at IBM he convinced senior management to initiate the development of home office capabilities, and he helped pioneer this practice at IBM. He still regards IBM as a "terrific" employer, but he struck out on his own in the early '90s to enter the financial services business and to found his own company, whose team of financial advisors provided investment and financial advice to personal and corporate clients. He sold this business and retired in 2011. From a telephone interview with Jeff, May 9, 2020.

Fourth Form (1958-59)

I can remember doing reasonably well with this "do-it-by-yourself" format, and was able to meet most of the challenges, but on one occasion I went to Mr. Herman with a problem I just couldn't solve. It was a construction problem: given any four points on a plane, present a method by which you can construct a square so that the sides of that square or their extensions pass through each point. I worked a lot on this absolutely infuriating problem. I was sure that the solution employed the fact that a triangle inscribed in a circle with one side being the diameter of that circle was a right triangle. But beyond this I could make no headway. In exasperation, I went to Mr. Herman for the solution. He refused to give it to me. Back to the drawing board. I finally gave up, and to this day do not know how to solve that problem—which was right there, unsolved, in our textbook.

Somewhere along the way during this year, the axiomatic method, together with the procedure of reducing mathematical problems to memorized rules and formulae suddenly gave me a series of other epiphanies regarding algebra. Geometry had interested me in math, and math had acquired a lot more meaning for me than it had for a long time. There was something about geometry that made algebra much more cognizable, as the various formulae became tools and the problems themselves became logic problems, really games, in which we would figure out how to use the memorized formulae to structure a solution.

I'm not sure what went on here. I know that geometry started me thinking of exercises and problems as puzzles and games, and not as routines to be memorized. I probably had been resistant to the memorization of formulae, and had been slow to perceive the interconnectedness of various different formulae or procedures. However, as soon as geometry started me thinking of math problems as challenges in deductive logic, the perspective changed. I gradually developed the practice of taking a relevant formula (such as $D = RT$) and expressing the circumstances of the problem in terms of the formula. The fun of puzzling out geometric problems became translated to algebraic problems. Memory then kicked in, and the experiences and methods in solving one problem were stored in memory for help in analogous circumstances. Each solution made subsequent problems more manageable. As I began to get some answers right, confidence built, and then the challenges seemed to be less daunting and more possible: bring 'em on! When things went in new directions, I would take serious time to puzzle them through, and the exercise of figuring them out locked the new procedures more solidly in memory than would have been the case had I simply been given the procedure (or even a clue to the procedure) as a formulaic guide. I think this was what Mr. Herman's maddening procedure of seldom presenting a solution was aimed at. Even simplifying and factoring complex expressions became fun (and "second nature")—in these cases, memory of previous procedures helped trigger recognition and played a much bigger role. In a strange sort of way, most of this process seemed spatial—even for algebra—and, although I cannot explain it, geometry seemed to play a role in developing algebraic skills in a fundamentally spatial way. Geometry also contributed to algebra in terms of building confidence, motivation, deductive skills, and relevant repertoires.

During this year, I also began to read Martin Gardiner's "Mathematical Games" column in the *Scientific American*. This was an imaginative, witty, and, to me, partly comprehensible monthly treat, and it reinforced the "gaming" aspect of mathematics. The experience in Fourth-Form Geometry, and its attendant impact on my understanding of algebra, helped out immeasurably on the Scholastic Aptitude Tests and other standardized quantitative reasoning tests taken that year which were relevant to college admission decisions. By end of the Fourth Form, I was at the top of the heap in math. Little did I expect that in Fifth-Form Math (trigonometry, etc.), I would barely scrape through.

English. Fourth-Form English was divided into two sections, one taught by Mr. Corbett, the other by Mr. Meserve. The assignment of students to one or the other was purely a matter of scheduling imperatives: those who took Second-Year German with Justin had Corbett; the rest had Meserve. Hence Bill Brehm, Barry Fain, Roy Maletz, Jim Rigney, and I, among others, were in Mr. Corbett's class.[245]

Mr. Corbett was a delight—he was both engaged with the subject matter and interested in us as students. He wore a bow tie, a sartorial practice that seemed to be largely the province of the English Department. He had a marvelous sense of humor, and he brought to the classroom the perspective of a published author of fiction, largely fiction aimed at our age group.

---

245 It met in Room 2, the province of the English Department, where we had had Mr. Taber and later were to have Mr. Paxton.

W. Scott Corbett

Just as Third-Form English had focused on American novelists, essayists, playwrights, and poets, Fourth-Form English focused on their British counterparts. As I recall, the whole class read a set of the same works, and then each of us read other works on our own, so there was a serious range of English literature covered throughout the class. During our previous three years, we had used anthologies from the same series in each Upper School English class. There was an appropriate one for British literature in this series that, I believe, had been used in the Fourth Form the previous year. Our class, however, did not use it. We read original sources and had no text or dedicated anthology *per se*.

Mr. Corbett spent a lot of time on Joseph Conrad. We read his novel *Victory*, and a set of short stories, including "The Lagoon," "The Secret Sharer," "Youth," "Typhoon," and "First Command." Corbett was a great admirer of Conrad, and he taught us much. I can remember biographical details of how Conrad became an author, interspaced with autobiographical details from Corbett's own experiences as an author. He once remarked to us that Conrad would have writer's block and spend lots of time, perhaps a whole day, searching for exactly the right word to use in a given sentence: "This may seem like a lot of wasted time—but, believe me, he usually did find the right word!" Conrad's stylistic accomplishments were all the more remarkable since his original tongue was Polish. Corbett showed us how the substitution of one synonym for another could subtly alter the whole meaning of the sentence. He also pointed out double entendre: for instance, the double meaning in the title "Secret Sharer"—was this a story about someone sharing secrets, or about a hidden or stealthy person who shared? It could be viewed as both—and how did this double meaning frame the story? He also introduced us in a more intimate way than we had experienced before to the use of symbolism, especially in *Victory*—what did the knife really stand for?

Mr. Corbett demonstrated that strong works of fiction could be subjected to many different forms of interpretation. This led, initially, to a kind of free-for-all, in which we could try, often facetiously, sometimes cynically, to force any interpretation whatsoever on a passage, and then try to justify it. Corbett cut us some slack in this regard, but then gently pushed us back to serious interpretation and an awareness of the limits which an author's identifiable narrative purpose imposed on the range of possible interpretations.

I remember him lecturing on Conrad's "Youth" and telling us (then in our teens) that we were about to experience the energy, the drive, the exhilaration, the sense of power, the sense of mastery, the sense of unlimited possibility, indeed the sense of infallibility and immortality, which came to men in their twenties and early thirties—as shown in Conrad's story. In making his point, Corbett drew upon his own recollections of this period in his life, and told us how marvelous this time of life would be for us. He also told us it would not last—and to enjoy it to the full before we gradually grew into more sedate maturity. On the other end of the age scale, he discussed sympathetically the challenges facing Captain MacWhirr in "Typhoon," as he encountered unfolding circumstances totally beyond his control.

While discussing Conrad, Mr. Corbett drew on his own nautical experiences (he had spent time at sea and had written about it). He also shared with us the challenges of creative writing that he himself had experienced (he eventually became the nationally recognized and widely acclaimed author of over ninety books, largely novels, many aimed at adolescents like us). His comments on creative writing were not lengthy or self-serving, but lightly anecdotal—and hence, probably better understood and absorbed by us. Generally speaking, he communicated on our wavelength, and this was very much a part of his success.

Corbett, in fact, used personal anecdote more effectively to make points than any other teacher I have had. I remember on one occasion he was discussing some of the gallows humor in Shakespeare—and the ways in which grim events can create very different emotional impacts in different people. He had served in World War II and had seen the death camps. He gave us a very graphic description of how bodies had been stacked up like cordwood. He told us a story about a time when he and some of his buddies had been standing around and a starving survivor had approached them while they were eating and asked for some food. They had a bag of donuts and they gave him several, which he devoured—and then clutched his stomach and died right there in their presence, presumably as a result of eating too many of those donuts. These had been given to the unfortunate person with the best of intentions, yet the result was horribly contrary to expectations. The point of his story was that some of his friends were horrified, some largely indifferent (they had recently seen so much of death), and others found it grimly humorous, a sort of emotional release in the ever-present stresses of war. He added, as an afterthought—which I have recalled many times—"Never let anyone tell you that the death camps did not exist—they did. I was there. I saw." According to *Wikipedia*, he was on the staff of an armed services newspaper, and was one of the first reporters into Dachau.

We read *Macbeth* with Mr. Corbett, and this was the first time I really enjoyed Shakespeare on a mature level. As I recall, we did not act it out, nor did we do in-class readings, as we had in the Second Form. Corbett himself read from the play and lectured, taking us through it act by act and discussing the text in great detail. He expounded at some length on the relationship between Macbeth and Lady Macbeth with respect to courage, ambition, and imagination. He elaborated on the discussions between them and the hesitations with respect to the plotted murder. He discussed the gatekeeper scene with its puns and grim humor. He pointed out how Macbeth was rescued by his wife's fainting when he was arousing suspicion and getting into deep waters after the murder. He showed us how Macbeth casually extracted from Banquo the details of his planned foray into the woods (accompanied by his son) so he could arrange for their murder: "Ride you this afternoon? ... Is't far you ride? ... Goes Fleance with you?"

Mr. Corbett also discussed the interaction between ambition and guilt in Macbeth's psyche. He then discussed the slow breakdown of Lady Macbeth, and how her lack of imagination, among other things, undermined her ability to confront the reality and immediacy of the shedding of blood—and the significance of blood as her mind broke down. He read us the famous scene featuring "Out, out, brief candle....." Corbett, however, spent little time on the witches' prophecies and let their ironies speak for themselves. This was the first time I had heard an analysis of Shakespeare at this level—and it was an eye-opener. Somehow movies, theater, and TV had always been simple entertainment to me—in which you sat back and passively let all come at you. Your role was to absorb. In this spirit, I had watched movie versions of *Hamlet* and *Richard III*. Now Mr. Corbett was teaching us the rewards of active engagement with the play—reading people and their motivations, analyzing circumstances, guessing at outcomes, sensing roadblocks to ambition, asking what you would do if you were in a character's position, deeply relating at an emotional level to the eventual triumphs and tragedies. This was strong stuff in a new dimension.

In Fourth-Form English, we also read a selection of quality essays.[246] Mr. Corbett's selections fell into two categories: the didactic and the humorous. In the first category we read essays by Francis Bacon on reading and books, and also on friendship. We read Emerson's "Self-Reliance," with Mr. Corbett tying this into his previous discussions of "Youth." We read Faulkner's Nobel Prize acceptance speech at the height of the Cold War as the implications of the atomic age were coming home to America: "I refuse to accept the end of man. ... I believe that man will not only endure, but will prevail. He is immortal, not because he alone among creatures has an inexhaustible voice, but because he has a soul, a spirit capable of compassion and sacrifice and endurance." We read an essay by Walter Lippmann on the failures of American foreign policy during the first half of the twentieth century, which he attributed to America's lack of realism, its failure to recognize that rivalries between countries are the norm and must be managed, not resented. In this same vein, we read an essay by E. M. Forster on "Tolerance," in which he argued that tolerance is a more important guideline for behavior than love because it is more attainable. I remember Mr. Corbett strongly endorsing this conclusion—love might

---

246 Robert U. Jameson, ed., *Essays Old and New*, New York: Harcourt Brace and Company, 1957.

Fourth Form (1958-59)

be the ultimate human objective, but tolerance, simply getting along with those you may not like, is the immediate one. I recall that Roger Williams played a part in this discussion.

Mr. Corbett had a wonderful sense of humor and some of his essay selections reflected this. Naturally, we read Thurber's "Macbeth Murder Mystery" as well as his "The Night the Bed Fell." We read Twain's famous (and scathing) essay on Cooper's literary offenses. We read Churchill's self-deprecating account of his admission to Harrow and his experiences there. We read Broun's "The Fifty-First Dragon" which everyone loved. We even read Stephen Leacock's "A, B, and C—The Human Element in Mathematics," in which he took typical math problems involving the above-named characters and wove stories around them: how they dug ditches, walked, ran, wagered, operated locomotives, pumped water into and out of cisterns, etc.; how A always seems to be the alpha character in the problem, B the quiet subordinate, and C the puny victim, etc. We got a good laugh from these light critiques and parodies of the literature and math we were learning. Corbett, too, had fun with them.

In the spring, we read poetry, scanned some of it, and learned about many of its structural aspects, not just the sounds created by alliteration and onomatopoeia, but the more important stylistic techniques, such as metaphor, simile, symbol, and irony. I believe our text was *Sound and Sense*,[247] but we may have used this in Fifth Form. I remember selections from Housman, Dickenson, Robinson, and Frost. I also recollect Mr. Corbett reciting Ogden Nash's pithy "Candy is Dandy, but Liquor is Quicker," and I recall his quoting Byron's shortest poem: "Mary Lamb—God Damn." I responded to his pithy quotes by handing in a brief Nash-style poem which ended with the line: "Said Corbett, 'Absorb it!'"

We read Hardy's *Return of the Native* that spring. I found it insufferably boring, and I do not remember Corbett discussing it. Perhaps it was at the end of the year and we spent little time on it. We did, however, plow through it out of class.[248]

---

247 Laurence and Perrine, New York: Harcourt Brace and Company, 1956.
248 In my own mind, I can't remember if we read this with Corbett or Paxton, but since Russ Carpenter remembered reading it with Meserve, I'm assuming it was read in the Fourth Form.

Composition was heavily emphasized—at least an essay a week. We wrote book reviews. We wrote essays about past experiences. We were drilled in writing precis. At times we were told to write about any topic we wished. On one of these occasions, I remember writing a frivolous piece on how to select a topic for an essay, an old dodge. I also remember writing a very serious, scholarly (and recognizably fraudulent) essay on how the colon had emerged as a form of punctuation (from diligent printers in Cologne, Germany, of course). Corbett got a big kick out of this. He enjoyed anything imaginative.

As I recall, Roy Maletz and I won the English prizes that year—Roy got first prize;[249] I got second. Roy fully deserved the honor. I suspect that some in the other section might well have deserved second prize ahead of me, but I did not complain.

English with Meserve. Since I never took a class with him, I cannot describe Mr. Meserve's teaching style firsthand, nor his approach to the literature read in Fourth-Form English. Any account of instruction at Moses Brown would be incomplete, however, without inclusion of Meserve's instructional style. From all accounts, he was a memorable presence in the classroom with a distinct style of instruction. Dave London,[250] Dave

---

249 Roy Maletz joined our Class in the Third Form. A graduate of Brown University, he earned his MD at Johns Hopkins University. A Vietnam-era veteran, he served as a major in the Air Force. Living in Andover, Massachusetts and practicing throughout the Merrimack Valley, he became a leading specialist in nephrology (kidney diseases), and was based at the Lowell General Hospital. As noted in his obituary: Francophile, military history buff, classical music and opera lover, art collector, pianist, photographer, carpenter, sailor, audiophile, wine connoisseur—these were just a few of the passions Roy embraced in his unyielding desire to live life to the fullest. Active in many civic affairs, he continued to practice until his final illness. He passed away in 2021.

250 Dave London joined our Class in the Third Form. He graduated from Brown University, where he served as News Director of the *Brown Daily Herald*, meeting his wife, Toby, at the newspaper. They were married right after graduation. Based in Attleboro, Dave enjoyed a very successful career in retailing, trade association management, and real estate development. He has been active in a wide range of professional, charitable, and religious organizations, and remains very active in Brown University Alumni affairs. He currently serves as Trustee and Treasurer of the Brown/RISD Hillel Foundation and the Brown Chaplain's Religious Life Association. He is the recipient of the Providence Hebrew Day School Community Service Award, several Brown/RISD Hillel Special Project Awards, and a Brown University Alumni Service Award. He has also served as Brown Alumni Class President. He is an active supporter of the performing arts in Rhode Island, enjoys tennis, gym, skiing, and pool, and has participated four times in the National Amateur Billiards Championships.

Chaffee,[251] Bruce Henkle, and Russ Carpenter ('59) shared their sets of largely positive classroom recollections with me. In light of what we now know, however, as noted below, Meserve had a deeply divided personality that included a very dark side. All of the interviews recorded here took place before this became public knowledge.

Dave London remembered Meserve as being a person with a lot of charm and style, an "avuncular guy, a consummate gentleman," reminiscent of the main character in the current movie *History Boys*.[252] In Dave's own words:

> I loved the way Meserve taught. He had a manner that I don't think you could duplicate—unless you were there. When the books opened in class, he had a soft, gentle way, not like Herman or Raines, who were challenging you with intensity. Meserve was trying to nurture you. He had an elegant and soft way of talking and a very gentle, very encouraging, nature.
>
> He used the Socratic Method. He didn't tell you anything; you had to find it out for yourself. For example, he would have someone read a sentence or a paragraph and he would then work that individual, or a group of us, or the whole class, until they had explored that passage from all sides and could see a full range of possibilities in it. He would never say, "I think the author is trying to do this," until the class had come to the conclusion that the author was indeed trying to do this—or trying to do two things at once, or trying to show ambivalence, or trying to use words for their assonance or consonance. Whatever it was, whether it was the content or the style, Meserve would get the class to figure it out. It was a method of making you think—and it was a wonderful way of teaching.
>
> He got everybody to read with a mind to explore—and it was a delight to read these books with him. He didn't ask us to agree with him or with each other. That was the very antithesis of his method. He was the first teacher I encountered who wasn't trying to get people to agree. He wanted us to see that there were many different ways to look at something. He would tell us that some critics had interpreted things in one way, and others in another

---

251 Dave Chaffee, who organized the Broadcasting Club (described in Volume II) founded his own advertising agency, as noted in Volume II.
252 Interview, Dave London, August 29, 2010.

way. He would introduce us to different interpretations of Shakespeare or Conrad to get us to see that in literary criticism there was no "right" and "wrong," but differences in perspective.

And, in this regard … you were not afraid to offer an opinion in class. You could tell him what you thought without being afraid that he would put you down. He also developed an atmosphere in which you were not afraid that someone else in class would put you down either. This was a tremendous gift—to be able to have everybody feel that if you concluded something about a word or passage or chapter or whole book (or a character's inner self, for that matter) that this opinion of yours had value. He got you to feel comfortable thinking outside of the box a long time before people in education wanted people our age to think outside of the box.[253]

Russ Carpenter also remembered Meserve as a "gentle presence" in the classroom with a nonaggressive teaching style, but a person totally in control of the class. According to Russ, the Class of 1959 occasionally gave a lot of grief to some instructors, especially those who gave them an opening, or exhibited some form of weakness. This practice started in the Seventh Grade with George Kenyon, who lasted only one year at Moses Brown (and who really lost control of the class). It continued into the Upper School, with rebellious conduct in the English classrooms of George Mayer (whose association with Moses Brown did not survive the experience) and Bill Taber (whose association did). Russ remembered Mr. Taber losing control of things on one occasion when he was teaching as a replacement instructor down in the music room. The class went wild. The topic was poetry, and at the end of the raucous session, Taber was heard to exclaim, "You have ruined Shelly." But such antics never occurred in Meserve's classroom. He never let students dominate the proceedings. There was a level of respect for Meserve that would preclude antics or rebellion. His questions were controlling, and it was through questions that he put his points across. It was through questions that he controlled the class.[254] As Dave Chaffee recalled, "He was pretty strict. Some teachers today would love to have the power over a class that he had."[255]

---

253 Interview, August 29, 2010.
254 Telephone interview with Russ Carpenter, May 23, 2011.
255 Interview, Dave Chaffee, August 2, 2013.

Fourth Form (1958-59) 311

There may have been no right and wrong in literary criticism, but there certainly was in grammar: as Dave Chaffee recalled, "Meserve insisted on accuracy. He did not believe that you should promote creativity in violation of the basic rules of expression."[256] Bruce Henkle,[257] in this context, remembered exercises with three or four questions that were referred to as Mr. Meserve's "goose egg" tests. If all questions were answered satisfactorily, then you received a score of 100. If any one question was answered unsatisfactorily, you received a zero, but the goose egg conveying the disappointing news was usually decorated with a little personalized cartoon.[258] I have in my yearbook what may be an example of such—Meserve's self-inscribed initials (BGM) in the form of a bird.

Russ Carpenter also remembered that Meserve in many ways aimed his teaching efforts at the individuals in the class, rather than at the class as a whole. For example, although there were books that the entire class was expected to read, there were also other books that Meserve would assign on an individual basis, tailored to a specific student. He would challenge his best students with more difficult readings.[259] Russ recalled that Meserve also used this technique in vocabulary drills. He would pick words for students to define by level of difficulty, and also occasionally by personal relevance—at least this is what Russ thought was happening when Meserve asked him to define "supercilious"![260]

Russ recollected that both Paxton and Meserve taught him how to write, but he remembered that Meserve's comments were more personally

---

256 Interview, August 2, 2013. Dave Chaffee still has a copy of the style book written by Paxton and Meserve, and he still consults it occasionally.
257 Bruce Henkle joined our Class in the Second Form. He graduated from Colby College (where he met his wife) and entered the Air Force, rising to the rank of Captain. He served at Plattsburgh Air Force Base, and later was the officer in charge of base procurement at Loring Air Force Base in Maine. Upon leaving the service he joined Universal Oil Products in Connecticut, a company specializing in air pollution control. He rose to take charge of the Personnel Department, and specialized in human resources for most of the rest of his career. In 1980 he joined ACCO in this capacity, and later became the Vice President for Administration at Barns Engineering in Stamford, Connecticut. After EDO bought out Barnes, he continued in a top management position in the Human Resources Department of this aerospace company until retiring in 2000. Returning to Maine after retirement, he joined JW Walsh Publishing Company, and has had an enjoyable career in a part-time management capacity there. Like many classmates, he is an avid golfer. From a telephone interview with Bruce, May 10, 2020.
258 Telephone interview, August 7, 2014.
259 Telephone interview with Russ Carpenter, May 23, 2011.
260 *Ibid.*

perceptive, and hence more memorable. Meserve once told Russ's mother that her son was "much more forthcoming and personally candid" in his papers than any other student he had had in class. Russ once wrote a paper in which he admitted that his "egocentric satisfaction" was the most important thing to him in the circumstances he was describing. Meserve in his comments on the paper praised the author's candor, but asked Russ whether the person he was describing in this self-portrait was likeable, and whether he really wished to present himself in this way. Consistent with Meserve's style of teaching, the question taught the lesson.[261]

Russ cited memorable treatments of Conrad's *Victory*, Hardy's *Return of the Native* (which he had read before), and *Macbeth* in Meserve's class. He also recalled reading an essay by Matthew Arnold on "Art for Art's Sake"—lessons from which stayed with him all his life.[262] Dave London remembered that "In terms of the contents of his classes, Meserve focused much more on writing style than on plot, more on the craft of the writer as a stylist, as a shaper of language, than on the larger structure of the work. He emphasized how individual passages were formed, rather than how the work as a whole was assembled. He asked us to write a lot in his class, and he expected our grammar to be perfect. But his emphasis was not on grammar, it was on literary style."

Dave continued, "It was interesting to see the different approaches to English our different instructors had. They all taught us literature, style, grammar, and writing skills, but with a different emphasis. Bennett emphasized the content of the literature, its social context, the plot, the big picture, in both poetry and prose, in both short stories and novels; Meserve emphasized the author's style, writing skills, use of imagery, hidden meanings, symbolism, and poetry within the prose; Paxton emphasized *our* writing skills, our vocabulary, and our grammar (if you mastered Paxton, you had nothing to worry from the SAT's)."[263] Russ Carpenter added that the difference between Paxton and Meserve was that the latter "pushed his

---

261 *Ibid*.
262 *Ibid*.
263 Interview, 2010. If I might make a personal observation here, Meserve was certainly successful with Dave London—who wrote two descriptive pieces for the *Delphian* in our junior year that exhibit an excellence and maturity of style that must have come to Meserve's notice since he almost certainly was the one to recommend them for publication. Dave later went on to edit the Brown *Daily Herald*.

students," while Paxton's primary aim was to cover the basics and ensure that all were up to speed on a range of skills he deemed important.

To add Corbett to the group, I would argue that he was more interested in an author's ability to resonate with the reader, to speak directly, to convey messages, both direct and subtle. In this regard, Corbett was like Meserve in terms of discussing specific passages and specific words at some length. Corbett, however, instead of giving major emphasis to the different ways small passages might resonate with readers, focused more on the ways in which the whole story itself would resonate in terms of its large messages. In emphasizing the whole over the parts, Corbett was similar to Bennett, but more than Bennett, he was interested in direct, passionate connections between author and reader—in contrast to Bennett's more cerebral concerns for plot structure and historical context, largely in the abstract. Corbett also showed us that English could be fun—echoing the basic perspective of Taber from the First Form, who wished to expose us to a smorgasbord of interesting and engaging literary forms and practices. Nichols, to complete the set, emphasized, not surprisingly (given his interests), the emotional, the dramatic, and the theatrical in literature—and how writing could be adventuresome, arresting, even shocking. Plot, presentation, and dramatic impact were therefore his specialties.

Dave London wonders if this variety in approach and interest was deliberately created through Moses Brown's hiring practices—with teachers being hired to complement, not replicate, those who were already there. This we will never know, but I do believe that Dave is absolutely correct in concluding that we were great beneficiaries of this diversity of interest and of classroom emphasis.

And, in terms of variety of approach and opinion, we might add that Meserve was also willing to experiment with new methods that would directly expose his students to the opinions of others. Bill Barrett remembered that he took his classes down to Alumni Hall (which had audio-video equipment) and showed them a series of televised programs in which critics evaluated readings under discussion in class. He was probably the first Moses Brown instructor to use this new medium as an important component of a course.

All our English teachers emphasized writing, although Corbett, Meserve, and Nichols seem to have encouraged creativity more than Bennett and Paxton. The set of compositions appearing in the *Delphian* from that time include a wide range of offerings in many modes, including poetry, descriptive prose, short stories, didactic essays, humor, and literary criticism, as discussed in more detail in the chapter on the *Delphian* in Volume II. Presumably most of the pieces were the result of assignments in English classes. They vary a bit in quality (although to appear in the publication, each had to meet a standard). The reader, however, is struck by the fairly frequent recurrence of truly imaginative pieces appearing in many different modes—but especially in poetry and fictional short stories. English classes, true to a liberal arts tradition, encouraged imagination, and those at Moses Brown probably did so more than those in any other field of teaching. Meserve's teaching style certainly contributed to this result, but that, unfortunately, is not the end of his story.[264]

---

[264] In January 2019 Moses Brown School announced that it had received reports of teacher abuse of students, and it launched an investigation to be conducted by the firm of T&M Protection Resources. The report of that investigation was released to members of the Moses Brown community on February 3, 2020, after much of this book manuscript had been written. Included in the Summary of Findings is the following statement: "Former teacher Basil Meserve, one of the subjects of the original complaint, engaged in sexual misconduct, inappropriate physical touching and other boundary-crossing behavior with at least nine Moses Brown students between the ages of 13 and 19 in the 1950s, 1960s, and 1970s. Most of the witnesses interviewed by T&M shared that they did not report Meserve's behavior to the school at that time. One witness reported that he had shared information about Meserve with the school, but T&M was unable to corroborate that information. The investigation found that one Moses Brown employee had reason to believe that Meserve had a sexual relationship with a senior in the 1960s but did not report that information to anyone else at the school." The report also listed four other former employees who engaged in inappropriate behavior with a combined total of eight students between the 1960s and the 2000s. These four were not identified by name to protect the confidentiality of the survivors and witnesses. Given the dates, it is probable that at least three of these four individuals are nowhere mentioned in these three volumes. In its communication to the Moses Brown community, the school extended its sincere apology to the survivors, their families, and to the Moses Brown community as a whole. There was a follow-up investigation, and on November 18, 2020 the School sent another letter to the Moses Brown community that contained the following statement, "T&M's first finding corroborates information already known: between 1949 and 1966, former teacher Basil Meserve engaged in boundary-crossing and inappropriate physical touching with three additional Moses Brown students between the age of 14 and 16. There is no evidence to suggest that the school was aware of Meserve's inappropriate behavior." Again, the school extended its sincere apology to the survivors, their families, and to the Moses Brown community as a whole.

Fourth Form (1958-59)

Reading. Somewhere along the way—I think it was in the Fourth Form, although it might possibly have been early in the Fifth—we were asked to take a class in speed-reading and reading comprehension with Miss Helen F. Sadlier. It was really an adjunct course to English. I don't remember much about the course, but I do remember we were taught how to scan a page to recognize its main points, and we were actually timed to encourage ever more rapid reading. We had a text (which I cannot find), and I remember having difficulty making much progress. I could never sight-read music rapidly, and I wonder today if something basic was at work (or not at work) here. In any event, I could read fairly well to begin with (and enjoyed reading), but I was never able to speed-read. Others may have benefited more from this class.

We did, however, read stories from the *Atlantic Monthly*. I remember one written by Peter Ustinov, who was also an excellent actor. It was entitled "Add a Dash of Pity." The plot (it was fiction) described how a failed British military operation in World War II was very critically treated by an historian. Ustinov's main character addressed this criticism and made the case for more sympathy in terms of the circumstances faced by commanders in battle situations, and why bygones should be bygones when historians sit in righteous judgment on their subjects. I always remembered the lessons of this short story, but that is really about all I remember from this class.

Second-Year German. By our junior year, Mr. Cate had retired, and we took Second-Year German with Mr. Kenneth Justin.[265] He was an interesting person, a young man who had earned an MA from Harvard, perhaps on the GI Bill. He had a spent a lot of time in Germany in the Army, and had a young, very attractive, blonde German wife. They lived at School, and I remember her frequently pushing their young child around campus in a little baby carriage. She didn't speak much English and faculty, who couldn't easily chat with her, would nevertheless doff their hats in a friendly way and say hello as she perambulated the baby around campus.

---

[265] In the fall, we met in Room 4 where we had had math with Mr. Roberts and English for a term with Mr. Bennett. In the Spring Term, we met in Mr. Whitford's Room 5. Both were on the north corridor.

Mr. Justin left Moses Brown after a couple of years. We were never told the reason. Students, however, are curious about such things. Some speculated that objections had been raised to alleged risqué classroom comments, although I remember nothing really offensive or out of line. Certainly not by later standards. I do remember that Mr. Pezet, it was rumored, occasionally engaged in such misdemeanors, but he never was dismissed for them, so there may have been other things at work here. Justin was very right-wing and had many rough edges. I suspect that he ruffled feathers among some faculty colleagues, and this could have contributed to his departure at the end of our senior year.

He also had a bit of a chip on his shoulder. He may have come from a modest background, resented those from a more privileged one, and was never able to put this fully behind him. He also had some basic personality problems, and he was not subtle about expressing his likes and dislikes. I suspect that Mr. Cunningham may have been one of his dislikes—and word of this would get back quickly in a small community like Moses Brown. A larger man than Cunningham would have counseled Justin, given him emotional support, helped him mature, and produced an excellent permanent member of the faculty, but perhaps Cunningham's own insecurities precluded this.

There were indeed rough edges here, and Mr. Justin was not always willing to adapt to community expectations. There is no doubt he lacked judgment on several levels, but he did not lack intelligence, and it was a shame that the latter did not grow the former. It is also possible that he took some bitterness over his Moses Brown experiences away with him. I don't know what happened to him eventually. I hope he got his act together and had an enjoyable, productive career.

Justin was a good instructor, when all was said and done, and most of us learned a lot. Our Second- and Third-Year German classes had about ten to twelve students, possibly as many as fifteen. These included Bill Brehm and Jim Rigney. I think Jeff Forman also took German. I can't remember who else did. Over half of Mr. Justin's class got a 560 or higher on their German SATs, and thereby qualified for the college language requirement (so they did not have to take a language in college). This was well above the Moses Brown average for foreign languages at that time. Mr. Herman, who was Director of Testing, told me this. In addition, it should

Fourth Form (1958-59)

Kenneth F. Justin

be mentioned that Jim Rigney won a Rhode Island statewide German competition award.[266] So Mr. Justin's class learned German well. For this reason, Mr. Herman was not happy about his departure.

In the Fall Term, we had a standard text together with a reader containing short stories and brief biographical sketches of German figures, such as Kant, Schiller, and Schopenhauer. Mr. Cate had probably ordered this, and Mr. Justin was not an admirer of it. For the Spring Term he substituted a novel: Remarque's *Drei Kameraden* in a condensed version for our level of reading. This we worked our way through carefully.

The text taught basic grammar—I remember memorizing the prepositions and which case they took: *aus, auser, bei, mit, nach, seit, von,* and *zu* took the dative, for example. We reviewed tenses and expanded our knowledge of them. We learned the subjunctive: "*es wehre*"—"it might have been."

---

[266] Jim Rigney joined our Class in the Fourth Form. He earned his MD from Georgetown Medical School and became a specialist in internal medicine, practicing in Doylestown, PA, directly north of Philadelphia.

We were also asked to write a lot of papers. I attempted to produce an erudite treatise on Secretary Dulles's foreign policy, and was promptly shot down for composing an overly ambitious tract, not written in good German. We were instructed to go back to simple language and build up our capabilities.

In addition to the text, Mr. Justin gave us a series of idioms which we memorized. These involved special usages, turns of phrases, and other colloquialisms. I don't know if these were the product of his own efforts, or if he collected them from another text (I think they were his own), but they were exceedingly helpful. I think there were about a hundred or so of them. We put them on little file cards and memorized them a few at a time. They were turns of expression that you would expect to find in normal conversation, and we could easily understand why they might come in handy—so there was little resistance to learning them. They really introduced us to spoken German and proved very useful on tests and other exercises. They also helped you read a newspaper.

Mr. Justin emphasized the contemporary in all of his German language instruction, and that was very much to the good. His style of instruction was straightforward. He read to us. He used anecdotes. He often used the blackboard to list words or phrases. Although we did learn traditional grammar, the emphasis was more on usage than strictly on grammar itself. Vocabulary was always a problem for me, but from frequent encounters with Mr. Justin's idioms, I remember beginning to "get a feel" for the language, and this was a new experience.

Chemistry. First-Year Chemistry was taught by Mr. Jeffers ('52), a very genial person, a nice guy, and a good teacher.[267] It was an enjoyable course. He had been hired to replace Mr. Hutton who had left to become Headmaster of another Quaker school, and this was his first year as an instructor at Moses Brown. However, he was a Moses Brown alumnus and the son of Mr. Allen's secretary, so he was familiar with the School and its personnel. Mr. Jeffers was also a proud Brown graduate and athlete, and he immediately became the Moses Brown wrestling coach. He had an excellent sense

---

[267] We met in the chemistry lab, the middle room in the new Thomas Science Building.

John H. Jeffers

of humor and obviously loved his chemistry. We had a text that was very readable and clear. I don't remember its name, and I haven't yet located it, but I do remember that it proceeded in a logical way, beginning with a great deal of description of chemical phenomena, and then moving into equations. I remember it being well-illustrated.

As Mr. Jeffers recalled, the post-Sputnik period was "an exciting time to be teaching," when national attention was given to science instruction, with a focus on the upgrading of science curricula. Teachers were encouraged to return to school for refresher courses both in substance and in methods of instruction. Mr. Jeffers did so as an incipient teacher, taking such a course at Brown the summer before he started teaching. Here he learned advances in both the "chemical bond" and "chemical study" approaches to teaching; the first emphasizing atomic and molecular structure, the second emphasizing laboratory learning. He brought the fruits of both to the Moses Brown classroom.[268]

---

268 Telephone interviews, December 7, 2010 and April 23, 2011.

Mr. Jeffers was fully on top of the text, and he followed it carefully in class. Not that he read from it, but he used it to systematize his class discussions. He also supplemented it a lot in class, following it topic by topic. He was a solid lecturer, often illustrating his lectures with examples and punctuating the class with an occasional experiment. Some of these were for show or for fun, but all were good basic science. I remember his "spit on eleven cents" demonstration of how an electric charge could be created with pocket change, and I remember him creating a very impressive explosion (with aluminum oxide, I think). On at least one other occasion, he put chemicals into a test tube, added other chemicals, and the color changed dramatically. Bill Barrett remembered the "Nassau experiment" where chemicals were mixed to produce an orange and black result—the colors of Princeton. He put sodium into water and produced a great fizz. Somewhere along the way he demonstrated atmospheric pressure with mercury, and he created his own "spheres of Magdeburg" by evacuating air from matching spheres which we then could not pull apart.

Chemistry was mathematically a more demanding subject than biology or those subjects we had encountered in the social sciences. There were certainly more correct (or incorrect) answers. It was important to memorize facts, but it was also important to develop intellectual techniques and understand procedures. By the second semester of the course we were using simple chemical equations to show how combinations of elements would produce other substances in certain specified ratios. We also used algebra to solve problems involving volumes of gases at certain pressures and temperatures. Descriptive memory, which could carry one through biology, was not enough for chemistry. Rigorously abstract concepts and math were needed.

Mr. Jeffers covered a lot of territory in this class. We were introduced to the Periodic Table of the Elements; we were taught the then-current understanding of atomic structures (the only important subatomic particles taught at the high school level then were protons, neutrons, and electrons); we were also taught molecular theories and were introduced to organic chemistry with its carbon/hydrogen molecules and their hexagonal structures; we spent a lot of time on solids/liquids/gases, and Dalton's discoveries; we were taught about moles, Avogadro's number, and absolute zero.

Fourth Form (1958-59)   321

Mrs. Full congratulates (L–R) Dave London, Stan Armington, Fred Schwartz, Ed Vieira, and Lyle Fain for RI Science Fair Awards.

We had labs once a week. Mr. Jeffers liked the modern facilities in the Thomas Building's new labs, but the walls were mostly glass. This was great for light, but in the winter the building could be quite cold during school sessions—unlike the steam-heated classrooms in the rest of the plant.[269] In biology class, our labs had principally focused on observation. Here there was more emphasis on actual experimentation and demonstration. They began with very simple procedures, and from the start each required a lab report. Mr. Jeffers gave us close guidance as to what to do. He would hand out an instruction sheet and we were issued certain pieces of equipment. We would hook up the equipment in the demonstrated way, following directions. Then we would begin the experiment. My recollection is that we paired off and did this two by two, but I might be wrong about that.

---

269 He remembered once working in the Thomas Building lab on experiments for his master's thesis during a cold spell before classes resumed after Christmas break. Suddenly sirens screamed nearby. He investigated and discovered a dozen fire engines out in the circle. The School had reduced the heat during the break, the sprinklers on the fourth floor had frozen, and the pipes had burst, triggering the call to the fire company. There was a cascade of water, some of which had frozen. They were pitching ice out of the fourth floor windows for quite some time after that.

I remember test tubes, beakers, retorts, and Bunsen burners. We made oxygen and collected it. We also made hydrogen, put it into an inverted test tube, and used it to put out a burning splint (demonstrating that pure hydrogen, lacking oxygen, would not burn). We then inverted the tube so the hydrogen could escape into the air—and at this point a burning splint would produce a pop as the hydrogen exploded.

We repeated Dalton's experiment with expanding gases. We created vacuums. I'm sure we did many other experiments, but at this time I do not remember them. Towards the end of the year, we did some analysis—taking a sample and trying to identify what it was by using various experimental methods. We didn't have a lot of time at the end of the year to get far into these types of procedures, but we did some of them.

After each lab, we wrote reports on the results, paying special attention to measurements. All this was a preliminary attempt to develop an acquaintance with lab procedures, and it was interesting—but most learning in this class came from the lectures and the textbook. All in all, it was an enjoyable class and built on our understanding of the scientific method we had learned from Mrs. Full.

Modern European History. One of the most enjoyable courses I took at Moses Brown was Modern European History, taught by Mr. Frederick Pratt, another young teacher with an AB from Harvard.[270] This was his first year at the School.[271] I remember that before school began I interviewed

---

270 It met in Room 8 at the end of the north corridor where we had had Tinker and Nichols.
271 He had been hired in August by Mr. Cunningham, who interviewed him in Dusseldorf, as Mr. Pratt recalled. Cunningham, who had been grouse hunting, or whatever, in Scotland, was on a European tour that took him to Britain, Scandinavia, Germany, and Paris (*Moses Brown Bulletin*, August, 1958, p. 1.). He was looking for a history teacher and a hockey coach. Mr. Pratt was both; this combination was, no doubt, a factor in his being hired. Mr. Cunningham also was looking for someone to teach German. Since Mr. Pratt could do this, it was an added asset. "Cunningham was very charming," recalled Mr. Pratt, "and I agreed to come" (Interview with Mr. and Mrs. Pratt at their home in South Duxbury, Vermont, December 16, 2010). According to Mr. Jeffers (phone interview, December 7, 2010), Cunningham thought some of the older faculty were in a rut, were teaching from an older perspective, and were teaching the same material over and over, so he hired Mr. Pratt to bring some new training and perspectives on board.

Fourth Form (1958-59)

Frederick A. Pratt

him for a story in the *Quaker*. Mrs. Pratt was present, and agreed to be interviewed as well. He was an excellent teacher, fresh from Harvard College and army duty in Europe, as I remember.

This was his first teaching job and we were his first class. He also taught ancient history, and later, German. His New England roots ran deep and he spoke with precise diction in a proper cultivated Massachusetts accent. He had gone to Middlesex, Andover, and Harvard.[272] He was a descendant of Bronson Alcott, the religious reformer, and a great-grandnephew of Louisa May Alcott, the writer.[273] After their arrival at Moses Brown, the Pratts soon became young parents.

---

272 His father taught and coached hockey at Middlesex. His grandfather was its founder and Headmaster. He graduated in 1950, and was accepted at Harvard. But he was only 17 at the time and his parents urged him to take a year at Andover before matriculating at Harvard. He did not think it was a good idea then, but he does now. Hence, he was Andover, '51, and Harvard, '55. Interview, December 16, 2010.

273 Louisa May Alcott was Mr. Pratt's great-great-aunt. Her older sister Anna married John Bridge Pratt. He had two sons, one of whom was Frederick Alcott Pratt, who was Mr. Pratt's grandfather. Mr. Pratt was named for him. Louisa May Alcott had no children, and she adopted his grandfather. She was a canny New England woman, and this kept the royalties in the family. Many of her books are still in print. Interview, December 16, 2010.

Mr. Pratt, when interviewed, had a good recollection of his inaugural class, which contained juniors and seniors. He remembered Allan Cokin sitting right in the middle of the room. He remembered Jerry Kroll ('59) sitting in the back row on the right complaining about "your Harvard questions." He remembered Tom Paolino ('59) and Bill Murdock[274] sitting next to each other and conspiring to test "this young guy of a teacher." So they dropped a marble or coin or something onto the floor: "I just said authoritatively, 'This is no place for that,' and they didn't repeat it. I didn't send them out—and it was just as well for them I didn't. It was a lecture course, and it was not good to miss one session."[275]

Mr. Pratt constructed this course himself. We did have a textbook, but it was used only sporadically—mostly to cover the nineteenth century at the very end of the course. I skimmed it throughout, however, and one feature of the text struck me as very odd. It carried modern European history up to the year 1940—not exactly a year in which the major issues of the day had been definitively resolved. Continental Europe, with the exception of the Soviet Union, was almost totally under Nazi formal or informal control, and Britain stood with its back to the wall. There was a map illustrating this. The book concluded by stating that only time would tell if Britain would be able to survive, maintain itself, and then rescue the continent. By 1958, this question had been answered definitively. The final events described in the book were nearly twenty years out of date. Surely a subsequent edition was called for—or another text! I had strongly suspected that Mr. Pratt had not chosen the text, but had inherited it from his predecessor.[276]

All this was really irrelevant, however, because the course was largely taught in class. Mr. Pratt organized a very detailed study of Western Europe, beginning in the Middle Ages and running solidly through Napoleon. He started with the feudal system, its structure, and its network of personal relationships. He discussed Charlemagne and the establishment of the Holy Roman

---

274 Bill Murdock joined our Class in the Third Form. He came from Jamestown, RI, and returned there to work in the family business after graduating from Hobart College. The Murdocks had a specialty hardware store in Jamestown which served the Narragansett Bay sailing and boating culture. They also operated a large wholesale business specializing in stainless steel and copper fittings for boats, with a boat-building and boat-repairing clientele nationwide. He was a lifelong sailor and expert navigator on Narragansett Bay.
275 Interview, December 16, 2010.
276 He confirmed the truth of this surmise.

Empire—and its drastic fragmentation by the Treaty of Verdun after his death. He then carried the story down through the individual histories of England, France, and the remaining Empire in Germany and Italy.[277]

In the English story, he discussed the unique features of its originally centralized feudal system, the gradual development of English law, the rise of Parliament, the travails of the late fifteenth century (including the War of the Roses), the resumed centralization of authority under the Tudors, and then the great religious and constitutional disputes of the seventeenth century culminating in the English Civil War, Cromwell, and the eventual Restoration.[278]

With respect to France, Mr. Pratt discussed its many early efforts at centralization, the Hundred Years War with England, the Babylonian Captivity of the Papacy at Avignon, the consolidations of Louis the Spider (to whom we had been introduced by Mrs. Bluhm), the religious wars of the sixteenth century, and the eventual emergence of the Bourbons and their mastery of France under Henry IV, Richelieu, and Louis XIV. With respect to Germany and Italy, we learned about the rise of the Hapsburgs and the Hohenzollerns, and the disputes between popes and emperors, including the significance of benefices and the investiture controversy.[279] We studied the Crusades, the Great Schism, the Reformation, the Counter-Reformation, and the horrible Thirty Years' War.

---

277 Mr. Pratt recalled, "To build my lectures, I suspect, although I don't remember, that I used Wallace Ferguson and Geoffrey Bruun, *A Survey of European Civilization*, published by Riverside Press. I had this at Harvard as a text. I also used *The Middle Ages 395-1500*, by Joseph Strayer and Dana Carleton Munro, both at Princeton, 1942. My wife had used this text at Middlebury when she took a course with Pardon Tillinghast, a Moses Brown graduate, whom she remembered as an instructor 'who scared us all.' I also used Crane Brinton's book. I had taken a class with Brinton. He was a rambling lecturer, but he wrote an excellent book. I used the Durants. I also had both Master Perkins and David Owen at Harvard. I don't remember my medieval course. At Harvard, my specific area in history was English history—and I took all of David Owen's courses." Taped interview, December 16, 2010, South Duxbury, Vermont.

278 English history was Mr. Pratt's specialty at Harvard, as noted. Stephen Graubard (later longtime editor of *Daedalus*, the journal of the American Academy of Arts and Sciences) was his thesis advisor. His thesis topic was British parliamentary reactions to the American Civil War. He remembered that upon submission of his first chapter draft, Stephen [for whom I worked in the summer of 1970 – CWB] had "lots of suggestions on how to improve!" Interview, December 16, 2010.

279 He remembered Vic Field ('59), who sat in the back row of this class: "I remember his saying that I would not be allowed to teach a lot of what I was teaching in a public high school. I did not spare the papacy." Interview, December 16, 2010.

Mr. Pratt ended the course with a detailed analysis of the eighteenth century—the developed Westphalian international system with its alliance structure, its diplomatic revolutions, its several "world wars"; the Industrial Revolution in Britain, and finally the French Revolution, which we covered in great detail, including its most famous product—Napoleon.

All this provided an excellent factual and interpretive background for the future study of European history. I remember taking a course in my sophomore year at Harvard on Western European intellectual and social development, and Mr. Pratt's course was very helpful as background for this. His lecture style was different from that of earlier instructors we had encountered. He always gave us an outline at the start of class, usually written on the board, although sometimes handed out, and he followed that outline faithfully. He didn't make us copy it down, but it helped if we put the outline in our notebook and filled in the details as he lectured. I remember my technique was to write his outline on a page leaving lots of space between the lines. Then as he spoke, I filled in the spaces between the main topics. You never knew how much space to leave, so often you would need more space than the original distance between the topics afforded. I therefore wrote all over the page while trying to keep the relevant material adjacent. When Mr. Pratt finished a topic, my notes about it would then be circled with a line to separate them from the notes for other topics covered on the same page. This led to strangely shaped areas filled with scribble, sort of like countries on a map of a fictitious continent whose boundaries were even more illogically formed than those of Austria-Hungary. I think these strange topological constructs had a mnemonic significance to them and helped me remember the subject matter.

Mr. Pratt also began to introduce us to the kind of examinations we might expect in college social science classes—identifications and essay questions. For the first, we were told to "identify and give the significance of" a number of items. The responses required a very brief "who, when, what, where" format.[280] The responses to the essay questions had to be well-argued with evidence for each point made.

This approach to examinations liberated us even more than Mr. Odell had from the true/false or short answer format we had been used to in much of

---

280 As Mr. Pratt himself recalled. Interview, December 16, 2010.

Fourth Form (1958-59)

the past. We therefore developed an ability to write succinct short answers as well as half-hour-long or even hour-long responses. We also began to get a sense of proof in answering questions—assertion, evidence; assertion, evidence. The exam strategy was to master the data and then respond creatively to the question by marshaling that data in support of an argument. No doubt the reasoning structure in geometry we were experiencing at the same time contributed subliminally to the development of this process. Thus we were taught to assemble or organize concepts—and we began to develop a sense of examsmanship in the process. The methods developed in Mr. Pratt's class became very useful in college. Looking back on this class from a great distance in time, Mr. Pratt remembered, "I would not have considered using true-or-false or one-word questions. They may be a challenge to your memory, but they are not an intellectual challenge. You guys needed an intellectual challenge."[281]

This logical ordering of evidence was important to Mr. Pratt. Once he returned an exam of mine with a low grade scratched out and a higher grade substituted with the following comment written on the side: "your exam makes a lot more sense when the pages are arranged in the proper order." We also wrote one or two major papers in this course. I remember doing a lengthy report on the Spanish Armada with a detailed map of the English Channel.[282]

Looking back at the ten years I spent at Moses Brown, we were taught history in eight of them. We learned about American history in the Third, Fifth, Seventh, and (as shall be seen) Twelfth Grades, with the last two really being very impressive and detailed courses. We learned about ancient history in the Fourth, Sixth, and Ninth Grades; and we learned about medieval history in the Fourth, Sixth, and Eleventh Grades. We

---

281 Interview, December 16, 2010.
282 Mr. Pratt liked maps as instructional tools because of the details they provided, and because they were difficult to fake—and provided models of intellectual honesty—"unlike the level of contemporary social discourse." He also experimented after our years at Moses Brown with case studies. For example, he taught a unit on the Norman invasion of England using original documents so the students could compare different accounts (even including an ancient hoax written shortly after 1066). This enabled them to understand different viewpoints on the conflict. (He observed wryly that most students tended to revert to the first viewpoint they read, assuming it was the standard one.) He also had one of his classes conduct a mock trial of Charles I.

learned about modern European history in the Eleventh Grade. The Western historical tradition was therefore very well treated at Moses Brown, with the exception of nineteenth and twentieth century European history (including international relations), and American foreign policy in the twentieth century. American domestic policy in the twentieth century was not neglected, but given light treatment.

In my sophomore year in college, incidentally, I filled these gaps—with an introductory course on American government, taught by Randall Ripley; a course on American diplomatic history from 1890 through the Second World War, taught by Ernest May; and a course on international relations with a very heavy emphasis on nineteenth and twentieth century diplomacy (Metternich, German unification, the Bismarckian balance-of-power system, and then the origins of both world wars), taught by Henry Kissinger (who later became my senior thesis advisor).

The history courses taught at Moses Brown, especially those of Monahon, Pratt, and Raines, supplemented by Odell's geography class, provided a very solid background for a college major in American government and international relations. They did not provide a basis for understanding non-Western history and culture. This was, of course, a very important gap, but the presumed trade-off was that we studied the Western tradition in serious depth, and we might not realistically have had the time to study other cultures well without sacrificing that depth or sacrificing other subjects outside of history. Contemporary curricula no doubt commendably try to resolve that tension. It might indeed have been fun to have learned more Latin American, African, and Asian history (two of these regions were given serious attention in Mr. Odell's geography class), but I have always appreciated the level of depth at which Western history was taught at Moses Brown.

XIV

Interludes
(1956-60)

In the early years of Upper School we spent our summers principally the same way we had in Lower School—at camp, at the shore, doing odd jobs, traveling, or simply at home. For example, during the summer of 1956, following our first year in Upper School, at least eleven of us were at summer camps, primarily outside of Rhode Island, mostly in northern New England.[283] Depending on their locations (in the woods, in the fields, at the shore), these camps offered a wide range of activities, many of them athletic, often in the form of organized sports. Hiking, swimming, tennis, soccer, golf, archery, boating, skin diving, fishing, and the camping experience itself provided opportunities for growth, and as the years passed, many classmates graduated from being attendees to being counselors.

Continuing in the Lower School pattern, at least eleven classmates also were at home or at family summer homes, most either up-country or by the shore, primarily in Rhode Island and Massachusetts.[284] Activities in many cases paralleled those at camp. A few traveled in the summer of 1956: Frank Abella and Hernan Franco returned home to their native

---

283 Ahmed, Barrett, Corris, Dean, Fain, Forman, Koffler, Oster, Saywell, Schwartz, and Alan Volkman, who was at Boy Scout camp. Information about our summer activities comes primarily from August issues of the *Moses Brown Bulletin*.
284 Carney, Dieroff, DiLibero, Fischer, Huntoon, Kilton, Littlefield, Marcello, Marshall, Najarian, and Stenmark.

Vin Marcello enjoying the summer with a Chevy.

Puerto Rico, Bill Brehm went to Florida, and Vin Marcello joined the Moses Brown bicycling expedition to Nova Scotia.

Several classmates spent time in more responsible jobs and apprenticeships. Herb Sawyer served as "mate" on this father's boat, Brian Broderick spent time in a lab at MIT, Jack Nixon caddied at the Pawtucket Golf Club, Tom Clark worked as a licensed lobsterman in Rockport, and Ned Young and I worked, at least part-time, on a farm. Most of these jobs were on the cusp between recreation and serious work, but they did point to the direction where we were headed.

A couple of years later, by the summer of 1958, the ratio of work to recreation was changing. Although our sample of those reporting is a bit smaller, by now ten were working at serious jobs and only eight were reporting recreational activities—and even these eight included some who were part-time caddies, presumably for compensation, and others whose

Interludes (1956-60) 331

camping experiences now involved counseling.[285] On payrolls were: Bill Criss,[286] in the die casting department of Alco Jewelry; Steve Dashoff,[287] working as a soda jerk; Bruce Henkle and Vin Marcello performing daily cleanup duties at public beaches; Ted Malley,[288] working at his father's gear manufacturing plant; and Bob Marshall, working at a First National Store on the Cape.[289] Lyman Davenport spent the summer engaging in odd jobs and participating in serious remodeling construction work at home.[290] Three of us (Ned Young, Ernie Meuser, and I) worked on a farm,

---

285 Presumably due to the upheavals concerning the departure of Mr. St. John, the August 1957 *Moses Brown Bulletin* was much abbreviated and the traditional account of student and faculty summer activities was omitted.
286 Bill Criss joined our Class in the Second Form. He had a distinguished career in banking. Joining Chase Manhattan Bank in New York, he was subsequently posted to Tokyo and London before arriving in Los Angeles in 1976. He was tasked with opening their San Francisco branch in 1981, and remained with Chase until 1988, at which time he moved to Honolulu to found and become Chairman and CEO of East West Bank. Returning to Chase in 1992, he became Chairman of Chase Manhattan Trust Company of California, and after their merger with JP Morgan, the chief credit officer of JPM/Chase for their western region. Retiring from JPM/Chase in 2004, he subsequently became Managing Director of HSBC Private Bank in San Francisco. He was a patron of the arts, serving on the board of directors of the San Francisco Opera, the Philharmonia Baroque Orchestra, San Francisco Performances, and the Stern Grove Festival. From Bill's obituary on the internet.
287 Steve Dashoff joined our Class in the Third Form. He built and owned a large packing goods business in Virginia or West Virginia, specializing in the production and sales of packing goods. From a telephone interview with Jan Moyer, May 9, 2020.
288 Ted Malley joined our Class in the Third Form. He went to Colby College. While in college and following graduation, he rented a plane and made good money flying over the ocean spotting schools of fish and reporting their location to fishermen who then closed in for the catch. In fact he made enough money to buy his own plane—and from then on he was a plane owner for most of the rest of his life. Not long after his fish-spotting venture, he went to work helping his father manage a manufacturing plant on Boston's South Shore that produced parts and equipment for the Ford Motor Company and for the government. Ted tragically died of Lou Gehrig's disease around 2018. From a telephone interview with Bruce Henkle, May 10, 2020.
289 Bob Marshall joined our Class in the First Form. He went to URI where he became a champion javelin hurler, setting a URI record for that event. He went to work in his family construction business and had a very successful career as its CEO. He also was President and CEO of Marshall Consultants, Inc., a national business development firm specializing in the construction industry based in California. After our graduation, his construction firm built the new Lower School building at Moses Brown.
290 Lyman Davenport joined our Class in the Third Form. He graduated from Brown University and then from Boston University Medical School, where he specialized in radiology. He interned at Boston City Hospital. After doing his stint in the Army, Lyman joined X-Ray Associates (later Diagnostic Imaging), a large practice with 50 doctors in Providence, and remained with this company for the rest of his 36-year medical career. He specialized in x-ray and later CT technologies. He now has retired to Richmond, VA. From a telephone interview with Lyman, May 10, 2020.

Barry Fain, front row, far left, at Camp Brunonia.

and by this time we were doing serious work there. Thus by the end of our sophomore year real summer jobs were becoming the norm.

Scouting. A summer activity that also took place during the school year itself was scouting. The camping experiences which so many of us had undergone throughout the Lower School and early Upper School years were closely related in terms of activities to the Boy Scout experience that many of us underwent during this same period. Many of us were into scouting, and for many of us scouting activity took place during the school year as well as during summers. Alan Volkman and John Dieroff were serious scouts with many badges. There were probably many more in our class, but the only ones I know for sure were those in my own troop, Rhode Island Troop Eight: Bill Barrett, Tom Clark, Bill Fischer, Chad Gifford, Harrison Huntoon, and Nick Littlefield. It met at Central Congregational Church on Angell Street, and drew its membership primarily from the East Side.

Gus Anthony, the statewide Boy Scout chief, whom I remember well, had been instrumental in starting this troop right after the First World War. We began as tenderfoots and then moved up to Second Class. Some went further. We met on the first and third Wednesdays of each month during the school year in the church's large recreation room. We were organized into four patrols: Owl, Alligator, Flying Eagle, and Jaguar. Each was expected to have its own separate camping activities, including hikes.

The Wednesday troop meetings featured games, and especially the acquisition of skills. The latter included Morse code signaling, devising our own methods of encoding and decoding messages, ropes and knots, map reading (and mapping itself), and the use of a compass. The last exercise we did outside of the building in the adjacent field. The troop also published a newspaper, and I remember having a hand in this. After a close vote on the name, we called it *The Echo* because it played back what it heard—a name that we were encouraged to adopt by Chief Anthony because it had been the name of a predecessor paper. The runner-up suggestion was *Alowljagfly*, named after the four patrols. The paper contained announcements, reports of activities, patrol reports, and a Fun Page, edited by Nicky Littlefield, containing codes to decipher, riddles, trick questions,[291] and a small crossword puzzle.

Nicky, Tommy Clark, Bill Barrett, and I, all close neighbors, always walked to Boy Scouts together if the weather permitted. We took a shortcut through the grounds of Dexter Asylum, the Providence City poor farm, then still in operation, with a few souls still in residence at its huge multi-story Victorian yellow-brick manse, lit by dim lights, some of them red. The site now contains the Brown University athletic complex. The entire property then was enclosed by a very high stone wall (much of which is still there). The building had a Charles Addams atmosphere about it and was very spooky to us young kids.[292] If any structure was ever haunted, obviously this was it! One night on our way back home after a session where we learned about

---

[291] Sample: Is it legal for a man to wed his widow's sister?

[292] The poor farm was located right across the street from Moses Brown. Its residents were elderly, and many went to their heavenly reward while there. Mr. Thomas recalled that on more than one occasion an undertaker arrived in his office at Moses Brown and inquired respectfully and in solemn tones where he could pick up the remains. Mr. Thomas, after a momentary concern that perhaps one of his students had come to grief, quickly sorted things out and directed the gentleman to the poor farm across Lloyd Avenue.

knots, we were stopped by a carful of plainclothes Providence Police, who were curious as to why this group of boys was walking around the East Side with lots of knotted rope in their hands. I remember speaking up and asking them for identification, which they provided. They asked us what we were doing (since we were in scout uniform, this should have been evident). As we started to explain, Tommy's father chanced to appear on the scene (he might have been looking for us). Mr. Clark was a lawyer with Edwards and Angell, a noted Providence law firm. When we saw him, we all turned and pointed at him—"There's our lawyer," we exclaimed. The plainclothes officers took one look at Mr. Clark, and then back at us. Apparently deciding that we no longer posed a potential threat to the peace of the neighborhood, they slowly drove off. Mr. Clark, therefore, was not called upon to resort to his professional persona.

One of the highlights of our Boy Scout year was an expedition to Purgatory Chasm in Sutton, Massachusetts. During the morning we descended into the chasm itself with its rocky sides. In the afternoon we walked along a trail up to the north of it, with each of us being asked to identify signs of ten different kinds of animal wildlife. We were told at the onset that one of the best signs was the animal itself. Birds were included. This proved to be an easy challenge to meet. At suppertime we encamped across the road, lit fires, and cooked a meal. This was a greater challenge. I don't remember what we ate, other than potatoes, which were greatly undercooked and quite hard. We returned to Providence late that evening. It was a lot of fun and we earned several credits towards our promotions, which took place in a ceremony that spring.

Work. By the summer of 1959, although only eight of us reported their activities to the *Moses Brown Bulletin*, seven of these had employment or positions of responsibility, and the other (Gerry Tow) was in summer school at Andover.[293] Bill Barrett and Lanny Brooks were counselors. Vin

---

293 Gary Tow joined our Class in the Third Form. His parents operated the Ming Garden restaurant in Providence, and later the family operated the Great House in Warwick. Gary participated in this family enterprise for many years, and we held many memorable Class gatherings at the Great House, where we enjoyed the extraordinary hospitality and the extraordinary cuisine.

Marcello and Bruce Henkle worked to maintain beaches in Narragansett and New London. Ted Malley worked at a boatyard. Ernie Meuser and I worked on a farm.

By 1960, with forty-two (of forty-six) classmates reporting on their summer activities following graduation, six were traveling, six were "at camp," and thirty were at work—including five of the thirty working as counselors at camps and four working at "odd jobs." There was a good range of activities: working in hospitals, at stores, as clerks, in manufacturing, on farms, as a radio announcer, and especially in construction jobs, where seven of us were employed.[294]

Although summer jobs may have contributed to our personal and family incomes, it is probable that our parents viewed our holding real jobs primarily as developmental experiences—preparing us for the adult world. Jobs obviously brought many lessons with them (in addition to the specific skills developed), including taking responsibility, giving fidelity to tasks, and responding to directions from superiors. Holding a summer job also seemed to ratify our evolving maturity, and by our senior year, it seemed a bit socially embarrassing not to have one. Although these jobs were almost all off campus, the tasks at times blended in with many experiences we had had on campus outside of the classroom—but it was still a different world. Summer camp had been a lot more like school than an actual job.

I cannot speak here about the lessons learned by my classmates on their summer jobs, but I can recount a few important lessons that I learned working during summers, weekends, and vacations on the family farm in Chepachet, operated by grandparents during most of Lower School, and by aunts and uncles during Upper School. I expect that my six other classmates who worked on farms throughout the years learned similar lessons.

First, there were the simple lessons that came from watching adults working on the job—in my case including adults from my own family who seemed to have a different state of mind while working than when relaxing on social and recreational occasions. They were recognizably the same people, but you saw different dimensions to them. On one occasion Uncle

---

294 *Moses Brown Bulletin*, August, 1960.

Walt (Steere), normally a very relaxed and low-key person, told a farmhand not to drive the hay truck across a certain part of a field because it was muddy from a recent rainstorm. The man ignored the direction, and (to cut corners, literally) drove into the forbidden area. He got stuck in the mud with a thunderstorm approaching, imperiling our ability to get the hay safely into the barn before it was ruined by the rain. Uncle Walt was furious. He turned to me and shouted, "Go get the tractor and a chain." He turned to the offending driver and said, "And you—go up to the house, collect your pay, and don't come back." I had never seen anyone fired before; the memory lasted. One saw adults under the stress of work-related events—when machinery broke down or failed to perform adequately. I was introduced to adult vocabulary, often directed at "Henry Ford" for employing "dumb engineers." I assume classmates also were impressed by their experiences of working in an adult environment for people with business and professional motivations. And for those who worked in a family business, I expect that they, too, noted the difference between a parent's behavior in a family context and in a professional one.

Second, the farm culture taught us to have curiosity about why things were done the way they were, why things worked the way they did, or why things were constructed in a given fashion—whether a farming practice, a machine, or a building. Knowing such answers was important to family economic success and survival. I expect that this was true of most manufacturing or hands-on productive enterprises that my classmates worked in. My relatives at the farm were excellent teachers who loved to explain things. Questions were encouraged and always answered. You were seldom asked (and almost never ordered) to do something without an explanation as to why it was important: you plow this way to prevent erosion; you have to get hay fully dry or it will mold (or even combust); you tar your corn seed to prevent crows from digging it up and eating it; you stomp down the silage in a silo to get as much air out of it as possible—the less air, the better the fermentation and the less spoilage; you use a wooden pitman rod on a mowing machine because if the blade jams, you want something to break before the rest of the machine is ruined; you wash a cow's bag with warm water before milking because she will let the milk down easier; you put a cow's grain into the manger before letting her into the barn so she will put her head right into the stanchion; it pays dividends to treat animals decently—if, from birth, you don't mistreat a bull, odds are, he won't turn on you. The family was filled with mechanics, and I can remember uncles pointing out why pieces of farm machinery were built the way they were—and why International Harvester machinery at that time was better designed (in their opinion) than Ford's or John Deere's. On one occasion Uncle John (Steere) showed me a special bearing for the paddles on a manure spreader, and explained why it was fashioned differently than other bearings were. This intergenerational teaching passed on not only farming traditions and techniques but also a way of thinking centered on curiosity about what makes things work. I am sure this went back deep in the New England culture of farming and manufacturing—and many of my classmates certainly experienced similar lessons.

Third, if you had a tradition of asking why something was done in the way it was done, it led you to evaluate the process and look for alternatives. One feature of this results-oriented attitude was to look for substitutions—my mother recounted using a hairpin as a substitute for a cotter pin that fell out of her Model T. A bent nail might do the same job as well. A strong plank and stones substituted for a jack. If you lost brakes, down-gearing and careful driving might get you home. If you knew the battery was dead, you parked your tractor on a hill and when you needed to use it, started the engine by turning on the ignition, putting the tractor in gear, depressing the clutch, rolling down the hill until you got some speed, and releasing the clutch to let the momentum from the wheels turn over (and hopefully start) the engine. If you stalled on a flat surface, you got a tow to start the engine. If your automatic transmission went, you usually could use reverse and drive backwards to get home—or get help. In an emergency, you could pull many farm machines with a truck instead of a tractor. Or, as Uncle George (Steere) once demonstrated, if your dog gets into an altercation with a skunk and there is no tomato juice handy, hitch a rope to the dog's collar, take him down to the pond, get into the rowboat, and row around the pond with him swimming behind. He'll enjoy the swim and come out smelling, if not like a rose, at least not like a skunk.

A fourth lesson learned from farm work was to respect folks who might not have had the same educational advantages as you—but who still could accomplish. People were evaluated according to their abilities. What counted was not style but substance. If they could do something well, no matter what the skill, it earned respect: "He sure knows how to weld."

"Nobody can dig a ditch like Mason." "Good workman." "He knows cows." "He knows machinery backwards and forwards" "Nobody can stack a load of hay as fast as Buster." I imagine this was the case in many other workplaces. Once Aunt Amey and the hired man started to unload and stack a large truck full of hay. Long before they were finished, the hired man had another important errand to do, so he left her alone at the task, vowing to come back to help as soon as possible. Shortly afterwards, my father and I appeared on the scene to pick up a package. Seeing Aunt Amey at work, the two of us pitched in, helped her finish the task, grabbed what we had come for, and left. Soon the hired man returned with a companion, just as Aunt Amey was walking back to the house. He took one look at the finished job, took one look at her, turned to his companion, shook his head, and remarked in near-disbelief and great admiration, "Rugged woman." Bill Goddard, who served in Vietnam as a GI, not an officer, came to understand and greatly respect the men he worked with in the field, and regards this learning experience as one of the most important in his life.[295] I'm sure that summer jobs helped my classmates acquire similar perspectives.

Fifth, the farm experience taught me how to make a game out of work. Most everyone in the family was a workaholic, but this was not some compulsive obsession. They enjoyed work. This, in part, was because they knew how to turn it into a pastime. It helped that there is a lot of variety in farm work. But there are also a lot of routines. One way of making games out of routines is competition—seeing who can get a task done soonest, best, or most imaginatively. Another way is to play solitaire—testing different tedding and raking patterns, seeing how high you can stack bales of hay without them falling off the truck, seeing how you can maximize the number of sweet corn ears you can stack in a wheelbarrow by building walls of upright ears around the edges and then filling in the center. And speaking of having fun, if you were sent on a mission to get a tractor part halfway across the state (which in Rhode Island can't be all that far), if it was not an emergency, you could route the return trip to pass by a favorite ice cream stand where you were obliged to treat yourself to a coffee cabinet or an ice cream cone—and everyone would understand the brief detour.

---

295 Conversation, with Bill Goddard, December 2017.

Another lesson I learned from the New England farm culture was how helpful its participants could be to one another. Theoretically, they were competitors, but they didn't behave that way. They would lend equipment to each other. They would share new techniques that proved to be improvements. They would help out in emergencies. I remember how a farmer, Russell Knibb, Moses Brown ('45), and a graduate of RPI, who enjoyed running his very successful dairy operation in Burrillville, dropped everything and rushed over to help my aunt deal with a sick cow when no vet was available. Farmers understood each other's problems. They didn't want to be taken advantage of, but when this was not the case, they were there to help when needed. The lesson learned was that sympathy and understanding will emerge from shared experiences and circumstances.

And yet another lesson involved the pluses and minuses of task orientation—a rigid focus on getting a task done, often at the expense of other objectives and values. This, I am sure, was a cultural inheritance from earlier days when the New England farm economy operated near a subsistence level and there were no safety nets. Getting the crops in was essential to survival—literally. Hence the task was paramount. When the occasion demanded it, this could mean working after hours, forgoing recreational time, being blunt with shirkers, including relatives, and thereby threatening family and personal relationships—all in the name of getting the job done effectively. I'm sure the pressures of competition imposed similar perspectives on supervisors in the manufacturing plants my classmates worked for, although their apprentices' hours were probably more predictable and the personal intensity lower.

Finally, farm work taught you a sense of realism. Farms lived in reality, not fantasy. I assume most successful businesses where my classmates worked summers did also. On a farm, there were deadlines to be met. Crops had to be planted in timely fashion. Hay had to be harvested before it was rained on—or it would lose half its nutrients. Machinery had to be serviced and kept in working order. Cows had to be bred in a timely fashion and otherwise be properly taken care of. A lot depended on dealing with nature, and nature was outside of your control. There were few good excuses or alternative options if you failed. Even good excuses would not change the results. If rain threatened your hay, you had no choice but to rush to meet the time deadline imposed by the impending approach of dark clouds in the west. You could not get a time extension. Alternatively, if a machine was broken, you could not just coax it into working. If there was not enough feed for the cows at the end of the year, you had to reach into your pocketbook. In this world of realism, you could not cut corners without cutting them on yourself. Or, as Bert Smith, our hired man, once explained it to me, "You can fool people—some people most of the time. But you can't fool a cow. Give her bad hay and she'll either stick up her nose at it or give less milk."

XV

Fifth Form

(1959-60)

The Fifth Form was an intensely busy year for most of us seniors. In addition to our five classes, some of which were being taught at advanced levels, we had publications to bring out, plays to act in, clubs to run, and sports to mainstay. It was a very fast-moving year. In my case, I was Editor of the *Mosaic*, Executive Editor of the *Quaker*, Historian of the *Delphian*, manager of the soccer and baseball teams, and assistant manager of the swimming team. Bill Carney,[296] Al Cokin, Lanny Brooks,[297] Bill Brehm, and Mark Saklad were equally busy with publications, and most of them also with sports. Al Brenner was heavily invested time-wise in the performing arts.[298] Vin Marcello, in addition to his normal governance duties, was spending lots of time organizing and promoting a new Judicial Board. And then there were our sports teams themselves—and the huge time commitment they represented for the athletes and even the managers.

---

296 Bill Carney joined our Class in First Form. He graduated from Colgate and received his MD from the School of Medicine at Thomas Jefferson University in Philadelphia. He interned and did his residency at the Tufts Medical Center in Boston, practicing surgery at Boston City Hospital. He went on to become a widely recognized vascular surgeon, practicing in Rhode Island and Massachusetts.

297 Lanny Brooks joined our Class in the Third Form. He went to Brown and then to the University of Vermont, where he taught and earned his PhD in physics. He then became Professor of Physics at Hartford University in Connecticut where he had a long and distinguished career.

298 Alan Brenner, who joined our Class in the Third Form, graduated from the College of Medicine at the University of Cincinnati. He specialized in rheumatology, and practiced in Framingham, MA.

342 Fifth Form (1959-60)

Class of 1960 Senior Photograph

Row 1: V. A. Marcello, President; B. A. Henkle, Vice-President; W. I. Carney, Jr., Secretary; A. Holoff, Treasurer; A. I. Brenner, S.A.C. Representative. Row 2: W. S. Barrett, A. J. Cokin, D. O. DeVlieg, R. J. Marshall, W. N. Murdock, C. W. Criss, Jr., J. R. Moyer, E. W. Malley, III, W. G. Tow. Row 3: R. J. DiLibero, P. R. Parker, B. H. Perry, J. R. Nixon, J. H. Ladd, Jr., C. W. Brown, Jr. Row 4: G. L. Brooks, Jr., J. L. Forman, R. M. Maletz, F. W. Schwartz, Jr., M. S. Saklad. Row 5: J. H. Ottmar, D. S. London, J. A. Tomlinson, R. W. Crawford, J. E. Hooper, S. F. Armington, D. S. Chafee, A. T. Crandon. Row 6: S. A. Estee, J. L. Costa, C. B. Smith, H. R. Franco, S. L. Dashoff. Row 7: J. H. Rigney, Jr., E. A. Corris, R. B. Buckley, W. J. Brehm, L. A. Davenport. Absent from picture: B. W. Fain, S. A. Koffler, H. C. Sawyer.

Most seniors my year took English, math, American History, a language (typically French or German), and a science (physics or advanced chemistry). I had English with Mr. Paxton, math with Mr. Herman again, American History and Government with Mr. Raines, Third-Year German with Mr. Justin, and Advanced Chemistry with Mr. Jeffers. I was familiar with three of these instructors from previous classes; Messrs. Raines and Paxton were new to me in a classroom setting, although I certainly was familiar with them outside of the classroom context. In terms of time spent and responsibilities assumed, this year was truly a culminating one. I can remember working steadily from September to June with little time off for any form of relaxation. Every afternoon was spent on managerial duties in sports. Evenings were for homework. Every weekend was consumed either by the *Quaker* or by the *Mosaic*—or both. The *Mosaic* devoured all vacations, and especially Christmas vacation. And then there was time spent writing for the *Delphian*, going to the Model UN in New York, and occasionally helping out at the farm. My only regular indulgence was an hour for *Perry Mason* every Saturday night after the family's traditional meal of beans and hot dogs, often with an apple pie for dessert. This I looked forward to and seldom missed. Mr. Corbett had been right about youth and its energies.

Math. With the exhilarating experience of Fourth-Form Math recent in memory, I looked forward to an encore in my senior year. This, however, was not to be. I returned to my accustomed chair next to the south wall in the front row of Room 11, but the magic had gone. The subject matter was much less enjoyable to me than the material we had experienced in the Fourth Form—partly because it seemed boring and very formulaic. Mr. Herman's classroom presence was undiminished and always enjoyable, but the math itself was somewhat repellant.

Our text was *Foundations of Advanced Mathematics*.[299] We did a lot of trigonometry, and this involved not just calculating distances, but also manipulating a lot of trigonometric equations, with all their sines, cosines, and tangents. I never quite understood the purpose of all this, and to make things worse, we had to do lots of calculations by hand. Today with modern

---

299 Kline, Oesterle, and Willson, New York: American Book Company, 1959.

calculators, I might have fared better, but we were somehow back to long multiplication and long division, with all the opportunities of careless mistakes that this retrocession produced. Slide rules helped to some extent, but not fully, since I could not always figure out how to use them for trig.

We also did a lot of logarithms, and those, too, required tedious calculations. We did have to do some thinking, but a lot more of what we were expected to do involved routines, which were always boring and often incomprehensible to me. Somehow I found it difficult to make a game out of them. Since Mr. Herman never explained anything, but left that to us and the text, we were totally reliant on the book, which I often found to be obtuse. We did coordinate geometry, which was interesting and manageable, but not as interesting as Euclidian, and we did some solid geometry (which I did like).

Mr. Herman also had us do determinants, a matrix-based way of solving advanced quadratic equations, as I recall. This was very fussy. We also were introduced to probability and sampling theory, but did not spend much time on them, and again I never really got the hang of things in this area—until college.

There was a section in the text on calculus, but Mr. Herman was determined not to teach us calculus—he argued that the colleges wanted to do this themselves. I'm not sure he was right about that: a half year's introduction to the principles of calculus would have been very useful.

Fortunately for me, Mr. Herman did do an extensive review of algebra and geometry. He used Tower and Sides again—with factoring and other forms of algebraic manipulation. He also used a more up-to-date equivalent, *Mathematics Review Exercises*, written by David Smith and Leslie Fagan, who taught at Lawrenceville.[300] This was aimed at College Entrance Exam level math. Exercises in these two books were more cognizable, and they saved me from disaster. Senior-year math, however, was a big comedown from junior-year math. Perhaps things would have been different had I had more time to spend on figuring things out, but the senior year was very full, and time was scarce.

---

300 Boston: Ginn and Company, 1956.

Fifth Form (1959-60)

I was not alone in regarding Fifth-Form Math as complex and often bewildering. Dave London remembered being advised by Mr. Herman not to take it: "The Babe knew I was applying to Brown. He called me in and said he didn't want me to take senior math—my grades would hurt me with admission to Brown. I had skipped a year of math, and this had been a mistake. Herman said, 'I wish I could back up the clock and do this right, but I can't. Because of this, you will be disadvantaged by taking senior math—the colleges look at the Fall-Term grades, and it will hurt your chances for Brown.'"[301] This was good advice and Dave took it.

We had lots of standardized math tests in our senior year—the SATs, Merit Finals, and at least two others I recollect that Mr. Herman administered (one of these, I think, was sponsored by the American Mathematical Association). By and large, these were structured around knowledge of algebra and geometry, and not around knowledge of trigonometry or probability, and I did well on them—and that helped with college admissions. But in class, I barely scraped through.

Mr. Herman was Director of Testing at Moses Brown, and standardized testing grew in importance as our Upper School years advanced. In the junior year we began to take standardized tests looking forward to college entrance. I think we took practice SATs in the junior year, and the real McCoy in the senior year—Aptitudes only in the junior year and both Aptitudes and Achievements in the senior year. We also were tested for the National Merit Scholarship Program—once to qualify for semifinalist status and then for finalist status if you had achieved semifinal. Mr. Herman also administered a special math aptitude test to the Upper School. Some of these exams were taken in the study hall; others were done in Sayles Hall over at Brown.

I never took a "Kaplan-style" course in how to take the SATs. To some degree, these courses were even considered a form of cheating or taking unfair advantage over those who lacked the financial resources to enroll in them. All we did was review the sample questions provided by the CEEB itself. However, in all fairness to those who did take Kaplan, Mr. Herman's courses, in part, had SAT math in mind and acquainted us with the type

---
301 Taped interview, 180 Brown Street, August 29, 2010.

Helen F. Sadlier

of math (algebra, plane geometry) we were expected to encounter on the exams. What we never practiced, however, were the fairly extensive logic and analogy-type questions we were to encounter on the SATs.[302] Today Kaplan courses are commonplace: in some schools, a lot of time is devoted just to preparing for these tests. I might have had somewhat higher SAT scores had I taken a Kaplan, but I did well enough to get admitted to the colleges I applied to, and I was a National Merit finalist. With respect to the verbal SATs, we did have Miss Sadlier's course, and there was an emphasis on vocabulary in fall Senior English. Each can be regarded as forms of School-sponsored preparation for the SATs, but we did not formally practice for the SAT itself in either math or English.

Advanced Chemistry. Somewhere along the way it was announced that Mr. Jeffers had decided to offer a course in Advanced Chemistry so that those taking it might get advanced placement standing in college. This was, as far as I know, Moses Brown's first experiment with advanced courses of this nature, and was probably part of a plan by Mr. Cunningham to

---

302 This is to that as something else is to what?

Fifth Form (1959-60)

upgrade the curriculum. It took place in the new chemistry lab, the center room of the Thomas Science Building.

It was almost certainly a mistake for me to have taken this course. I did so because of the challenge, but I badly miscalculated my ability to master an advanced course while taking four other courses and engaging responsibly in all the extracurricular activities on the schedule. I was able to get through the course, but if I had taken physics (the alternative) it would have been a lot easier, given the preparation in Mr. Herman's algebra and geometry classes.

I do not remember a lot about Advanced Chemistry, probably because I had other things on my mind that year, and probably because I did not really enjoy struggling through it. I did not do particularly well in it. This was not the fault of the instructor—I remember Mr. Jeffers as an excellent and patient teacher. We had an advanced text—a college text—with a much higher level of explanation than we had had in First-Year Chemistry.[303] There were lots of chemical equations to solve or to balance and lots of calculations based on measurements. There were many exercises. We covered a fair amount of organic chemistry: methane, ethane, polymers, acetones, ketones, and the like.

We also were taught about buffer solutions and the equations needed to describe them. These always remained a mystery to me—I understood the concept, and could somehow understand what was expected of me in terms of solving the equations, but nothing ever seemed to turn out right. They were my undoing. I never could get the expected answer. The more I tried, the worse it got. If I had understood them, I might have become a chemist. *C'est la vie.*

The one part of the course that I did enjoy, and did fairly well in, was the section on nuclear chemistry—which was almost nuclear physics. We studied shells, valences, atomic stages, and so forth. Needless to say, science's understanding of the atom has increased mightily since this time—everything we learned in 1959 and 1960 is now probably quite obsolete, but nevertheless for the time it was a good state-of-the art section of the course, and very interesting.

---

303 I cannot seem to find this text.

We had lots of labs. These involved the setting up of equipment, a careful measurement of each material to be used, an experiment, and then additional careful measurements of the resulting materials afterwards. All this would be written up in a lab report. In most cases, the point was to achieve a measurable result closely predicted by the theory we were testing, and then to explain the extent of the difference between theory and result. I remember that it became routine to include the shortcomings of the lab equipment in the explanations for that difference—to the point where Mr. Jeffers, in good-humored exasperation, asked us to take some responsibility ourselves, and stop blaming his equipment for our shortfalls and longfalls. Towards the end of the course we did some analysis—to identify what chemicals were in a given compound—but we did not have time to do a lot of this.

The above is about all I remember about this course. I believe that I barely got advance placement credit for it, but I never did pursue chemistry in college.

Conversations with Mr. Jeffers in recent years have put Moses Brown science in better perspective for me than was the case when I was there. The sequence of biology-chemistry-physics was fairly universal, and reflected an expected level of mathematical competence, as students moved through high school. Biology was mainly descriptive. Classification was a central concern based on a sense of structure. Causal explanation, another central concern, was based on a sense of system and function. In both cases, little or no serious mathematics was required.

Chemistry at Moses Brown was taught in a traditional way, based both on chronology (the evolution of chemical discoveries) and on experimental and "industrial" chemistry—how chemistry is useful in producing results and products (the Haber process, for example). The molecular theory was used, but primarily for establishing the ratios of elements combined into chemicals that would produce predictable amounts of other chemicals upon reaction. Equations based on algebraic expressions would relate the initial combination of molecular configurations to the resultant combination. Thus math at the level of algebra was expected and used, but not extensively. Advanced Chemistry required more math (for those miserable buffer solutions, for example) and advanced algebra was certainly important.

Physics came last in the sequence because by the time high school students took it, they had been exposed to algebra and geometry and were studying trigonometry. Physics at Moses Brown (which, regrettably, I did not take) was, I believe, highly dependent on both geometry and algebra. I can remember some senior physics students puzzling over geometric exercises based on squares inside of circles which, in turn, were inside triangles, and so forth. I also assume that Newtonian mechanics were taught—models of acceleration, for example, that enabled Science Club members to estimate the height to which their rockets rose. I imagine that today physics is taught at Moses Brown using introductory calculus.

Third-Year German. In Third-Year German we had Mr. Justin again, and in the Fall Term he seemed more in control of things than he had been the previous year. He was building on his own previous course, and by this time we had been systematically exposed by him to a full range of grammar and to his long list of frequently used idioms. In the first half of the year, he reviewed much of what we had done in the previous year—exercises and composition. But we also began to read serious books, and therefore concentrated on vocabulary building.

I remember three books read this year—although it is possible one of them had been read at the end of the previous year. Two were murder mysteries. The first, *Der Richter und sein Henke*, by Durrenmatt, was set in Switzerland with the aging, but canny, Inspector Berlach eventually deducing that one of his fellow inspectors had done the murder. He confronted the guilty party with this conclusion at an elegant dinner in the final scene. The second, *Der Nachtmensch*,[304] another murder mystery, was set at a ski lodge or such, and featured a rowdy party with wealthy playboys and lots of girlfriends bouncing back and forth between the bedrooms, with an obnoxious host who was murdered, as I recall, by one of the girls. Although there was nothing obscene in it as far as my limited German could tell, perhaps this book was the source of Mr. Justin's undoing! The third novel was *Die Sterbende Jagd*,[305] an account of a German fighter squadron on the Russian Front during the Second World War.

---

304 Bernhard Borge, West Berlin: Ullstein Bucher, 1958.
305 Gerd Gaiser, Frankfurt am Main & Hamburg: Fischer Bucherei, 1959.

I remember reading the first with a modicum of comprehension, plowing through the second with difficulty, and attempting the third with no success whatsoever. In fact, I got a "C" on my Fall-Term final exam in German, a fact that was made known to me minutes before I took the Fall-Term final in Advanced Chemistry. There was a major problem on the chemistry exam involving the metalloid "germanium"—so all I could think of when taking the chemistry exam was the disaster in German. When I mentioned this to some of my classmates, they found it hilarious, but I failed to see the humor!

In the second half of the year, Justin gave us a course in German history (in English) from the Middle Ages through the eighteenth century. I was never sure what was going on here—why did he do this? Mr. Pratt had given us a lot of German history in the previous year in his Modern European History course, and surely Mr. Justin must have known that. In many respects it was, on Justin's part, a repeat performance of Pratt. I think by this time he knew that he would not be returning to Moses Brown and that Mr. Pratt (whom he may have disliked) would be teaching German in his place. Perhaps he was demonstrating that he could have taught history in Pratt's place (trying to get back at Pratt by trying to one-up him). It is even possible that there was a serious pedagogical reason behind teaching German history in a German language class, but it was nevertheless a curious turn of events.

In any event, Mr. Justin gave a perfectly solid course on German history—basically Otto the Great through Frederick the Great. It was not a waste of time, rather a refresher course. We reviewed the Holy Roman Empire in some detail, with its investiture controversies and the Germany-Italy connection. We covered both the Reformation and the Thirty Years' War and then went on to the rivalry between Austria and Prussia in the eighteenth century. I don't remember Justin doing Bismarck, so I assume we did not make it far into the nineteenth century—but if we did so, it would have been late in the spring when we were all concentrating on other things, and little attention, if any, would have been paid to the Schleswig-Holstein crisis. For me, with my difficulties in German, this diversion on Justin's part was a godsend. German was tough for me, but history was a blast, and I recouped some of my earlier losses.

Despite his problems, Justin gave us a very good grounding in German, and I remember that on the SATs I was able to squeak by and reach the score at which I did not have to take a language course in college. In fact, I took a couple of German literature classes my freshman year in college, and actually enjoyed them.

Also in the Spring Term we had an exchange student (Uwe Massmann) from Germany living with us. This had been somehow arranged through the School. There was a family in Providence by the name of Higgins and their son John had spent time in Germany with the Massmann family. When that family's scion was old enough to come to America in exchange, the Higginses could not take him in—probably because John ("Higgsie," as Bill Barrett recalled) had by then graduated from Moses Brown and it would have been awkward for Uwe to live in a household with no contemporary. The Higginses appealed to Moses Brown with their problem, and the School asked my folks if they were interested. I was taking German and someone at the School thought this might be helpful to me. As things turned out, Uwe was a nice kid, and talking German to him certainly did not hurt. He came in the spring and stayed through the summer, occasionally attending classes at Moses Brown. My mother talked the Rhode Island Division of Motor Vehicles into giving him a driver's test and a license—which was probably against policy, if not illegal, but she could be persuasive. From his standpoint, it was the high point of the visit. It also turned out that John Higgins, Sr., was head of the Harvard Club of Rhode Island, and after I was accepted for admission he strongly urged me to go there instead of to Brown or Princeton. Other factors were involved, but his ministrations were one factor in my decision.

English. Fifth-Form English was designed to be the culminating experience of a dozen years of native language instruction. It was taught to all seniors by the formidable William Paxton. Mr. Paxton was an excellent instructor and a very powerful presence, both in the classroom and on campus. His undergraduate degree was from Brown, and he had done graduate work at Harvard and Chicago. He later served as Acting Headmaster the year after Mr. Cunningham resigned in 1964. There was a strong air of assurance about him, and he certainly was a very intelligent

William Paxton

and erudite person, well-read in English literature. He was the coauthor of a textbook on English composition published not long before we had him in class.[306]

Mr. Paxton's approach to the world was one of genteel cynicism, and he was quick to detect hypocrisy, which he searched for, both near and far. He hated pretense, and laid traps to identify it. These qualities, however, were softened by a sense of humor, albeit an ironic one. There was often a thin smile on his face. You had the feeling that he had the full measure of you, and that he understood you better than you understood yourself, but his sense of quiet superiority was tempered by benign professional motives. He did not play favorites. I think he was equally hopeful about all our prospects, and equally helpful to us as we struggled with the requirements of the course.

---

306 Smith, Reed, Paxton, William, and Meserve, Basil G., *Learning to Write*, Boston: D.C. Heath and Company, 1957.

Mr. Paxton moved deliberately and spoke slowly, often thoughtfully. He looked directly at us, and each observation seemed like an arrow pointed in our direction. His eyes penetrated. There was an air of formality about the man, perhaps more so than in the case of any other Upper School instructor. You would not expect familiarities from him. His smiles were frequent and he chuckled fairly often, but you would never expect him to do a handstand on the desk, call his students dizzy apes (or babbling babies), or josh with them informally. He was not distant: the teacher-student relationship in Paxton's classroom was intense, not detached, and no one was bored, but the intensity was fully controlled and unidirectional. His formality fell short of stiffness, but it still precluded intimacy. Mr. Fuller could be quite formal in Latin instruction, but he could at times unwind. Mr. Paxton seldom unwound, at least not in class. Many of his sentences could be styled "pronouncements," and he had a habit of repeating these in front of the class. He would state something, pause, and then repeat it in a slightly different tone of voice. Sometimes he would make his point a third time. I don't know if this was to help us take notes, to vary his emphasis, or whether it was just from the force of some ancient habit, but it was recurrent and could be downright funny at times. In fact, Russ Carpenter ('59) lampooned the practice in a humorous *Quaker* column. Mr. Paxton was a devotee of White Owl cigars, and our corrected papers were always returned with a strong scent reflecting his addiction. Some wags among the student body referred to him as "Willie White Owl." But he knew syntax, grammar, and literature very well, he loved his subject, and he presented it to the class with emotionally controlled enthusiasm.

Paxton's justly renowned Fifth-Form English course concentrated on three different areas: vocabulary, the techniques and mechanics of writing (especially grammar, syntax, usage, and punctuation), and literature—understanding and evaluating it at a relatively sophisticated level of literary criticism. In all three areas, he made major efforts to raise our standards and our skills.

In the fall, we spent serious time on English vocabulary, with a special text and daily quizzes at the beginning of each class. This was probably designed to help us on our SATs. Many of the words studied were familiar to me, but certainly not all of them. I remember learning *cynosure* (a favorite of his that I seldom use today, since it reminds me of cyanide), *synergy* (at that time soon to be a Madison Avenue favorite), *sinecure* (which I had trouble differentiating from cynosure), and *pseudonym* (easy to remember when you make a set of it with *synonym* and *antonym*). My father had already taught me *syzygy,* and this word seemed at least as erudite as any word learned in Senior English. Mr. Paxton was quite demanding. When I defined tenacity as "stick-to-it-iveness" he rejected this out of hand and insisted on "unyielding firmness." I still like my definition better, but he wouldn't accept it. To him precise meaning was important. Obviously all this had a much wider area of useful application.

Our vocabulary text, as I recall it, defined the word and used it in a sentence or two. I was not particularly adept at learning English vocabulary this way—no more than I was adept at learning Latin or German vocabulary by rote. In my own experience, I learned vocabulary best in conversation with those who used sophisticated words and from reading good literature—namely, in active context. This exercise of Paxton's was therefore of marginal utility in my case. Moreover, even though he was also giving us an easy means to improve our grades, I did not take full advantage of that either.

Mr. Paxton also taught grammar, syntax, usage, and punctuation—emphasizing the proper construction of English sentences, paragraphs, and, ultimately, essays. We wrote a lot of papers in the Fifth Form. I don't remember how many we wrote in a typical week, but it was more than one. Mr. Paxton had developed an alphanumerical system to classify errors in grammar, usage, and punctuation. He went through our papers very carefully and put abbreviations or a number in the margin that corresponded to the error we had committed. "WW" stood for "wrong word."[307] "AWK" stood for "awkward expression." He handed out a sheet with these coded, so we could look up the abbreviations or the number on the sheet and identify our mistake. He kept a chart recording our grammatical and punctuation errors so he could identify recurrent soft spots, and plot our progress or lack thereof. This involved a great deal of drudge work both for him and for us, but I'm sure my own writing abilities improved slowly throughout the year as a result. As *Quaker* editor Bill Carney recalled, it built self-confidence in our ability to write.[308]

---
307 I was reminded of this by Bob Smith ('58), taped interview, March 26, 2014.
308 Taped interview, July 15, 2015.

Mr. Paxton also evaluated our papers on substance as well as on grammar and punctuation. With respect to usage, he introduced us to Strunk and [E.B.] White's *Elements of Style*, a short and pithy monograph on effective writing. He had his own pet peeves. For example, he had serious objections to our utilizing "one" as an indefinite pronoun in the German sense of "man" (e.g., "One should not be surprised at the result" or "He did not let one easily get away with something" or "It made one think."). He also did not like us to use the word "contact" in the sense of "get in touch with" or "communicate with." I had written something to the effect that someone had "contacted" someone else about something, and he wrote in the margin, "Leave that usage to the Bread and Butter people"—meaning people in the business world. In this same vein, the Eisenhower-era neologism "finalize" was treated by Mr. Paxton (and others at Moses Brown) with haughty disdain. I can only begin to imagine how he may have responded later to Secretary McNamara's use of "phase out" which became popular in the '60s after we graduated. Mercifully, he did not live to see the way "problematic" and "enormity" have been transformed and traduced by modern writers, nor the way in which split infinitives have become common occurrences in the *Wall Street Journal*, the *New York Times*, and even, God forbid, the *New Yorker*. Discovering the "F-word" in a publication like *Time* magazine would have produced an end-life crisis, curable in his case only by a massive dose of cynicism regarding the drift of American culture.

When it came to punctuation, Mr. Paxton had a bird-sized bee in his bonnet with respect to the "comma blunder" (or comma splice), which is joining two independent clauses with a comma instead of a semicolon. This appeared in capital letters on his chart of errors, and it was considered to be the most heinous of crimes—right up there with arson and murder. I don't know why this was the case. I will admit that it is indeed an offense, but why, for example, should it be a more heinous practice than dangling a participle? Since Moses Brown days, I have come across people who said this practice was considered an abomination in other New England prep schools. The concern for the comma splice may therefore reflect a very long regional tradition in American English instruction that goes back into the nineteenth century. Perhaps someone in Boston before the Civil War, no doubt out of total exasperation with a student, decreed that this would deserve the Puritan equivalent of excommunication, and the tradition propagated throughout the New England private school culture.

In any event, the 1950s featured nuclear deterrence, and Mr. Paxton's equivalent was an automatic "C" grade for a paper containing a comma blunder. Somehow I missed incurring this penalty, but I do remember an unfortunate upperclassman, "Rat" Ratensky ('58) who committed the crime: his otherwise "A" paper received a "C." I recall Mrs. Paxton saying that she had spotted this in advance and that her New England conscience had prevented her from pointing this out to the hapless Ratensky. Whether this was true or whether she had just missed it and was covering, I do not know, but I do remember the incident. I suspect that Rat may also.

At one point we had an exercise in how to place apostrophes in the proper place, and almost no one in class had a perfect score. Most of us had a very pedestrian score. A second attempt produced unsatisfactory improvement. Mr. Paxton was sufficiently aggravated by this that he founded the "Apostrophes Club." This consisted of First Class, Second Class, and Third Class members. If you got it right the first time, you became a member, First Class. If you got it right the second time, you became a member, Second Class, and so forth. Stan Armington, who had a little print shop at the time, produced membership cards for us.[309] A photograph of one appears next to Mr. Paxton's picture in the 1960 *Mosaic*.

Mr. Paxton was very concerned not only with the mechanics of good English usage, but also with the structure of exposition: how sentences, paragraphs, and essays were properly constructed. Strunk and White helped a bit here, but more important was Mr. Paxton's commentary on our individual essays. To him, teaching lucid writing took precedence over teaching creative writing, and he read our productions with this in mind. His comments on substance were aimed in that direction.

In this regard, I felt that our essay topics never allowed much creativity, although I do remember writing one about the disappearance of Pluto, our pet dog. The problem may have lain more with me than with the subjects themselves, but I remember criticizing a list of topics in the book Mr. Paxton coauthored—and he challenged me to produce a better list. I

---

309 Stan Armington joined our Class in the Third Form. He may have been the most adventuresome of our classmates. After college, he decided to be a professional mountain climber, and moved to Nepal where he became a sherpa and set up a business organizing mountain-climbing expeditions, operating out of Katmandu. He has returned for a few reunions.

had in mind current events, and the like. When I dodged the request, he smiled with that thin smile of his and observed that my evasion was not a problem: if I could learn to write well about his dull topics, then I would do even better when I found interesting ones. The many creative and imaginative offerings in the *Delphians* from that era suggest that others found little difficulty in being imaginative.

Mr. Paxton did not ignore current events altogether when it came to papers. Perhaps in response to my criticisms, he once asked us to "put yourselves in Congress—either house, representing any state," and respond to a constituent concern involving some matter of policy—I forget what the policy was. I accepted the challenge, assumed the guise of Senior Senator from New York—then the largest state—and wrote what I thought was a valid philippic on the topic. Mr. Paxton was impressed with neither my syntax nor my policy position. His comments, in the form of a letter back from a constituent, were gently sarcastic and ended with the query, "Might the voters of New York State have erred in sending you to the Senate as their representative to that august body?"

The third major focus of Senior English was literature. Although Mr. Paxton clearly regarded the mechanics of writing as the central mission in his course, the most enjoyable parts of Fifth-Form English (to us, and no doubt to him as well) were in the areas of literature, poetry and criticism. We read a lot in the senior year and we read it critically. Mr. Corbett's forays into literary criticism had been interesting and instructive. He taught from the perspective of an author, reflecting his own experiences. His comments were more spontaneous and free-flowing. Mr. Paxton's, by contrast, were much more structured, and located solidly within the traditions of literary criticism itself. Both approaches were valuable—I don't intend to demean Mr. Corbett's efforts (which were shrewd and perspicacious), but Mr. Paxton's were systematically grounded in the mainstream of contemporary literary thinking.

I believe we started the year by reading Rolvaag's *Giants in the Earth*, a novel about Scandinavian immigrants to the upper plains states. I don't remember spending a lot of time in class on this, but I think we had to write a book report on it. We also definitely read Edith Wharton's *Ethan Frome*. I found neither of these tragedies very interesting.

We read several plays. These included *Hamlet*, and I can remember Mr. Paxton going into great detail regarding the play, describing for us the hidden meaning of some of the obscure references and allusions. He took it scene by scene. I remember him discussing some of the puns that we would have missed. He would read various passages and then explain them. He described the Shakespearian theatre and how his plays were produced. I remember him demonstrating how the final act of Hamlet could be staged so that Hamlet's and Laertes's swords got exchanged (Laertes's sword might have been knocked out of his hand by the swordplay, Hamlet would then graciously offer him his own, while picking up Laertes's off the floor to use for himself).

This was a very interesting section of the course. Building on Corbett's discussions the previous year, we were expected to read Shakespeare not just for its entertainment value, but for intellectual development. The point was not just to see if Hamlet could make up his mind or to find out who would survive the final scene, but to appreciate the structure of the play, the techniques of the writing, and, of course, the lessons about life to be found there.

We read other plays from an anthology entitled, *Drama in our Time*.[310] This began with Lillian Hellman's *Watch on the Rhine*, which we read and discussed at some length. It made a great impression on me. I still use the expression "We have fallen out of the lilacs" on appropriate occasions, and I will never forget the implied lesson that being highly cultured is no excuse for inaction. Thornton Wilder's *Our Town* made an even greater impression when I read it for the first time. I remember Mr. Paxton playing a recording of a Clifton Fadiman critique of the play which put it in perspective. I also remember discussing it with Paxton after class. In addition, we read and critiqued Karel Capek's *RUR*, Arthur Arent's *One Third of a Nation*, and Robert Sherwood's *Abe Lincoln in Illinois*. There were other plays in this collection which I read, including Sidney Howard and Paul De Kruif's *Yellow Jack* and Norman Corwin's *El Capitan and the Corporal*, but I don't remember us discussing them in class.

We also used a book of essays written by eminent English and American essayists.[311] We read Matthew Arnold on "Hellenism and Hebraism," an

---

310 By M.M. Nagelberg, New York: Harcourt Brace, 1948.
311 Douglass S. Mead, ed., *Great English and American Essays*, New York, Rinehart & Company, 1959.

Fifth Form (1959-60)

essay that traces the intellectual foundations of the West, and which classmates today remember as being important to the development of their intellectual perspectives. We read John Galsworthy[312] on "Quality"—a wonderful story about aging shoemakers with a strong commitment to produce the finest of "boots," and how they were being eased out of business by the mass production of shoddy goods. We read Swift's famous description of warfare from *Gulliver's Travels*. We read Thomas DeQuincy's essay on "Literature of Knowledge and Literature of Power," the purpose of the first being to teach (or inform) and that of the second being to move (or influence). This dichotomy, a first cousin of the modern concept of "teaching truth to power," impressed many of us. We read William Hazlett's "The Indian Jugglers," an essay about perfection and greatness. We read Aldous Huxley on "Comfort," which contained marvelous sections on "Central Heating and the Feudal System" and "Baths and Morals." We read a seventeenth century essay on learning by Francis Bacon, and a thought-provoking 1925 essay on "Science and the Faith of the Modern," by Edwin Conklin. The latter, written during the Scopes trial era, is a defense of science and its proper place in culture; some points it makes speak to many debates in twenty-first century America. Bruce Perry still remembers this essay today as an interesting source of ideas and perspectives.[313]

Although these essays were works of "letters," and not strictly of "philosophy," they did introduce us to thinking critically and analytically—and at a much higher level of sophistication than we had been used to. They opened new venues for thinking. They made new connections. I remember them as lofty mountains to climb. How much we actually retained—how many of the lessons they contained we internalized—is difficult to remember, and different readers certainly were struck by different points, but this set of essays represented a level of quality and excellence that was easy to recognize, and that itself created an impression.

---

312 Later famous among American PBS audiences as the author of *Upstairs, Downstairs*.
313 Bruce Perry joined our Class in the Fourth Form. He graduated from the University of Virginia, went into the Army, and was stationed in Korea as a member of the First Cavalry Division (whose specialty was rappelling out of helicopters). He graduated with an MBA from the University of Denver and entered the banking business in Connecticut where he worked for Society for Savings Bank in Hartford in the mortgage and commercial real estate business. He became a mortgage broker and consultant for asset management, and then worked for the Connecticut Housing Finance Authority specializing in the funding of affordable housing.

Whittemore Whittier

We also read poetry in the spring from an anthology. It was either *Sound and Sense*, mentioned above, or *12 Poets*.[314] We had learned some of the stylistic elements of poetry with Mr. Corbett in the Fourth Form. Here we read more for content and criticism. We read a set of Shakespeare's sonnets ("Shall I Compare Thee to a Summer's Day") and some of Donne ("Death Be not Proud") and a bit of Wordsworth, including "Westminster Bridge." We read Keats's "Ode to a Grecian Urn" and Browning's "My Last Duchess." I remember Mr. Paxton reading the last to us in class. We read a few poems of Emily Dickinson, including "I Love to See It Lap the Miles," and A.E. Housman's "Is My Team Ploughing?" We read Edward Arlington Robinson's "Richard Cory" and "Miniver Cheevy," both of which we had encountered before. We read quite a bit of Frost, including "Stopping by Woods," "The Death of the Hired Man," and "The Road Not Taken." We also read a smattering of T.S. Eliot. I did not respond particularly well to poetry. Frost was an exception, but that was probably narrowly cultural, and at that time, I did not recognize the savagery in some of his poems. Mr. Paxton had someone come up from Brown and deliver a lecture in Alumni

---

314 Edited by Glenn Leggett, New York: Rinehart & Company, 1958.

Hall on Whittier, the Quaker poet who wrote "The Quaker Alumni," a poem about Moses Brown School, delivered at a gathering of alumni and alumnae exactly one hundred years before our own Commencement. Its final section begins with the invocation "Long Live the Good School," which we often sang on ceremonial occasions. Mr. Paxton read this to us with pride.

Mr. Paxton indeed seemed proud of his Moses Brown affiliation. Once or twice in Chapel, he read from a recently published biography of Moses Brown describing his shrewd dealings and public spiritedness. Several times he mentioned "For the Honor of Truth," explaining that this meant a lot more than just transparency—it meant the pursuit of truth as an honorable intellectual objective. He did not expand greatly on speaking truth to power, but that was among the points he made. He did not sermonize anywhere nearly as much as Mr. Raines or Mr. Herman, but he seemed to have strong values. He asserted that intellectual honesty was high among them: as noted above, he was critical of hypocrisy and impatient with naivete. Above all, he emphasized standards of excellence in his own performance and in ours.

In senior year, we were asked to write an essay about civil rights, and I remember writing about Martin Luther King, Jr., who was just beginning to come to national fame. Mrs. Paxton helped me find materials on him. At Allan Cokin's suggestion, I also submitted a "peace essay." There was a prize for the best peace essays, no doubt the result of a legacy left by well-meaning Quakers. Writing for it, however, was not part of the regular curriculum. Allan wanted to go for the prize, and I think he needed someone else to enter the competition in order for the prize to be awarded. In any case, he came to me about it, and I assented. We both wrote on the causes of war—and we talked about this a bit in advance. We agreed that there had been many such causes throughout history, most of which were still with us. We did conclude, however, that there was one traditional cause of war that was no longer extant (and that would probably never again emerge in this capacity during our lifetime): religion. We concluded that there were no more religious wars in prospect. The idea that religion, in our liberal age, might again become the motivation for war and mayhem seemed preposterous. We were the only two contestants. Allan won the prize; I came in second. He wrote passionately in support of peace; I wrote

Helen J. Paxton

in defense of military strength as a source of peace, with Munich and Cold War deterrence in mind. Mr. Paxton, no doubt, made the right choice. I recall that my "peace" essay was quite bloodcurdling.

Mrs. Helen Paxton was the librarian for the Upper School. She had been a college classmate of Aunt Amey's at Brown, and so she knew my family. She was very bright, cheerful, and always helpful. Her contributions to our intellectual development can easily be overlooked because she was not a classroom instructor, but she was a very learned person, erudite, imaginative, very well-read, and conversant in a wide range of intellectual topics, especially literary ones. She was easy to talk to, and a source of many useful comments, criticisms, and suggestions, especially for papers. She was very helpful to me in choosing paper topics, and especially in finding resource materials for articles I wrote as Historian of the *Delphian*. She was almost like a special tutor for those who took advantage of her helpfulness. She was very supportive and eminently approachable. She was an often overlooked major contributor to the School's educational enterprise.

Fifth Form (1959-60)

The Library itself was located at the rear of Alumni Hall. There were shelves on the back wall itself and then a set of stacks standing a few feet from that wall (and parallel to) it, one on each side of the wide entranceway to the hall. These had shelves on both front and back. There was also a room behind the stacks on the east side of the building where the rarer books were kept. There was a table out front where Mrs. Paxton sat with her paraphernalia.

As seniors, we could escape study hall and go to the library to study. This was a welcome change. It was more pleasant than in the study hall room. Some quiet conversation was permitted. We just signed out and went over. There were tables near the stacks at the back of the room for our use. We could read, write, study, or prepare for class. I can remember several of us going down to the front of Alumni Hall on occasion to quiz each other on Mr. Paxton's vocabulary exercises.

Mrs. Paxton had good suggestions for reading. In the senior year, we were expected to do outside reading, largely of our own choice. I remember reading Churchill's *Triumph and Tragedy*—and then not long after this, reading the remaining five of his World War II volumes. I also read Conan Doyle's *The White Company*, and Charles Reade's *The Cloister and the Hearth*. I read Dickens's *Hard Times* and was also permitted to reread Dickens's *Tale of Two Cities*. Mrs. Paxton recommended the story of Abelard and Eloise to me, but I didn't enjoy it. Although I was unaware of Twain's critique of A & E at that time, I subsequently came to agree with him. Mrs. Paxton was quite disappointed—clearly I was just not mature enough to appreciate the story at that time! But frankly, I still think Twain had it right. There were also books in the library about the School itself, and she gave me access to them for my *Delphian* articles discussed in Volume II below.

American History and Government. Everett B. Raines was another commanding figure at Moses Brown. Like Mr. Paxton, he served briefly in the administration, in his case as Dean for one year under Mr. St. John, and two years under Mr. Cunningham. Like Messrs. Paxton and Howe, he often wore a vest. He took his undergraduate degree from Wesleyan and did graduate work at Brown. He was a very strong presence in the

Everett B. Raines

classroom, yet a delightful person, outgoing, and quite adept at handling us. Whereas Mr. Paxton stood relatively still and made his pronouncements from on high, Mr. Raines was constantly in relaxed motion, whether standing or seated—which was often his teaching posture. His expressive hands, his very large head, and his whole upper body seemed to be always in slow flux, and this fluid quality helped set the class at ease. No matter whether he was agreeing or disagreeing with you—or whether he was admonishing you for ignorance (or for misbehavior)—he spoke to you in a strong, directly personal, yet calm, friendly, and informal, manner. Most of the time this was with a smile and the proverbial twinkle in the eye, sort of like a patient grandparent or uncle who takes a generous view of your shortcomings and an immediate interest in your well-being. He never undermined our perception that no matter what you did—or what he did to you—he still liked you. This was the mark of an experienced politician, and Mr. Raines certainly was that—in the best sense of the word.

He also took an intense interest in each of us as individuals. Jim Rigney recalled that early in the term he was a bit frightened of Raines and

Fifth Form (1959-60)

therefore refrained from class participation. Mr. Raines took Jim aside and asked him, "What am I doing wrong not to capture your interest in class?" They had a brief chat, and from that point on, Jim became much more engaged in class proceedings. Dave London recalled that when he headed for Brown, Mr. Raines took him aside and told him to take a certain course with a certain professor that Raines knew he would enjoy.[315]

Mr. Raines needed no help when it came to handling people. If someone misbehaved in class, one of his favorite tricks was to take a coin out of his pocket, flip it, and ask the miscreant to call it heads or tails—heads you leave the room, tails you stay, or whatever. Mr. Raines controlled the outcome, and the student always won the toss, but Mr. Raines had made

---

315 This advice led to a memorable outcome. When Dave got accepted to Brown, Raines took him aside, congratulated him, and said that the one thing he wanted him to do at Brown was take James Hedges's course, the History of American Economic Life. "I want you to take that course," Raines said with emphasis. He knew of Dave's interest in business and knew he would like this course. Dave remembered the advice, but at the end of his freshman year, he saw a write-up in the Brown paper that Hedges was retiring at the end of the next year. So he rushed around and pulled the papers for the course, but was told that he couldn't sign up—it was for seniors and graduate students only.

So he went to Hedges and told him that his favorite teacher at Moses Brown said that he had to take this course. He went in and explained the whole thing to him. Hedges, however, responded that the course was open to seniors and graduate students only. Dave argued his case, but Hedges bluntly told him, "You'll never be able to pass—you don't have enough background." Dave asked if he could audit. Hedges waved dismissively and said, "I don't let anyone audit. I don't want to waste the oxygen in the classroom on someone not taking the course."

Dave then wrote him a beautiful letter—vowing to work as hard as it took, and saying it would be okay if he didn't get a good grade. This did not move Olympus. So Dave went to Hedges during the summer and begged him once more. Hedges finally relented, but said, "You'll never pass the course."

Dave loved the course. It was all about the American Revolutionaries getting out from under the king's taxation and the hidden agenda of economics throughout American history. Dave sat there amongst the seniors and grad students, but he worked his proverbial tail off. He had a perfect attendance record—the only class at Brown for which he attended more than half of the lectures. At the end of the first semester, however, he got an "F". The only basis was one submitted paper returned with the scrawl, "I told you. Not enough scholarship."

So he redoubled his efforts. All other courses went to pieces, but this one received more time and attention than he had ever given to a course, then or later. It was an all-consuming challenge. The final was an in-class written exam. The next week, when he got it back, the grade was a "B-". Dave recalled that this was his happiest moment in college. Then a week later he got his final grade for the course—and it was an "F." He drove back to Providence and made an appointment to see Hedges. "I suppose you have come to see me about your final grade," the professor said before Dave could open his mouth. "Yes," Dave responded. "Well, I told you that you were not going to pass my course, and I keep my promises." Apalling.

his point and the problem receded. I can remember once being nailed by him in the study hall for some infraction—one that produced a Saturday morning penalty—but he hailed me with a "gotcha" smile followed by a chuckle, as if he had just scored a point in a friendly game and it was all great fun. All this while still announcing my penalty on the spot. How could you dislike such a person?

He enjoyed mixing with people, but he dealt with them from a position of emotional strength. He was a very secure person, and never let anyone get under his skin. In fact, he was one of the most secure persons I ever met— secure almost (but not quite) to the point of smugness. Part of this security came from his mastery of facts. He knew the text; he knew the record; he knew the evidence; he knew the dates—and in all cases this to him was unassailable knowledge. Self-awareness of the possession of unassailable knowledge can be an enormous source of emotional security, and it was in his case.

To many of us boys, all this meant that Raines had the voice of unimpeachable authority. And he did earn a lot of respect from his enormous command of the factual basis of American History. I remember once he was lecturing on some topic—I forget the actual topic, but let us say it was the extent of American military production in the Second World War. He called on someone in the back of the classroom and asked him to take down such-and-such a book from the shelf behind him. He told him from memory to turn to such-and-such a page, and began to recite the data appearing there. "Correct me, if I am wrong, but I believe you will find listed there that in 1942, the US produced 44,350 planes, 352,400 trucks, 1,258,000 jeeps ... liberty ships ...."—or whatever the data were. From memory he went down the list, with the student checking his numbers. When he came to the end, he said, "Is there any other important category of production that I have missed?" The student had to admit that Mr. Raines had forgotten nothing. It was a real tour-de-force. Such demonstrations happened more than once.

He loved to pose specific factual questions in class. During the first few days of the Fall Term, he asked us to draw a different continent from memory every day—and then the United States with all the states depicted. Sometimes his questions were about historical events and sometimes they were about an aspect of American history or culture that he thought was important for us to know. He taught, among other things, what today would be called cultural literacy. This was long before the days of Trivial Pursuit, but Raines's course was good training for it. Instruction at times was sort of like a game, and he treated it as such. Some of these questions could end up on his daily quizzes, and we had to pay attention. Bill Brehm recalled that on one occasion Mr. Raines asked us, "Who was the largest manufacturer of locomotives in America?" This stumped everyone, and there was a noticeable pause. Mr. Raines was about to provide the answer when Jack Nixon's hand went up, Mr. Raines called on him, and Jack said, "Lionel?"[316] Everyone roared, including Mr. Raines, and for once he had no comeback.

He not only had a command of facts and dates, but he could make those facts and dates appear terribly significant by dint of his own personality. Often he would give emphasis to the significance of his remarks by saying "Now, put that down," or "Make a note of that."[317] Because he boomed out his points with such extraordinary confidence, they acquired an importance that they somehow might have lacked in any other context or from any other source. When he talked about the Wilmot Proviso or the Peggy Eaton affair, he did it in such tones that they suddenly acquired striking significance. When he told you that Jackson fired two Secretaries of the Treasury before he found one (Taney) who would withdraw federal funds from the Bank of the United States, this suddenly became an astounding event. The "Dred Scott Dezision" as he called it, could have stood out on its own in this regard, but Mr. Raines's tone of voice, not to mention his pronunciation, certainly ratified the importance placed on it by history. When he recounted the episode of Teddy Roosevelt's telling Congress (which was objecting to funding an around-the-world trip for the Navy) that existing appropriations would take the Navy halfway around the world, and unless they wished to leave it there they had better appropriate the money to bring it back, this acquired cosmic constitutional importance in Mr. Raines's manner of presentation—and you could see how much he would have enjoyed making that threat himself.

He also employed authoritative-sounding epigrams in support of his points, ones that made you feel superior because they seemed to let you in on

---

316 The leading toy train manufacturer at that time.
317 Recalled by Bill Carney, taped interview, July 15, 2015.

important political secrets: "power corrupts and absolute power corrupts absolutely," "figures lie and liars figure," or Twain's famous trilogy, "lies, damn lies, and statistics." In this manner, Mr. Raines connected well with adolescent boys on the verge of maturity. If history was important to a person such as this, then it must be important to us. And so was acting responsibly. Admonishing us not to get our girlfriends pregnant, he memorably repeated several times, "If you sow wild oats, don't count on crop failure."

Dave London remembered an amusing episode involving Mr. Raines.[318] We were studying the origins of the First World War and the famous Zimmerman telegram. At the end of class, Raines turned to Dave and said, "London, your homework assignment for tonight is to find out what the Zimmerman process is, not the Zimmerman telegram, mind you, but the Zimmerman process." This was long before the days of Google, so Dave went home and looked in the encyclopedia—nothing on the Zimmerman process. He checked in a few other places—still nothing. So he enlisted his dad who said, "I'll ask around."

Dave came to class the next day and Raines called on him: "What did you find out about the Zimmerman process?" Dave had to admit he had drawn a blank. Raines responded, "Have you asked your dad to help?" Dave replied, "Yes, he's probably working on it right now." Raines asked again the next day and again the day after. When Friday came, he said, "I want a full report by Monday. Tell your dad to ask his broker."

With this clue, Mr. London solved the mystery. The Zimmerman process was a means of turning waste water into recyclable water (or something like that). It was in its infancy, and there was a company on the stock market that was developing the process. Mr. London finally found out about it through his investment person. On Monday, Dave gave the answer. "Tell your dad to look into that stock," advised Mr. Raines. He did, and the stock went up. Mr. London later sold it, made a nice profit, and donated the profit to Moses Brown.

Mr. Raines taught the full spectrum of Western history at Moses Brown—from ancient to modern, both European and American. Bruce Henkle

---

318 Interview, August 29, 2010.

remembered studying medieval history with him in a class of three students.[319] But most of us had him for American political institutions and American history in our senior year. In the Fall Term we studied American government. This was an important introduction to civics, which had gone unstudied systematically in the classroom since Mrs. Monahon in the Lower School. I enjoyed it greatly. It was taught as a basic factual course in the institutions of government, both national and local. We learned about presidential nominating conventions and the Electoral College (Mr. Raines predicted that Symington would be the Democratic nominee in 1960, and that Kennedy, if nominated, would lose to Nixon on the religious issue). We were taught a list of presidential powers and a lot about the history and structure of the executive branch. We learned the advantages and disadvantages of the committee system in Congress and about how a bill becomes a law, including the roles of the Speaker and the Rules Committee in the House, the possible roles of filibusters and cloture in the Senate, and the potential role of presidential vetoes and how they might be overridden. We learned how the House was apportioned and how senators used to be appointed by state legislatures before the Seventeenth Amendment. We learned about the treaty-making power and modern executive agreements. We learned about executive sessions of Congress. We also were taught the vocabulary of the legislative process—lame duck, teller vote, logrolling, tabling, discharge, pork-barreling, adjourning *sine die*, etc. Such vocabulary terms were fair game for a quiz.

Mr. Raines also talked about the court system and judicial review on the national level, citing Marbury against Madison in this context. He mentioned Roosevelt's court-packing scheme. He also described dual federalism and the system of state and federal courts. On the local level, we learned about strong mayors, city managers, and traffic courts—the last of which he urged us to attend as observers. Finally, in the larger institutional context, he talked about checks and balances.

This was very basic, very factual material, and a good introduction to the constitutional underpinnings of the system and how it was designed to work. It was a course on the rules of the political game. Raines was not particularly interested in abstract concepts of government and political

---

319 Telephone interview, August 7, 2014.

theory, except to the extent that these concepts could be summarized by a word or phrase (e.g., "representation," "progressivism") and thereby encapsulated as a briefly defined fact. We learned these facts and factoids because he made them seem terribly important—not that he directly said they were important (although when he ordered us "to make a note of it" we knew that was what he meant), but they just came across as important in his manner of presentation. He taught as someone who was letting us in on a secret—something that those in the know knew—words and concepts used by adult insiders behind the closed doors of smoke-filled rooms, the idiom, style, practices, and rules of legislators and other politicians that we needed to learn if we wished to be a player. The message was that this was how adults played the game in the real world—and he made us want to be a part of it.

We had a text of which we read sections,[320] but in this department, Mr. Raines dominated the learning process. He used to open each class with a small quiz—a "ten-second" special (that may not be its exact name—I forget what he called it) where we had ten seconds to answer each question. This tested our factual knowledge of the reading. Sometimes he would toss in a ringer or two. At the end of these exercises, we would exchange papers and correct each other's answers. During class itself, he continually asked questions about the facts and details he wanted us to understand. He would parlay our answers (or lack of them) into class instruction itself. The class was very interactive and personal—he seldom lectured in a formal way or used the board during this part of the course. He often told brief anecdotes or stories that kept the flow interesting. Classes passed quickly.

The second part of the year—it may have been more than half—focused on American History. Raines used Thomas Bailey's *American Pageant* as a text, probably one of the most readable books ever written on the subject. Frankly, I could not put it down. It was filled with maps and charts and political cartoons—Dave London remembered that he "became a freak, admiring political cartoons" because of Bailey[321]—but its attractiveness was in its narrative style. History was taught as a series of stories, occasionally interrupted by statistics and data.

---

320 William McClenaghan, *Magruder's American Government*, Boston: Allyn and Bacon, 1959.
321 Interview, August 29, 2010.

Fifth Form (1959-60)

This book had a point of view very compatible with Mr. Raines's own outlook: American history, despite America's many problems, embarrassments, and shortcomings, was an exercise in unfolding progress—establishing a democratic republic, ending slavery, settling a continent, controlling monopolies and political corruption, creating a mass-consumption economy, beating the Depression, winning two world wars, containing communism, and basically overcoming all obstacles to enlightened capitalism and enlightenment liberalism (in the old meaning of the word). There was a basic sense of optimism in Bailey that reflected Mr. Raines's own optimistic outlook on politics and on life.

To be sure, he recognized problems in American democracy and he had his likes and dislikes (FDR was one of the latter). He was also more than a bit proud of the presumed Protestant origins of American democracy. These perceptions, however, only occasionally shaped his conclusions, and he certainly tried to be fair within the context of his own values. He had a right-of-center political vantage point, and he made sure the class understood the errors of left-wing ways, but this was done with good humor and even grace. He could be faulted for not recognizing and not conveying to us the plight of African-Americans at that time, but he endorsed Eisenhower's Little Rock intervention, and one might note that he was not alone in coming late to recognize America's widespread deprivation of civil rights. I had little contact with him after graduation, and I do not know how his thoughts evolved in this respect during the 1960s.

As far as I could tell, Mr. Raines played no favorites in class. I don't believe he ever discriminated against anyone on any grounds that would be regarded then or now as illegitimate—nor do I remember any other Moses Brown instructor doing so. Neither personalities nor differing perceptions entered into his grading equations. With respect to personalities: his wife and my mother had had a dustup over the Plantations Club, to which they both belonged. Mrs. Raines (how shall I put it gently?) had come to dislike my mother quite strongly. Both Raines and I, of course, were very aware of this circumstance, and it was always there in the wings, but we never mentioned it, and as far as I could tell, it never influenced his treatment of me in any substantive way.

With respect to differing perceptions, Pete Parker recalled, "Raines wasn't exactly totally impartial. He presented a view of the world that obviously corresponded to his own. If you think about it in this regard, there is no more difficult class than one in recent history and contemporary events because everyone has a point of view—and he did too. I think he tried to keep his views out, and he tried not to penalize us for expressing contrary views. He was more interested in scholarship than in views, even though he could be very forceful. It even made me uncomfortable at times. I tried to do something different and support some things not in sync with his views. He would in these instances return my paper without comments. But he graded the paper like everyone else's."[322]

In this part of the course, Mr. Raines gave us extensive, but very terse, notes—starting with the Age of Discovery and the Colonial Period. These were a summary of the items he considered to be most important. For example, he would list four dozen explorers, where they came from, and what they discovered—and then on to the next topic. All this was fairly easy for me because of Mrs. Monahon, but others may have found his method daunting. We were expected to organize these notes in a neat format with appropriate indentations and present them to him at the end of the year either in typed form or in very legible handwriting. Mark Saklad remembered that his did not meet Mr. Raines's standard for legibility, and he was ordered to type them up. He enlisted the aid of his entire family in this enterprise, and the task was accomplished. He remembered that this was exceedingly convenient for his younger brother, Jim, who took Mr. Raines's class a couple of years later—until somebody stole the notes.[323]

Mr. Raines discussed the founding of each colony, its type of government, and colonial attempts at union. He covered the causes of the Revolution, the war itself, the "critical period" under the Articles of Confederation, and the writing of the Constitution (with its various plans, compromises, and features).

The rest of American history was organized in two intersecting ways. The first was chronological, the second, topical. In the first, he presented the challenges, the accomplishments, and the failures of each presidential administration from Washington to Franklin Roosevelt. The second approach was to organize events topically around important problems in

---
322 Taping session at the 50th Class Reunion, May 8, 2010.
323 Taping session at the 50th Class Reunion, May 8, 2010.

Fifth Form (1959-60)　　　　　　　　　　　　　　　　　　　　　　　　　　　373

American history. Some of these were from the early republic: territorial acquisition, states' rights, pre-Civil War judicial decisions, the formation and evolution of political parties, the tariff. Others came from the post-Civil War period: labor, big business, banking, silver and gold, the tariff (again), transportation, civil service, Prohibition, and immigration. He would give us notes for both approaches, and the cross-referencing of these topics with presidential administrations would provide a good matrix for understanding and remembering each. The topical discussions came more towards the end of the course, as he summarized the evolution of the great issues.

He did spend a lot of time on the first half of the nineteenth century: the Louisiana Purchase, the War of 1812, the age of Jackson, Polk and the Mexican War, and the events leading up to the Civil War. He covered American expansion, the development of the party system from the Federalists on, the Industrial Revolution during this period, and the rise of the slavery issue. Throughout, he emphasized the importance of economics. He was certainly no Marxist, and he did not buy Charles Beard's economic theory of American history lock, stock, and barrel, but clearly it had influenced his thinking about how interests formed and events unfolded. Many of the topics we studied (Hamiltonian debt assumption, the tariff, banking, Civil War finance, bimetallism, canals and railroads, antitrust, etc.) were related to economic forces, and he was not naive about their impact. Raines did not spend a lot of time on the Civil War itself—he let Bailey cover that—but he did go into good detail on the Gilded Age and the period between the Civil War and the First World War. It was here that he developed his topical discussions to help summarize the main political, social, and economic events of the period: the populists, the progressives, the socialists, the mug-wump Republicans, the rise of monopolies and of the labor movement, Bryan and silver, the ICC, Teddy Roosevelt's famous "chocolate éclair" characterization of McKinley, the Spanish War, and Roosevelt's own imperialism. This coverage was new to my experience, and it filled a big chronological gap.

Mr. Raines did not spend a lot of time on these topics. None was discussed or elaborated in great detail. Nor could we have had many such elaborations and still completed the course. He was not really teaching social or economic history. He was giving us an outline. He was providing a structural basis for understanding the period and its main movements and events. He would give a sentence or two authoritatively as to what populism was and where it fit into the larger scheme of things, but he did not explain it in detail. He would provide a long list of progressive reforms (antitrust legislation, Australian ballot, referendum, recall, primaries, the civil service system, political professionalism, competitive bidding, banking regulations, Federal Reserve, etc.), and give a sentence or two explaining what they were, but would not go into great detail as to how these reforms came about or what their political implications were. He would mention Debbs and the Socialist Party or Gompers and the Labor Movement (and give us a few sentences as to what their aims and accomplishments were), and we would write it down in our outline—but he would not elaborate in detail.

In sum, Mr. Raines did not discuss the conceptual underpinnings or important interpretations of the great political or social movements in American History—such as how Calvinism, the Enlightenment, Transcendentalism or Social Darwinism helped influence American political perceptions and practices. He did not discuss in detail the significance of the frontier, or the intellectual currents behind imperialism and anti-imperialism at the turn of the twentieth century—or the sources of isolationist thinking in the '20s, or the philosophical underpinnings of the New Deal and its critics. Such phenomena would be mentioned, but not explained in depth. What this course did do, however, was to put them on the table, so to speak, in ways that would give us not just a list, but a structure, an armature, on which to hang concepts and details should we wish to pursue them in greater depth at a later time. This was valuable if you regarded the structure he provided as a starting point, not as an endpoint—and I'm sure he knew what he was doing in this regard.

Mr. Raines's lectures were well-supplemented by Bailey, who did cover a lot of territory and provided a more interpretative account of American history. Bailey gave us some flesh for Raines's skeleton, so to speak. The combination was a good one. The only potential drawback to Bailey was his very positive attitude about the unfolding of events. American history was one triumph after another, and where triumph was lacking—one hundred years of Jim Crow, for example—this did not get major treatment.[324] All in all, however, Mr. Raines gave us what was in most respects a good course in American history for this stage of our intellectual development. We read a lot and we were tested a lot. We did not write frequently, but we did have to write a lengthy biography on an important American figure. I chose Theodore Roosevelt—whom Raines described more than once as "manic." It was not a particularly impressive paper, but the exercise of writing it did expose me to some of the more fascinating events in this person's very full life.

In later years, I heard criticisms of Mr. Raines's fact-based approach from some who went on to study history and politics, and they did make a valid point. In his partial defense, however, let me suggest that having a basic factual acquaintance with events, institutions, and political/economic/ social movements, not only gives you a structure for ordering more sophisticated data and interpretations, it also carries with it enormous forensic advantages. It is always quite valuable to have factual training when you are conversing with someone who lacks it, because if he or she makes a factual error, you can often catch it—and derail the argument. If you know a great deal of factual detail, not only can you trip up opponents, but you can also generate good starting points for your own arguments. It may be difficult to argue with a philosopher on this basis, but if you have a strong factual grounding you can usually get a head start on a lawyer and will have a good edge on almost anyone else.

There is a tendency today to teach, shall we say, the soft dimensions of history—the social aspects, the philosophical aspects, the intellectual aspects—without first providing the factual framework *a la* Raines. There are good reasons for focusing on the more interpretive aspects of history at the college and graduate level, but without the "hard" basis in events and strong data, you can get some very bizarre comments from people who will put someone in the wrong century or in the wrong country, or in the wrong war, or they will have somebody responding to someone not yet born, or attacking the writings of someone who had not yet published— things like that. I have had students ask in all seriousness about World War I, saying that they assumed there must have been one, since they had heard

---

324 It was, however, mentioned briefly.

about World War II. I have had other students ask me whose side we were on in World War I. I have had students attribute the invention of the light bulb to Benjamin Franklin. Colleagues have traded such stories with me. None of these questions or comments would have come from an attentive person in a class taught by Mr. Raines.

In another vein, many incoming college students do not know that it takes two-thirds of the Senate and House to override a presidential veto, or even how the Electoral College operates. Many cannot locate Prague on a map of Europe or Singapore on a map of Asia. These are bright students from excellent high schools. At least part of the problem is the nature of their high school training. When such events occur, I inevitably think of Mr. Raines and the training he gave us, not to mention Mr. Odell, Mr. Pratt, or even Mrs. Bluhm and Mrs. Monahon with their courses in basic geography and history.

It is true that in good colleges what I have characterized as "soft" history is regarded as ultimately more valuable—and I agree with this—but since the colleges teach less of the "hard" history anymore, and many high schools have long departed from Mr. Raines's approach, an important gap opens up in a student's background. Although some might argue that it would have been better for Raines to have supplemented his facts and chronologies with some in-depth analysis, had he done this he would have had to abandon some of his matrix, and that would have been a shame. I guess the bottom lines are that I am glad to have had Mr. Raines, I remember much of what he taught me, his historical matrices were excellent foundations on which to build more sophisticated and interpretive superstructures, and his inspirational classroom style fueled an enhanced interest in the subject.

The experiences with both Mr. Raines and Mr. Pratt were valuable preparations for college and afterwards, not only conceptually in their very different ways, but in simple terms of examsmanship. Mr. Pratt introduced us to the then-current features of a college examination, and in Mr. Raines's case, I remember beginning to learn how to guess in advance what questions he might ask. I recall that he promised us that on our final exam he would ask us to write a biography of an important American historical actor. I remember deducing that it would probably be John Quincy Adams. Mr. Raines throughout the year had mentioned the importance of

Adams, who had helped his father with work on treaties at the end of the American Revolution, who had served the Federalist Party in the Senate, who had been involved with settling the War of 1812, who had written the Monroe Doctrine, who had become president in America's first disputed election under the current Electoral College system, who had been a strong opponent of the gag rule, and who concurrently had lit the torch in Congress for the fight against slavery—so he covered very well the whole first half of the nineteenth century.

I shared this guess with Jim Rigney, and we both carefully reviewed Adams's long professional life. I remember that the exam was in the afternoon, and Jim came over to my house for lunch beforehand so we could do some last-minute studying for it. We reexamined Adams with great care. When the exams were handed out, Jim sat a couple of rows in front of me and got his exam first. I can remember him glancing at the exam and turning to me with a huge grin on his face. That said it all: I knew then that we had been right about J. Q.

Examsmanship is something one became adept at—namely figuring out in advance the type of questions one could expect. If you went over your notes very carefully, if you understood the basic structure of the course and the main points the instructor was trying to cover, by the time you had done this, you could probably formulate the kinds of questions you would be asked. Thanks to the outline form of Mr. Raines's class, this was a technique that I had perfected by the time I graduated from Moses Brown, and it served me well in college. Hence there were very few surprises on our history final exam—and I did well on it. This performance enabled me to share the senior history prize with Jonathan Costa.[325] We were awarded, first, a copy of Langer's one-volume *Encyclopedia of World History*—still a valuable reference and source of Raines-style facts—and, second, a subscription to *Foreign Affairs* magazine, which I have kept up to this day. My experiences in Mr. Raines's course in American Government and History were certainly the most enjoyable academic ones in my senior year, which saw uphill fights in most classrooms because I did not have the time to give academics the attention they intrinsically deserved.

---

325 Jonathan Costa joined our Class in the Second Form. He graduated from Harvard. We lost touch with him, but believe that he became a psychiatrist.

Mr. Thomas and Upper School faculty and staff, 1949–1950

Front row (L–R): Mr. W. Paxton, Mr. A. W. Cate, Mr. S. H. Waughtel, Mr. L. R. Thomas, Mr. O. J. B. Henderson, Mr. F. W. Howe, Jr., Mr. E. B. Raines. Second row: Mr. E. F. Armstrong, Mr. L. H. Cole, Mr. W. J. Kennedy, Mr. M. L. Herman, Mr. T. S. Whitford. Third row: Mr. C. F. Mulkey, Mr. F. E. Fuller, Mr. D. F. Clapp, Mr. L. E. Stout. Fourth row: Mrs. E. B. Monahon, Mrs. H. J. Paxton, Miss E. B. Angilly, Miss M. L. Shaw, Miss E. G. Weeks, Miss R. N. Cook. Back row: Mr. C. H. Hutton: Mr. E. H. Jernquist, Miss N. B. Keach, Mr. B. G. Meserve, Mr. W. H. Goffe, Mr. D. J. Blackwell, Mrs. G. M. Seidel.

XVI

The Upper School Classroom Experience

Looking back upon the whole Moses Brown classroom experience, it must be remembered that it was an all-boys school when we were there. Moses Brown had been coed for more than a hundred years before the arrangement with Lincoln was made in 1926—although "coed" historically did not mean what it does now. There was very little social interaction between boys and girls at Moses Brown in the nineteenth and early twentieth centuries—my uncle, Robert Steere ('20), had to get permission from the authorities to speak to his sister, who also attended Moses Brown at that time. The history surrounding the Lincoln arrangement is well set forth in Mr. Thomas's book. What role did this circumstance play in our education? It was such a given that I seldom contemplated the alternative at the time, although today, looking back, I wish we had been coed with expanded facilities and schedules.

Obviously, the athletic program would have been structured differently, although this was before Title IX. Clubs and organizations would have been run a lot differently, and there would probably have been an expanded set of them. Social circumstances would have been very different, and life on campus outside of the classroom would also have had a very different flavor.

What about in the classroom? I remember talking with Mrs. Paxton about this one afternoon. I forget how the subject came up. It was an issue of interest to Mrs. Paxton, one of the very few female faculty members in the

Upper School. She had apparently discussed it at some length with Mr. Paxton. He had made the point to her that there would be a big difference in his classroom if it were coed—and in the way he would teach. She said to me, "I was angry with him for saying this, and responded, 'Why? Do you spend all your time in class telling dirty stories?'" He had answered her, that no, he didn't spend all his time telling dirty stories (which he didn't—he never came close to telling a dirty story in class), but that the whole atmosphere and ambience would be different with women in his classroom. She remained unconvinced that this was a decisive argument, but she did to some extent recognize what he was saying.

I guess this goes back to the question raised earlier of whether one teaches a subject or teaches a student. Many of these faculty members felt their function went beyond teaching a subject to include being a role model for us boys, giving us advice to deal with life, including its social circumstances, and serving to some degree, if not *in loco parentis*, at least as a supplement to them. Furthermore, good teaching depends on achieving a certain level of communication, and in this case there was, in subtle ways, a sort of "male bonding" phenomenon in many classrooms that enhanced certain levels of communication, although this varied from classroom to classroom.

I do not know how many of the teachers we had in the 1950s were still there when Moses Brown became coed in the 1970s—many retired in the 1960s—but it would be interesting to find out how those who were still there adapted to the new circumstance. I think some classes would have been very similar to ours and some would have been quite different.

I expect that classes taught by Cate, Whitford, Fuller, Pratt, and Taber would have been very much the same with women in them as they were in our time. We had Mr. Odell as eighth graders, and his efforts at socialization were aimed at raising our maturity to a level where he could effectively teach his subject. They were not particularly "gendered." He probably made the transition very easily. Mr. Corbett might have revised his reading list a bit, but he would have been at ease in a coed classroom. Mr. Paxton, despite his comments, would have done the same. Mr. Tinker took life as it came, and would have adapted, but his class would have been different (less Damon Runyon, for sure!). Nichols, Pezet, and Justin would each have had to teach in a different idiom. Mr. Herman's classroom would also have been very different, but Mr. Herman (who could be exceedingly polite when the occasion required it), after a year or two of treating his women students impeccably according to the dictates of the chivalric code, would have relaxed into the new circumstances, guided by his sense of humor, his sense of fairness, and his basic decency. The same can be said of Mr. Raines, although, of all these teachers, his style would have had to undergo the most dramatic evolution to remain effective, since it depended so heavily on his ability to connect with adolescent boys as a strong role model and a strong authority figure.

Turning to the actual educational experience as offered by Moses Brown, I would argue that Upper School instruction, although not uniform, was largely excellent, and the occasional soft spot was often remedied later. Our teachers for the most part created the impression that what they taught was important to them, and therefore should be important to us. Although we did not always take full advantage of their efforts, they did offer us a strong foundation on which to build. Where we went with it was up to us.

The requirement that we take math and English every year in Upper School paralleled the emphasis that these subjects had received in the Lower School. They certainly gave important preparation for college admission, college itself, and life thereafter. Although we did not practice for the SATs in a formal way (with the possible exception of Mr. Paxton's vocabulary exercises), our Moses Brown classroom experience certainly helped prepare us for them. The Class of 1960 had four National Merit Finalists and one-third of us went to an Ivy League college—with the rest having the opportunity to go to other excellent schools. That is not a bad record. Moses Brown in no way let us down, and I believe that those of us who remained at Moses Brown throughout the Upper School (instead of going off to other elite boarding schools) received as good an education as those who went. As noted above, I never regretted that choice.

The heart of the Moses Brown intellectual establishment in our time was in the humanities: Cate, Paxton, Whitford, and Fuller. These are the people who kept on top of their subjects through intellectual cross-fertilization. Mr. Raines was certainly very much a part of the social establishment at Moses Brown, but I doubt that he was part of the intellectual establishment. I suspect that Mr. Herman, though a senior person widely respected for his talents, was part of neither. The junior faculty (including Doc Odell early in our day) probably fitted themselves into this structure as best they could.

In English, each one of us was fortunate to have a set of five very different instructors (from a larger pool of seven or eight) with a wide range of skills, experiences, and interests, but all exceedingly well-read, enthusiastic, and committed to their subject. We had very solid training in grammar, usage, and composition, and had lots of practice in writing, both creative and analytic. We were exposed to a wide variety of high-quality literature (English, American, and in translation), both fiction and nonfiction, including essays, poetry, and drama. As the years passed, this was read critically and with increasing sophistication. Our instructors also put literature into a wider cultural context that taught us much beyond the story line itself. We were certainly well-prepared for college literature courses, and to read on our own.

In foreign languages, we were given a traditional three-year course in Latin, no doubt built around perceived college expectations (which were in the process of transformation at that time). At Moses Brown, English grammar set the stage for the study of Latin, which, in turn, set the stage both for building English vocabulary and for learning the Romance languages. Our instruction in modern languages began very late—I wish it had begun much earlier, and I wish these classes had included more of an experiential "total immersion" language-lab approach. That said, our language instructors were, by and large, very accomplished people who knew their subjects well, were well-read in the literature of their languages, and conveyed to us their enthusiasm for language along with very solid traditional grammar-based instruction.

The extended Moses Brown curriculum offered serious opportunities in the humanities, many outside of the classroom, and especially in the performing arts. The Glee Club and the Proscenium Club were both very active during our stay at Moses Brown. Declamation and the Debate Club offered their own special opportunities in this area. Individual music students gave recitals. Some pursued studio art on their own after the Second Form outside of the course structure. What was lacking from the curriculum in both Lower and Upper School was art history and art appreciation, and there was only a smattering of music appreciation. We got a small amount of art in our history courses, which touched on ancient art and Renaissance art, but nothing from the post-Renaissance era. In only one Upper School course was music appreciation seriously taught.

In the social sciences, which were called "social studies" in our early years, we had world geography and three history courses, which covered ancient, modern European, and American history. Mr. Odell's course was the only one that exposed us to cultures in the "third world" beyond the European tradition, and, given that this was a geography course, the focus was understandably on the physical, the political, and the economic, more than on the cultural. This was the only class I took in the Upper School that spent serious time on Latin America, East Asia, and South Asia, and one of the few that used current events in a systematic way to contribute directly to the purposes of the course. The three history courses provided a solid factual chronology of historical events. In Mr. Pratt's course we also were exposed to good causal analyses of the political, economic, social, and intellectual forces that shaped those events. In Mr. Raines's course, we were taught about American institutions, and were given a long chronology of important events together with a set of intersecting lists of episodes and accomplishments relevant to specific economic or political topics. The two combined gave us a very useful matrix on which to build a deeper understanding of American history in college, but presenting a range of hypotheses as to why things happened was less emphasized.

Turning to the mathematical and scientific culture, I believe we could have advanced in math more quickly and reached the foundations of calculus by the senior year without skimping on anything important that we did learn. To do this (or just to do well what we did) we also could have had more directed instruction in math early on, better showing the purposes and uses of algebra as incentives for studying it, and better reviewing and drilling specific algebraic techniques—the way we drilled computational techniques in Lower School. But overall, in terms of developing deductive logic and reasoning skills, developing the ability to manipulate symbols, and applying math to the solution of a bounded range of given problems, we had a very solid grounding by the time we graduated.

Upper School science lost its chief patron with the retirement of Mr. Thomas, but the structure he had established was strong, and science was required (or very strongly encouraged) in every year, starting with the Second Form. Mrs. Full's General Science course that year was not only a good general introduction to many topics in science that we were to revisit in subsequent years; it also was a basic course for future citizens in how the technologies of modern civilization work. We were exposed to a small amount of practical engineering in this course. Later, Mr. Howe's Mechanical Drawing class developed some specialized engineering skills, but we were not exposed to engineering or technology more broadly. Still, I expect that we were introduced to applied science and engineering to a greater extent than are most students pursuing a liberal arts track in today's high schools. To the extent this is true it is a serious gap in their preparation for citizenship and for life.

With respect to the traditional hard sciences: we were well-introduced to the vocabulary of biology and to its basic use of structural and functional concepts; we were given a good non-quantitative introduction to chemistry, with a few forays into the quantitative. In physics, it is my understanding that mathematics was used liberally to provide a good foundation for classical mechanics, but little was done with quantum mechanics. We were not taught earth sciences. Nevertheless, we had challenging courses that were well-taught by professionals on top of their subject. They introduced us to the vocabulary of science; to the scientific method; to many contemporary principles, conceptualizations, and findings in each discipline; and to the life of the laboratory.

A Moses Brown education in the 1950s was more than a well-taught set of disciplines. It also developed intellectual and social skills in preparation for college and for life. In the American tradition, the concept of "skill" itself as a major educational objective was deeply grounded in nineteenth and early twentieth century roots. Moses Brown not only educated, it also trained. In both Lower and Upper Schools, it undertook the development of skills as the starting point of its curriculum: computational skills, reading skills, writing skills, foreign language skills, and communication skills more generally, including vocabulary and oral expression. Even in the Upper School, these skills were acquired primarily through demonstration, memorization, and recurrent exposure with practice and repetition—leading to internalization. This whole process, however, grew fairly quickly to include in many cases the demonstrated application of skills—which provided both incentives to learn them and opportunities for practice. No one could successfully complete the Moses Brown course of study without extensive exposure to all these skills, taught as skills in a developmental and relatively systematic way with a strong commitment to ensuring that all Moses Brown graduates had mastered them. This was the basic set of building blocks on which all else rested, and in the educational philosophy of the day, the most important objective. If one thing was to be taught extensively and well, it was a set of basic skills that enabled one to cope with life in any venue. Many of these skills in this pre-electronic age were even more important than they are now, when we have access to handheld computational devices, word processing, spell-check and grammar-check, Google, and the vast informational resources of the internet.

Training, of course, was the genesis of education. We were taught to think critically and to think on our own. In this connection, we were taught to reason and to seek proof as the basis for reaching our own judgments or assessing prevailing conclusions. At first, the ability to reason and to prove grew out of simple problem-solving in mathematics (practical logic, so to speak). We then learned simple applications of formulae. By the time we were in Upper School, we were using symbolic manipulation and we revisited in a much more sophisticated way the applications of formulae. We then were exposed to syllogistic reasoning in geometry, and also (using proportion) to reasoning by analogy. Branching out from mathematics, we were also exposed in English classes to reasoning by analogy and, in many essays, to sophisticated analyses and arguments based on synthesizing experiences and drawing abstract conclusions from them. This form of analysis enabled us to move from empirical conclusions to moral judgments.

In both the natural and social sciences we were exposed to concepts of causality, evidence and proof. In the social sciences, interactive factors were occasionally identified as causes of social and political results, but the paradigm was basically linear, not structural/functional (equilibrium models of historical explanation, for example, were not presented). I am being descriptive, not critical, here—I do not advocate the use of many such models at this level of study in the social sciences (although there are those who do).

The natural sciences were a bit different. The linear-causal model was dominant in chemistry and physics, but we were introduced to a structural/

functional model in biology. In all three sciences, we were explicitly introduced to the "scientific method" of hypothesis-testing by experimentation as a refinement of the concept of proof. Despite a half century of relativity, however, the general paradigm in both chemistry and physics was more Newtonian than relativistic, more deterministic than probabilistic. Relativity itself was mentioned, but not expanded on in a serious way; quantum theory in chemistry and quantum mechanics in physics were also mentioned, but not developed in either case as a major basis for understanding physical reality.

Memory was central to almost everything. Early on, repetition was a major aid to memory; later, association grew to become very important. Memory itself lay at the heart of skill acquisition. It was central to success in the social sciences, as they were taught. It lay at the heart of foreign language instruction. It was a great help in mathematics and geometry, since so much was built upon prior understanding. It was, of course, very useful in English as well, although here there was a serious attempt to build critical skills that relied as much on aesthetic judgments as on memorizable formulae.

Aesthetics themselves, as normally defined, however, were not emphasized at Moses Brown (although they were not totally ignored). We did read poetry and were asked to evaluate it. In a sense, Mechanical Drawing, with its emphases on presentation and precision gave to those who took it an introduction to aesthetic evaluation. Even geometry helped in this regard. There was not, however, an emphasis on design in the curriculum, with neither art appreciation courses nor engineering courses (although we did have some of its rudiments in General Science). To be sure, art was taught in the first two Forms, but it was studio art, and there were no regularly scheduled Upper School courses in art appreciation or aesthetic evaluation. Computer Science, which could have contributed much in this regard, was not, of course, even a discipline at this time.

Moses Brown also taught values in the classroom. Whether it was Odell telling us to act maturely, or Raines advocating personal standards of responsibility, or Herman reminding us that there were high levels of expectation, or Whitford invoking precision in linguistic accuracy, or Paxton affirming the importance of intellectual honesty, or these instructors and so many others (like Fuller, Taber, Full, and Pratt) themselves demonstrating a genuine standard of excellence in the classroom, there came across to us not only a set of defensible values but also a sense of quality and commitment: teachers cared—and whatever else may have gotten through, this always did.

One important value Moses Brown taught was good citizenship. The American history courses, going way back into the Lower School, taught some civics (albeit mostly informally) and the unfolding processes of American democracy throughout its history; Mr. Raines provided a capstone course for all this in our senior year. But citizenship as taught at Moses Brown went far beyond courses in civics. Many courses right across the curriculum gave us components of what today has come to be called cultural literacy, closely related in many ways to a larger concept of citizenship. The Quaker tradition reinforced civic obligation and a tradition of civic advocacy. Current events and presentations about the great issues of the day lay at the heart of a large percentage of Chapel talks. Discussion, debates, and our own recurrent elections to leadership positions in every sort of organization were an unquestioned part of school life.

Even more important: I think it can be argued that there was a very strong undercurrent throughout the whole operating ethos of the School that it was the duty of the citizen to try to improve society—to observe its workings critically, to become involved, to try to make a difference, to try to make things work better. In a very quiet way the School taught us a strong sense of patriotism, not the unexamined "Rah! Rah!" kind, but a deeper sense of patriotism, grounded in traditional liberal values (freedom, democracy, equality, justice), based on pride in historic American accomplishments (both social and economic)—a patriotism that was not blind to America's faults, but that motivated citizens to make America stronger and better, both at home and in the eyes of the world. This was accompanied by the very important set of beliefs that citizens could understand how political and social systems operated, and that with such understanding, they could work cooperatively with others to help improve the country. People—including us—could make a difference. Perhaps our understanding was more than a bit naive, but our motivation to achieve better results ourselves (or to applaud others who did) was genuine. In this respect, we were familiar with corruption and were prepared to combat it, but we were strangers to demagoguery beyond a few brief mentions in ancient contexts.

As noted, another value was excellence. In most cases, although admittedly not all, there was a strong emphasis in the classroom on excellence, not only in terms of motivating us to perform better, but in terms of praising quality in larger historical and cultural terms: great inventions, good literature, historic achievements, generous contributions to society, great sacrifices, and heroic attempts, even if they were unsuccessful. This created an atmosphere that praised effort and achievement. Again, we were not beaten over the head with this, but the implications of classroom value judgments in this regard were unmistakable, and they carried beyond the classroom to our organizations, our publications, and to our playing fields.

We were very fortunate—not only to attend a school like Moses Brown, but to have the strong support of our parents, most of whom were very interested in participating in our educational growth. They were committed to us. Not only were they willing to send us to a private school, but also they were willing to take the time to interest themselves in what we were doing there and to share with us their own experiences and knowledge. We also had many opportunities to witness this level of interest among the parents of our classmates. They paid attention and they encouraged. This level of engagement was a very important resource and motivator. On many dimensions we were truly privileged.

Finally, related to both values and skills acquired at Moses Brown in the Upper School, there was a set of interpersonal and organizational talents that emerged not only from classroom contact, but from social relations outside the classroom, from our student organizations, from work on our publications, and from our athletics. These, too, were important parts of the educational process, and to them we now turn in Volumes II and III.

Appendices

Appendix I

The Upper School Setting

———

The study hall chamber contained about 175 student desks bolted to the floor in rows. On the north wall, there was an elevated large desk with a bell on it for the study hall master, and in front of the room on the east wall there was a lectern desk, behind which sat the Chapel speakers. The wall behind this desk was paneled in yellow oak. There was a plaque in the middle, with Moses Brown World War I veterans on it, as I recall. Above the center woodwork was the clock. On either side were large heating ducts rising from the floor, also covered with the same oak paneling, each surmounted by a bust. Burke was inappropriately on the left as we faced them; I forget who his counterpart was on the right. Several other busts stared out from high shelves around the room. Agassiz, I think, resided above and to the right of the rear exit from the room. The paneled right heating duct was separated from the central podium by the door going into Room 1.

In the front left hand corner of the room as we sat at our desks, and next to the door, was a small set of blackboards at right angles, which met in the corner. These were used for writing the day's announcements and other important messages. When Mr. Whittemore Whittier, a graduate of Haverford, with a master's degree from Harvard, and a relative of the poet, joined us in the Fifth Form as Assistant Headmaster, he used to pin up lists of students he wished to see in his office on the door jamb next to the blackboards.

The student seats were divided into two sections, a front section for the First through Third Forms, and a rear section for the Fourth and Fifth Forms. Thus we started in the front ranks and proceeded year by year through the middle ranks to the rear ranks in our senior year. These two sections were separated by a cross-aisle going north to south in front of the study hall master's desk. There were aisles between all the files of desks, except for those on the south wall of the study hall chamber, where two desks were adjacent, and you had to climb over your neighbor's hopefully unoccupied seat to get to your window-seat desk. There was also an aisle along the north side of the study hall room leading to the cross aisle, and a door near the rear in the southwest corner of the room that led to both a stairwell and a corridor across the archway, so you could walk in from the lounge area, proceed along the north wall, cross the room in the middle, north to south, then walk westward down an aisle between two files of desks, and then exit the rear door to the left into the corridor that led across the arch.

The entire Upper School met every morning for Chapel, each student at his desk and the boarders on benches along the north wall. We then broke into a series of classes with study hall times between them. My recollection is that the classes were relatively short in the Eighth Grade, and there were quite a few of them. I think each class was forty minutes. There was a five-minute break for passing. In later years, the School went to fifty-minute classes—either in our Second or Third Form. In the Upper School we had a buzzer system to announce the end of a period, with buzzers all over the building.

In our freshman year, as I recall, there were thirteen classrooms in the Upper School building, plus the art studio, the shop, the music room in the power house, and Alumni Hall, where Upper School students met for a few classes, such as Bible.

First, there was the Arch room located above the arch connecting the Lower School building (now the Gifford Building) and the Upper School buildings. The room itself was on the west side of the space above the arch, with a corridor on the east side. Then, east of study hall on the south side of the building were three relatively spacious rooms with doors opening into the lounge area. The westernmost of these, Room 1, also had a door

The Upper School Setting

opening directly into study hall. In our freshman year this was principally the province of Mr. Fuller. Room two, to the east of Room 1, was the domain of Mr. Paxton, but was used by other English teachers, including Mr. Taber and Mr. Corbett. Room 3 beyond, was used by Mr. Raines, but also by other history teachers.

There were five rooms leading off the North Corridor, which ran north from the west end of the lounge area, past a small stairwell on its right which led down to the chemistry lab below. Room 4 was the first on the left, and was used by several teachers from different departments, including Mr. Roberts who taught us math during our First Form, Mr. Bennett, who taught us English in the Third Form, and Mr. Justin who taught us German in the Fourth Form. Room 6 was in the middle on the left, and was the domain of Mr. Cate for the first three years we were there. The last room on the left, Room 8, was used by various teachers from different departments, including Mr. Tinker, who taught us math in the Second Form; Mr. Nichols, who us taught English, also in the Second Form; and Mr. Pratt, who taught us History in the Fourth Form.

On the right side of the North Corridor, beyond the staircase mentioned above, was Room 5, the domain of Mr. Whitford, who taught French in our upper three Forms. Finally at the end of the corridor on the right was Room 7, the biology lab, the province of Mrs. Full, who taught us General Science there in the Second Form and also biology in the Third Form until the Thomas Science Building opened in the Winter Term of that year.

On the upper floor of the North Wing (the Third Floor, if the ground level is considered to be the first floor, with study hall being on the second floor), there was also a classroom on the right (east) side of the corridor—Room 12. We had Latin with Mr. Fuller in this room during our Second and Third Forms, and later we worked there on the *Quaker*, which he advised.

During the first years we were there, the chemistry lab was located in the basement of the North Wing, and was reached by the above-mentioned stairwell near the lounge. Its aromas would occasionally drift upwards and fill the North Corridor with the appetizing odor of rotten eggs. This was probably Room 9. The physics lab, I believe, was next to the chemistry lab.

Downstairs under study hall was Room 11, Mr. Herman's Ape Den, in the northwest corner of the first floor. Back and to the left of it as you faced it (also under study hall), was the door to a smaller classroom, Room 10, used by various teachers, including Mr. Jansen, who taught English to upper formers (while we were lower formers), Mr. Westland, who taught us ancient history in the Second Form, and later Mrs. Sadlier, who taught us speed-reading in the Fourth or Fifth Forms.

When the three-room Thomas Science Building was built west of the Upper School main building (it opened in January 1958 during our Third-Form year), it housed (south to north) biology, chemistry, and physics, with each room equipped with lab facilities. It no longer stands. The Studio and Shop were described above. The Music Room was the west half of the Power House (it had housed the dynamos when the School generated its own electricity). Its walls were painted brick, and I remember that it had risers on which stood chairs with desk arms. These chairs could be removed so the Glee Club could practice on the risers.[326] It contained blackboards and at least one piano down front.

---

326 Pictures in the Catalogue from a slightly earlier era show no risers. Either they were installed later (or my memory is incorrect on this point) but I will stand by my recollection.

Appendix II

The Class of 1960

Graduating Members of the Class of 1960

Stanwood Francis Armington (10-12)
William Sisson Barrett (2-12)
William James Brehm (8-12)
Alan Ira Brenner (10-12)
Glidden Lantry Brooks (10-12)
Clifford Waters Brown, Jr. (3-12)
Richard Bennett Buckley (9-12)
Wilfred Ignatius Carney, Jr. (8-12)
David St. John Chaffee (10-12)
Allan Jay Cokin (9-12)
Edward Alan Corris (6-12)
Jonathan Leeds Costa (9-12)
Alan Tebbe Crandon (11-12)
Richard William Crawford (11-12)
Charles William Criss, Jr. (9-12)
Stephen Leigh Dashoff (10-12)
Lyman Alan Davenport (10-12)
Daniel Owen DeVlieg (9-12)
Ralph John DiLibero (8-12)
Stephen Ames Estee (9-12)
Barry Wald Fain (3-12)
Jeffrey Lee Forman (8-12)
Hernan Ramon Franco (8-12)

Bruce Alexander Henkle (9-12)
Alan Holoff (9-12)
James Emery Hooper (12-12)
Stephen Alexander Koffler (6-12)
Joseph Howard Ladd, Jr. (8-12)
David Saunders London (10-12)
Roy Martin Maletz (10-12)
Edward William Malley, III (10-12)
Vincent Anthony Marcello (PP-12)
Robert John Marshall (8-12)
Jan Rodney Moyer (12-12)
William Newton Murdock (10-12)
John Richard Nixon (4-12)
James Howard Ottmar (9-12)
Peter Ross Parker (9-12)
Bruce Hayward Perry (11-12)
James Herbert Rigney, Jr. (11-12)
Mark Stuart Saklad (PP-12)
Herbert Covell Sawyer (6-12)
Frederic Willard Schwartz, Jr. (8-12)
Cleveland Bryden Smith (10-12)
John Austin Tomlinson (12-12)
Wellington Gerry Tow (10-12)

Upper School Members of the Class of 1960, Never in Lower School, Who Left the Class before the 1960 Graduation

Iqbal Ahmed (8-8)
Brian Toye Broderick (8-8)
Clinton R. DeConti, Jr. (11-11)
Philip Robert DeSano (8-9) (To Class of 1959)
Stephen Edwin Kindelan (8-8)
Ernest August Meuser, Jr. (9-11)
Kenneth Robert Neal (8-8) (To Class of 1961)
Frank Norton Ray (11-11)
Kempton D. Razee (11-11)
Frederick William Walters II (9-11)
Silas Charter Weeks (9-9)

Members of the Class of 1960 Who Graduated from the Lower School, June 1955

Frank Andrew Abella (7-11)
William Sisson Barrett (2-12)
William Theodore Batchelder (1-3; 6-7)
Clifford Waters Brown, Jr. (3-12)
Vincent Joseph Buonanno (7-8) (to Class of 1961)
Frederic Read Chesebrough (1-7)
Thomas Laing Clark (PP-9)
Edward Alan Corris (6-12)
Peter Briggs Darrah (PP-8)
Robert Arthur Dean (6-9)
John Walter Dieroff (5-8)
Barry Wald Fain (3-12)
William John Henry Fischer, III (PP-9)
Charles Kilvert Gifford (6-7)
William Holland Drury Goddard (PP-7)
James Vincent Hoye, Jr. (5-7)
Harrison Hibbert Huntoon (PP-9)
George Williams Kilton, Jr. (2-10)
Stephen Alexander Koffler (6-12)
Bancroft Littlefield, Jr. (PP-9)
Vincent Anthony Marcello (PP-12)
William Clarke Stevens Mays, III (6-7)
Leon Andrew Najarian (5-9)
John Richard Nixon (4-12)
Stephen Alan Oster (6-8)
Mark Stuart Saklad (PP-12)
Peter Amyor Sanderson (7-9)
Herbert Covell Sawyer (6-12)
Robert Morse Saywell, Jr. (6-9)
David Helmar Stenmark (6-10)
Theodore Herman Vetterlein, III (4-7)
Alan Blair Volkman (7-9)
Edwin Parson Young, III (7-11)

Lower School Members of the Class of 1960, Who Left the Class before Lower School Graduation in 1955

David Hall Barstow (1-2)
Peter Michael Eteson Bergne (5-5)
Alan Garrott Cameron (4-5)
David Collin Campbell (2-4)
Maurice Chen (3-3)
Stuart William Eddy (PP-1)
Joseph Franklin, Jr. (4-6)
Henry Louis Lavaur (PP-6)
Leo Henry Leary, III (PP-1; 4-4)

Pete Taft Moses (1-2)
Samuel Douglas Mott (4-7)
Glenn Bruce Neumann (PP-5)
Kent Howat Painter (5-6)
Jeffrey De Laval Plante (6-6)
Bruce Stephen Pansey (PP-4) (to Class of 1959)
Stephen Louis Spear (PP-3)

Index

Page numbers in *italics* indicate illustrations.

"A, B, and C - the Human Element in Mathematics" (Leacock), 307
Abe Lincoln in Illinois (Sherwood), 358
Abelard and Eloise, 363
Abella, Frank Andrew (Joe), 121, *168*, 198, 242, 272, 329–330, 396
Adams, John, 26, 80, 377
Adams, John Quincy, 376–377
"Add a Dash of Pity" (Ustinov), 315
Addams, Charles, 333
Addams, Jane, 26, 233
advanced placement courses, 171
"The Adventure of the Six Napoleons" (Doyle), 227
Aeneid (Virgil), 270
African Americans, race, and racism
    abolitionist Quakers, 3, 142
    Brown v. Board of Education, 161
    Civil Rights Movement, ix, 161, 361, 371
    Dred Scott Decision, 367
    historical study of, 142, 143, 161
    Jim Crow, ix, 143, 161, 374–375
    1950s era and, ix, 160–161
    slavery and slave trade, 80, 139, 142, 161, 371, 377
    textbooks, African Americans in, 26, 197
Agassiz, Louis, 391
Ahmed, Iqbal, *168,* 329n283, 396
Alcott, Bronson, 323
Alcott, Louisa May, 26, 323
Alfred the Great, 113
algebra, 102, 134, 170, 215, 216–219, 251–254, 299, 301, 302, 344, 345, 349, 383
Algebra Course 2 (1955), 251n180
Allen, J. Drisko (Dick)
    admission of C. Brown to Moses Brown School and, xxiii, xxiv
    at Commencement exercises, 154, 155
    under Mr. Cunningham, 243
    First Intermediate and, 63
    Fourth Intermediate and, 146, 151, 153
    F. Fuller compared, 187
    as head of Lower School, xxiii, 3–6
    J. Jeffers and, 318
    office of, 7n11
    photos of, *2, 5*
    Second Intermediate and, 90
    as summer camp supervisor, 122, 129
    Third Intermediate and, 115, 116, 117
    Third Primary and, 44
Allen, Mrs. J. Drisko, 122, 154
Alliance Francaise, 294
"*Alouette, Gentille Alouette,*" 58
Alumni Hall
    Bible class in, 170n121, 207, 392
    Book Fair in, 27, 100–101

Christmas Pageant in, 40–41
classical busts in, 156
Commencement exercises in, 154, 156
Eisenhower's inauguration watched on television in, *82*
fair/exhibition/exposition in, 35, 60, 64
Glee Club concert in, 207
lectures in, 360–361
movies and TV programs shown in, 3, 90, 313
music classes in, 61, 88
"America (My Country 'Tis of Thee)," 17–18, 32, 155
"America The Beautiful," 32, 155
American history, 26, 27, 53, 79–80, 109, 140–143, 159, 170, 343, 363–377
American Mathematical Association, 345
American Pageant (Bailey), 370–371, 373, 374–375
American Revolution, 79, 80, 138, 141, 365n315, 372, 377
America's Cup, 125
Amherst College, 238, 284, 288, 293
Amos and Andy (radio program), xx
Ancient History (Robinson, 1951), 221
Ancient Peoples (Morey), 221, 222
ancient/classical history, 53, 104, 106, 110–112, 113, 159, 170, 191–192, 215, 219–224
And Not to Yield (Villiers), 99
Anderson, Arthur, 129n101
Anderson, John B., 174n125, 398
Andover (prep school). *See* Phillips Andover
Angilly, Ethel B., R.N., *378*
Anglicanism/Episcopalianism/Church of England, 178, 239, 253n188
Anna Karenina (Tolstoy), 227
Anthony, Gus, 333
Ape Den (classroom), 247, 394
Apostrophes Club, 356
Appalachian Mountain Club, 64
Applegate, Bill, xv
Arch Room, 169, 170n121, 175, 392

Archimedes, 224
the Arena (Rhode Island Auditorium), Providence, 65–66
Arent, Arthur, 358
Aristophanes, 223
Aristotle, 110, 159, 223
arithmetic. *See* math
Armington, Stanwood Francis, *321, 342,* 356, 395
Armstrong, Edmund F., Jr. (Ted), xiv, 250n178
Armstrong, Edmund F., Sr. ("Army"), 129, 172, *378*
Arnold, Matthew, 312, 358–359
Around the World in Eighty Days (Verne), 99
art
   in First Form, 170n121, 203–204
   in First Intermediate, 61–62
   in First Primary, 15
   in Fourth Intermediate, 144
   in Lower School, 162
   in Second Form, 203–204, 215–216
   in Second Intermediate, 62, 86–87
   in Second Primary, 15
   in Third Intermediate, 114–115
   in Third Primary, 30–32, *31*
   in Upper School, 170n121, 171, 382–383, 386
"Art for Art's Sake" (Arnold), 312
Aslakson, Ken, xv
astronomy, 114, 144, 234
Atlantic Monthly, 315
atom bomb. *See* nuclear weapons
Atomic Pearls, 175
Atwood, Lois, xv
Atwood, Preston, xv
Audubon Society, 64–65, 84–85, 127
The Autobiography of Benjamin Franklin, 197, 257
automobiles. *See* transportation and automobiles
Avon Theater, Providence, 90
awards. *See* prizes
Awful-Awful frappe (or cabinet), Newport Creamery, Wayland Square, Providence, 151
axiomatic proof, 300–301

Index 401

Bachman, Frances M., xxiii, *2,* 15, *21,* 21–22, 25, 29
Bacon, Francis, 306, 359
Bailey, Thomas, 370–371, 373, 374–375
Bain, Tommy, 123
Balboa, Vasco Núñez de, 79
ball toss, 43–44
Barrett, Amy, ii
Barrett, Bill (William Sisson)
   on basement of Lower School, 7n11
   in Boy Scouts, 332, 333
   at Commencement exercises, 155, 156n115
   in Fifth Form, *342,* 351
   in First Form, *168,* 175, 178, 181, 184n135
   in First Intermediate, 48n45, 49, 60, 65–66, 67, 68
   in Fourth Form, 250, 313, 320
   in Fourth Intermediate, 134, 140, 155
   graduating member of Class of 1960, 395
   graduating member of Lower School Class of 1955, 396
   higher education and career, 23n27
   pencils, on younger students' restriction to, 8
   in Pre-Primary through Second Primary, 11–15
   in Second Form, 234
   in Second Intermediate, 74, 81, 84, 85, 90
   as source of information, xiii
   on sports, 145–146, 147, 147n112, 151
   at summer camp, 121–122, 329n283, 334
   in Third Form, 242, 248n176, 252, 259, 278, 288, 289, 290, 293
   in Third Intermediate, 95, 97n72, 102, 149–150
   in Third Primary, 18, 22, 23n27, 34, 37, 145–146
Barrett, Mrs. John (mother of Bill), xii, 140, 229
Barstow, David Hall, 397
"Bartleby the Scrivener" (Melville), 259
Barton, Clara, 26

baseball
   at Father and Son Day, 45
   Little League, 121
   in Lower School, 147, 150
   Red Sox, xx, 45
   softball, 146, 147, 149
   on television, 91
   World Series, 90, 137
baseball cards, 66
A Basic German Reader (1943), 275
Basic Ideas of Mathematics (1953), 133
basketball game, class outing to, 65–66
Batchelder, Bill[y] (William Theodore), 37, 121, 122, 129, 149, 396
Bates College, 224n160
"A Battle over the Teacups" (short story), 196
Beard, Charles, 373
Becker, Rhonda, xv
Beecham, Sir Thomas, 89–90
Beecham's Pills song, 89–90
Beethoven, Ludwig von, 86
Bell, Alexander Graham, 26
Belmont Hill School, 35n35, 215
Beloit College, 15n19, 203n150
Benet, Stephen Vincent, 257, 258
Bennett, E. Kenneth ("Buzzy Bennett"), 247, 254–261, *255,* 312, 313, 314, 315n365, 393
Benny, Jack, xx
Bentham, Jeremy, 155
Bergne, Peter Michael Eteson, 397
Berry, Mr. (at Mapleville public school), xxiiin6
Bessemer steel process project, 143
Bible class, 170n121, 171, 207–211, 209n153, 392
Bibles sold at Book Fair, 101
bicycle club, 151, 330
bicycles, 67
Biddeford Pool, ME, xxi
The Big Story (TV show), 91
Bikini H-Bomb explosion, 137
"Billy Budd" (Melville), 259
biology
   memorization exercises in, 108
   in Upper School, 170, 232, 234–235, 247, 261–267, 384, 386

Bird Room, Moses Brown School, xxiii
birthday parties, 45–46, 114, 186
Bixby, William C., 238
Black Americans. *See* African Americans, race, and racism
blackboards, 8, 18–19, 30, 206
Blackmore, Richard Doddridge, 135
Blackwell, D. J., *378*
Blackwell, Elizabeth, 197
Blank, Barry, 149
Bleak House (Dickens), 197
Blues (intramural sports), 146
Bluhm, Eleanor (Ellie; Mrs. William T. (Ted) Bluhm), 53, 93n71, 94–95, *95*, 104, 106, 109–114, 179, 223, 376
boarders at Moses Brown School, 22, 129n101, 172, 185n139, 212, 255, 281, 392
boarding/prep schools, Moses Brown students departing for, 215, 216, 237–239, 241–242, 381
Boer War, 61
"*Bonne Nuit, Bonne Nuit*" (Hugo), 58
Book Fair, 27, 77, 100–101, *136*, 229, 293
book reports and reviews, 27, 51, 73, 99, 135, 197, 201, 226, 258, 259, 357
Book-of-the-Month Club, 99
"Boomalay, Boomalay, Boomalay, Boom" (Lindsay), 199
Boone, Daniel, 26
Borge, Bernhard, 349n304
Borge, Victor, 89
Boston Braves, 91
Boston Latin School, xxiii, 191
Boston Museum of Fine Arts, 86
Boston Tea Party, 80
Boston University, 114–115, 216, 220
Boston University Law School, 174n125
Boston University Medical School, 331n290
Bowditch, Nathaniel, 233
Boy Scouts, 67, 68, 121, 329n283, 332–334
"A Boy's Will" (Longfellow), 258
Braddock, General George, 90
Brando, Marlon, 227

Brehm, Bill (William James)
  appendectomy, 269
  college applications, 269
  in Fifth Form, 341, 367
  in First Form, 195, 204–205
  in Fourth Form, 302, 316
  graduating member of Class of 1960, 395
  higher education and career, 221n158
  Mr. Howe visiting, 269
  photos of, *168, 342*
  in Second Form, 221, 222–223
  as source of information, xiii
  in summer vacations, 330
  in Third Form, 259, 267–269
Brenner, Al (Alan Ira), *264,* 341, *342,* 395
Bricker Amendment, 115
Brinton, Crane, 325n277
Broderick, Brian Toye, 396
Brooks, Lanny (Glidden Lantry), 334, 341, *342,* 395
Broun, Heywood, 307
Brown, Clifford, grandparents of, xx, xxi, xxii, 66, 126, 127n99, 257, 335
Brown, Clifford W., Sr. (father of C. Brown)
  baseball, interest in, xx, 45
  on child's book about Philadelphia, 27
  corner cupboard built by C. Brown, transportation of, 237
  crossword puzzles, assisting C. Brown with, 115
  Mr. Cunningham and, 242
  "Darius," on pronunciation of, 222
  driving C. Brown to school/school trips, 66, 70–71
  educational background, xxiii, 191, 230n166
  Eisenhower/Stevenson election (1952) and, 81–82
  enlarging drawings, teaching C. Brown technique for, 184
  erector set of C. Brown and, xxi
  Father and Son Day, 43, 44, 45
  Mr. Fuller and, 189

Index 403

  limerick taught to C. Brown by, 198
  V. Marcello's father and, 66
  math and, 49, 71, 72
  occupation and employment of, xx, xxii, 77, 139, 241
  Mr. Odell and, xvi, 185
  pipe stand made by C. Brown for, 62
  relatives and, 41, 43
  on Russian novels, 227
  school parties hosted by, 186, 187
  Union Station, visit to, 35
  vocabulary learned from, 354
  Miss Wilson and, 19
Brown, Mrs. Clifford W., Sr. (Helen Steere Brown, mother of C. Brown)
  Book Fair, involvement in, 27, 100–101, 229
  class outings, involvement in, 67, 86
  driver's license for German exchange student obtained by, 351
  electric typewriter used by C. Brown for school projects, 183
  gavel made by C. Brown for, 206
  hairpin used to replace cotter pin in Model T, 337
  presidential election button collection of, 81
  Mrs. Raines, disagreement with, 371
  relatives and, xx, xxii, 62, 125n97
  school parties hosted by, 46, 114, 186
  school supplies provided by, 30, 44
  Miss Wilson and, 19
Brown, Clifford Waters, Jr., xv–xvii, 398. *See also specific grades/years, from* Third Primary
  admission to Moses Brown School, xxiii–xxiv
  alibi, denial of, 71
  attendance slips taken to office by, 116–117
  before attending Moses Brown School, xix–xxiii
  Beecham's Pills song, 89–90
  birthday parties of, 45–46
  in Boy Scouts, 67, 68, 121, 329n283, 332–334

  braces and orthodontia, 48
  Miss Chappell's encouragement of, 70
  Chepachet, RI, family farm at, xxii–xxiii, 45, 62, 66–67, 126–128, 226, 335–340, 343
  class newspaper in Third Intermediate, involvement in, 115
  as class officer, 84, 116, *168,* 186
  classmates and friendships, 22–23, 241–242
  clay snake made by, 64
  college applications, 246, 248
  at Commencement exercises, 154, 155
  corner cupboard built by, 235–237
  Cuba, Panama, and Colombia, trip to (1952), 68, 186
  on David (biblical king), 209
  Delphian, as historian of, 341, 343, 362, 363
  early childhood illnesses of, xxii, 35
  essays and other compositions by, 28, 51, 73–74, 98–99, 201–202
  geography bee won by, 109–110
  German exchange student (Uwe Massmann) living with, 351
  graduating member of Class of 1960, 395
  graduating member of Lower School Class of 1955, 396
  at Harvard, 225, 238, 246, 325n277, 326, 328, 351, 398
  "Home News" issued by, 28–29
  informant, Mr. Cunningham's attempt to recruit as, 244
  interviewing F. Pratt for *Quaker,* 322–323
  lathe, articles made on, 205–206
  Latin, father's assistance with, 191
  lunch, going home for, 18, 67
  on Memorial Day in Webster, MA, 257–258
  mild dyslexia of, 75
  money, fellow students asking for loans of, 243–244
  Mosaic, as editor of, 255, 341, 343
  naps, avoidance of, 18–19

novel, failed attempt to write, 54
number computation game taught by father to, 49–50
Mr. Odell on ponderousness of, xvi, 185
papier-mâché bottle made by, 30–31
penmanship, failures at, 30, 53
photos, *168, 342*
pig, blind drawing of, 67–68
pig breadboard created by, 35
poison ivy contracted by, 226–227
political science, interest in, 39, 81, 83
prep school urged on parents of, 239
pronunciation issues of, 100
Quaker, as executive editor of, 341, 343
Republicanism of parents, 39
sports, involvement in, 146, 282, 341, 343
summer vacations and jobs, 121, 123, 125, 126–128, 331–332, 335–340
television and movies, access to, 91–92
Third Form, difficulties in, 241–242
tonsils, removal of, xxi
The Union (recess sports), involvement in, 150–151
Mrs. Wilson, difficult relationship with, 19–22, 25
Brown, Frederick D. (Fritz; cousin of C. Brown, Sr.), 257–258
Brown, John, 142, 155
Brown, Moses, 1–3, 139
Brown, Obadiah, 1, 74
Brown University
　C. Brown considering attendance at, 351
　Carr's catering for, 186n140
　college faculty of, 95, 113, 221, 239, 365n315
　Dexter Asylum land bought for athletic grounds, 268, 333
　East Side Monthly and, 201n149
　geology display room at, 144
　grandfather of Chad Gifford playing football at, 150
　Harvard-Brown hockey game, 65
　Lower School students cutting across campus of, 67
　Model UN at, 255
　Moses Brown from originating family of, 1
　Moses Brown School alumni attending, 21n26, 81n67, 123n93, 246, 291n232, 308nn249–250, 331n290, 341n297, 345, 365
　Moses Brown School teachers educated at, 219, 232, 351, 362, 363
　Sayles Hall, standardized testing at, 345
　students hired by Moses Brown as sports assistants, 146–147, 149
Brown v. Board of Education, 161
Brownell, Marilyn, ii, xv, 398
Browning, Robert, 360
Bryant, William Cullen, 258
Buckley, Dick (Richard Bennett), xiv, *342,* 395
Bulldogs (intramural sports), 150
Bunsen burners, 62, 203, 322
Buonanno, Vinny (Vincent Joseph), 65, 122, 137, *168, 208,* 396
Burgess, Perry, 197
Burke, Edmund, 391
Burnham, Dave (David), 8, 295
Burnside, General Ambrose, 139, 142
Burton, Ted, 174
"Bus Stop" (Steinbeck), 259
Byron, George Gordon, Lord, 307

Cabot, Henry, 79
The Caine Mutiny Court Martial (play), 228
calculus, 344, 383
The California Gold Rush (McNeer), 51
Calvinism, 252, 374
Calvo, Cait, xv
Cambridge University, England, 209
Cameron, Alan Garrott, 397
Camp Bauercrest, Amesbury, MA, 121
Camp Brunonia, Casco, ME, 122
Camp Monomoy, East Brewster, MA, 121

Index 405

Camp Tecumseh, Center Harbor, Lake Winnipesaukee, NH, 122
Camp Westwood, Coventry, RI, 121
Camp Wigwam, Harrison ME, 122
Camp Wyonegonic, Denmark, ME, 122
Camp Yawgoog, Hopkinton, RI, 121
Campanella Football Field and track, 246–247
Campbell, David Collin, 147, 397
Canada, bicycle club tour to, 151, 330
Canobie Lake, NH, xxii
Capek, Karel, 358
Carney, Bill (Wilfred Ignatius), Jr., xiii, *168*, 329n284, 341, *342*, 354, 367n317, 395
Carpenter, Russell Higson, Jr. (Russ), xiv, 229, 280, 283, 286–289, 291–292, 294, 307n248, 309–313, 353
Carrington House, Providence, 140
Carroll, Lewis, 200
Carr's (catering company), Providence, 186
cars. *See* transportation and automobiles
Carver, George Washington, 26
"Casey at the Bat" (Thayer), 198
cat skeleton, Lower Gymnasium, 44
Cate, Arthur W., *58,* 159, 170, 238, 247, 271–277, *273,* 315, 317, *378,* 380, 381
Catholicism, 62, 369
Cavanaugh, Joe, 23n27
"The Celebrated Jumping Frog of Calaveras County" (Twain), 258
Celtics, 65–66
Centennial History of Moses Brown School (Kelsey), viiin1, xii
Chaffee, Dave St. John, xiii, 308–309, 310, 311, *342,* 395
Chapel
 addresses at, 172–175, 210, 212, 361
 biblical texts at, 210
 eulogy for Madame Warge at, 292
 student criticism of headmaster in, 246
 in study hall room, 171, 212, 213, 391
 in Upper School, 170n121, 171–175, 206–207, 392

Chappell, Elsie E., *2*, 26, 69–73, *70,* 75, 76, 82, 83, 86, 87, 94
Charlemagne, 324–325
Chase, Edith Buffam, 142
cheating, 29
chemistry
 Fifth Form, advanced chemistry in, 343, 346–349, 350
 in Fourth Form, 299, 318–322
 in Fourth Intermediate, 144
 in Upper School, 170, 232, 386, 393
Chen, Maurice, *36,* 39, 397
Chepachet, RI, C. Brown's family farm at, xxii–xxiii, 45, 62, 66–67, 126–128, 226, 335–340, 343
Chesebrough, Derric (Frederic Read), 122, 123, 139, 146, 154, 215, 396
chicken pox outbreak, Third Primary, 39
Childs, Laura C., *2*
A Child's History of the World (1951), 110, 112, 113
Choate (prep school), 215, 238
chocolate pudding, Mr. Howe's fondness for, 204–205
Christmas, writing histories of, 51
Christmas cards, making, 59, 87, 203
Christmas carols, 40, 89–90, 227
Christmas decorations, making, xxiiin6
Christmas Pageant, 3, 17, 32, *38, 39*–41, 87
Christmas presents
 Book Fair and, 27
 making, 31, 35, 62
Church of England/Episcopalianism/Anglicanism, 178, 239, 253n188
Churchill, Winston, 41, 307, 363
Cicero, 192, 270
cinema. *See* movies
citizenship and civil obligation, teaching, 387
civil defense drills, 145
Civil Disobedience (Thoreau), 257
Civil Rights Movement, ix, 161, 361, 371
Civil War (American), 79, 80, 141, 142, 161, 180, 257–258, 325n278, 373
Civil War (British), 325
Clapp, David F., *378*

Clapp, Nicholas (Nick), xiv
Clark, Mrs. John (mother of Tommy), 229
Clark, Mr. John (father of Tommy), 334
Clark, Tom[my] (Thomas Lang)
  as Boy Scout, 332–334
  in First Form, *168*
  in First Intermediate, 67
  graduating member of Lower School Class of 1955, 396
  higher education and career, 35n35
  prep school, departure for, 215
  in Pre-Primary, 11
  in Second Form, 215
  in Second Intermediate, 80, 81, 83, 85
  as source of information, xiv
  in summer vacations, 124, 332–334
  in Third Intermediate, 95, 115, 116, 149
  in Third Primary, 18, 22, 35, *36, 37*, 45
Clarke, John, 138
Class of 1960. *See also specific school years*
  Fifth Form class photo, *342*
  50th Reunion of, xi–xii
  First Form class photo, *168*
  graduating and non-graduating members, 395–397
  size of, 8, 86, 170
  T. Whitford, yearbook dedicated to, 280, 296–297
class officers
  in First Form, *168*
  in Fourth Intermediate, 155
  in Second Intermediate, 84–85
  in Third Intermediate, 116
classical/ancient history, 53, 104, 106, 110–112, 113, 159, 170, 191–192, 215, 219–224
clay animals made for annual exhibition, 62, 63–64
clocks and timekeeping, 9, 18
The Cloister and the Hearth (Reade), 363
clothing. *See* dress
Clue (board game), 23, 123
Coddington, William, 138
Cody, Buffalo Bill, 26

Cokin, Allan Jay, 245–246, 255, 256, 259, 260, 324, 341, *342,* 361–362, 395
Colby College, 3, 187, 238, 311n257, 331n288
Cold War, communism, and Soviet Russia, ix, 82, 104–105, 107, 109, 145, 160–162, 180–181, 199, 306
Cole, Mrs. (at The Garden of Children school, Lawrence, MA), xxii
Cole, Leo H.
  as Lower School teacher, 33, 35, 44, 62, 63, 101, 115, 131, 144
  photos of, *34, 378*
  student recollections about, xiv
  as Upper School teacher, 170n121, 186, 195, 203
Coleridge, Samuel Taylor, 229
College Entrance Exams, 344
College Hill mural, the Studio, 62
college placement. *See also specific universities and colleges*
  classical emphasis and, 159
  successes of Moses Brown School in, 154, 238, 256, 381
  Upper School curriculum aimed at, 171
Colonial Daughters, 206
Columbia Business School, 15n18, 201n149
Columbia School of Architecture, 203n150, 204
Columbia University, 69, 131, 247
Columbus, Christopher, 26, 79
"Comfort" (Huxley), 359
comic books, 23
comma splice/comma blunder, 355–356
Commencement exercises, 32, 74–75, 87, 140, 154–156
communism and Soviet Union. *See* Cold War; McCarthy, Joe
Comodoro Rivadavia, Argentina, 179
comparative advantage, concept of, 180–181
composition, writing, and essays
  creative writing, 158, 314, 356–357
  in Fifth Form, 354–357, 361–362, 375

Index 407

in First Form, 195, 201–202
in First Intermediate, 51, 54, 64
in Fourth Form, 308, 314
in Fourth Intermediate, 137, 140
in German class, 318
in history class, 375
letters, how to write, 74
in Lower School, 158
in Second Intermediate, 73–74, 77
in Third Form, 259, 260
in Third Intermediate, 98–100
in Third Primary, 27–28
in Upper School, 158
computer science, absence of, 386
Conklin, Edwin, 359
Connell, Richard, 75–76, 227
Connolly, Bruce, xv
Conrad, Joseph, 303–304, 306, 312
conscientious objection, 173, 175
Constitution, U.S., 26, 51, 115–116, 138, 369, 372
Cook, Ruth N., 154, *378*
Coolidge, Calvin, 293
Coolidge, John, 293
Cooper, James Fenimore, 307
coordinate geometry, 344
Copley, John Singleton, 86
copper beech tree, as playground, 147
Corbett, W. Scott, 238, 299, 302–308, *303*, 313, 314, 343, 357, 358, 360, 380, 393
Cornell University, 221n158, 256n189
Corpus Christi College, Cambridge, England, 209
corridor duty, 154, 293
Corris, Mrs. (mother of Ed), 229
Corris, Ed (Edwin Alan), xiv, 120–121, 124, 129, *168*, 241–242, 329n283, *342*, 395, 396
Cortez, Hernan, 79
Corwin, Norman, 358
Costa, Jonathan Leeds, *342*, 377, 395
The Count of Monte Cristo (Dumas), 135
Country Day School, 150
"The Courtin'" (Lowell), 258
Cousey, Bob, 65
Coutanche, Phil, 41–42, *42*, 67
Coveney, Richard, 147, 150

Cox, Wally, 193
The Cradle of Liberty, 27
Cragged Mountain Farm, Freedom, NH, 121–122
Crandon, Al[an] Tebbe, xiv, 203–204, *342*, 395
Crane, Stephen, 258
Crawford, Dick (Richard William), xiv, *342*, 395
creative writing, 158, 314, 356–357
"The Cremation of Sam McGee" (Service), 198
Crevecour, Eugene de, 260–261
Crime and Punishment (Dostoevsky), 226
Criss, Mrs. (mother of Bill), 229
Criss, Bill (Charles William), Jr., xiv, 331, *342*, 395
Cromwell, Oliver, 325
Cronkite, Walter, 81
The Crucible (Miller), 259
Crusader Rabbit (TV show), 91
Cub Scouts, 67–68
Cullen, Florence S., 2, 93–97, *94*, 99, 100, 104n77, 114, 116, 189, 243
Cum Laude Society, 293
Cumberland Valley State Normal School, Shippensburg, PA, 21
Cunningham, Griselda H., 244–245, *245*
Cunningham, Robert N., 174, 175, 242–247, *243*, 295, 316, 322n271, 346–347, 351, 363
current events
Bricker Amendment, class newspaper article on, 115
Chapel addresses on, 174
Cold War, communism, and Soviet Russia, ix, 82, 104–105, 107, 109, 145, 160–162, 180–181, 199, 306
Eisenhower/Stevenson election (1952), ix, 80–82, *82*
Fifth Form, American history and government in, 343, 363–377
Fifth Form, English essay writing in, 357, 361–362
in First Form, 181
in Fourth Intermediate, 137

Mr. Herman on political parties, 249
Kennedy/Nixon election (1960), 369
Rhode Island, gubernatorial and senatorial elections of 1950 in, 39
senatorial elections of 1958, 249
in Third Intermediate, 109, 110
Truman election (1948), 39
Current Events (magazine), 81, 109
cursive writing, 53. *See also* penmanship
Czechoslovakia, mnemonic for spelling, 102

Daedalus (journal), 325n278
Dalgliesh, Ron, xiii
Damien of Molokai, 197
Darrah, Peter Briggs, *168,* 396
Dashoff, Steve (Stephen Leigh), 331, *342,* 395
Daughters of the American Revolution (DAR), 206
Davenport, Lyman Alan, 331, *342,* 395
David Copperfield (Dickens), 197
Davis, Ann, ii, xv
De Gaulle, Charles, 284
De Kruif, Paul, 358
de Soto, Hernando, 79
Dean, Bob (Robert Arthur), 121, 137, *168,* 178, 201, 242, 329n283, 396
Dean of School, E. Raines as, 175, 213, 220, 238, 242, 363
"Dear Lord and Father of Mankind" (Whittier), 74, 155, 258
"Death Be not Proud" (Donne), 360
death camps, Mr. Corbett as eye witness to, 305
"The Death of the Hired Man" (Frost), 360
deaths
　of Vin Marcello's father, 66
　of Madame. Warge, 60, 292
　of T. Whitford, 295
debate and oral skills, 228–229
Debate Club, 225, 229, 382
decimals, 71, 72, 133
Declamation Contest, 229, 283, 382
Declaration of Independence, 256
DeConti, Clinton R., Jr., 396

Defoe, Daniel, 99
Delphian (school literary magazine)
　C. Brown as historian of, 341, 343, 362, 363
　creative writing in, 357
　family/family experiences as central topic of, xx
　First Primary work in, 51
　Fourth Form work in, 312n263, 314
　Fourth Intermediate work in, 137
　Second Intermediate work in, 73
　as source for school history, xii
　Third Intermediate work in, 98, 99
demerit system, 152
"Democrat Party," improper use of, 102
DeQuincy, Thomas, 359
DeSano, Philip Robert, *168,* 396
determinants, 344
Detlefsen, Bruce B., 215
Developing Your Language, 50–51
"The Devil and Daniel Webster" (Benet), 258
DeVleig, Dan (Daniel Owen), xiv, 229, *342,* 395
Dewey, John, 233
Dewey, Thomas E., 81
Dewey decimal system, 202
Dexter Asylum, Providence, 268, 333–334
Dias, Bartolomeu, 79
Dick and Jane, 14, 15, 25, 190, 277
Dickens, Charles, 101, 132, 197, 363
Dickinson, Emily, 258, 307, 360
Dickinson College, 247
dictionaries, 29, 75
Dieroff, Jay, 122
Dieroff, John Walter, 45, 122, *168,* 329n284, 332, 396
DiLibero, Mrs. (mother of Ralph), 229
DiLibero, Ralph John, xiv, *168,* 229n164, 329n284, *342,* 395
DiMaggio, Dom, xx
DiMaggio, Joe, xx
discipline
　by J. Drisko Allen, in Lower School, 4–6
　Alsace and Lorraine, student jokes about, in French classes, 56

Index 409

in Chapel, 172, 175
Class of 1959 and, 310
confiscation of objects, 6
corridor duty, 154
demerit system and Saturday punishments, 152
dismissal from school, 295
in Fifth Form, 365–366
for fighting in class, 219
in First Form, 172, 175, 176, 178, 189
in First Intermediate, 48
in Fourth Form, 295, 310, 324
informants recruited by Mr. Cunningham, 242, 244
leaves of absence, 295
maturation of student perception of, 98
money, fellow students asking for loans of, 243–244
office, being sent to, 5–6
for passing notes, 116
recess, missing, 6, 116, 117
removal from class, 218, 279, 324, 365
Saturday punishments, 152, 366
in Second Form, 218, 221, 224, 238–239
in Second Intermediate, 70–71
smoking rules, 173–174
for snowball fighting, 46
sperm brought to biology class, 266
Mr. St. John, disciplinary issues under, 238–239
in study hall, 212–213
for talking in class, 218
in Third Form, 242, 270
in Third Intermediate, 94
in Third Primary, 19–22, 35, 164
by T. Whitford, 279, 286, 295–296
writing out a hundred times, 48
Discussion Club, 199
diversity of student body, 160, 211
Dodgers, 90
Donne, John, 360
Dorna (novel), 51
Dorr Rebellion, 138, 139
Dostoevsky, Fyodor, 226

Down to the Sea in Ships (movie), 90
Doyle, Arthur Conan, 135, 196, 227, 363
Dr. Doolittle books, 125
Drake, Sir Francis, 79
drama. *See* plays and theatricals
Drama in our Time (1948), 358
Dred Scott Decision, 367
dress
 at Christmas Pageant, *38,* 40
 at Commencement exercises, 156
 Cub Scout uniforms worn to school, 68
 of students, 14
 of teachers, 6, 248
Drexel University, 229n164
Drums Along the Mohawk (Edmond), 135
Dulles, John Foster, 318
Dumas, Alexandre, 135, 197
Durrenmatt, Freidrich, 349

Eagles (intramural sports), 150
Earlham College, Richmond, IN, 69, 193
earmuffs deposited in tree, 117
The East Side Monthly, 201n149
East Stroudsburg Teachers College, PA, 93
Eastman, Eleanor, *2,* 7n11, *13,* 13–14
Eaton, Peggy, 142, 367
The Echo (Boy Scout troop newspaper), 333
Eddy, Stuart William, 397
Edmond, Walter, 135
The Egyptian (novel), 53
Eiffe, Mary, xv
Eighth Grade. *See* First Form
Eisenhower, Dwight D., ix, 80–82, *82,* 371
El Capitan and the Corporal (Corwin), 358
elections, class. *See* class officers
elections, governmental. *See* current events
Elements of Style (Strunk and White), 355, 356
elevator shoes attributed to Mr. Pezet, 279

Eleventh Grade. *See* Fourth Form
Eliot, George, 227
Eliot, T. S., 360
Elizabeth II (queen of England), coronation of, x
Emerson, Ralph Waldo, 233, 258, 306
Encyclopedia of World History (Langer), 377
English. *See also* composition; grammar; literature; penmanship; reading; spelling; vocabulary
   in Fifth Form, 343, 351–363
   in First Form, 170n121, 195–202
   in First Intermediate, 50–52
   in Fourth Form, 299, 302–315
   in Fourth Intermediate, 135–137
   in Lower School versus Upper School, 158
   oral skills and debate, 228–229
   Queen's/Oxford English, not taught at Moses Brown, 275
   in Second Form, 215, 224–229
   in Second Intermediate, 73–76
   speed-reading and reading comprehension, 171, 232n168, 299, 315, 394
   in Third Form, 247, 254–261
   in Third Intermediate, 96–102
   in Third Primary, 25–29
   in Upper School, 170, 381, 382
   Upper School teachers compared, 312–313
Enriching Your Language (1951), 73
Ensign, Walter, xiv
Episcopalianism/Anglicanism/Church of England, 178, 239, 253n188
Erie Canal, 79, 141
essay writing. *See* composition, writing, and essays
Essays Old and New (1957), 306
Estee, Steve (Stephen Ames), xiv, *342*, 395
Ethan Frome (Wharton), 357
Euclidian geometry, 250, 344
Euripides, 159, 223
European history, 53, 105, 112–114, 159, 170, 299, 322–328, 350
examinations. *See* testing

excellence, as Moses Brown School value, 162–164, 388
Exercises in Writing Latin to Accompany Using Latin III (1957), 270n199
Exeter Academy, 40n38, 215, 239, 242
exhibitions/expositions. *See* fairs/exhibitions/expositions
Exploring Life Through Literature (1951), 227n162

faculty. *See* teachers at Moses Brown School
Fadiman, Clifton, 358
Fain, Barry Wald, xiii–xiv, 45, 115, 122, *168*, 201, 242, 250, 302, 329n283, *332*, 395, 396
Fain, Lyle, *321*
fairs/exhibitions/expositions. *See also* Book Fair
   in First Intermediate, 60, 62, 63–64
   Rhode Island Science Fair, 262, *321*
   in Third Primary, 35–37
Falklands War, 179
Father and Son Day, 43–45, 56, 108, 149
Father Damien of Molokai, 197
Faulkner, William, 259, 306
Field, Vic, xiv, 325n279
field trips and class outings
   bicycle club tour to Canada, 151, 330
   in First Intermediate, 65–66
   in Fourth Intermediate, 65–66, 139–140, 144
   from The Garden of Children school, Lawrence, MA, xxii
   geology display room at Brown University, 144
   Model UN expedition to New York, 246, 255, 343
   Purgatory Chasm, Boy Scott trip to, 334
   in Second Intermediate, 86, 87–88
   in Second Primary, 15
   in Third Primary, 35, 37
   T. Whitford leading, 293–294
Fields, W. C., 250

Index   411

Fifth Form (Twelfth Grade)
   advanced chemistry, 343, 346–349, 350
   American history and government, 343
   Class of 1960 senior photograph, *342*
   course load in, 171, 341, 343
   English, 343, 351–363
   extracurricular activities, 341–343
   geometry in, 251
   German, 343
   math, 343–346
   testing in, 344, 345, 350, 351, 353, 370, 375, 376–377
Fifth Grade. *See* Second Intermediate
50th Reunion of Class of 1960, xi–xii
"The Fifty-First Dragon" (Broun), 307
films. *See* movies
Finding New Neighbors, 26
finger painting, 32
Finley, John H., 225
fire drills, 18, 145
"First Command" (Conrad), 303
A First Course in German (1952), 275
First Form (Eighth Grade), 169–213
   ancient history in Latin class, 191–192
   art classes, 170n121, 203–204
   Bible class, 170n121, 207–211
   Chapel, 170n121, 171–175, 206–207
   Class of 1960 photo, *168*
   class officers, *168,* 186
   course load in, 170n121, 171
   English, 170n121, 195–202
   geography, 170n121, 175–187
   Geography Banana Party, 185–187
   grading in, 182–183
   homework in, 182, 183, 192, 212, 213
   introduction to Upper School, 169–171
   Latin, 170n121, 187–192
   math, 170n121, 193–195
   music, 170n121, 206–207
   science, 170n121
   sentence diagramming in, 97
   shop class, 170n121, 204–206
   study hall, 211–213
   teachers in, 170n121
   testing in, 183, 187, 192, 195, 198, 200
First Intermediate (Fourth Grade), 47–68
   activities, 64–68
   art, 61–62
   birthday parties, 45
   exams, 49, 59
   French, 56–60
   geography, 54–56
   history, 53–54
   homework in, 49, 52, 54, 59
   language, reading, and spelling, 50–52
   location of, 7, 47
   math in, 23n29, 48–50
   music, 60–61
   penmanship, 52–53
   science, 60
   shop, 61–63
   sports in, 146, 147
   teachers of, 47–48
   testing in, 49, 59
First Primary (First Grade), 7, 13–14
The First Transcontinental Railroad, 73
First World War. *See* World War I
Fischer, Bill[y] (William John Henry), III
   at Commencement exercises, 155, 156n115
   in First Intermediate, 66, 67
   graduating member of Lower School Class of 1955, 396
   higher education and career, 40n38
   in Kindergarten through Second Primary, *12,* 13
   prep school, departure for, 215
   in Second Form, 215, 221
   in Second Intermediate, 73
   summer vacations, 126, 129, 329n284, 332
   in Third Intermediate, 115, 116, 149
   in Third Primary, 18, 29, *38,* 40, 45
Fischer, Mrs. William (mother of Billy), 229

Fish, Guy R., *2*
Fisher, Dorothy Canfield, 51
flash cards, 14
Flash Gordon (TV show), 91
Fletcher School of Law and Diplomacy, Tufts, 95
football
   Campanella Football Field and track, 246–247
   in Lower School, 145, 147, *148,* 149, 150
"For all the Saints who from their Labors Rest" (hymn), 206
Ford, Henry, xiv, 26, 98, 336
Foreign Affairs magazine, 377
foreign languages. *See also* vocabulary, in foreign languages; *specific languages, e.g.* French
   grammar study as preparation for, 201
   literary versus commercial/conversational, 274–275, 318
   Lower School lack of emphasis on, 162
   in Upper School, 170, 171, 382
Forman, Mrs. (mother of Jeff), 229
Forman, Jeff[rey] Lee, xiv, *168,* 300, 316, 329n283, *342,* 395
Forms, in Upper School, 3. *See also specific forms*
Forster, E. M., 306–307
Foundations of Advanced Mathematics (1959), 343
fountain pens, 8–9
four-color conjecture, 184n135
Fourth Form (Eleventh Grade), 299–328
   chemistry, 299, 318–322
   course load in, 171, 299
   English, 299, 302–315
   geometry, 250
   German, 299, 302, 315–318
   homework in, 300
   Latin, 299n243
   math, 299
   Model UN, 255
   modern European history, 299, 322–328, 350
   speed-reading and reading comprehension, 299, 315
   teachers in, 299
   testing in, 299, 311, 326–327
Fourth Grade. *See* First Intermediate
Fourth Intermediate (Seventh Grade), 131–156
   activities, 65–66
   American history, 140–143
   art, 144
   civil defense drills in, 145
   class officers, 155
   Commencement exercises, 140, 154–156
   English/language skills in, 135–137
   as First Form, in mid-1960s, 170n120
   French, 56, 58, 115, 144
   geography, 143–144
   history, 53, 79, 137–143
   location of, 8, 69, 131n102, 137
   math, 133–135, 157
   music, 144
   Rhode Island history course, 137–140
   science, 144
   shop, 63, 144
   sports, 150–151
   teachers in, 131–133, *132, 133*
   tennis instructor criticized for coaching practices, 5
   Upper School, introduction to, 151–154
Fourth of July, 125, 128
fractions, 71, 72, 102, 133
Franco, Hernan Ramon, xiv, *168,* 221, 244, 272, 295, 329–330, *342,* 395
Franklin, Benjamin, 26, 197, 233, 257, 376
Franklin, Joey (Joseph), Jr., 122, 129, 149, 397
Frederick the Great (Holy Roman Emperor), 350
French
   Mr. Cate and, 272
   in First Intermediate, 56–60
   in Fourth Intermediate, 56, 58, 115, 144

Index

Quebec, bicycle club tour to, 151
  in Second Form, 215–216
  in Second Primary, 15, 56, 215–216
  in Third Form, 247, 277–280, 284, 285–294
  in Third Intermediate, 115
  in Upper School, 170
  vocabulary in, 280, 288
French and Indian War, 80, 90, 138, 141
French Revolution, 326
"*Frere Jacques*," 58
Freshman year. *See* Second Form
Friend's Academy, 149, 150
Friends' Boarding School (original name of Moses Brown School), 1
Friends Hall, 246
Frost, Robert, 258, 307, 360
Fulbright scholarships, 176n126
Full, Ada T., 129, 170, 215, 232–235, 238, 247, 254, 256, *261,* 261–267, *321,* 322, 384, 387, 393
Fuller, Frank E. ("Doc")
  classrooms used by, 170, 393
  in First Form, 172, 186, 187–192, 206
  in Fourth Form, 299n243
  moral education and values, teaching, 387
  in Moses Brown intellectual establishment, 381
  W. Paxton compared, 353
  photos of, *188, 378*
  as school historian, xi
  in Second form, 215, 230, 231, 238
  Shadows of the Elms (1983), viin1, xii
  single-sex versus co-ed schooling and, 380
  in Third Form, 247, 254, 270–271, 293
fungos and fungo bat, 4, 151

Gaiser, Gert, 349n305
Gallic Wars (Julius Caesar), 230
Galsworthy, John, 359
The Garden of Children (Lawrence, MA school), xxii

Gardiner, Martin, 302
Garrison, Molly, xii
Gaspee, burning of, 138
Gehrig, Lou, 197
gender and sexuality
  co-educational institution, Moses Brown School as, x, 1, 379, 380
  dime novels, Mr. Tinker on, 219
  girls, exposure to, 120, 122
  Latin, grammatical gender distinctions in, 190
  math problems divided by, 194
  matriarchal teacher tradition, advancement through grades and separation from, 131, 133, 232
  the Pill, arrival and availability of, xi
  E. Raines advising Seniors not to get their girlfriends pregnant, 368
  sexual references in class, teacher handling of, 178, 197, 224, 279, 316
  sexual revolution, xi
  single-sex education, concept of, x, 379–381
  single-sex institution, Lincoln School as, 1, 379
  single-sex institution, Moses Brown School as, x, 1, 379–381
  sissies and sissy behavior, 4, 18
  sperm brought to biology class, 266
  teacher sexual abuse, 314n264
  women's history, 26
  women's rights in 1950s, ix
geography. *See also* maps and mapmaking
  in First Form, 170n121, 175–187
  First-Form Geography Banana Party, 185–187
  in First Intermediate, 54–56
  in Fourth Intermediate, 143–144
  in Lower School, 159, 160–161
  in Second Intermediate, 76–78
  in Third Intermediate, 104–110
  in Upper School, 171, 383
Geography around the World (1948), 54n51
geography bees, 109–110
Geography of a Working World (1951), 143
Geography of the Americas (1950), 76

geology, 144, 234
geometry, 134, 170, 194, 250, 251, 254, 299–302, 344, 345, 349, 386
Georgetown Medical School, 317n266
Gerhan, David, xv
German
 in Fifth Form, 343, 349–351
 in Fourth Form, 299, 302, 315–318
 Mr. Pratt as teacher of, 322n271, 323
 in Third Form, 247, 271–277
 in Upper School, 170
 vocabulary in, 275–277, 318, 349, 354
GI Bill, 315
Giants in the Earth (Rolvaag), 357
Gifford, Charles Kilvert, Jr. (Chad), 66, 68n57, 104, 115, 116, *124,* 149–150, 215, 332, 396
Gifford, Charles Kilvert, Sr. (father of Chad), 68n57
Gifford, Mrs. Charles Kilvert, Sr. (mother of Chad), 68
Gifford, John, *124*
Gifford, Seth K., 7, 140, 153, 156n116
Gifford Building, Moses Brown School, 392
The Gillette Cavalcade of Sports (TV show), 91
Glee Club, 207, 382, 394
Glendinning, Matt, xiii, 169n119
Gmelch, George, xv
"God of our Fathers, Whose Almighty Hand...." (hymn), 206
Goddard, Mrs. (mother of Bill), 123
Goddard, Bill[y] (William Holland Drury)
 in First Intermediate, 63
 in Fourth Intermediate, 137
 graduating member of Lower School Class of 1955, 396
 in Kindergarten through Second Primary, 6, *12,* 13
 at prep school, 215
 in Second Intermediate, 85, 86
 as source of information, xiv
 summer vacations, 122–123
 in Third Intermediate, 115

 in Third Primary, 23, *36,* 37
 working men, respect for, 338
Godfray, Nancy Rapelye, xv
Godfray, Tom, xiv, 150
Goff, Wilfred H., 154, 156, *378*
Golden, Nancy Hayes, xiii, xiv–xv
Gompers, Samuel, 27
Gone with the Wind (book and movie), 135
Good Times through Literature (1951), 195–196, 198, 201
Goode, J. Paul, 178
"goose egg" tests, 311
Gordon, Emalyn, xii
Gordon School, 150
Gorgas, William, 26
Gorton, Samuel, 138
Grade School. *See* Lower School
grades or years, at Moses Brown, 3. *See also specific grades/years*
Graham, John, 172
Graham, Pierpont, 172
grammar
 in Fifth Form, 353, 354–356
 in First Form, 195, 199–201
 in Fourth Form, 311
 in Fourth Intermediate, 135–137
 in German class, 317, 349
 in Latin class, 190–191, 231, 270–271
 Lower School emphasis on, 158
 in Second Form, 200n147, 225–226
 in Second Intermediate, 73, 74
 sentence diagramming, 97, 199–200
 in Third Form, 260
 in Third Intermediate, 96–98, 135
Grant, General Ulysses S., 26, 142, 233
Grapes of Wrath (Steinbeck), 259
Graubard, Stephen, 325n278
Great English and American Essays (1959), 358n311
Great Expectations (Dickens), 101, 197
Great House, Warwick, RI, 334n293
Greek language, 159, 171, 271
Green, Theodore Francis (Senator), 80n66
Greenville, RI, 66
Groton (prep school), 238

Index 415

grove, Father and Son Day held at, 44
"Guides to Study," 178n129, 182–183
Gulliver's Travels (Swift), 359
Guys and Dolls (musical), 219

Hahnemann University Medical
   School, 229n164
Half Deck (classroom), 137
Halloween and trick or treating, 51, 67
Hamilton, Alexander, 72n59
Hamlet (Shakespeare), 306, 358
Hampton Beach, NH, xxi
"hangman," in French class, 58–59
Hannibal of Carthage, 111–112
"The Happy Journey to Trenton and
   Camden" (Wilder), 259–260
Hard Times (Dickens), 363
Hardy, Thomas, 307, 312
Hart, Bret, 258
Hartford University, CT, 341n297
Harvard Business School, 241n171, 246
Harvard Club of Rhode Island, 351
Harvard *Crimson,* 177
Harvard Law School, 23n27
Harvard University
   C. Brown at, 225, 238, 246,
      325n277, 326, 328, 351, 398
   Brown-Harvard hockey game, 65
   Moses Brown alumni attend-
      ing, 23n27, 85n70, 177, 238,
      323n272, 377n325
   production of Moliere in French at,
      Moses Brown students attending,
      293–294
   teachers at Moses Brown attending,
      3, 209, 220, 315, 322, 323, 324,
      325nn277–278, 351, 391
   Whittemore Whittier at, 391
Haverford College, 391
Hawes Gymnasium, 117, 247
Hawks (intramural sports), 150
Hayden, Carl, 80n66
Hazlett, William, 359
H-bomb. *See* nuclear weapons
Headmaster's Cup, 23n27
health issues. *See* medical issues
health science, 234–235

hearse driven by J. Tinker, 216
Hedges, James, 365n315
"Hellenism and Hebraism" (Arnold),
   358–359
Hellman, Lillian, 358
Hemingway, Ernest, 260
Henderson, O. J. B., *378*
Henkle, Bruce Alexander, xiv, 309, 311,
   331, 335, *342,* 368–369, 395
Henry, O., 198
Henry Aldrich (TV show), 91
Henry Barnard School, xxiii
Henry IV (king of France), 113
Henry IV, Part I (Shakespeare), 228
Henry the Navigator, 79
Herman, Babe (baseball player), 247
Herman, Marion L. ("Babe")
   classroom used by, 170, 394
   compared to other teachers, 309, 361
   as Director of Testing, 154, 248,
      316–317, 345
   in Fifth Form, 343–345, 347
   in Fourth Form, 299, 300, 301
   in study hall, 212–213
   moral education and values, teach-
      ing, 386
   in Moses Brown intellectual estab-
      lishment, 381–382
   origins of nickname, 247
   photos of, *248, 378*
   rubber stamp of, 248
   in Second Form, 218, 238
   single-sex versus co-ed schooling
      and, 380–381
   in Third Form, 247–252, 254, 270
Herreshoff, Halsey, 125, 269n197
Higgins, John, Jr. (Higgsie), 351
Higgins, John, Sr., 351
High School. *See* Upper School
Hindenberg, demise of, 90
history
   American, 26, 27, 53, 79–80, 109,
      140–143, 159, 170, 343, 363–377
   American achievements, emphasis
      on, 160–161
   ancient/classical, 53, 104, 106, 110–
      112, 113, 159, 170, 191–192,
      215, 219–224

European, 53, 105, 112–114, 159, 170, 299, 322–328, 350
Fifth Form, American history and government in, 343, 363–377
in First Intermediate, 53–54
Fourth Form, modern European history in, 299, 322–328, 350
in Fourth Intermediate, 53, 79, 137–143
gaps in, 159–160
in German class, 350
in Latin class, 191–192, 231
in Lower School, 159–162
medieval, 53, 104, 110, 112–113, 159, 324–325, 350, 369
of Rhode Island, 78, 137–140
in Second Form, 215, 219–224
in Second Intermediate, 79–80
teaching pattern of, Primary classes to Upper Forms, 327–328
in Third Intermediate, 53, 110–114, 223
in Third Primary, 26–27
in Upper School, 170, 383
History Boys (movie), 309
History for the Beginner (1948), 53n50
History of Young America (1951), 79n65
Hit Parade (TV show), 91
Hitler, Adolf, 41
Hobart College, 324n274
hockey game, class outing to, 65
"*hocus pocus*", 191
Holmes, Oliver Wendell, Sr., 228
Holmes, Virginia, 114–115
Holoff, Al[an], xiv, 279, 342, 394
Homer, 159, 271
homework
in First Form, 182, 183, 192, 212, 213
in First Intermediate, 49, 52, 54, 59
in Fourth Form, 300
in Second Intermediate, 72, 91
in study hall, 212, 213
in Third Form, 270
in Third Intermediate, 95–96, 103–104, 106, 111
in Third Primary, 24–25, 27
Hooker, General Joseph, 142

Hooper, James Emery, *342,* 395
Hoover, Herbert, 81
Hope High School, Science Fair at, 37
Hopkins, Esek, 138
Housman, A. E., 307, 360
Houston, Sam, 19
Howard, Sidney, 358
Howdy Doody (TV show), 91
Howe, F. Warren, Jr. ("Junie")
chocolate pudding, fondness for, 204–205
compared to E. Raines, 363
photos of, *235, 236, 378*
student recollections of, xiii
as summer camp counselor, 129
Third Form, Mechanical Drawing class, 267–269, 384
track team, as coach of, 204, 295
Upper School shop classes with, 170n121, 186, 195, 204–206, 215, 235–237, 238
visiting B. Brehm at home, 269
Howe, Mrs. F. Warren, Jr., 269
Hoye, Jim[my] (James Vincent), Jr., 124, 147, 396
Huckleberry Finn (Twain), 258
Hudson, Henry, 79
Hugo, Victor, *58,* 226
Hunchback of Notre Dame (Hugo), 226
Hundred Years War, 325
Huntoon, Mrs. (mother of Harrison), 229
Huntoon, Harrison, xiv, 66, 95, 115, 122, *168,* 215, 271, 329n284, 332, 396
hurricanes in Rhode Island, 137, 139, 283
Hutchinson, Anne, 138
Hutton, Mr., 129, 170, 318, *378*
Huxley, Aldous, 359

"I Love to See It Lap the Miles" (Dickinson), 360
I Remember Mama (TV show), 91
Indian Hill camping facility, Little Compton, RI, 129n101
"The Indian Jugglers" (Hazlett), 359
Industrial Revolution, 326, 373

Index 417

industry and labor
    in American history, 142
    factory system in US, introduction of, 1–3
    in geography, 77–78, 143–144, 180–181
    Industrial Revolution, 326
    mechanics, in Second Form general science, 232–233
    in 1950s, viii
    in Rhode Island history, 138, 139–140
    Rhode Island industry project, Fourth Intermediate, 139, 155
informants recruited by Mr. Cunningham, 242, 244
ink inkwells, and ink bottles, 8–9, 139, 184–185
Intermediate levels, in Lower School, 3, 18. *See also* Lower School; *specific grade/year*
Intruder in the Dust (Faulkner), 259
Irving, Washington, 257
"Is My Team Ploughing?" (Housman), 360
Isabella Stewart Gardner Museum, Boston, 86
Island of Peril (novel), 99

"Jabberwocky" (Carroll), 200
Jackson, Andrew, 26, 373, 467
Jackson, Helen Hunt, 27
James, Henry, 233
James I (king of England), 141
Jamestown, 26
Jansen, Walter E., 173, 283, 394
Japanese beetles, 128n100
Jeffers, Elizabeth Lee, 2
Jeffers, John H., xii, xiii, 238, 254, 260, 299, 318–321, *319*, 343, 346–348
Jefferson, Thomas, 26
Jenckes, Joseph, 139
Jensen, Patricia
    as First Intermediate teacher, 47–48, 51–55, 60, 169
    as Second Intermediate teacher, 69, 70, 76, 78, 80, 83, 85

    as summer camp counselor/instructor, 129
Jernquist, E. Harold, 154, *378*
Jim Crow, ix, 143, 161, 374–375
Joan of Arc, 113
John Brown House, Providence, 137, 140
John Brown's Body (Benet), 258
Johns Hopkins University, 238, 308n249
Johnson, John George (Grandpa; step-grandfather of C. Brown), 28, 40–43, 89
Jones, Janet Chase, xv
Journey to the Center of the Earth (Verne), 135
Journey to the Moon (Verne), 135
Judicial Board, 341
Julius Caesar, 192, 230, 231
Julius Caesar (Shakespeare), 228
Jungle Book (Kipling), 99
Junior Audubon Society, 64–65, 84–85
Junior High per se, Moses Brown's lack of, 3
Junior year. *See* Fourth Form
Justin, Kenneth F., 260, 277, 299, 302, 315–318, *317*, 343, 349–351, 380, 393
Justin, Mrs. Kenneth F., 315

Drei Kameraden (Remarque), 317
Kant, Immanuel, 317
Kaplan-style SAT courses, 345–346
Keach, N. B., *378*
Keats, John, 360
Keene State Teacher's College, NH, 131
Keeney, Barnaby, 239
Keller, Helen, 197
Kelsey, Rayner W., viin1, xii
Kemalian, Drew, xiv
Kennebec Junior Camp, Denmark, ME, 122
Kennedy, John F., 369
Kennedy, Ted, 85n70
Kennedy, W. Jay, 207, *378*
Kent, Rockwell, 99
Kenyon, George, 310

Kidnapped (movie), 90
Kidnapped (Stevenson novel), 99
Kilgus, Mr., 237
Kilton, Mrs. (mother of George), 229
Kilton, George Williams, Jr., 46, 117, 122, 329n284, 396
Kindelan, Stephen Edwin, *168,* 396
Kindergarten. *See* Pre-Primary
King, Martin Luther, Jr., 361
King George's War, 138, 141
King William's War, 138
Kipling, Rudyard, 99
Kissinger, Henry, 328
Kit Carson (movie), 90
Knibb, Russell, 339
Knight, Jonathan, xv
Knowles, Mike, xiv
Koffler, Steve (Stephen Alexander), 121, 124, 244, 329n283, 395, 396
Korean War, ix, 82–83, 107
Krause, Bob, 280, 281, 287–288, 290, 294–295nn238–239, 295
Krive, Anne, xiii
Kroll, Jerry, 324
Kukla, Fran, and Ollie (TV show), 91

labor. *See* industry and labor
Ladd, J. H. (Joseph Howard), Jr., *168, 342,* 395
Ladd Observatory, 174
"The Lagoon" (Conrad), 303
Landen, Alf, 81
Landmark series books, 26, 27, 51, 73
Langer's *Encyclopedia of World History,* 377
language skills. *See* English
languages, foreign. *See* foreign languages; *specific languages*
LaSalle, René-Robert Cavelier, Sieur de, 79
Latham, Dorothy and Hubert, 186, 187
Latin
    Mr. Cate and, 271–272
    college admissions and, 159, 382
    in First Form, 170n121, 187–192
    in Fourth Form, 299n243
    in Second Form, 215, 230–231
    in Third Form, 247, 270–271
    vocabulary in, 230, 270, 271, 354
Latin for Americans (1950), 230n165
Latin Poetry (1040), 270n198
Lawrence, MA, xx–xxii
Leacock, Stephen, 198, 307
Learning to Compute, 24, 71, 251
Learning to Write (1957), 311n256, 352n306, 356
Leary, Leo Henry, III, 397
Lee, General Robert E., 26
letters, composition of, 74
Levaur, Hank (Henry Louis), *36, 85,* 121, 122, 397
Levy, Austin T., 39
Lewis and Clark, 26
library and library instruction, 202, 362–363
The Life of Riley (TV show), 91
Life on the Mississippi (Twain), 258
limericks, 198
Lincoln, Abraham, 26, 79, 142, 256, 358
Lincoln School
    as all-girls school, 1, 379
    B. Barrett's siblings at, 34
    mock election at, 80–81
    New England Yearly Meeting of Friends acquiring, 1
    M. Pezet's wife teaching at, 280
    sources of information about, xii
    spelling bees with, 29
Lindsay, Vachel, 199
Lionel trains, 22, 367
Lippman, Walter, 306
"Listen to the People" (Benet), 258
literature. *See also* reading; *specific books and short stories*
    in Fifth Form, 357–361, 363
    in First Form, 195–199
    in Fourth Form, 302–307
    in Second Form, 226–229
    in Third Form, 256–260
"Literature of Knowledge and Literature of Power" (DeQuincy), 359
Little League baseball, 121
Littlefield, Mrs. (mother of Nicky), 229
Littlefield, Bancroft, Sr. (father of Nicky), 191

Index 419

Littlefield, Margaret, 154
Littlefield, Nick[y] (Bancroft Littlefield, Jr.)
    as Boy Scout, 332, 333
    in First Form, *168,* 190
    in First Intermediate, 45, 51, 54, 67
    in Fourth Intermediate, 155
    graduating member of Lower School Class of 1955, 396
    higher education and career, 85n70
    in Kindergarten through Second Primary, *12,* 13
    in Little League, 121
    prep school, departure for, 215, 238
    in Second Form, 215, 228
    in Second Intermediate, 84, 85
    as source of information, xiv
    sports played by, 149, 150
    summer vacations, 121, 126, 129, 329n284, 332, 333
    in Third Intermediate, 95, 99, 115, 116, 149, 150
    in Third Primary, 18, 22, 32, 37
Livy, 230
logarithms, 344
London, Dave (David Saunders)
    in Fifth Form, *342,* 345, 365, 368, 370
    in Fourth Form, 308, 309–310, 312, 313, *321*
    graduating member of Class of 1960, 395
    higher education and career, 308n250
    as source of information, xiii
    in Third Form, 255–256, 258, 278, 279
London, Mr. Harry Leopold (father of Dave), 368
London, Toby, 308n250
London School of Economics, 85n70
London Symphony, 89
long division, 23n29, 48–49, 68, 71, 102, 344
Longfellow, Henry Wadsworth, 258
Lord's Prayer, 17, 58
"Die Lorelei", 276–277
Lorna Doone (Blackmore), 135
Louis the Spider (Louis XI, king of France), 113, 325

Louis XIV (king of France), 113
Louise de la Villaire (Dumas), 197
Louisiana Purchase, 79, 373
Love Story (movie), 23n27
Lowell, James Russell, 258
Lower School, 3–10, 157–165. *See also specific grades/years*
    J. Drisko Allen as head of, 3–6, *5*
    art and shop in, 162
    basic skills versus creativity and self-expression in, 158, 163–165
    class size in, 8, 86, 170
    clocks and timekeeping in, 9, 18
    composition, writing, and essays in, 158
    Mr. Cunningham and, 242–243
    daily routine, 17–19
    English/language skills in, 158
    excellence, as value of, 162–164
    faculty and staff (1950), *2*
    foreign languages, lack of emphasis on, 162
    geography in, 159, 160–161
    grades in, 3
    grading in, 182
    history in, 159–162
    math, emphasis on, 157
    moral education and values in, 164
    physical surroundings, 7–10
    practical knowledge, emphasis on, 103, 113, 133, 134, 162, 164–165
    reading, emphasis on, 158
    science, lack of emphasis on, 162
    sports in, 145–151, 162
    summer vacations during, 119–129
    Upper School compared, 170–171
Lower School building, 7–8
Lower School Gymnasium, 44, 147–149
Lower School Student Council, 116
Luck of Roaring Camp (Hart), 258
Ludlum, Robert, 141n109

Macbeth (Shakespeare), 305–306, 312
"Macbeth Murder Mystery" (Thurber), 307

Mackenzie, Will, xiv
MacLeish, Archibald, 258
Madison, Dolly, 26
Magellan, Ferdinand, 79
Magruder's American Government (1959), 370n320
Maine, class project on, 78
Maletz, Roy Martin, xiv, 302, 308, *342,* 395
Malley, Ted (Edwin William), III, 331, 335, *342,* 395
Man, Money, and Medicine (DiLibero), 229n164
Man in the Iron Mask (Dumas), 197
Manera, John, xv
Manlius Military Academy, NY, 284
manners and politeness, 59–60
Manual Training. *See* shop class
Mapleville, RI, public primary school in, xxii–xxiii, 24
maps and mapmaking, 55–56, 76–79, 83, 95, 104–109, 178, 179–180, 183–185, 222, 327n282, 366
Marbury v. Madison, 369
Marcello, Mrs. Albert (mother of Vin), xii, 20
Marcello, Mr. Albert Peter (father of Vin), 66, 123
Marcello, Vincent (Vin, Vinny) Anthony
  in Fifth Form, 341, *342*
  in First Form, *168*
  in First Intermediate, 66
  graduating member of Class of 1960, 395
  graduating member of Lower School Class of 1955, 396
  higher education and career, 15n18
  Judicial Board promoted by, 341
  in Kindergarten through Second Primary, *12,* 13, 15
  photos of, *12, 168, 330*
  in Second Intermediate, 84
  as source of information, xiii
  sports played by, 146, 150
  in summer vacations, 122, 123, 329n284, *330,* 331, 334–335
  in Third Form, 242
  in Third Intermediate, 115, 150
  in Third Primary, 20, 45, 146
La Marseillaise, 58, 289, 291
Marshall, Mrs. (mother of Bob), 229
Marshall, Bob (Robert John), xiv, *168, 264,* 329n284, 331, *342,* 395
Martin Kane, Private Eye (TV show), 91
Massachusetts College/School of Art, 33, 86
Massmann, Uwe, 351
Master Teacher Development Fund, xvii
math. *See also specific branches, e.g.* algebra
  in Fifth Form, 343–346
  in First Form, 170n121, 193–195
  in First Intermediate, 23n29, 48–50
  in First Primary, 13, 14
  in Fourth Form, 299–302
  in Fourth Intermediate, 133–135, 157
  Lower School emphasis on, 157
  new math, 157, 194
  problems and problem-solving, 50, 71–72, 102, 133, 134–135, 194, 251–254, 300–302
  science curriculum, tracking with, 170–171
  Second Form, algebra in, 215, 216–219
  in Second Intermediate, 24, 71–72
  in Second Primary, 15
  in Third Form, 247–254
  in Third Intermediate, 71, 102–104, 157
  in Third Primary, 23–25
  in Upper School, 170–171, 381, 383
"Mathematical Games" column, *Scientific American,* 302
Mathematics Review Exercises (1956), 344
May, Ernest, 328
Mayer, George, 310
Mayflower, 26
Mays, Maxwell, 126n98
Mays, Skip[per] (William Clarke Stevens Mays, III), 126, 128, 149, 396
McCarthy, Joe, ix, 102, 137, 259
McClellan, General George B., 142

Index   421

McKinley, William, 373
McNamara, Robert, 355
McNeer, May, 51
Meade, General George G., 142
meals and snack breaks, 18, 44, 67, 91, 154, 204–205
Mechanical Drawing, 162, 171, 204, *236,* 267–270, 384, 386
Medea (play), 228
medical issues
    appendectomy (Bill Brehm), 269
    braces and orthodontia, 48
    C. Brown, early childhood illnesses of, xxii, 35
    chicken pox, 39
    dyslexia, 75
    field trip injuries, 15, 67
    get-well cards for sick teacher, 61
    poison ivy, 47, 57, 127, 226–227
    polio epidemic, 17n21
    tonsils, removal of, xxi
medieval history, 53, 104, 110, 112–113, 159, 324–325, 350, 369
Melville, Herman, 99, 259, 261
Memorial Day in Webster, MA, 257–258
memorization exercises
    in Lower School, 74–75, 79, 87, 107–108, 109, 141
    in Upper School, 178–179, 180, 223, 256, 262, 266, 288–289, 386
Mercator, Gerhard, 79, 178
Mertes, Kate, xv
Meserve, Basil G., 302, 307n248, 308–314, 311n256, 352n306, *378*
Methuen, MA, xx–xxii
metric system, 134
Meuser, Ernie (Ernest August), 331, 335, 396
Mexican War, 79, 373
The Middle Ages 306-1000 (1942), 325n277
Middle House, 1, 8, 10, 18, 69, 145, 154, 212, 283
Middle School, at Moses Brown, 3, 243
Middlebury College, 325n277
Middlesex (prep school), 323

A Midsummer Night's Dream (Shakespeare), 197–198
Miller, Arthur, 259
Milton Academy, 85n70, 215, 238
Milton Berle's Texaco Hour (TV show), 91
mimeographed worksheets, 25
Ming Garden restaurant, Providence, 334n293
"Miniver Cheevy" (Robinson), 360
Le Misanthrope (Moliere), 293–294
The Miser (Moliere), 228
Les Miserables (Hugo), 226
MIT, 15n19, 238
Mitchell, Margaret, GWTW, 135
Mitchell Junior College, 124n96
Moby Dick (Melville), 99–100, 259
mock elections, 80–81
Model UN, 246, 255, 343
Modern Biology (Moon, Mann, and Otto, 1956), 262, 267
Modern Language Association, 226
modern languages. *See* foreign languages; *specific languages*
Modern Practical Arithmetic (1926), 193
Moliere, 228, 293–294
Monahon, Clifford, 137
Monahon, Mrs. Eleanore, 53, 79, 131–133, *132,* 137–144, 155, 156, 159, 223, 234, 328, 369, 372, 376, *378*
The Monitor and the Merrimack, 73
Monroe Doctrine, 377
Moore, Carolyn, 144
Moore, Louise Winsor, *2,* 32, 61, 129
Morey's *Ancient Peoples,* 221, 222
Morris, Andy, xv
Morse, Karin, xii
Mosaic (school yearbook)
    Mr. Bennett as advisor to, 255
    C. Brown as editor of, 255, 341, 343
    on Miss Chappell, 70
    on Christmas Pageant, 39n37
    First Primary in, 14
    Pre-Primary photo from, 11–13, *12*
    Second Primary in, 15
    Mr. Tinker as advisor to, 219
    T. Whitford, Class of 1960 dedicating yearbook to, 280, 296–297

Moses, Peter Taft, 397
Moses Brown Bulletin
    attenuated edition following departure of Mr. St. John, 331n285
    as source for school history, xii
    standardized test statistics in, 238
    on summer vacations, 120, 121, 122, 127n99, 129, 334
Moses Brown School, vii–xvii. *See also* Lower School; teachers at Moses Brown School; Upper School; *specific buildings and rooms; specific grades/years*
    50th Reunion of Class of 1960, xi–xii
    administration of, 152–154
    author's entry into, xxiii–xxiv
    boarders at, 22, 129n101, 172, 185n139, 212, 255, 281, 392
    as co-educational institution, x, 1, 379, 380
    college placement, achievements in, 154, 238, 256, 381
    diversity of student body, 160, 211
    excellence, as value of, 162–164, 388
    founding and early history of, 1–3
    fundraising efforts, 239, 246, 247
    Middle School, creation of, 3, 243
    New England intellectual/cultural tradition at, 233–234
    1950s, as historical era, and, viii–x
    prep/boarding schools, students departing for, 215, 216, 237–239, 241–242, 381
    published histories of, viin1, xii
    "The Quaker Alumni" (Whittier), 361
    as Quaker school, vii, x–xi, 1–3, 6
    school history, style of, vii–viii, xv–xvi
    school song and Psalm, 74, 75, 155
    school year at, 17
    as single-sex institution, x, 1, 379–381
    source materials for study of, xi–xv
    Mr. St. John, departure of, 237–239
    tuition at, xxivn7
Moses Brown School, A History of its Third Half Century (Paxton, 1974), viin1, xii, 245n173, 246

"The Most Dangerous Game" (Connell), 75–76, 227
Mott, Lucretia, 61n54
Mott, Samuel Douglas, 397
movies. *See also specific movie titles*
    Class of 60's childhood access to, xix, 90
    shown at Lower School, 3, 90–91
    television, Hollywood responses to, ix
    United Fruit documentary, 186, 187
Moyer, Jan Rodney, xiv, 21, *342,* 395
Mulkey, C. F., *378*
multiplication table, 24, 48
Murdock, Bill (William Newton), 125, 324, 395
Murray, Miss, 13–14
Muscente, Louise E., *2,* 14, 30
music
    Book Fair, records sold at, 100–101
    in First Form, 170n121, 206–207
    in First Intermediate, 60–61
    in Fourth Intermediate, 144
    Glee Club, 207, 382, 394
    in Second Intermediate, 87–90
    in Third Intermediate, 115
    in Third Primary, 17, 32–33
    in Upper School, 382–383
Music Room, 394
Mustard, Mr., 146–147
Mutter, Bonnie Riker, xv
"My Financial Career" (Leacock), 198
"My Last Duchess" (Browning), 360
My Weekly Reader (periodical), 20, 27
The Mysterious Island (Verne), 135, 233
"A Mystery of Heroism" (Crane), 258

Der Nachtmensch (Borge), 349–350
Najarian, Leon Andrew, 99, 117, 122, 129, *168,* 329n284, 396
Napoleon, 324, 326
naps and naptime, 18–19
Nash, Ogden, 198–199, 307
Nassau experiment, in chemistry class, 320
national flags, facsimiles of, 185
National Geographic Society, 184
National Merit Scholarships, 213, 345, 346, 381

Index 423

Native Americans, 3, 138, 142, 159
Neal, Kenneth Robert, *168,* 396
neologisms, 355
Neumann, Glenn Bruce, 397
New Deal, 142, 374
New England accents, 28, 29, 323
New England Conservatory, 60
New England farm/work culture, 31, 156n116, 283, 335–340
New England intellectual/cultural tradition, 135, 189, 233–234
New England literalist style, xv
New England Yearly Meeting of Friends, vii, x–xi, 1, 247
The New Hymnal for American Youth (1930), 172n123
new math, 157, 194
New York Times, 189, 355
New Yorker, 355
newspapers, student. *See also* Quaker
  The Echo (Boy Scout troop newspaper), 333
  "Home News" issued by C. Brown, 28–29
  The Student Weekly News (Third Intermediate), 115–116, 149
Nichols, Paul A. ("Pig Eyes"), 200n147, 215, 224–229, *225,* 313, 314, 322n270, 380, 393
"The Night the Bed Fell" (Thurber), 307
A Night to Remember (movie), 202
1950s, as historical era, viii–x
Ninety-Three (Hugo), 226
Ninth Grade. *See* Second Form
Nipper (RCA dog), 101
Nixon, Bruce, 81
Nixon, Jack (John Richard)
  graduating member of Class of 1960, 395
  graduating member of Lower School Class of 1955, 396
  higher education and career, 81n67
  in Lower School, 45, 81, 115, 116, 121, 124, 129, 139, 149, 150
  as source of information, xiii
  in Upper School, 224, 242, 286, 291, *342,* 367
Nixon, Richard, 81, 369

Norfolk Music School, Yale, 32n33
notes, passing, 116
nuclear chemistry, 347
nuclear weapons, ix, 109, 137, 145, 162, 181, 306, 356

"October's Bright Blue Weather" (Helen Hunt Jackson), 27
"Ode to a Grecian Urn" (Keats), 360
Odell, King B. ("Doc")
  C. Brown misspelling name of, 182
  compared to other teachers, 254, 326
  on R. Cunningham, 246
  Debate Club formed by, 229
  First Form geography class of, 169, 170n121, 172, 175–179, 181–187, 189, 204, 376
  Latin American and Asian history in geography class of, 328, 383
  leaving and returning to Moses Brown after Doctorate program, 169n119, 238
  moral education and values, teaching, 386
  in Moses Brown intellectual establishment, 382
  as native Rhode Islander, 283
  photo of, *176*
  on ponderousness of C. Brown, xvi, 185
  as School Historian, xii, 169n119
  single-sex versus co-ed schooling and, 380
O'Donnell, Barbara, *2*
Of Mice and Men (Steinbeck), 259
Ogden, Chris, 123
Ohio State University, 241n171
Ohio Wesleyan University, 241n171
The Old Man and the Sea (Hemingway), 260
Old Stone Bank series, 138
Oliver Twist (Dickens), 197
Olney, Stephen, 138
Omoo (Melville), 259
"Once to Every Man and Nation Comes the Moment to Decide," 206–207

One Third of a Nation (Arent), 358
"Onward Christian Soldiers," 206
oral exams, 260–261
oral skills and debate, 228–229
Oregon Trail, 90
Oreos, as Primary School snack, 18
Oster, Steve (Stephen Alan), 121, 329n283, 396
Ottmar, James Howard, *342,* 395
Otto the Great (Holy Roman Emperor), 350
Our Earth and Man (1951), 104
Our Independence and the Constitution (Fisher), 51
Our Miss Brooks (radio program), xx
Our Town (Wilder), 358
Out of the Past (1950), 110
Ovid, 270
Owen, David, 325n277
Oxford University, 242

Painter, Kent Howard, 73, 84, 85, 121, 122, 149, 397
Palmer, David, 41
Palmer Method, 30
Pansey, Bruce Stephen, 43, 45, 61, 229, 397
Paolino, Tom, 324
papier-mâché bottle, 30–31
paragraph design, 74
Parents Council, 229, 242
Parents Open House, 185
Parker, Pete[r] Ross, xiii, 281, *342,* 371–372, 395
passing notes, 116
Pastore, John O. (Senator), 39
Pawtucket cotton mill, 1–3
Paxton, Helen J., 80–81, 202, 356, *362,* 362–363, *378,* 379–380
Paxton, William
   as acting headmaster, 351
   classroom used by, 170, 302n245, 393
   compared to other teachers, 238, 311, 312–314, 357, 361, 363, 364
   R. Cunningham and, 243
   Fifth Form English with, 226, 260, 307n248, 343, 351–358, 360–363
   on Mr. Herman's nickname, 247n175
   Learning to Write (1957), 311n256, 352n306, 356
   moral education and values, teaching, 386
   in Moses Brown intellectual establishment, 381
   Moses Brown School (1974), viin1, xii, 245n173, 246
   photos of, *352, 378*
   on single-sex versus co-ed schooling, 380
peace essays, 361–362
Peggy Eaton Affair, 142, 367
Pembroke College, Brown University, 232
penmanship
   in First Intermediate, 52–53
   in First Primary, 15
   fountain pens and ink, use of, 8–9
   pencils, younger children restricted to, 8
   in Second Intermediate, 75
   in Third Intermediate, 96
   in Third Primary, 8, 30
   writing out a hundred times, as punishment, 48
Penn State, 144, 193
percentages, 71, 102, 103, 134, 194
Perry, Bruce Hayward, xiv, 295–296, *342,* 359, 395
Perry, Oliver Hazard, 139, 140
Perry Mason (TV show), 343
Petticoat Scandal (Peggy Eaton Affair), 142, 367
Pezet, Maurice L., 277–280, *278,* 316, 380
Phillips Andover (prep school), 242, 251–253, 323, 334
phonics, 29
physics, 170, 347, 349, 384, 386, 393
pi, concept of, 103
Pickett, William, 60–61, 88, 131
Pictorial History of World War II (Life Magazine), 80

Index 425

The Pirate Laffite and the Battle of New Orleans, 73
Pitman, Sophia, 61
Pixley, Marion P., xxiii–xxiv, *2,* 22, 47–48, 49, 50, 51, 60, 68, 72, 76, 129
Pizarro, Francisco, 79
plane geometry, 299–302
Plantations Club, 371
Plante, Jeff[rey] De Laval, 121, 397
Plato, 110, 159, 223
The Players, xv, 87
plays and theatricals
    Christmas Pageant, 3, 17, 32, *38,* 39–41, 87
    A Midsummer Night's Dream (Shakespeare), 197–198
    Mr. Nichols, as drama coach, 225, 228
    one-act plays based on scenes from famous books, 101
Pledge of Allegiance, 17, 161
Pliny, 299n243
Poe, Edgar Allan, 196, 198, 258
poems and poetry, 27, 43, 51, 58, 198–199, 229, 257, 258–259, 307, 360–361, 386
poison ivy, students and teachers contracting, 47, 57, 127, 226–227
polio epidemic, 17n21
politeness and manners, 59–60
politics. *See* current events
Polk, James, 373
Polo, Marco, 79, 80
Ponce de León, Juan, 79
Pope, General John, 142
Porter, Dawn, xv
Porter, Steven, xv
Portsmouth, RI, Moses Brown School originally in, 1
potato prints, 31–32
potato race, 43
Potter, Dr. Edgar S., 67
Power House, 206, 394
practical engineering, 384
practical knowledge
    Lower School's emphasis on, 103, 113, 133, 134, 162, 164–165
    in Upper School, 193, 194, 233–235, 254, 385
Pratt, Anna Alcott, 323n273
Pratt, Frederick A., xii, 112, 238, 254, 260, 299, 322–328, *323, 350,* 376, 380, 383, 387, 393
Pratt, Mrs. Frederick A., xii, 323, 325n277
Pratt, Frederick Alcott (grandfather of Frederick A.), 323n273
Pratt, John Bridge, 323n273
prayers, at school, 17
pre-calculus, 170
precis exercise, 289
prep/boarding schools, Moses Brown students departing for, 215, 216, 237–239, 241–242, 381
Pre-Primary (Kindergarten), 3, 7, 11–13, *12*
Presley, Elvis, 174
Primary levels, in Lower School, 3, 18. *See also* Lower School; *specific grade/year*
Princeton University, 242, 287, 320, 351
prizes
    ball toss, Father and Son Day, 44
    at Commencement exercises, 154–155
    Declamation Contest, 229, 283
    essays, 74
    Fourth Form English prizes, 308
    Headmaster's Cup, 23n27
    National Merit Finalists, 213
    peace essays, 361–362
    Red Feather/United Fund campaigns, 65
    Rhode Island Science Fair, 262, *321*
    senior history prize, 377
    spelling, 29
    statewide German competition award, 317
    word-making games, 52
projectors, 262
Proscenium Club, 229, 382
Providence, RI. *See also specific locations*
    author's move to, xxi, xxii–xxiii
    East Side of, 22, 90
    new Master Plan for, 293

relocation of Moses Brown School to, 1
Providence Police, Boy Scouts stopped by, 334
punctuation. *See* grammar
puns, 198, 358
Purgatory Chasm, Sutton, MA, 334
"The Purist" (Nash), 198–199
pushball, 146
Pythagorean theorem, 103

quadratic equations, 344
Quaker (student newspaper)
  C. Brown as executive editor of, 341, 343
  B. Carney as editor-in-chief of, 354
  on A. Cate, 272
  classroom used by, 393
  F. Fuller as faculty advisor to, 188
  W. Paxton lampooned in, 353
  F. Pratt interviewed by C. Brown for, 322–323
  as source for school history, xii
"The Quaker Alumni" (Whittier), 361
Quakers and Quakerism
  abolitionists, Quakers as, 3, 142
  Bible course and, 209, 211
  Chapel addresses and, 172–173, 175
  civic obligation, importance of, 387
  consistency of school curriculum perspective with, 162, 211
  on faculty, 172–173, 195, 197, 209, 239, 281
  military, attitude toward, 6, 82, 144, 172–173, 206, 361
  Moses Brown School founded by, vii, x–xi, 1–3, 6
  nonindoctrination, principle of, 211
  in Rhode Island history class, 138
"Quality" (Galsworthy), 359
quantum mechanics, 384, 386
Queen Anne's War, 138, 141

race/racism. *See* African Americans, race, and racism
Radcliffe College, 207

radio, xix–xx
Raines, Everett B.
  Chapel addresses by, 172
  classroom used by, 170, 393
  compared to other teachers, 224, 238, 249, 255, 309, 328, 361, 363, 364
  as Dean, 175, 213, 220, 238, 242, 363
  Fifth Form, American history and government class in, 79, 224, 343, 363–377, 383, 387
  Mrs. Monahon's class compared, 141, 142
  moral education and values, teaching, 386
  in Moses Brown intellectual establishment, 238, 381
  photos of, *364, 378*
  single-sex versus co-ed schooling and, 381
Raines, Mrs. Everett B., 371
"The Ransom of Red Chief" (O. Henry), 198
Ratensky, Alexander K. ("Rat"), 356
"The Raven" (Poe), 198, 258
Ray, Frank Norton, 396
Razee, Kempton D., 396
Reade, Charles, 363
The Reader's Digest, 115
reading. *See also* literature; *specific books and short stories*
  Bibles sold at Book Fair, 101
  in First Intermediate, 51
  in First Primary, 14
  in Fourth Intermediate, 135
  Lower School emphasis on, 158
  in Second Intermediate, 26, 71, 75–76
  in Second Primary, 15
  speed-reading and reading comprehension, 171, 232n168, 299, 315, 394
  in Third Intermediate, 96, 99–101
  in Third Primary, 25–27
  tracked reading, 26, 158
reading music, 32–33
recess, 6, 18, 67, 71, 117, 150–151

Index 427

Recollections (Thomas, 1994), viin1, xii, 188, 379
The Red Badge of Courage (Crane), 258
Red Feather campaign, 65
Red Rover, 146
Red Sox, xx, 45, 91
Reifsnyder, William, 170n121, 206–207
religion. *See also* Chapel; Quakers and Quakerism
   Anglicanism/Episcopalianism/ Church of England, 178, 239, 253n188
   Bible class, 170n121, 171, 207–211, 209n153, 392
   Bibles sold at Book Fair, 101
   Calvinism, 252, 374
   Catholicism, 62, 369
   diversity of faiths of Moses Brown students, 211
   nonindoctrination, Moses Brown School principle of, 211
   presidential election of 1960 and, 369
Remarque, Erich Maria, 317
Renaud-Barrault Company, France, 294
Rensselaer Polytechnic Institute (RPI), 242n172, 339
repetition, as instructional method, 24, 30, 49, 57, 72, 95, 386
Return of the Native (Hardy), 307, 312
Revere, Paul, 86
Reviews and Examinations in Algebra (Tower and Sides, 1953), 251–254, 344
Reynold, Quentin, 51
Rhode Island Auditorium (the Arena), Providence, 65–66
Rhode Island Audubon Society, 64, 65
Rhode Island Historical Society, 137
Rhode Island history, study of, 78, 137–140
Rhode Island hurricanes, 137, 139, 283
Rhode Island Independence Day, 138
Rhode Island industry project, 139, 155
Rhode Island Philharmonic, 86, 88
Rhode Island School of Design, 30, 99n75, 201n149, 268
Rhode Island School of Design Auditorium, 88
Rhode Island School of Design Museum, 53
Rhode Island Science Fair, 262, *321*
Rhodes Scholars, 242
"Rhodora" (Emerson), 258
"Richard Cory" (Robinson), 360
Richard III (Shakespeare), 283, 306
Richardson, John, 37
Der Richter und sein Henke (Durrenmatt), 349–350
Rigney, Jim (James Herbert), Jr., xiv, 302, 316, 317, *342,* 364–365, 377, 395
Rime of the Ancient Mariner (Coleridge), 229
Rinky Tinks (recess sports), 151
Ripley, Randall, 328
"The Road Not Taken" (Frost), 360
Roberts, Howard M. ("Mr. Peepers"), 170n121, *193,* 193–195, 256, 315n265, 393
Robin Hood (movie), 90
Robinson, Charles Alexander, 221
Robinson, Edward Arlington, 258, 307, 360
Robinson, Frank, 221
Robinson Crusoe (Defoe), 99
Robison, Dorothy L., *2,* 7n11, 14–15
Robots (recess sports), 150
Rochambeau, Jean-Baptiste, 138
Rod and Gun Club, 246
Roger Williams Family, 206
Roger Williams Park Museum, field trips to, 37
Roll, Paula, xv
Rolvaag, Ole Edvart, 357
Romance of Helen Trent (radio program), xix
Romeo and Juliet (Shakespeare), 198
Roosevelt, Franklin Delano (FDR), 26, 81, 369, 371, 372
Roosevelt, Theodore, 26, 142, 367, 373, 375
Rose, Elizabeth, 154
Ross, Betsy, 26
rubbers, importance of wearing, 4

Runyon, Damon, 219, 380
RUR (Capek), 358
Russia. *See* Cold War, communism, and Soviet Russia
Russian language, 171, 272
Russian Revolution, 181
Rutgers University, 93
Ruth, George Herman "Babe," 247

SAC, 246
Sadlier, Helen F., 232n168, 299, 315, *346,* 394
sailing club, 125
Saint Exupery, Antoine de, 280
Saklad, Mrs. (Mark's mother), 45, 229
Saklad, Jim, 372
Saklad, Mark Stuart
  in Fifth Form, 341, *342,* 372
  in Fourth Intermediate, 151
  graduating member of Class of 1960, 395
  graduating member of Lower School Class of 1955, 396
  higher education and career, 15n19
  photos of, *12, 168, 342*
  in Pre-Primary through Second Primary, *12,* 13, 15
  as source of information, xiii, xiv
  on summer vacations, 120–121, 122
  in Third Form, 242, 287, 288
  in Third Intermediate, 115
  in Third Primary, 45
Saltonstall, William G. (Bill), 239
Sandburg, Carl, 258
Sanders, C., *2*
Sanders Theater, Harvard, 293–294
Sanderson, Mrs. (mother of Peter), 229
Sanderson, Peter Amyor, *168,* 212, 396
Saratoga, Battle of, 80
Sargent, Joe, 156
SATs, 291n232, 312, 316, 345–346, 351, 353, 381
Saturday punishments, 152, 366
Saugus Iron Works, MA, 139–140
Sawyer, Herb[ert] Covell, xiv, 98, 108, 124, *168, 208,* 241–242, 395, 396
Sawyer, Judith, 124n96

Saywell, Mrs. (mother of Bob), 229
Saywell, Bob (Robert Morse), 5, 122, *168,* 329n283, 396
Schatz, Mrs. P., *2*
Schiller, Friedrich, 317
scholarships and scholarship students, 34
school histories, types of, vii–viii, xv–xvi
school nurse, 154
school year, 17
Schopenhauer, Arthur, 317
Schwartz, Fred[eric] Willard, Jr., xiii, *168,* 174, 197, *208, 278,* 283, 289, 290, *321,* 329n283, *342,* 395
science. *See also specific disciplines, e.g.* biology
  Fifth Form, advanced chemistry in, 343, 346–349, 350
  in First Form, 170n121
  in First Intermediate, 60
  Fourth Form, chemistry in, 299, 318–322
  in Fourth Intermediate, 144
  lab classes, 233, 262, 263–265, *264,* 321–322, 393
  Lower School lack of emphasis on, 162
  math curriculum, tracking with, 170–171
  1950s, science and technology in, ix–x, 319
  Second Form, general science in, 215, 231–235
  in Second Intermediate, 83–85
  Sputnik and increased emphasis on, 174
  Third Form, biology in, 247, 261–267
  in Third Intermediate, 114
  in Third Primary, 33
  in Upper School, 170–171, 383–386
"Science and the Faith of the Modern" (Conklin), 359
Science Club, 349
Scientific American, 302
scientific method, student introduction to, 385–386
Scipio Africanus, 111–112

Index

Scorpions (intramural sports), 150
Scott, J. Parker, 150
Second Form (Ninth Grade), 215–240
    ancient history, 215, 219–224
    art classes, 203–204, 215
    course load in, 171, 215–216
    English, 215, 224–229
    French, 215–216
    general science, 215, 231–235
    Latin, 215, 230–231
    math (algebra), 215, 216–219
    shop class, 203, 204, 215, 235–237
    St. John headmastership, end of, 237–239
    teachers in, 215
    testing in, 216, 224
Second Intermediate (Fifth Grade), 69–91
    art classes, 62, 86–87
    class officers, learning democratic procedure, and how to conduct a meeting, 84–85
    current events and election of 1952, 80–83, *82*
    English/language skills, 26, 73–76
    exams, 76, 83
    field trips and class outings, 86, 87–88
    geography, 76–78
    history, 79–80
    homework in, 72, 91
    location of, 8, 69
    math in, 24, 71–72
    movies and television, *82*, 83, 86, 90–91
    music, 87–90
    penmanship, 75
    science, 83–84
    sports in, 149–150
    teachers, 69–71
    teachers of, 48
    testing in, 76, 83
Second Primary (Second Grade), 7, 14–15, 39, 56
Second World War. *See* World War II
"The Secret Sharer" (Conrad), 303, 304
Segal, Dan, 228
Segal, Erich, 23n27

Seidel, Gertrude N., 154, *378*
"Self-Reliance" (Emerson), 306
Senior year. *See* Fifth Form
Service, Robert W., 198
Seth K. Gifford Building, 7
Seurat, Georges, 86
Seven Years' War. *See* French and Indian War
Seventh Grade. *See* Fourth Intermediate
sex and sexuality. *See* gender and sexuality
Shadows of the Elms (Fuller, 1983), viin1, xii
Shakespeare, William, 197–198, 228, 283, 305–306, 312, 358, 360
"Shall I Compare Thee to a Summer's Day" (Shakespeare), 360
Sharpe, Henry, 139
Shaw, Marian L., *378*
Shawn (Irish setter belonging to Thomases), 87
Sherlock Holmes stories, 135, 196, 227
Sherwood, Robert, 358
shop class
    in First Form, 170n121, 204–206
    in First Intermediate, 61–63
    in Fourth Intermediate, 63, 144
    in Lower School, 162
    in Second Form, 203, 204, 215, 235–237
    in Third Intermediate, 63, 115
    in Third Primary, 33–35
    in Upper School, 170n121, 171, 394
show and tell, 72
significant figures, concept of, 194–195
Silas Marner (Eliot), 227
silence, moment of, 17
the "Sirs," 146–147
sissies and sissy behavior, 4, 18
Sisson, Margaret Gifford (daughter of Seth K. Gifford, grandmother of Bill Barrett), 7, 140
Sixth Grade. *See* Third Intermediate
Slater, Samuel, 1–3, 139
slavery and slave trade, 80, 139, 142, 161, 371, 377
Smiley, Charles, 114, 174
Smith, Bert, 340

Smith, Bob (Cleveland Bryden), xiv, 177, 250n179, 262, 266, *342,* 354n307, 395
Smith College, 83
smoking by students, 173–174, 278
snowball fights, 46, 147
soccer, 117, 146, 150
social studies. *See* geography; history
sociological and attitudinal changes, ix, xi
Socrates, 110, 159, 223
Socratic Method, 309
softball, 146, 147, 149
Sophocles, 159, 223
Sophomore year. *See* Third Form
Sorbonne, Paris, 287
Sound and Sense (1956), 307, 360
Soviet Union and communism. *See* Cold War; McCarthy, Joe
Spanish language, 171, 272
Spanish War, 373
Spear, Stephen Louis, *12,* 13, 397
"The Speckled Band" (Doyle), 196
speedball, 150
speed-reading and reading comprehension, 171, 232n168, 299, 315, 394
spelling
  in First Intermediate, 51–52
  in Second Intermediate, 75
  in Third Intermediate, 96, 101–102
  in Third Primary, 29
spelling bees, 29, 102
split infinitives, 200, 355
sports. *See also specific sports*
  class outings to sports games, 65–66
  Mr. Cunningham's support for, 246
  at Father and Son Day, 43–45
  in Fifth Form, 341
  N. Littlefield's debate defense of, 228
  in Lower School, 145–151, 162
  playing fields, 145, 147n112, 246–247
  at single-sex versus co-ed schools, 379
Sprague, Lloyd, 56, 65–66, 129, 131–135, *133,* 151
Sputnik, 114n84, 174, 272, 319
square dance, in Third Intermediate, 115

squares and square roots, 102, 194
St. Andrews School, 150
St. George's School, Middletown, RI, 23n28, 37n36, 75, 123n93, 125, 215
St. John, George C.
  Bible class taught by, 170n121, 207–209, 211
  Chapel addresses by, 173–174
  R. Cunningham and, 242, 246
  departure of, 237–239, 331n285
  discipline, problems with, 175, 238–239
  dismissal of Mr. Nichols by, 225
  encountering C. Brown standing in hallway, 218
  photos of, *173, 208*
  as Quaker, 195, 209, 239
  Raines as Dean under, 363
St. John, Mrs. George C. (Nancy), 170n121, 195, 207–209, *208*
Stalin, Joseph, 181
stamps and stamp collecting, 22, 66, 137, 140
standardized testing, 104, 238, 345
Stanford Achievement Test, 104
Stanford Graduate School of Business, 221n158
Stapleton, Miss, 71, 75, 76, 81, 93n71
Steere, Amey (aunt of C. Brown), xx, 28, 75, 83, 127, 191, 338, 362
Steere, Bradley (cousin of C. Brown), 45
Steere, George (uncle of C. Brown), xxi, 337
Steere, John (uncle of C. Brown), 337
Steere, John P., Sr. (grandfather of C. Brown), 126
Steere, Philips (Phiddy; cousin of C. Brown), 45
Steere, Robert (uncle of C. Brown), 379
Steere, Walter (uncle of C. Brown), 335–336
Steinbeck, John, 259–260
Stenmark, David Helmar, 99, 120–121, 126, *168,* 329n284, 396
Stephenson, William, 41n40
Die Sterbende Jagd (Gaiser), 349–350
Stevenson, Adlai, ix, 80, 81, 83
Stevenson, Robert Louis, 99, 135

Index

"Stopping by Woods" (Frost), 360
"Stories Read from the Rocks" (1948), 144
Stout, L. E., *378*
Streets and Roads, 25
Strunk and White, 355, 356
The Student Weekly News (Third Intermediate), 115–116, 149
the Studio (room), 30, *31*, 33, 61–62, 394
studio art. *See* art
study hall
  busts in, 391
  disciplinary issues in, 238
  in Fifth Form, 363
  in First Form, 211–213
  homework in, 212, 213
  location and physical space, 170, 211–212
  physical layout of, 391–392, 393
  in Upper School, 170, 391–392
Sullivan Dorr mansion, Providence, RI, 140
summer camps and camp culture, 121–122, 129, 329, *332*
summer jobs, 120, 126, 128–129, 330–332, 334–340
summer vacations
  during Lower School years, 17, 28, 119–129
  during Upper School years, 329–340
Sunday School, 43
A Survey of European Civilization (1942), 325n277
"sward," meaning of, 75
Swayze, John Cameron, 83
Swide, Emily H., 62, 86–87, 162
Swift, Jonathan, 359
swimming team, 282, 293, 295–296
Swiss Family Robinson (Wyss), 99
Sydlowski (Class of 59), 212
Symington, Stuart, 369

Taber, William P.
  Class of 1959 and, 310
  classroom used by, 393
  compared to other English teachers and classes, 225–226, 238, 254, 258, 302n245, 313
  in First Form, 170n121, 172–173, 175, 186, 195–202
  moral education and values, teaching, 387
  photo of, *196*
  single-sex versus co-ed schooling and, 380
Taft (prep school), 215, 271
A Tale of Two Cities (Dickens), 197, 363
Taney, Roger, 467
T-Bird owned by Mr. Odell, 176
teachers at Moses Brown School. *See also specific grades; specific teachers by name*
  Chapel, attendance at, 172
  on corridor duty, 154, 293
  criticism of school under St. John by, 239
  dismissals of, 219, 225, 239, 245n173, 316
  dress of, 6
  Lower School faculty and staff (1950), *2*
  Master Teacher Development Fund, xvii
  matriarchal tradition, advancement through grades and separation from, 131, 133
  Quakers and Quakerism, association with, 172–173, 195, 197, 209, 239, 281
  quality of, xvi–xvii, 238
  sexual abuse incidents, 314n264
  summer camps, working at, 122, 129
  Upper School faculty and staff (1949-1950), *378*
telephone, use of, 91, 95–96, 300
television. *See also specific shows by title*
  at-home access to, xix, 83, 91
  classroom use of, x, *82*, 86, 313
  Hollywood responses to, ix
  "Mr. Peepers" (TV character), teacher nicknamed for, 193
  science specials on, 114
"Telltale Heart" (Poe), 196

Ten Years After (Dumas), 197
tennis, 5, 149, 150, 247
Tenth Grade. *See* Third Form
testing
 College Entrance Exams, 344
 examsmanship, 376–377
 in Fifth Form, 344, 345, 350, 351, 353, 370, 375, 376–377
 in First Form, 183, 187, 192, 195, 198, 200
 in First Intermediate, 49, 59
 in Fourth Form, 299, 311, 326–327
 "goose egg" tests, 311
 Mr. Herman as Director of Testing, 154, 248, 316–317, 345
 National Merit Scholarships, 345
 oral exams, 260–261
 SATs, 291n232, 312, 316, 345–346, 351, 353, 381
 in Second Form, 216, 224
 in Second Intermediate, 76, 83
 standardized testing, 104, 238, 345
 in Third Form, 260–261
 in Third Intermediate, 104
 in Third Primary, 25, 29
textbooks. *See also specific texts by title*
 in Fifth Form, 343, 344, 346, 347, 353, 354, 358, 360, 370
 in First Form, 178n129, 182, 183, 190, 191, 192, 193, 194, 197, 199, 213
 in First Intermediate, 50, 53, 54
 in Fourth Form, 300, 301, 303, 305, 306, 315, 317, 318, 319, 320, 322, 324, 325n277, 352
 in Fourth Intermediate, 133, 134, 135, 138, 140, 141, 142, 143, 144
 in Kindergarten through Second Primary, xxii
 photos and illustrations in, x, 104
 in Second Form, 221, 223, 224, 226, 230, 232n167, 234
 in Second Intermediate, 73, 76, 77, 79n65, 80
 as source materials, xi
 in Third Form, 251, 256, 261, 262, 263, 265, 268, 270, 271, 272, 275, 277

 in Third Intermediate, 95, 104, 105, 106, 107, 110, 111, 112, 113
 in Third Primary, 26
"Thanatopsis" (Bryant), 258
Thatcher, Margaret, 123, 179
Thayer, Ernest L., 198
theater. *See* plays and theatricals
Theroux, Paul, 179
They Made America Great, 26–27
The Thin Man (movie), 90
Third Form (Tenth Grade), 241–297
 biology, 247, 261–267
 course load in, 171, 247
 Cunningham headmastership and, 242–247
 English, 247, 254–261
 French, 247, 277–280, 284, 285–294
 German, 247, 271–277
 homework in, 270
 Latin, 247, 270–271
 math, 247–254
 Mechanical Drawing, 162, 171, 204, *236,* 267–270
 teachers in, 247
 testing in, 260–261
Third Intermediate (Sixth Grade), 93–117
 activities, 115–117
 art classes, 114–115
 birthday parties, 45, 114
 class newspaper, 115–116, 149
 class officers and elections, 116
 English/language skills in, 96–102, 135
 French, 115
 geography, 104–110
 history, 53, 110–114, 223
 homework in, 95–96, 103–104, 106, 111
 ink bottles allowed to students in, 9
 location of, 8, 69, 93n71
 math in, 71, 102–104, 157
 music, 115
 passing notes in, 116
 polio epidemic in, 17n21
 science, 114
 shop, 63, 115
 sports in, 149–151

Index 433

standardized testing in, 104
teachers in, 93–95
Third Primary (Third Grade), 17–46
activities, 35–39, *36, 38*
art classes, 30–32, *31*
birthday parties, 45–46
Christmas Pageant, *38,* 39–41
classmates and friendships in, 22–23
daily routine in, 17–19
exams, 25, 29
Father and Son Day, 43–45
history in, 26–27
homework in, 24–25, 27
Hope Street Gate, fights at, 41–42
location of classroom, 7, 17
math, 23–25
music classes, 17, 32–33
penmanship, 8, 30
science, 33
shop (Manual Training), 33–35
sports in, 145–147
teachers in, 19–22
"Thirty Days hath September," 33
Thirty Years' War, 113, 350
This is America's Story (1954), 140–142
Thomas, Edith Maxham, 40, 87–90, *88,* 115, 144, *153, 208*
Thomas, L. Ralston
admission of C. Brown to Moses Brown School and, xxiii
barn converted into Lower School gymnasium by, 147–149
at Commencement exercises, 155
Dexter Asylum and, 333n292
dress of, 6
as headmaster, 152–154
office of, 69n58
photos of, *2, 152, 208, 378*
Recollections (1994), viiin1, xii, 188, 379
retirement of, 90, 152
secretary of, 64
Mr. St. John and, 239
teachers hired by, xvi
Upper School, introducing Lower School students to, 152
Upper School science program, development of, 162
Upper School science under, 383

Thomas Jefferson University School of Medicine, Philadelphia, PA, 341n296
Thomas Science Building, 256, 261, 318n267, 321, 347, 393, 394
Thoreau, Henry David, 257
Thornton, Steve, xiv
Thorpe, Miss (at Henry Barnard School), xxiii
The Three Musketeers (Dumas), 135
Thucydides, 159
thumb-wrestling, 212
Thurber, James, 258, 307
Thurmond, Strom, 80n66
Tillinghast, Pardon, 325n277
Time magazine, 161, 355
Tinker, Joseph W., 129, 215, 216–219, *217,* 251, 322n270, 380, 393
Tinker, Tommy, 216
T&M Protection Resources, 314n264
Tocqueville, Alexis de, 260–261
Toilers of the Sea (Hugo), 226
"Tolerance" (Forster), 306–307
Tolstoy, Leo, 226–227
Tom Sawyer (Twain), 99
Tomlinson, John Austin, *342,* 395
Tow, Gerry (Wellington Gerry), 334, *342,* 395
Tower and Sides (*Reviews and Examinations in Algebra,* 1953), 251–254, 344
track team, 204, 295
tracked reading, 26, 158
Transcendentalism and Transcendentalists, 257, 274
transportation and automobiles
corner cupboard built by C. Brown, transportation of, 237
farm tractors, C. Brown's experience with, 127–128, 335–340
hairpin used to replace cotter pin in Model T of C. Brown's mother, 337
hearse driven by J. Tinker, 216
internal and rotary combustion engines, study of, 232
Vin Marcello with car, *330*
in 1950s, ix–x
Paris, T. Whitford on driving in, 290–291
M. Pezet arrested for speeding, 279

M. Pezet's car, in pushing contest, 278–279
radios, xx
snow, getting stuck in, 70–71
T-Bird owned by Mr. Odell, 176
travel by students outside New England, 68, 120–121, 151, 329–330
Treasure Island (movie), 90
Treasure Island (Stevenson novel), 99, 135
trigonometry, 134, 170, 343–344, 345
Trinity College, 241n171
Triumph and Tragedy (Churchill), 363
Trivial Pursuit, 367
Truman, Harry, ix, 39
Tufts University, 15n18, 95, 238, 279n208
tuition at Moses Brown School, xxivn7
Turner, William, *88,* 154
Turner, Mrs. William, *88*
Twain, Mark, 99, 233, 257, 258, 307, 363, 368
Twelfth Grade. *See* Fifth Form
12 Poets (1958), 360
Twenty Years Later (Dumas), 197
20,000 Leagues under the Sea (Verne), 135
Typee (Melville), 259
"Typhoon" (Conrad), 303, 304

The Union (recess sports), 150–151
Union College, xv, 95, 398
Union Station, Providence, 35–37
United Fruit, 186, 187
United Fund/United Way, 65
United Nations, 110, 196, 246, 255, 343
The United States in Literature (1957), 256n191
University of California, 254
University of Chicago, 238, 281n212, 351
University of Cincinnati, 341n298
University of Denver, 349n313
University of Dijon, 277
University of Miami, 124n96
University of Michigan, 187
University of Missouri, 176n126
University of New Hampshire at Durham, 216
University of Pennsylvania, 85n70, 174n125, 201n149, 229n164, 284
University of Pittsburgh, 195
University of Rhode Island (URI), 81n67, 174n125, 331n289
University of Rochester, 95
University of Southern California, 300n244
University of Vermont, 216, 341n297
University of Virginia, 349n313
Upper School, 379–388. *See also specific grades/years*
  academic curriculum, 170–171
  advanced placement courses, 171
  art, music, and aesthetics in, 171, 382–383, 386
  Bible class, 171
  Chapel in, 170n121, 171–175, 206–207, 392
  class size in, 170
  clocks and timekeeping in, 9, 392
  course loads in, 170n121, 171
  English in, 170, 381, 382
  excellence, as value of, 388
  faculty and staff (1949-1950), *378*
  geography in, 171, 383
  grades or forms in, 3, 170
  history in, 170, 383
  intellectual and social schools imbued in, 384–386
  introduction to, 151–154, 169–171
  languages in, 170, 171
  Lower School compared, 170–171
  math in, 170–171, 381, 383
  Mechanical Drawing in, 162, 171, 204, *236*
  moral education and values in, 386–388
  physical layout of, 391–394
  practical knowledge in, 193, 194, 233–235, 254, 385
  quality of instruction in, 381–388
  science in, 170–171, 383–386
  shop class, 170n121, 171, 394
  as single-sex versus co-ed institution, 379–381
  Study Hall in, 170
  summer vacations during, 329–340
Upper School gymnasium, Lower School students discouraged from playing on steps of, 4–5

Index   435

Upper School library, 202
Using Latin, Book I (195?), 190n143
Ustinov, Peter, 315

Valentine's Day cards, 32
Van Bever, Louise (aunt of Clifford Brown), xxii, 20n25
Vasco da Gama, 79
Vassar, 64, 95
Veragua (ship), 68
Verdun, Treaty of, 325
Verne, Jules, 99, 135, 233
Verrazano, Giovanni da, 80
Vespucci, Amerigo, 79
Veterans Auditorium, Providence, 87–88
Vetterlein, Ted "Dutch" (Theodore Herman), III, 122, 178, 396
The Vicomte de Bragelonne (Dumas), 197
Victory (Conrad), 303, 304, 312
Vieira, Ed, *321*
Vietnam War, 23nn27–28, 35n35, 107, 123n93, 203n150, 308n249, 338
Villiers, Alan, 99
Virgil, 270
vocabulary, English
  in American history and government, 369
  in biology, 266–267, 384
  in Fifth Form, 312, 346, 353–354
  in First Form, 190–192, 201
  in First Intermediate, 51
  in Fourth Form, 311
  in Lower School, 158
  in Second Intermediate, 76, 95
  in Third Intermediate, 100
  in Third Primary, 26, 27
vocabulary, in foreign languages
  French, 280, 288
  German, 275–277, 318, 349, 354
  Latin, 230, 270, 271, 354
Vol de Nuit (Saint Exupery), 280
Volkman, Alan Blair, *168,* 215, 329n283, 332, 396

Walden (Thoreau), 257
Wall Street Journal, 355

Wallace, Mrs. David (Aunty Wallace), 28, 31, 41, 62
Walters, Frederick William, II, 396
Wankel rotary combustion engine, 232
Wanton Lyman Hazard House, Newport, RI, 140
War and Peace (Tolstoy), 226–227
War of 1812, 139, 142, 373, 377
War of the Roses, 325
Warge, Mme. Emma Ducimetiere, *2,* 15, 56–60, *58,* 90, 115, 144, 162, 292
Warren, Earl, 161
Warwick High School, 215, 243
Washington, Booker T., 197
Washington, George, 26, 72n59, 79, 90, 138, 372
Watch on the Rhine (Hellman), 358
Waters, Loring Davis (Great Uncle Lo), 257
Waughtel, Samuel H., *378*
Waughtel-Howe Field House, 246
Wavus Camps, Jefferson, ME, 122
"We Are Marching to Pretoria," 61
We Walk Alone (Burgess), 197
weather and climate studies, 234
Webster, Noah, 275
Webster's Dictionary, 29, 75
Weekly Reader (periodical), 51, 81
Weeks, Elizabeth G., 64, 84, *84,* 154, 155, *378*
Weeks, Silas Charter, 396
Wesleyan College, 238, 363
Westerly High School, 284
Westland, William, 215, 219–224, *220,* 394
"Westminster Bridge" (Wordsworth), 360
Wharton, Edith, 357
"What I Did Last Summer" essays, 28
Wheeler School, 29
Wheelock College, 11, 14
"When Lilacs Last in the Dooryard Bloomed" (Whitman), 257–258
White, E. B., 355, 356
The White Company (Doyle), 363
Whites (intramural sports), 146
Whitford, Mrs. Theodore (Ruth), xii, 284, 293, 294

Whitford, Theodore S., (Ted), xii, xiii, 60, 129, 170, 238, 244, 272, 278, 280–297, *281,* 315n265, *378,* 380, 381, 386, 393
Whitman, Narcissa and Marcus, 26
Whitman, Walt, 257–258
Whitney, Eli, 26
Whittier, John Greenleaf, 74, 258
Whittier, Whittemore, *360,* 361, 391
Wilder, Thornton, 259–260, 358
Wilkie, Wendell, 81
Wilkinson, David, and Wilkinson families, 139, 155
William Penn College, 195
Williams, Roger, 138, 307
Williams, Ted, xx, 146
Wilmot Proviso, 79, 142, 367
Wilson, Harriet M.
   compared to other teachers, 47, 70, 94, 176
   as disciplinarian, 19–22, 35, 164
   location of classroom desk of, 17n20
   photos of, *2, 19*
   as Third Primary teacher, xxiii–xxiv, 19–25, 28, 30, 35, 37, 39, 44
Wilson, Woodrow, 26
Winchell, Walter, xx
Winsor, Edward, 293
The Wonder World of Science, 33
Woodbury, Otla M., *2,* 7n11, 11, *12,* 13, 18–19
Woodman Center, 117
Wordsworth, William, 360
World Book Encyclopedia, 77, 143, 183
World Series, 90, 137
World War I, 79, 80, 142, 159, 160, 161, 181, 275, 326, 328, 333, 368, 371, 373, 375–376, 391
World War II
   Grandpa Johnson in, 41
   "Kindergarten," American use of, xxii
   in Lower School classes, 80, 105, 108, 142, 159, 160, 161
   1950s era and, viii
   teachers at Moses Brown as veterans of, 173, 284–285, 296, 305
   teachers at Moses Brown mostly hired before, xvi, 275
   in Upper School classes, 181, 258, 277, 315, 326, 328, 349, 363, 366, 371
Worthington-Witczak, Tammy, xii
Wouk, Herman, 259
wrestling, 44–45, 318
Wright Brothers, 26
The Wright Brothers (Reynold), 51
writing. *See* composition, writing, and essays
Wyss, Johann David, 99

Yale University/College, 23n28, 40n38, 206
Yankees (baseball team), 90
years or grades, at Moses Brown, 3
Yellow Jack (Howard and De Kruif), 358
YMCA summer camp, 121
You and Science (1955), 232n167
Young, Ned (Edwin Parson), III, 121, *168, 264,* 331, 396
Young, Thelma, 154
"Youth" (Conrad), 303, 304, 306
yo-yos, 15

Zama, battle of (202 BC), 111–112
Zane, Elizabeth, 26
Zeke's stamp shop, Providence, 66
Zeoli, Jerry, xii, xiii, 245n173
Zimmerman process, 368
Zimmerman telegram, 368

www.ingramcontent.com/pod-product-compliance
Lightning Source LLC
Chambersburg PA
CBHW051615010526
44107CB00037B/1433/J